DELTA PUBLISHING COMPANY
Chicago, Illinois

Copyright 2020 by Charles J. Martinez, MD
Cover by Touchstone Graphic Design, with special thanks to artists Jason Patrick Miller (front cover) and Frank Simon Herrmann (1866-1942) (back cover) for their cover images.
Manuscript layout by Kevin Theis, Fort Raphael Publishing

The narratives in this book are based on recorded conversations and I have recreated other events, locales and conversations from my memories of them. In order to maintain their anonymity in some instances I have changed the names of individuals and places. In addition I may have changed some identifying characteristics and details such as physical properties, occupations and places of residence.

UNDER THE L

*A Chronicle of
Growing up in the Near North Side of Chicago
in the 1930s, 1940s and 1950s*

by Charles J. Martinez MD

CONTENTS

INTRODUCTION	1
CHAPTER ONE: BEGINNING	6
CHAPTER TWO: ROOTS	21
CHAPTER THREE: FAMILY LIFE AND ETHNICITY	73
CHAPTER FOUR: PREPARATION	147
CHAPTER FIVE: WORK	193
CHAPTER SIX: TIME EATERS	241
CHAPTER SEVEN: THE SOFT WALL	277
CHAPTER EIGHT: BEHIND OUR WORLD	310
CHAPTER NINE: THE PLAGUE	340
CHAPTER TEN: WELL MEANING	356
CHAPTER ELEVEN: THE GROUP	379
CHAPTER TWELVE: THE END OF THE LINE	440
Epilogue of how some of the guys turned out.	464

Dr. Charles Martinez was born 86 years ago and grew up under the elevated tracks in a tough working-class neighborhood on the near north side of Chicago.

He has lived a remarkable life, some of which is not apparent since this book focuses on its first three decades, the 1930s, 40s and 50s, but his recollection of growing up during those hard years of Depression and War, and his ability to sustain his connection to the colorful friends who enliven the pages of this book, strike him today, and the reader as well, as "awesome."

"I hold my childhood in awe. Awe that so much of the human condition can flow from such meager beginnings. I have been in touch with all those I interviewed and many others from the old neighborhood for many years and when we get together one comment that runs through our conversations is, 'How did we survive?' Behind this question is the realization that some did not survive; many brothers and friends fell by the wayside from drugs and crime."

In a way, his whole life was preparation for this book. Charlie Martinez was one of the lucky ones. He ended up going to college, and then medical school, becoming an internist, and then, after more years of study, a practitioner of Nuclear Medicine where he learned how to inject radioactive substances into the human body to better diagnose and help other doctors treat ailments. Toward the end of his career, he started the Old Irving Park Free Community Clinic and found a new way to continue what he had been doing his whole life, caring for those around him.

This is not just a book. It's a lesson for life.

       Leonard Aronson Documentary
       Producer WTTW (retired)

"That's right, Charlie. We weren't kids, we were like little men."

Jack La Brasca

"But you know, to be very honest, they were like golden years, those years. It was just like a holiday every day. You know, it was just ... it was beautiful. And it didn't last long. That's the funny part. I mean it only lasted from the time I was nine till nineteen. It's only ten years. Seemed like a lifetime Charlie. Seemed like a lifetime!"

Bunny Byrne

INTRODUCTION

Growing Up In The Near North Side Of Chicago is an oral history, turned into a chronicle, obtained by personal interviews with my childhood friends recorded on audiotape. This book is not a scientific social document. It is not a confession, nor does it try to achieve catharsis.

This book was written out of awe. I hold my childhood in awe. Awe that so much of the human condition can flow from such meager beginnings. I have been in touch with all those I interviewed and many others from the old neighborhood for many years, and when we get together at parties, weddings and funerals, one comment that runs through our conversations is, "How did we survive?" Behind this question is the realization that some did not survive; many brothers and friends fell by the wayside from drugs and crime.

The survivors' lives resulted in accomplishments that had not been predicted, encouraged, or nurtured. Most people equate success with attainment of a high socioeconomic status. What do I see as our accomplishment?

That we grew to manhood and led ordinary lives in spite of our background is something to brag about. And we do brag about it.

One interviewee, after I noted that we did so many adult things when we were so young said, "That's right Charlie, we weren't kids, we were like little men."

The term Near North Side needs clarification. I don't hear the term as often now as I did when I was young. We identified ourselves in three ways as youngsters, and especially as teenagers. Back then, when asked where we were from in Chicago, the most common reply was the name of our parish. Since almost everyone was Catholic in the area and the church was the center of our school, athletic, and social life, especially in grammar school but also into our teenage years, the most common reply was the name of our parish. So there was IC, for Immaculate Conception Church, St. Joe's for St. Joseph Church, St. Phillip's, and St. Mike's for St. Michael Church. The second common designation was to name an intersection of two important streets, e.g. North and Wells, or Division and Sedgwick. If the person asking was from an area farther away in Chicago or in a suburb, we would simply say we were from the Near North Side.

The Near North Side has definite borders. The area lies just north of the Loop, across the Chicago River with Lake Michigan as its eastern border, while south and west borders are formed by the Chicago River. North Avenue was our northern edge.

All of the subjects lived in these boundaries, at least until they got married or moved away with their families in their late teens or early twenties. Several lived just across the "border" but spent most of their time within the Near North Side.

When we were growing up, there were also socioeconomic designations. The "Gold Coast," from Dearborn Street and east to the lake was a middle-class to upper- middle class to a very affluent area with Michigan Avenue from Oak Street south to the river as its shopping center. Just west of the Gold Coast and north of Division Street were poor Appalachian whites who lived in large apartment/tenement buildings. They were especially concentrated where the huge Carl Sandburg condominium development is now situated, from North Avenue to almost to Division Street, fronting on Clark and LaSalle streets. At Wells

Street and west were lower-class and lower-middle-class whites with a sprinkling of different nationalities -- but mostly Irish.

Then, from west of Sedgwick to the North Branch of the Chicago River on the west, and south to the Chicago River and north to North Avenue, were large numbers of Italians left over from when the area was designated "Little Sicily." South of Division and west of Wells Street were the beginnings of a Black concentration. East of Wells was a mixture of middle-class and lower-class residents with several seedy hotels and some high-level night clubs and restaurants, especially along Rush Street.

None of us thought we lived in a slum or ghetto, yet in 1929 a large part of the Near North Side was labeled a slum in sociological terms. Within our Near North Side were several ghettos. There was a definite Italian ghetto as well an Appalachian white ghetto and a middle to upper-class white ghetto called the Gold Coast. No definite Irish or Black ghetto existed during these years. People settled in these areas because they wanted to live with their own kind. They felt no shame in seeking out a place where they shared the same culture and where support systems were available.

The interviews are presented as a sampling of young lives as played out in the Near North Side of Chicago from roughly the late 1930s into the late 1950s. We were born into the Depression, learned our first school lessons as the U.S. entered World War II, learned to read and write in the foment of patriotism, and became teenagers as the war ended. The Korean War and the Cold War tested our later adolescence.

Surprisingly, these cataclysms didn't greatly affect our lives.

I will present their testimony with minimal editing; however, I have changed some sentences to clarify sense and situation, but always trying to leave the character of each person's speech identifiable. The selection of the subjects was of course confined by availability and willingness. I sought interviews from those in different geographic sections of the Near North Side, from different nationalities, from different socioeconomic levels and tried to include both men and women. I did not seek out those who had "good stories" to tell but rather, I wanted ordinary people to talk about their everyday life as children..

Before the actual taping began, I reminisced with each person for a short time and we also looked at old photos the person had from that time in their life. I used a checklist of topics to make sure all aspects of the person's life, as far as possible, were covered. What did they eat? How did they dress? Who affected their lives the most? How did they play? I inquired about crime, love, race, school, religion, and other facets of their life.

The topics related to the time both before and during grammar school, high school, late teen years and into their early twenties. Comments were elicited, when not forthcoming on their own; however, I kept my questions short and as infrequent as possible to avoid becoming part of the remembrance.

Several subjects were reluctant to be interviewed; they worried whether painful memories or reciting stories about friends or relatives which could later cause controversies. I assured them that anything they found absolutely objectionable would be further edited to avoid recognition by other parties. I asked women but all refused to be interviewed, limiting my intention to completely cover the Near North Side by class, gender, and geography. Fortunately, some of those I interviewed bridged into other parts of the Near North Side.

The book is arranged into topics such as school, church, race, etc. I have placed the friend's name as a heading for his response to that topic. This way the variety of their experiences in each category adds contrast and irony to the reading. All seemed to relish the interview process once it started and several of the men choked back emotion at certain points in the interview.

These are not the stories of people born to privilege. They are those who, in the natural course of their lives, dictated by the culture into which they were born, were not destined to acquire a good primary education, go on to a fine high school, and then sit down with their family and decide on the college that best suited the family's budget and a future career for the son or daughter. Some, in spite of their humble beginnings, rose to higher levels of education and socioeconomic achievement, and even those few seemed to accomplish this more by accident than by design.

The home lives of those I interviewed was frequently characterized by a severe clash of the parents' ethnic culture with a modern American outlook. Most had disinterested parents who were harsh taskmasters, who provided no push to go on and accomplish. Their culture taught that life was about surviving until you were old enough to get a steady job and then to see how things went from there.

Almost all that I relate, in the final analysis, will appear to be commonplace, but as opposed to James T. Farrell's indictment in his short story *Studs,* where he has the narrator comment on his boyhood friends when he meets them again at Studs' wake, *"They kept on talking and more and more I thought they were a bunch of slobs. All the adventurous boy that was in them years ago had been killed. Slobs, getting fat and middle aged, bragging of their stupid brawls, reciting the commonplace of their days."* I believe there is not much else that we are that is not commonplace.

Since some of the stories are sure to arouse curiosity in the reader concerning the outcome of the storyteller's life, I have added a general epilogue and an epilogue for each interviewee. Please read the interview portions before peeking at the epilogue. The correlation will astound you.

Now, together, we will go "in search of lost time" (Proust) to taste the extravagant stew of our childhood.

CHAPTER ONE: BEGINNING

Part One: Earliest Memories

"The Child is father of the Man"
William Wordsworth, *"My Heart Leaps Up"*

Charlie Martinez

Sunny day with bloody red towels soaking in a crimson-watered roasting pan.

Patsy dropped a tin can with an open, sharp edge from the second floor window, aiming for the garbage can. Instead, my older sister missed the garbage and the empty container struck my head as I sat on an ancient potty chair in the backyard.. Blurred forms ran around gathering wet towels, applying pressure to stop the bleeding, and rinsing the towels in a large basin. The basin blushed bright red. I felt no pain, cried no tears. And I remember it was a sunny day as I looked out over the yard. I was three or four years old.

John Giovenco

I was about five. I got a job. I went to work for the butcher for a day and I killed chickens by wringing their necks and I gutted them and dipped them in hot water to pull the feathers off. Upside down, in order to drain the blood. And I remember he gave me a penny for that ... for a whole day. I brought the penny home to my mother and father. And my father got so pissed that he went over to the butcher and screamed and yelled at him for taking advantage of a young boy by giving him only a penny. And, ah, so I only had that job for one day. I was so proud to have made some money to contribute to the family ... I do remember being very, very proud of the fact that I was working.

Bunny Byrne

See my dad was working up in the Straits of Mackinac, I was four or five. And my uncle, who was my mother's brother, ah … let's see who the hell died. Somebody died … my dad's father died I think in the old country. My mother gave my uncle five bucks to go send my Dad a telegram to tell him that his father died. And, what does my uncle do but he goes out … it cost about half a buck to send a telegram … he comes back and tells my mother the telegram cost a fin. He drank the rest, see, over on Clark Street. So my dad got home and money was short at the time, you know, 'cause it was the Depression. She says, 'Well I had to give Pete five dollars to send the telegram.' And he says, 'Well didn't he give you change?' See my father was a lot smarter than my mother when it came to worldly stuff and she said, 'No, he said it was five bucks.' So my uncle happens to come to the door, just at that time and pow! My dad hit 'im.

He never got a step in the door. Well back then, Charlie, five bucks was like, be like a week's worth of food. Yes. And we had times where we didn't have lights on, we were using candles. You knew they were turning the lights off. Course we didn't know it at the time, but every once in awhile the house would be all lit with candles. So we knew damn well, you know.

John Owens

I can remember … we're moving into a house. I was like four or five years old. I was going through the living room and the shade flew up and it scared the hell out of me. I mean, that's the thing I can remember from my real early age, you know. I mean, I just flew back into the bedroom.

Pat Rogers

I can recall my younger brothers, Michael and Charles, feeding in the kitchen. And they were being milked by my mother. I came in there and I saw mom feeding … and she was doing double duty. All I could say was, 'God, I'm really hungry.' I had to be about four years of age…maybe that's why I have this eating disease that I have.

Peter Eichel

I remember three little kids sitting on the front steps next door or two doors down from the house on La Salle Street. We musta been four or five. One kid said, 'We're gonna die someday… you know that?' I felt a sense of wonderment at this. At home, I asked my mother was this true. She said, 'Yes, it does happen.' She said other things I don't remember but my sense was I came away feeling better about it.

Jake Pistone

And my parents used to go to the theater called the LaSalle Theater. When we were kids, on Tuesdays and Thursdays nights. And they used to give out dishes …they took us. I sat between my mother and father and my little brother sat on the end. And ah, those were the days, you know, that's how they got their dish sets. Ah, I was about six or seven years old.

Michael Lutazzi

And I can only guess at my age it had to be like six or seven. Cause I was living on Cleveland Avenue, in a two-flat and we were living on the first floor, and there was a family upstairs from us named Andrew.
…there was a commotion, my father went to the door and I can remember the cop. And he was like thirty feet tall. And I remember the uniform. I can see his face and him standing there and my father saying something to him. And they went upstairs and they got Andrew and they pulled him down. And I don't remember if they took him away or just had a talk with him because he had just popped his wife a couple a times. I remember … I was standing behind my father and I seen this cop in this uniform and

this big gun and this big man and he was tall and skinny. And he had this uniform and this hat, you know.

Yeah. Yeah, I was afraid. Cause there was some shit going on. Yeah, I was afraid. Ahm, I'm not sure if I was afraid of the cop. Maybe I was afraid of the cop, not Andrew because I was beginning to learn about Andrew. And I realized where I learned it. Andrew's real crazy, and he used to punch his wife around.

Ken Martinez

Bobby and Jerry and I slept on the floor in the dining room. Right off where Dad's radio was. Right under a window off of Ma and Pa's room. I got sick one night and I went by Ma, 'cause Pa slept on the inside and Ma slept on the outside. And I touched her and I said I don't feel good … I'm sick, I'm sick, I don't feel good. And I threw up right outside the door there. And I remember Ma cleaning it up. And then she put a pail by me and I kept throwing up. I was five, six. Five years old.

Jack LaBrasca

I hadda be like ah, four or five, three or four or five years old. I remember that in the summertime on the sidewalk for like a whole block they put white sheets. And they would fill it up with tomatoes that were squeezed already and they would make tomato sauce. And then they would put like screens over it. Like nettings so that the flies couldn't get at it. All the way up until about 1940 they did that. They made their own tomato paste. They called it 'astrada,' which means street. Astrada, it was made on the street. It was something they did in the old country and they brought it here. And I remember we'd be coming home from school and we hadda walk around these sheets. Like they'd be like two city blocks. White, all the way down. And the sun would be drying them. And they would ooze and then the juice would become almost pasty. Then they would gather all this up and separate the skin and they would put it in big jars. They made their own tomato paste.

Paul Temple

I was frightened. You could look out the first floor windows (of his apartment) and rats were coming out of the sewers at night. They were the size of alley cats. I mean, they were huge. And I was always thinking, God, we lived on the first floor and if one got up on a window ... You know I used to have nightmares as a kid about it.

Frank De Monte

...don't forget, I'm three or four years old now, and here's World War II. The earliest thing I remember is my mother putting a sailor suit on me and me going with her downtown for a parade. Armed Services parade for the war. That's the first thing I remember.

Jim Sullivan

Playing in a sandbox I guess at 1437 Wells Street. There used to be a vacant lot next door to it. And in the back they had sheds. And they had actually a sandbox there. You know, about six inches of sand in there and it was really kind of neat...I had to be five or six at the time...

Joe Olita

You know, the only thing that I remember (when around four years old), is that for some reason when I would wake in the morning, I would go into this chant.
Yeah. I would, and it would drive my mother and father crazy. And what I would do, I would rock back and forth in a chair and just go 'oh ma, ma ... oh ma, ma.' They would tell me to stop it, and I wouldn't stop it. And one day from what my mother tells me, my father got so upset with me, he picked me up and threw me

up towards the ceiling and scared the living daylights out of me and it was from that day on that I never did that again.

Jack Flaherty

Well, 221 W. Wendell was my first address and I guess my mother and I walked up to the corner to pick up our laundry at the Vail Laundry. This was on the corner of Wendell and Wells. I was about four years old. They had a dog that they let roam the shop. In the evening it acted as a watchdog. I guess I had some candy or something like that in my hands and I dropped it. So the candy rolled over or made its way over toward the dog. So I went over to retrieve the candy, but I guess at that point the dog felt that it was his … so he sort of swung his paw at me and caught me right on my eyelid to which this day I have a faint scar.

Joe Zummo

I had to be three years of age or so---my mother used to wash the clothes in the bathtub—and I dreamt she was washing the clothes and the water was turbulent and there was a little man in there drowning and that man was Sam and that man was the husband of the people who occupied the front of our apartment on Sedgwick Street. They had a beauty parlor in the front. Overall it was a very frightening experience.

Part Two: Locale

There was a time when meadow, grove, and stream,
The earth, and every common sight,
    To me did seem
    Appareled in celestial light,
The glory and the freshness of a dream.
It is now as it hath been of yore;—
    Turn whereso'er I may,
    By night or day.
The things which I have seen I now can see no more.

"Ode: Intimations of Immortality from Recollections of Early Childhood," William Wordsworth

Charlie Martinez

My backyard. The first five hundred square feet of the outside world that I would know in detail. Endless hours wandering through, playing with, climbing on, throwing around, wondering at, and asking about the things that were there.

Diagonally laid bricks with peeling paint set off a garden of broken glass and weeds on the east side with Grandma's mint and mother's four o'clocks struggling to survive. The mint cooled your mouth and cleaned your breath. Scattered rocks, broken glass, a few weeds, and the rest all a dry lake where you could dig dirt, pour dirt, move dirt, taste dirt and throw dirt. At times a platform of mud. Modest piles of trash rotted in the waste space between the horse barn, LoVecchio's fence and the lifeless 'backhouse' in the rear of the yard. Guarding the yard was a worn out Tree of Heaven whose thin branches were our whips for fighting.

One of our puppies with "rabies" shot in this garbage pile by a policeman as my brothers, sisters, cousins, friends and I watched in awe and curiosity. Boards laid out to mark off areas for games or pirate areas or for the circus we would stage. Curious mound of coffee grounds on the bare dirt outside the kitchen window between the houses. The side gangway had an accompanying river of dirt where I spent hours using a toy bulldozer to move those coffee grounds into ever-changing piles.

Fence misshapen, broken, needing repair. Ken chased another puppy into Mr. Kennedy's yard and threw the dog back over the fence, landing him on the diagonal bricks. Pitiful yelps. Swinging gate with no lock. In a brotherly rage, I slammed that gate into Ken's face, cutting it with protruding nails. Uncovered garbage cans revealing their rotting filth and feasting flies. To the east, a wooden fence separated our backyard from the forbidden green grass yard beyond. The fence was unpainted with a matching chicken coop set against it. And we ran, playing hide and seek and tag; sweat did not smell, dirt did not matter, and scratches and bruises were not felt.

Sometimes a few chickens, always a dog, perhaps a rabbit living out their childhood just like me. Smells and nuisance of dog crap. But always we kept one part of our awareness on the alert in case we came too close to the "backhouse." This was an unpainted, windowless, unlived-in, almost miniature, two-story house set in the far end of the yard. We entered into it a little ways when feeling brave. We smelled the dampness of this unused house, felt the coolness, and noted the mild urine odor that came from the corners of the rooms. And suddenly, like a flock of bolted birds, we ran out terrified and screaming. The horror was in our imagination. But soon we were back to playing in the dirt and all was well again.

Many sweaty children with puppy-dog smell, snot-soaked sleeves, bedraggled hair, and worn out shoes, mismatched, worn, hand-me-down clothes shared these hours. I knew, but could not say what dirt smelled like, tasted like, and felt like. Adults were for feeding you, calling you in, demanding quiet; but the yard was my life. My childhood went on with listening, listening, listening. Observing, observing, observing. And wondering, wondering, wondering.

#

In time, I left the refuge of the yard to enter our neighborhood realm: a mélange of sidewalks, empty lots, weeds, dirt, elevated structures, garage roofs, streetcar tracks, garbage cans, fences, trees, gangways, hallways, streetlight poles, alleys, empty schoolyards, asphalt streets, sewers, abandoned buildings, railroad yards, factory trash areas, curbsides, small stores, beaches, cement of the lakefront, grass of the park. All was more cement, tar, and steel than grass and flowers.

Scents came to us from Tree of Heaven whips, rotting rats, garbage cooking in the sun, dog crap, the unwashed, cocoa oil on female sunbathers' skin, snow-soaked winter wool clothes; heating oil on our hands, clothes and food, kitchen odors of roasting meat, garlic, baking, wine making; peppermint candy, jumbled smells of vegetables, cheeses, fish, and spices in congested family grocery stores.

A brotherhood existed that lived out the fantasy that no grownups had access to these places or things. Our special spaces were never discussed with parents, teachers, police, or church people but sometimes we used their spaces in a secret way.

We lived in a world of sensual joy:

> the concrete sidewalks scorching under our feet in the summer,
> the tasteless pleasure of chewing roofing tar taken from the workman's bucket,
> the burn of asphalt on our arms when we fell playing touch football,
> the constant battle with dog crap on our shoes,
> the cool, crisp whiff of grass,
> the glory of a Pepsi and Hostess Cupcake on a summer day,
> the excitement of eating stolen chunks of ice from the delivery truck,
> a taste of pure, new-fallen snow,
> belly flopping on a sled down the crunching snow on a still winter night,
> fierce street hockey on the packed snow with broken, taped sticks and a Mason jar top as the puck,
> roller-skating with wind in our faces as the metal clamps ripped off the soles of our shoes,

the pride and excitement of a scooter built with a two-by-four, peach crate, and old roller skates and decorated with bottle caps,
riding and crashing rented bikes down the hills at Lincoln Park by Grant's Tomb,
sharing a huge Italian sandwich with a couple of guys, swimming naked in Lake Michigan,
fighting and wrestling till our sweat-soaked clothes were covered with mud,
never a makeup discussion with an enemy,
the joy of junking in the railroad areas,
time-wasting wandering with a buddy in the alleys,
the exciting hunt for rats in garbage cans and along the riverbank,
turning into a cowboy after leaving the Plaza Theater,
turning into a Marine after leaving the Plaza Theater,
running fast without tiring,
the cruel pleasure of stoning dogs locked together after mating,
the wonder and power of a BB gun,
playing catch in the deserted street of an early Sunday morning,
getting up a ballgame whether we had 4 or 20 players,
no umpires, no parents, no grownups ever in our play,
spiking rats with a pointy nail broomstick,
the burst of stars when hitting your head on the sidewalk,
burning up caterpillars with a magnifying glass,
poking a dead horse in the alley,
whipping each other with Tree of Heaven branches,
the grand taste of salted potatoes after roasting them in a junk fire in the alley,
brutal game of capture the flag on a hot summer night,
the lights, the noise, the thrills of St. Michael's carnival,
begging stale bread from Piper's bakery to use as bait to fish in Lincoln Park lagoon,
solemn curiosity as we watched firemen pull a drowned man out of Lake Michigan,

the strange, pleasant sensation in the groin when sliding down the steel covering of a telephone pole guy wire,
group masturbation in the boys' bathroom,
mysterious attraction to girls,
the pleasant taste of spit when playing spin the bottle,
stealing from the fruit stand on North Avenue and Wells and running down the alley changing clothes to thwart the police,
harassing old ladies with snowballs,
incessant "draggin' the street" in heat, cold, snow, or rain,
the triumph when we got the police to arrest a driver who moved our patrol boy barrier,
swinging from the ceiling pipes in the altar boys' changing room,
the rush when jumping from Jimmy Foley's garage roof,
leaping onto a ten foot pile of old Christmas trees from Patty Irwin's second floor,
the skill and concentration when shooting marbles,
sitting and talking with your buddies at the curb,
sleeping overnight in Lincoln Park,
taping, retaping our league balls,
secretly saving money from serving weddings at Immaculate Conception Church to buy a fielder's glove,
sharing olive oil on Gus Johns' back porch to form a perfect pocket in the glove,
listening in awe in King's hallway as Gus Johns tells us what sex is like,
shooting dice in hallways and hidden areas of schoolyards,
playing football and softball in empty lots with gravel and glass for grass,
digging warfare trenches in IC lot,
garbage picking in alleys,
using the alleys as our toilets,
the sweet-sickening smell of rotting rats in the alley,
the recurrent, bouncing clank of 'kick the can' on the asphalt,
streetlights and cement and pain for a game of 'buck, buck,'
the otherworldly sensation of the Italian Feast,
choking and vomiting with the first puffs of tobacco,

ten guys sharing a quart of beer,
the mature feeling when shopping for clothes on Maxwell Street,
the feeling of confidence when dressed 'cool' with the guys on a Sunday morning,
playing handball at the lake in the sun in front of the girls,
stickball, fast pitching and ledge ball till too dark to see,
touch football on the streets for hours and hours and hours,
drop kick football with only two players,
the serious game of territory played with knives and a square in the dirt,
the taste of a muggy midsummer night,
sharing a cold Popsicle on a hot day,
the exotic smell of incense while serving a funeral mass,
gulping ice cold water from the water fountains in Lincoln Park,
the wind in your face when you got the front window on a streetcar,
endless varieties of softball depending on how many showed up to play in the hot sun,
the cuts, bruises, joint pain, mud, cold, rain, and fear of football,
the joy and triumph of a good tackle, block, catch or run of football in Lincoln Park,
the certainty of good luck when winning at dice in Franklin School yard,
the terrible left out feeling when running out of money at dice,
the sensation of entering another world when riding in a friend's car,
plodding back home after a long day in the hot sun at Lincoln Park,
the glorious cold power of water from an illegally opened fire hydrant on a hot day,
listening to the bark of the announcer for the fights or the Indy 500 race from a radio coming from somebody's apartment,
the distant, hollow boom of a firecracker thrown down the fireplug,

terrifying people when we popped up between the rails of the elevated trains,

the grinding of the junkman's wagon wheels on the alley dirt.

Snow, rain, hot or cold; any weather was good enough for us. Rain was fun. Snow was fun. A hot sun was fun. No weather was bad weather. Never tired.

Churches, parks, houses, schools and stores were interspersed incidentally throughout this secret (we thought) network of ours.

We had our lost Atlantis. At times we wandered below the streets to find the remains of an ancient city with its abandoned stores and apartments waiting patiently for the return of kids playing hopscotch, adults smoking and talking away a hot summer evening, customers coming and going to the family tailor shop or grocery store. Horses had plodded the mud-baked streets along this "lower level"; the "ghost town" left behind when the streets and sidewalks were raised years before for a new sewer system but now populated by rats and adventurous kids.

"But our greatest fun was trying to get the glass inserts out of the sewer covers. When you went down in the basement you could look up and you'd see these different colored lights coming down into the basement through the sewer covers. Mueller's bakery was actually a five-story building. But when they put the sewer system in, they buried all those stores. And one we used to look at and it used to say 'Tailor Shop.' Yeah, underneath there ... the doors and everything was there." (Ken Martinez)

And what did we talk about? That part is lost. We must have talked but talking seemed minimal and a lot of interaction was non-verbal. We didn't discuss the fairness of a situation but rather argued and fought when we understood something to be unfair.

Through this neighborhood ran a backbone of steel and wood. The L was the defining man-made structure of the Near North Side. This steel spine was suspended twenty feet in the air on brawny girder arms. Rugged, ancient, and available, it was generous with its gifts but potentially unforgiving to a misstep. This was our huge playground. We played 'It' in its structure, baseball on the ground beneath, roasted potatoes in fires against the girders, smoked our first cigarettes hidden in its shadows and held the long, quiet, secret conversations of youth behind the L station. We climbed the steel screening designed to keep us out and popped up between the ties and onto the platform in front of terrified adults for a free ride downtown or to Cubs Park. No one ever chased us; no one ever seemed to care what we were doing under the L.

Ken (my brother and little more than a pregnancy older) described the block on Schiller Street where we lived. He leaned back in his chair and his mind's eye withdrew sixty years and described his early childhood world which was only a block long.

"On Sedgwick Street, at the corner with Schiller, there was a flat limestone with horse rings in it." And you knew he saw the carriages and delivery wagons tying up to these rings with horse crap all around.

"Then you walked on the same side, the south side of Schiller Street, and you came to the old barn. There was a carriage inside of it. Dejesuri's yard with the wooden fence was next. And they had chickens in there. They had a brick staircase with brown apertures, which was my fort. Next it was LoVecchio's building and Mr. Poge lived on first floor, the LoVecchios lived on the second floor. Grew tomatoes. We had an old house in the backyard that Mr. Amau lived in. It was a two-story thing. Then our house. Then the Kennedys. Then Gus's grandmother's cottage. Then her house. Then the Degnan's and the 'L' station. Mr. Culbertson was the old man from World War I with one leg. He used to sell cigarettes and newspapers in the L station. Just east of the L station was a two-flat, I think it was brick and the Ellises lived there. Then there was the building on the corner, which was a three-story red brick. The Corbetts lived there. And across the street, going back west was Mary Joyce's store, a garage, the elevated, and the Temple Art Glass building. You crossed Orleans Street to an empty lot. Schlaw's owned the lot and lived next to it in a two-story frame. The Bushalakis owned the next two buildings. And there was another little house and then there was where Walter Gibbons lived with his mother and his sister and his little brother in that big apartment building above Mueller's bakery. And it seemed the whole neighborhood smelled from the bakery. A good smell of dough, cake, baking bread. And that was our block."

Once, in our daily alley wanderings under the L, an ivory mound appeared in the distance. Now, there always was a mound of garbage in the alley next to the L behind Degnan's house. Who replenished it, we did not know, but supposed hermit-like men came out at night to deposit their rubbish. But our mound of garbage was usually a dull gray with some red of tomato cans and green of beer bottles. This milky disturbance in our natural world urged us on faster in our single file.

Ken bounded ahead then slowed and stared at the alien mass. We joined him and watched as our eyes caused the heap to accept a form. It was in the garbage, but not yet of it. Four legs were thrust horizontally and a head was flattened against the ground. The head looked away. The eyes were dull, not like the harried, angry, frightened, probing eyes of the horses in the cowboy movies. The teeth were glazed yellow and the mouth was slightly open. There was no hideous smile of death. The white horse appeared tired but content. Was it glad there were no more whippings and straining to pull overloaded vegetable carts? No more winter snow or summer heat?

The horse produced no odor and the flesh was intact so we made the streetwise, scientific assumption that he was cast out the night before.

No parades; no romps in a glorious green retirement pasture. What will they do with Mr. Bartali, the owner of the barn and horses, when he has lost usefulness? But after these altruistic thoughts came male youth curiosity with the bizarre, dangerous, obnoxious and hideous. The swollen abdomen lured us.

What a chance to see if we could make it explode! What a story to tell! But rocks, bricks and pointy sticks would not get us our result as we beat the horse, kicked the horse, probed the horse and it said nothing in response to our insults.

We left, not wanting to look each other in the eye.

CHAPTER TWO: ROOTS

Part One: Grandparents

Charlie Martinez

My grandmother prayed daily, mumbling and stroking the beads of her rosary with her bleeding fingers.

I stood next to the gas stove and listened as my grandmother recited her prayers in French in the bedroom off the kitchen. She was dying. She was placed in the bed my brother Ken and I shared. Father Morrison attended her death, praying over her in English and Latin. She was eighty-eight; I was twelve. I heard her voice as a loud whisper with exaggeration of the "s" sounds. She had been blind for many years and was so hard of hearing that I had to shout into her ear to make her understand.

"Grandma, do you want some coffee?"

"Huh?" she said, staring straight ahead out of her opaque lenses.

"Coffee?" I shouted louder with my lips touching her ear.

"Alright."

She constantly picked at her fingers till they bled. I had seen her swollen legs with their weeping sores as she shuffled to the bathroom or kitchen in her oversized felt slippers. Her small body was bent over, making her appear the size of a child. Her gray-white hair sprayed out in all directions. I noted that all ancient ladies seemed to look alike. She had given up her duty of mending socks and now waited for the end, praying daily, mumbling and stroking the beads of her rosary with her bleeding fingers.

Then I noticed that her high-pitched whispering had stopped. Father Morrison continued to recite prayers in Latin in a grave monotone and as he finished them, I looked into the bedroom and saw him make the sign of the cross over her still body. My older brother Tommy sent me out of the house to play without any discussion of the drama taking place. I have no recollection of her funeral, or even if I attended her funeral.

This was the extent of my personal connection with any grandparent. My grandmother had come north to Chicago from New Orleans in 1910 with her husband, children and another family, the Rouzans. Later when my wife and I studied my father's genealogy we discovered that he was part black and we decided that the increasingly harsh Jim Crow laws likely had driven them out of New Orleans. I never saw my paternal grandfather. My mother's parents emigrated from Ireland and died before I was born.

Even with this meager relationship, my grandparents were giants in my mind's eye. They did not accomplish impossible things; it's just that to a child everything they did from my grandmother Teen coming north on a train from New Orleans to Chicago or grandfather Lonergan having his leg cut off when a horse-drawn beer wagon crushed it against a loading dock loomed as adventures and huge catastrophes. And that's the wonder of it.

Jack La Brasca

> *You had these two extremes. My paternal grandmother went to church every morning at 5:30 a.m. Mass, at the Italian Mass at St. Phillip Benizi. And my maternal grandmother did abortions.*

I was born at 1122 North Sedgwick Street 1935. My maternal grandmother was the one who brought me into the world at that residence.

Yes. She was a midwife. She was born in Villa Frati, Sicily. Bounced into New York City and wound up in Chicago working at County Hospital and learning midwifery.

She was mother's stepmother. She doubled as an abortionist. It was fairly well understood. Yeah. She went both sides of the track. They related it to me in a discreet way that she did abortions. They said she did a job ... usually for people with money. But I knew exactly what they meant. I was seventeen. She also trained in Bellevue Psychiatric Hospital in New York. She had instruments, 'cause I remember a black bag, like a doctor's bag. I can always remember that, yeah.

My paternal grandfather had a grooming and livery stable where the Fourth Presbyterian Church is now across from the Drake Hotel, on Michigan Avenue. Well we still had horse and buggies at the turn of the century. We hadn't moved into the mechanized world yet, so they cleaned horses, fed them, groomed them for the carriage trade. My paternal grandmother was a seamstress for the Potter Palmer family who lived in the Potter Palmer Castle at Schiller Street and Lake Shore Drive. So the two of them would venture from the old Sicilian neighborhood on Sedgwick Street and Oak Street to the Gold Coast every morning and one went to the grooming stable and one went to the Palmer family. My grandmother sewed dresses for the family and did drapes and that sort of thing. They walked. Yeah. All year around. Snow, ice winter. They'd get up at five in the morning and made tracks.

My father's mother wore very nondescript clothing. Long dark dresses with a apron in front … calico. Very thin woman. My grandfather wore blue work pants and long sleeve cotton shirts and long underwear … summer or winter. I remember my Dad's mother always smelled of spices. She ground her own coffee.

My mother's stepmother, who was a midwife, always had balm on her hands. Italian balm. Nice lemon smell. They told me tremendous stories about my grand stepmother who did abortions. You had these two extremes. My paternal grandmother went to church every morning at 5:30 a.m. Mass, at the Italian Mass at St. Phillip Benizi

And my maternal grandmother left the house to do abortions.

When my Dad's mother died in '43, I was eight years old. I knew how she died. A bunch of kids were running, playing baseball, knocked her down, broke her hip. She died of pneumonia in Henrotin Hospital, which was at LaSalle and Division. They had the wake at Barisi's on Clybourn Avenue, just north of Division on the east side of the street. They were from Tuscany. It was winter. The wake was not well-attended. I went to the cemetery and that was three days off school for me. That was nice. It was like a party. It didn't impact me much.

My overall contact with the grandparents was minimal. They were there and I was over here.

Michael Lutazzi

To say I loved my maternal grandmother more than my other grandmother wouldn't be fair. And it might be real.

Ah, yeah, my maternal grandparents, they lived behind Mr.Manfredi's candy store. Renzo Manfredi on Mohawk Avenue. You went in this gangway, behind the store and you made a left and it was also an entrance to some apartments upstairs above the candy store. So you went in the gangway, went up the stairs to the apartments.

My grandmother and grandfather lived on the ground floor. Another door and you walked in there and you walked into the kitchen. And then to the right there was a front room. And to the right of that a bedroom. It was a three-room apartment. I would go there after school. Especially in the winter and get the coal from the basement for them. And we were always back and forth anyhow. Matter of fact when we lived on Wells Street, the dog ran away, he went to my grandmother's house. And you know we knew where he was, you know. The apartment smelled like cigars. Yeah. Parodi. Yeah. You're right, cigar smoke. And ah, cooking.

My mother's father was a beautiful man. He was a singer, not professionally, but he loved the arts. He loved music, he loved opera. And he always had a nice tie on, you know. He's a laborer. And he saved his money, came to this country as a young man. And then he brought his wife and his two daughters. They all did that. They came alone for a few years and saved money. But my grandfather worked hard and saved money and bought a two-flat on Division Street and Mobile Street. Now Mobile's near Harlem Avenue. And that was all country in those days. He bought this two-flat. He was doing real well and he worked hard. He lost that two-flat during the Depression and never went back to work. He felt so screwed.

My maternal grandmother, I spent a lot of time with her. My mother was working and I dearly loved this woman. To say I loved her more than my other grandmother wouldn't be fair. And it might be real. But I spent more time with her. She used to hold me and if it was cold out, she'd rub my hands. She'd kiss me and you know, get my hands warm. When they were still on Mohawk Avenue, after we went to Wells Street, I would go over and spend time and sleep overnight. And every time I went there, you know, and I would go there a lot, I would go to the basement and pick up coal for them. Two buckets of coal. Every day … every other day. When I was going to school, I'd stop, go by Grandma's and get the coal.

When I slept over, when I was still a little guy, she always made sure there was a package of cinnamon rolls for me. That I loved, with coffee. You know, I used to drink coffee when I was a kid. And you know, you knew she loved you, she was crazy about you. And I knew that and as far as interaction on a intellectual level, naw we just felt comfortable. You know, I felt really good when I was with her. And her husband. He was a mild man and my father was not. So I could see the two of 'em and I was named after my grandfather. The artist. Benito Fabri.

My father's mother was a widow. She lived on the North Side up on Foster near California Avenue. In those days it was pretty nice.

Her daughters were all single. They all lived at home. Four of 'em. One stayed home, took care of Grandma and the other three worked and brought in the money. Then two got married and left. The two boys got married and left. Yeah. That's how she did it.

Jim Sullivan

But my grandfather died of cancer and it was like a one-year process of dying.

My father was Irish on both sides, yeah. My father's father married a girl, Catherine Sweeney, and they came over in the potato famine in the late 1890s or the late 1880s or early 1890s. But I don't have no background on them. I never met my father's parents. Dad was from Delaware. Wilmington, Delaware. I never visited them. Never went to their funerals. My father as far as I know never contacted his family.

The grandparents on my mother's side were German. They were always entrepreneurs. They always owned property and they got hurt pretty bad in the Depression. They lost a lot of stuff.

We always visited. You know, families always had like going to the grandparents' house. The kids used to come to our house all the time and on Sunday or whatever, we used to go to our grandparents' house. And they always threw parties and dinners and stuff like that.

I was close to them. When my grandfather got sick, I would like stay at the house and I would do like his chores. Like, I'd stoke the furnace, make sure there was coal in the hopper and stuff like that. I was in high school probably at that time. Up until then it was mostly visits, you know. Sometimes we'd sleep over an stuff like that.

I remember them dying. My grandmother died first. She had a sudden heart attack and she died probably you know, sixty-five, sixty six. I think my grandfather was older when he got married so he died when he was seventy-one or seventy-two. But he died of cancer and it was like a one-year process of dying, so. I was in high school.

My grandfather was a butcher all his life. He worked in Wilmette. So he walked like from Halsted Street to Clark Street, take a streetcar, take a train. Take it to Wilmette. Then you know, reverse the process at night, you know. Work ten hours a day, plus. He put in like fourteen-hour days as a butcher.

At one time he, you know, he owned a shop in Villa Park. In the twenties or thirties and stuff like that. That's when they had the money. You know, I don't know, it's pretty unclear what happened after they lost their shop and lost their property. I just think he worked as a butcher at some shop, you know, on the North Shore. Never retired. Worked until he died. You know, like he'd carry home a box of groceries every night. Big meat eaters.

My grandmother always had two pots of soup on the stove. One that she made yesterday and one she's making like today, you know. So that when one was over, the next one was on. My grandmother she was like the second or third generation German over here. So she was completely Americanized. And my grandfather was first generation so he had a German accent. He was "mitt der beer" and you know stuff like that.

My grandmother never worked, no, no. They had a rooming house. At 752 Schubert Street in Chicago. Yeah, I went there a lot. They had an apartment above the tavern. There was a tavern down below. Big tavern. My aunt had an apartment up above that and then on the other side of the staircase going up, there was like on each floor there was like three or four maybe five rooms that they rented out to single guys. You know people in those day, lot of people renting one, you know, one-room apartments. They did a lot of that. So that's how they supplemented their income.

Bedbugs were like the common foe at the time 'cause they would have transients that would come in and out. And they never knew who would bring what in with 'em. And I remember they just ripped the beds apart, lit newspapers and they would burn the shit out of everything that was in sight. It was like that's the way, I shouldn't say disinfected, but that's the way they cleaned up everything. If they couldn't find it on a curtain or a sheet or something like that, and clean it that way, then they went through the beds itself. In those days everybody had like springs. You know with the mattress on top of the springs. And the bedbugs used to like infest the springs. They'd put the springs outside or something like that. Then using newspaper, they would torch the whole area.

Jay Pistone

> *My grandmother's youngest son died in 1935 and from that day on she always wore black and every Sunday she would go to the cemetery. Catch the train, walk miles, you know what I mean?*

My dad's father died years ago before my dad got here. He got kicked by a horse in Sicily. And when my dad came here, he never seen his mother again. She died in Italy and two of his sisters died later on in Italy.

My grandmother lived next door, in the basement. 'Cause she used to come up and take care of me and my kid brother. That grandmother was my mother's mother. Yeah my mother was already deceased.

Oh, I was very close to my grandma. You know. When my mother first died, my grandma lived downstairs and she stayed with us, you know, for a couple a months at night. Then she always used to come up after work, check on us you know. And she went to church every day at St. Joseph's before she went to work. She wore black all her life.

Well her son died. Her youngest son died in 1935 and from that day on she always wore black and every Sunday she would go to the cemetery. Catch the train, walk miles, you know what I mean? I mean, they had a hard life. And she took the death of my mother pretty bad. She took it real bad.

Yeah, right. Son and daughter. Eight years apart. And she took it real bad. She had a tough life. She had a rupture and she never had it taken care of, you know what I mean. She wore the belt, you know, for a woman, yeah. But she was very beautiful. She had long, long hair. She had a braid, but at night she used to comb her hair. It'd be down to her butt. You know what I mean. Lot of the Italian women were like that.

Yeah. She was a tough little woman. One time my grandmother found a rat in the house. She lived in the basement next door. She was a remarkable woman. She just grabbed it by the neck. She put the rat in the toilet and drowned it. You know, just stuck it in the toilet.

What they do, the rats start making holes. And these homes were beneath the street level. And they had sheds and basement apartments facing the shed. So down there you had lotta rats. And that's why lotta people had cats and dogs. You know. To keep the rats away. There were a lotta rats around there 'cause the garbage didn't have containers, they had cement blocks. Yeah. Yeah. The poor garbage man had to shovel it out.

My brother married a Polish girl and that caused a little problem. Yeah, in those days it was not done. The Polish and Italians couldn't mix. My grandmother softened the blow. Oh, she told my dad, that, you know, it's my brother's choice and forget about what she is. Then my dad embraced her. They got along real good. Yeah, he gave in. He was a little perturbed at first. Yeah. Yeah, he listened to her. Oh, they were very close. They were very close.

My grandmother worked downtown sewing zippers. Five days a week. She brought zippers home at night and sewed to make extra money. Went to church every morning. It was not piecework. It was how much maybe you got per pants, you know what I mean.

Her husband didn't work. A lot of Italian men in those days didn't work. The wife went to work. He sat on the steps and spit. You know what I mean? See how far he could spit.

Frank DeMonte

But they saved everything. You know you make a dollar; they saved ninety-six cents.

Well, my grandparents on my mother's side came from a town called Chefelu.

Sicily. Northern part of Sicily about ten miles east of Palermo. But it's on the Mediterranean. It's a gorgeous town. Yeah we were there. But they never talked about it when I was young. When they came over to the United States, they went via Africa, then Marseilles.

He got a job, a political job. He was the maintenance guy for Navy Pier. That's where he used to take me a lot. He used to take me downtown to Navy Pier early in the morning. He would do some of the maintenance stuff and I'd go in with him. I remembered Navy Pier, which was fantastic back then. The ships and everything. Yeah.

A nice person. He was the nicest, nicest person. He got involved in politics you know like precinct captain. He was no ward committeeman, but he helped the ward committeeman out. In fact he was instrumental in certain times of passing food out. They would pass food out to the people who didn't have much food. And Joe Zummo always said that he helped them out. He came over to their house and gave the family some food.

My grandfather owned his own house; he had a four-flat house, with three in the front and a cottage in the rear.

They worked extremely hard in all the laboring type fields. But they saved everything. You know you make a dollar; they saved ninety-six cents.

He owned the building but we all lived together, my mother, my father, my maternal grandmother, and grandfather, and me. And then my brother came along later cause I'm five and a half years older than him. My grandfather was the one who really taught me how to speak Italian. Him and my grandmother. Since we lived there, they spoke Italian. So you had to speak Italian.

The thing that I remember is the smells in my grandfather's house on my mother's side cause we lived there. Man, there was a ton of garlic. There was garlic everywhere. The cooking smells were just fantastic. You know, I mean they would make pasta with the sauce. With what we call sugo. Now we pronounce it in Sicilian, zugo. Cause Sicilians kind of bastardize all, all the words anyway.

When I was growing up I spoke fluent Sicilian. Cause of my grandparents being there. Yeah. They taught me. My grandmother on my mother's side never learned English. Never. She knew maybe a couple a words. We had a small television set, and my buddy, I don't know if you ever met Billy Hague, he came over. He was a basketball player. Big spaghetti dinner. And we sat down in front of the TV and my grandmother said, "Francisco, put on Abugotz." Abugotz. Course I knew what she meant. But Abugotz was Arthur Godfrey. But my grandfather on my mother's side spoke pretty good English.

My father and my grandfather, they would speak Italian but I could understand Italian at that time. My grandfather you know he came from Italy and they used to talk about Il Duce (Mussolini) all the time. He didn't think too highly of Il Duce, especially fighting the United States.

But in the basement of the building he had a card room that all his compatriots from Italy would come and play cards. He also had the wine cellar next to where he made his own wine with his own press. My grandfather used to have me with him all the time when he was home. He had me at the card game. My grandfather on my mother's side was always interested in politics.

I was five, six, maybe even younger. They were talking about the war, and one of the Italian guys said that he thought Il Duce was right and United States was wrong. "What are you talking about Il

Duce for, the guy was a geek so to speak cause he didn't give anybody any jobs in Sicily and he tore the country up. He's fighting the United States who adopted us in this country and I love this country."

My grandfather whacked him in the mouth, knocked him down told him to leave. He says, if you don't know the difference between Italy and the United States you're not welcome in this place. I remembered it very clear 'cause I got startled when he hit 'em. You know I'm just a kid. I never seen somebody getting hit.

I could tell you one thing on both grandparents on the male part. They were kind of like laborers and had to go to work in kind of work clothes. Come home after that, they would take a bath, and they would dress up in suits and ties and ... yeah. I mean that's what they did. If you notice this picture of my grandfather, that's a picture of my mother's side, he has a suit and tie on. I mean, he's got a shirt with a tie on. I don't think I ever seen any picture of my grandparents that they weren't dressed up. And they were just laborers. Yeah. But they always wanted to be neat. And they always had a hat. I mean unbelievable.

I think I was thirteen, twelve, thirteen, when all my grandparents died. All died within a year. My grandmother's death was very painful. She had cancer. But my grandmother and my aunt were so close. My aunt Carmela. She was a midwife in Sicily. Carmela. That's my grandfather's sister. And she come over when my grandmother was dying and she would bring the leeches in this thing. She would put 'em on my grandmother's back and side and take out the bad blood. I remember her doing that. Yeah. Scared me to death. I saw it one time and that's it. It was kind of a normal. I mean they didn't even think about it. That was the remedy and that's it.

Ken Martinez

She was blind. She had white eyes. That fascinated the hell out of me.

I knew my grandmother, Grandma Teen. That was my father's mother. That's the only grandparent I knew. Lonergan, my mother's father, I think he died in the nineteen twenties. I didn't know the other three.

I don't know how old Grandma Teen was. I always thought she was a hundred years old. She was blind. She had white eyes. That fascinated the hell out of me. And she couldn't hear. But she would sew. So I used to sit on that little bench and I would thread her needles for her. She would sit there and sew socks. Uncle Paul's socks, or Ma would bring socks up and she'd sit there and sew by the window on the second floor. In that little bedroom. Couldn't a been more than four feet by eight feet with a linoleum floor. And she sewed. Let's see, there was a dresser in her room and the bed and then there was the door to the kitchen with four pieces of glass in it.

Joe Zummo

There was civility in their home, solidarity.

My grandparents were truly special to me. They were my father's parents. I walked to their house when I was four years old. About eight or ten blocks by myself and getting over there it was a little bit boring in a way because if my aunts or uncles weren't there you know it was strictly a Sicilian family that only spoke Sicilian. However there was always food and a treat there.

There was civility in their home, solidarity. My relationship with my grandfather wasn't that close. He was an authority figure. I saw him as a big husky man and I was very careful when I was around him but I felt much closer to my grandmother. My grandfather was a fruit peddler. He had a pushcart that he literally pushed through the city and when he emptied it he would go back home and reload. He did this three times a day. He had regular customers. He couldn't read or write Italian or English. My grandmother could read and write because she had a private tutor in Italy. And every day when he would come home he would put all the currency on the table and stack up all the coins. Never a paid holiday or vacation. They ended up buying a three story building and they bought the lot next where they had a little bit of Sicily where they had their garden. My grandfather came over from Italy first and the way the story was he worked seven years in the U.S. before he could afford to bring the whole family over. My father was about ten when he was brought over.

Charlie Martinez

All Saints Cemetery is the grassy area where a dozen or so of my close relatives are at rest. They sleep in the "old" section on the east side of River Road in Des Plaines, Illinois. I have visited it maybe six times, usually to attend a burial ceremony. But it was only as an adult that I really took notice of a grey, granite memorial with a black facing near a mature oak tree. In surprisingly large letters the name Martinez is chiseled into it. A ten inch cross rose from the top of the three by five foot stone and along the bottom, names of my ancestors were carved with dates of birth and death.

Ernestine "Teen" Martinez, my paternal grandmother, rested next to her husband Girard, whom I never met. "Teen" was born in 1860 in New Orleans. That engaged my young mind in figuring that one person -- my grandmother, could connect the time between Abraham Lincoln and me. Sleeping with them is sweet Uncle Paul Soraparu and his wife, my Aunt Nini. A hundred feet away, across a small path, are my parents, Max and Ellen, and between these two groups, my older sister Maryellen and her husband Marty McDonough are resting. Still farther to the west, a group of miniature headstones, flush with the ground, are lined up in narrow rows. Here lies my infant nephew, David, my sister Jackie's boy.

In winter and summer, All Saints Cemetery is sunny when I visit and a pleasant sadness overcomes me. Visitors I never saw. Perhaps they were hidden behind tombstones. But looking at the graves, I wondered what I had lost knowing my grandparents only through hearsay. My paternal grandmother's parents dated to 1840 and before. Did she hear stories about the black and white problem in my family? Had her aunt or mother described Maryann Picquery, the free black that lived with a white man, Michael Meffre Rouzan? That woman was my grandmother's great, great grandmother and my great, great, great, grandmother. A lot of history repressed and some forgotten to protect each following generation. I can't blame them.

Part Two: Father

Those Winter Sundays

Sundays too my father got up early
And put his clothes on in the blueblack cold,
Then with cracked hands that ached
From labor in the weekday weather made
Banked fires blaze. No one ever thanked him.

I'd wake and hear the cold splintering, breaking.
When the rooms were warm, he'd call,
And slowly I would rise and dress,
Fearing the chronic angers of that house.

Speaking indifferently to him,
Who had driven out the cold
And polished my good shoes as well.
What did I know, what did I know
Of love's austere and lonely offices?

Robert Hayden

Charlie Martinez

"What the hell's the matter with you? You got no sense?"

    My father brought the odors of his trade home with him. His splattered overalls gave off the aroma of shellac, paint, and turpentine. He was a painter and wallpaper hanger. From my brothers and sisters and friends, I got the impression that he did above average work as a painter and wallpaper hanger in his early years. I approached him in my late teens to suggest that he, several of my brothers and I open a painting and wallpaper business but there was no further discussion of this plan.
    My father was forty years old when I was born and I was the tenth of eleven children.

In my early years he seemed gruff and impatient with me. He took me to the Plaza Theater by myself when I was about seven. As we went north on Orleans Street, up the two blocks to the show, he stopped when we were under the elevated tracks and he said roughly, "If you have to go, go now under the L, I don't want to bother in the show." I remember another rough encounter when I was seven or eight. He had just finished painting the inside doorknob to the kitchen door and he turned to clean his brush just as I started to leave the kitchen. I grabbed the doorknob and smeared the paint. He responded as if I had ripped the door off its hinges.

"What the hell's the matter with you? You got no sense?"

He pushed me to the side and immediately began to reopen the can of paint.

I absorbed this with no comment, no backtalk, and so no communication with my father.

Ken Martinez

What does a child know? Fathers don't tell you all their problems.

My father was a painter. He painted houses. He was always going out to paint. And worked on the WPA. Worked on Lake Shore Drive. I really don't know what he did on Lake Shore Drive. I think he was a laborer. I was watching him one time putting newspapers in his coat. I don't know, I guess to keep the cold away. And I was standing there watching him put the newspapers up his sleeves and then he buttoned his coat.

Sometimes he would show me how to do stuff, and then sometimes he would lose patience with me. When I dumped his nails over because I wanted to see how many nails were in the bucket, he cracked me for it. Then I had to scoop up all those nails. Why he would save all those nails I have no idea.

I don't remember him ever really being mean. I really don't.

I don't think my father was religious at that time. I think he got more religious later, after my mother died. I remember my mother saying, Max are you gonna go to church. "Say your beads Nell, I'll go next week." See. But I always heard, "Go say your beads."

But he was always going out with those white overalls on. Painting things after a while, after he got off the couch. And then he used to let me clean his paintbrushes. He used to make wallpaper paste and he would put syrup in it. Then he would have me stir it. I'd stand there stirring it. It didn't taste bad. It was flour. Yeah. And I would taste it and I asked, why the syrup, he says it lets you take the paper off easier. See.

I was watching him cut wood. Him and I dragged railroad ties home to Schiller Street from underneath the L. Yeah. I was six, seven. And we dragged one home and we put it on the horse and he was sawing it. And I was trying to learn how to saw. He had one end, I had the other. We were going back and forth, back and forth. He went to do something else and I did it and I think I cracked the blade. The blade was hot. Yeah. Cracked it. So he cracked me. But I didn't cry. That's the funny part about it. I never cried when he hit me. I guess I cried too much when I was a kid, ah, when I was a baby.

I think I was six when I broke Pa's radio. Well, it had four legs and a piece of wood and the speaker was under there. And I put my hand under there ... I could feel the vibration and I poked a hole in the speaker and then I took ... I don't know where I got the toilet paper, but I put toilet paper in it to cover the hole. And he cracked my butt for it. Yeah. Then the next time I played with the radio I stuck my hand up and I touched the top of the tube when it was on. And I come flying out from underneath it. He said you won't touch it again will ya? I didn't.

Pa's moustache was black. He had dark hair and he had his Knights of Columbus ring on. That's the only ring I ever saw him wear. Sometimes he had his white overalls on. Pa was never tall. Pa was short.

Yeah. He would laugh. We had a funeral when I was a real small kid in the house on Schiller Street. Everybody came over after a funeral. And they were all there ... everybody, well all the Irish people were there talking. Uncle Mike would say something and Pa saying to him, "All you guys ever do is throw stones at the Black and Tan." Black and Tan were the Scottish troops in Ireland in 1924.

He was on the couch a long time. On the couch in the front room. Just lying there. For a long time. It was a blue couch. He got ruptured when he was working on the WPA on Lake Shore Drive. Lifting stuff. Exactly why he was on the couch, that I couldn't tell you. He didn't go to the hospital; I guess it had to heal. No. I really didn't know. He was sick, you know. What does a child know? They don't tell you all their problems.

Charlie Martinez

...but just having him to myself filled me with content.

Pa did some baking and Creole cooking and one Sunday night when I was nine, he baked cookies. That's when we lived on Schiller Street. We went into the living room where he turned out the lights and turned on the radio, a four-foot high, console type unit with a large face for the station numbers and four dials. He sat in a chair and I sat on the floor in front of the radio. Only the yellowish glow of the radio face lit the room. He tuned on the scary mystery show, "Inner Sanctum" with the horrifying squeaking door. That was a wonderful time. We didn't talk that I recall, but just having him to myself filled me with content. His affectionate nickname for me was Charles Ruggles, after an old movie star.

Bunny Byrne

He went through his whole life and he never, never came to a game or talked to us about sports. And we all played sports.

My father came here in 1920. He was twenty-three. He was a fisherman in the old country, in Ireland. See, so when he got here, why he was on boats since he was a young kid. He knew how to splice lines and you know, splice cable and everything. He came down and somebody told him, "Why don't you go down to the docks?" And he went down, he told me, he says, "I'm a seaman you know." And they said, "Can you splice?" "Yeah, I can splice." "Can ya do this?" "Yeah." Cause he used to make nets and everything. So they gave him the job. He worked on a tug. On a tugboat.

He was tough but I mean he just didn't get involved in disciplining us. He just, he let my mother handle it. He didn't believe in, John did this at noon and he's home at eight o'clock at night. He didn't believe in, I'm not going after him at eight o'clock tonight for something he done at noon,

Did he even come to my graduation? Maybe. High school he did. I remember him at high school. I'm not sure about grammar school. He could've been working. But if he wasn't working, he was there.

My father drank. Not bad, ah, he never missed work. You know, he never missed church. Always went to church.

But I mean, you know, a funny thing is, it's almost sad. My father never was at a ball game. Ever. Probably never was to a theater. To a movie. He just never did, you know, understand baseball. Didn't know what football was about. Didn't know what basketball was about. Didn't have a clue. You know, it's unbelievable that he went through his whole life and he never, never came to a game or talked to us about sports. And we all played sports.

Charlie Martinez

From age ten till my early twenties I assumed my father worked regularly. I would come home for lunch in grammar school and he was always there, also eating lunch and smoking a cigarette as he sat on the top of two stairs that led out of the kitchen to the back porch. In those years I thought he came home from work and then went back. That was all I needed to know and I knew he was just like the other fathers. Later I learned that he did not work regularly from about when I was born till he died at age eighty-nine. Actually he worked only occasionally for a friend or relative. Why he essentially stopped working so early in the depths of the Depression and with eleven kids was never questioned or explained.

Joe Zummo

We never had a discussion.

My father was basically a quiet, thin, selfless man who never missed a day's work and came home with his check and handed it over to my mother. His greatest value was education. That's all he talked about was getting an education and going to school. To my knowledge my father went to only third grade. He had to leave to work.

He never complained about paying my tuition even though we had very little. My dad was super quiet and I had no real interaction with him. The main thing he did for entertainment was to go to the local moviehouse and the other was to visit his mother and father and just sitting around and talking. And I would join him but it was pretty boring and there wasn't much interaction with him. I craved for it but didn't expect much from him.

He was a relatively good cook and it was not uncommon for him to come home and make his own meals. Of course everything he made was fried. He was short, about five seven, very gaunt and light complected. He would come home from work, shave, put on a clean shirt and tie and sit on the couch and read. Then he went to get his paper, read the Tribune and went to bed at ten o'clock. We never had a discussion.

John Giovenco

My parents never gave me any advice about school except that school was bad for your eyes.

My father was born in the United States and as an infant was brought back to the home of his mother and father which was in Sicily. And he lived there until he was about seventeen or eighteen at which time he was contacted by the American Consulate and had to determine whether he wanted to retain his American citizenship or his Italian citizenship. He chose American. He heard that the place to come was Chicago. So he came to Chicago. Arrived here and immediately went to work for Curtiss Candy Company for which he worked for the rest of his life. His first paycheck after working a six-day week was eight dollars. He saw that and told me he said "Now I'm never going back to Italy."

He worked in the section of Curtis Candy where they mixed the chocolate. Putting chocolate on the bars. When he retired he had that same job and very generous retirement benefits of seventeen cents a month. Seventeen cents a month! Nothing but Social Security for income.

My father went to visit my grandfather and saw my mother sewing and knitting and asked my grandfather if he could court her. They courted for a while, he taking the whole family to movies like they did in the old days. Go sit there but being constantly escorted around. So he married her. She was sixteen at the time they married. I think my father was twenty-two. That was one of those big Italian three-day weddings you know. Long thing.

In Italy, he went to school for one day. While in Italy he was responsible for maintaining the olive grove and so he would take a donkey to the grove, work there all day, come back and then go to school at night. And the teacher told him that he was just too tired, might as well just not come. So he didn't. And that was his entire education. He couldn't read or write, neither Italian nor English. But my mother or father never complained about their lack of education.

My father was small and bent over but had a pleasant smile on his face most of the time. He was about five foot three. He would always dress in pants and a polo shirt. When I was fourteen, my father tried to hit me, and I grabbed his arms and wrestled him to the ground and pinned him.

My contact with my parents in grammar school and high school was functional. They never gave me any advice about school except that school was bad for your eyes.

My father gave me one bit of advice in my whole life. It was on his deathbed. He said, "John, let me tell ya," he said, "a woman can be very gentle and they can be very nice to you and they can be very sexual but they will control you. Cause they did with me. They will control you and take all your money. Be the boss. And you're the guy always getting chewed on." That was his gift.

That was my inheritance. That was the only advice my father ever gave me about anything. He was not out of it at the time, but he died a few weeks later.

Charlie Martinez

My father was about five foot seven or eight with a moderately stocky build. He always wore a moustache. His smile was very appealing. He was extroverted with people but unassuming, forcing others to ask him about himself.

He always dressed neatly in the evening and on weekends. He wore a tie and sport shirt and appeared like a successful businessman to me. I don't recall any conversations with him during my grammar school years except somewhere in the mid grades. I believe I was to get a vaccination. He was against it and told me, "That stuff is made from cow pus." I know I received my vaccination anyway.

Early in grammar school he would entice us to take castor oil by holding up an orange as a reward. The castor oil was to "clean out our system," whatever that meant. I noticed that his hand that held the orange showed a badly nicotine-stained index finger and thumb from his heavy smoking. So I began to notice this disconnect between what he said and wanted us to do and what he actually did.

Pat Rogers

I think just the close contact of so many kids being in the same vicinity, he would just flip you know.

Dad was in construction. He was a hod carrier. Hod carrier was somebody who was a common laborer. Generally worked with plaster, brick, mortar. Hard labor. He was also -- as many of the people from Donegal, Ireland were -- a TNT man. They were dynamiters. They either were fishermen or dynamiters. So he had that experience and a lot of them worked in the wells in building the large buildings downtown. Like the Chicago Tribune. He was part of that, and even the Lawson YMCA.

Sometimes he worked seven days a week. If the work was there, and then again they could've been out of work for a goodly portion of time too. He didn't have the skills to work in the factories. I wouldn't even say he was literate. He only had two years of elementary school. Whereas mom had six years of elementary school. And although the schooling was superior to American education at the time, I wouldn't say that my dad was literate.

My dad never talked about Ireland at all. No. He was so irritated for some reason. It never really came out. And my mom didn't confide in us either. It was something deeper.

My dad and his friend, big Barney Gallagher, at fifteen found jobs digging British Naval bases. By hand. In Scotland. And of course all of them went over there for the Paddyhoken. You know, that was collecting potatoes at various places in Donegal patrolled by the landlords and also they found jobs in Scotland. It was quite common for many people to leave by a small boat. They carried twenty, twenty-five people over to Scotland. They stayed there for months.

My mother and father met here at an Irish dance. The people from Aranmoor, the people from Burtonport, and Kajue, and Acres and Mallenduff generally knew each other in common. But there was a stock of Aranmore men that generally associated together. Frequently. And again many of them got into the construction trade here, but also many of them worked the boats and especially in Beaver Island, Michigan.

My dad had a temper. He was very good as I can recall. But he was temperamental and there was so many of us, I think just the close contact of so many kids being in the same vicinity, he would just flip you know, and then he would scream and shout and so on and so forth. But he wouldn't bother you unless my mom suggested it that so and so did this and that. And then he gave the older ones a big crack, never the younger ones, you know. And I can remember as we grew older and when we got a crack we certainly deserved it, at least myself and Frankie did. Mom never touched anybody.

He did not work steady in the Depression. You know Chuck, and I can't really swear by this because there just weren't any jobs, but they were probably on the dole. My brother Jimmy worked, though. He was singing down at the Blackstone Theater.

That kind of saved the family. There's no question about it. It was probably like thirty-five dollars a month. And if they were down there and it was stage-connected, they probably had an agent. You know working for them. And essentially they were the kids from Holy Name Cathedral Choir. They were down there for about three years. And again, you have to understand, I wasn't around.

Charlie Martinez

When I was in high school in the late 1940s, my father and I occasionally had discussions about the White Sox since we were both fans. He did talk to me about his early baseball career and how he played semi-pro ball when the gloves were very thin with hardly any padding.

Also in early high school, when we lived on North Park Avenue, my younger sister and I were fooling around and as she leaned on the kitchen table, I knocked her hand away and she hit her lower abdomen against the edge. She was about eleven at the time and ran crying to my mother. My father said to me in a demeaning voice, "You are smart on book learning but you know nothing about women," or something to that effect. Of course I didn't know what the hell he was talking about except I felt in the back of my mind I had damaged her 'female organs.' I responded with silence, not knowing how to tell adults my feelings. I was confused and embarrassed. In those days he also passed another oblique remark to me. My older brother Ken hung around with a fellow named Gus Johns. For some reason my father didn't like Gus and implied to me there was something wrong with him because he abused himself too much. Now I can't remember his exact words, but this was the impression I got because my father vigorously moved his hand in his pocket as he spoke.

Jim Sullivan

You know, he was a thoughtful kind of guy. Sort of a neat guy. Everybody sort of liked him.

We lived at 1437 Wells Street when my father got sick at that particular time. He was in the sanitarium for a number of years. Had some major surgery while in the sanitarium with tuberculosis. It was the tuberculosis hospital that they had in Chicago at that particular time, on Peterson Avenue at Crawford, yeah, right.

So my father probably got sick when I was six or seven years old. And he was out of the unit, out of the family for a couple of years. You know, maybe, three of four years. Because in those days with tuberculosis they did radical surgery by taking all the ribs out in the back. So he had no bone structure in the back at all. It took that long to heal and then, you know, he'd be validated as cured.

No, I never was allowed to visit him. And there were also very extensive TB tests at that time that we had to go through. Shots. And periodically checking us out. One of my main jobs as a young kid, when my father came back, was scouring that silverware, you know. Well, in case he did use it, you know, that we were going to be transmitting the germ to ourselves. That was the job my mother gave me. You know, so whenever I did the dishes, at an early age, you know, I had to have kitchen cleanser on it and actually I rubbed the stuff down.

My father worked for a number of different companies. He was sort of like sickly so he didn't always have a job. But he worked for the longest for Link Belt. He was a draftsman. He was pretty good at numbers, had a fairly decent education, and good command of the English language. Could write very well. Had beautiful penmanship. And I think pretty well read.

The last ten years or twelve years of his life he worked in a tool shop in a manufacturing plant. And he'd be responsible for checking out tools that they needed at the time.

My father's first name was Harry. His real name might have been Henry. I never met my father's parents. He was from Delaware. Wilmington, Delaware. We never went to his parents' funerals. My father as far as I know never contacted his family. He didn't know his brothers or sisters.

When I had just got out of the service, my father and I took a trip to Wilmington Delaware. He showed me the places that, like he went to church and stuff like that but we never contacted anybody. He showed me where he was from and the school he went to. The only thing I remember about that trip, my father was a chain smoker and on that bus he must've had three packs of cigarette butts on the floor like in a pile. Yeah on the Greyhound bus.

I think the idea for the trip might be my father's. I think my father might of wanted to sort like touch base with something. He didn't say he didn't want to see his relatives. He looked in the phone book and said he couldn't find 'em. I think it was more for his edification than it was for mine, 'cause I didn't really get a lot out of it. Part of it might have been that we didn't have a lot of money. We were not able to take cabs anyplace so you know we had to walk or take public transportation or something like that. It satisfied his curiosity.

When it was cold and my father wasn't in the sanitarium, he warmed up the house in the morning. Usually a potbelly stove. He would stoke the fire so that when you woke up in the morning you could get the thing going again in short order, you know.

My father dressed, you know, pretty neatly. I shouldn't say spiffy but he never wore gym shoes. He always had a hat on. Fedora type of hat. He had black hair, parted down the middle. Brown eyes, about five foot eleven. Sort of like walked with a little bit of a humped back 'cause all the ribs were removed from one side, you know. A radical lung removal. Pretty even-tempered. When I was small, he drank a little bit. He was abusive in tone but not, you know, he wouldn't strike us. Sometimes my mother would get after him to get after me, but usually the disciplinarian in the family was my mother. He was a, sort of a quiet, very nice sense of humor type of guy. Pretty much into working crossword puzzles and stuff like that. He could amuse himself very well.

When I came out of the service my relationship with my parents was closer. My father wrote me letters all the time. He had a very good penmanship and he wrote long, nice letters. You know, he was a thoughtful kind of guy.

Sort of a neat guy. Everybody sort of liked him. He died in 1963.

Charlie Martinez

My father was born in New Orleans and migrated to Chicago in 1910 with the Rouzans and Soraparus. These were his relatives. My wife and I later found documents showing that he and probably the others were part black. This was never discussed with him while he was alive and since we found this out in the 1970s, we didn't know if the rest of the family could handle it.

He was very proud of his education in New Orleans. He claimed he finished high school and the Jesuit school was so good that he received the equivalent of at least one year of college. Throughout his life he had beautiful penmanship. He followed politics very closely and I heard him and my older brothers hollering at each other about politics. Not a good intellectual discussion, just a gut response. He read the newspapers every day but I don't recall ever seeing him read a book. I never heard him discuss religion and as far as I remember, he never went to church in those years.

Jay Pistone

...the good landlord.

I'm very proud of my dad, because here's a man who couldn't read and write but knew every street by the numbers. You know, he knew California was twenty-eight hunnert, Western was 24, he never got lost. You know, as long he knew the numbers, Y'mean? He invented the number system on the telephone before they did. You know I mean? Well, we'll say Mohawk 4, he had the 664 written down, so he could do it. Because he wouldn't know what Mo is, you know, on the dial.

He owned buildings and couldn't read or write. He was a fruit and vegetable man.

Here's how he did the peddling. What he did, he had customers on the norwest side. Ah, not Italian. He had his own customers. He wasn't a one of these peddlers that hollered out, you know. And what he'd do, he had a bag and draw a pitcher of every item on the bag that was on the truck. Y' I mean? He'd draw a pitcher of every item on the truck so he wouldn't miss; you know he might have thirty items on that truck.

He had one route on Tuesday, Thursday, Saturday. An on Monday, Wednesday, Friday anoder area. Were he'd go. An in those days women were home, they wasn't working, see. Yeah, he could add. He could add and subtract. That was no problem. He just couldn't read n write. I mean, 'cause he would go into the market an buy ah hunnert pounds of potatoes for a certain price and he know how much he had to sell them for.

I used to go on Saturdays with him. Or in the summertime. I'd deliver. He would fill the order up and I would deliver. And my oldest brother did it first, you know. He was growing up, and then I did it. In the wintertime they used to have a little oil container to keep the truck warm. You know you, you'd be freezing your butt off. No heater in the back but there was heat in the truck.

He drew a pitcher of an orange, an apple, banana, potata, you know. Any vegetable there was an he drew a pitcher of it and then he knew the price of it and he would tell em this is what he had on the truck, what they needed. Den he had annuder bag and he would draw the pitcher. And she'd say, well John I want one head of lettuce, he'd draw one, a head of lettuce one. And she'd say I want three pounds of potatoes, he would put a three and draw potatoes. But he knew the potatoes were ten cents a pound and he would draw the thirty cents.

People in those days didn't have that much cash either, ya'know what mean? They got paid twice a month, or once a month, so you run a tab. And then at the end of the month they would pay him, you know.

He was very handy with his hands. He could do anything. Where we had our truck, he put radiators in, so we had radiator heat in our garage. Ya know I mean? Ya come in from the porch and you go right inta garage. He had it built that way. Ya know I mean? He made seats. You know you can put over the radiator so you can sit on it.

Yeah. He smoked. As he got older, he got emphysema. Little bit, little bit, he stopped, but he couldn't go up and down the steps any more as he got into his fifties. So he became a janitor in the school system.

So my dad was working right at the Cooley's School. Right near the house. He was ten minutes from the house. So he would work the four in the afternoon till midnight shift. Me and my kid brother were very close to my dad. You know. Cause he was there for us and we were without our mother.

Well he was short, heavy set and bald, you know, a typical little Italian. I got pictures of him and his brothers. Right. He was a small man. You know, strong but small. No beard or mustache. I would say he was about five feet, five one. He wore a hat, pants and shirt. He wore a suit maybe at a wake. He wore some after-shave lotion, yeah.

They wrote an article years ago in the Herald American. A whole big page with his picture on it. About the good landlord. You know in those days there was a lot of slum landlords. He wasn't a slum landlord. Like ya say that building we lived in there was three Negro families in there with us and he had two other buildings with Negroes in there. You know what I mean? The Herald American picked on it because one of the tenants called up about how nice he was and how good he was and so they followed through and they went to see the other tenants. They took pictures and they wrote a nice article about him at the time.

My grammar school graduation was held at the St. Joseph Church. Ah, my mother was deceased. My dad and my grandmother were there. I don't remember them saying anything. I guess we had a party. I can't remember. See, my dad took my mother's death pretty bad. And that was a few years after she passed away and he was still ah, you know , they were very close. He had to raise me and my kid brother. He had his hands full just, you know.

Now when the grandchildren came, my dad became a whole different guy. He was really into it. Yeah. Oh, he loved the grandchildren.

Michael Lutazzi

He used to take a shovel to work with his lunch on the streetcar and come home with a shovel every day.

They were farmers in Sicily. There were two boys and five girls in his family. His father was kicked in the groin by a mule and died of complications. He was in his forties, his father. My father, being he was the oldest in his family and he was sixteen years old, they decided to send him to America by himself. So there were five girls, his mother, and his brother back in Sicily. And a woman in Sicily back in 1900 with no husband, you know times were tough even with fathers and husbands.

He came here under sponsorship of a man by the name of Joe Zucheroe. He was like a great uncle in Sicily and he was already here. And these people had to have sponsors. New York. Chicago. And he lived with Uncle. It was like a pet name for Joe, I guess, you know. Tu would be uncle, you know. Peeto. Uncle Peeto. Uncle Joe. And his wife. They were wonderful, wonderful people. His wife was my grandmother's sister. That's how they were related, yeah.

So he kind of watched out for my father and took him to work on the railroads. They were ditch diggers and laborers at that time. So it was 1911. It was before the war and they would follow the railroad. I remember him talking about Utica, Illinois working out there. I remember me thinking, I could have been living in Sycamore, you know, if my father decided to settle out there instead of Chicago. A lot of times I believe they slept with the railroad on jobs, you know, for some days, then they'd come home.

He left the railroad and he got a job on construction. Used to take a shovel to work and a lunch. On the streetcar, come home with a shovel every day. And he worked with concrete, you know.

As he got older, he started bringing his family over. I think he brought them all over at one time. 'Cause they were all kids. He brought his mother. He had an apartment for all of 'em. He was taking care of everything, you know. He was probably twenty years old, twenty-one and was considered the head of the family. This was before the war. 'Cause during World War One there was no traffic coming back and forth and my mother came after the war.

I had very little conversation with my father when I was younger. As a matter of fact, we walked on like, what do you call it, eggshells in my house.

Then he'd come home and he'd take his sponge bath after work, not in the morning. You know, he'd get all cleaned up and shaved for dinner not for work. And I could still see him, you know, in the bathroom, shaving, putting powder on, and talcum his body, getting kind of dressed up and sitting down at dinner with a bottle of wine. He'd sit there for an hour and you know we'd be done eating, the girls would be doing the dishes. My father would call to my sister Donna for a cigar.

His dinner hour was a probably the most important time of the day for him. Then he had a cigar and he drank about two thirds of the bottle every day, every night. He'd put the unfinished fifth back in the pantry. Then when he came home from work the next day, he'd take that bottle downstairs and fill it up. And put it on the dining room table. And he'd do the same thing every night. And he made his own wine.

My father as the first guy up would start that fire. You'd lift these iron lids and put your wood and your coal in there. Then this part of the stove was for heating, cooking stuff. You know, you could cook right on that stove, you know. It'd get pretty hot. And then the kitchen would warm up too, you know. We didn't have any storm windows I don't think. Just windows and they got icy.

My father didn't go on vacations. His vacation was working on the house. Two weeks off in the summer and he'd work on the house. You gotta remember he came from Sicily where it was close to impossible to have property unless you already had it or somebody handed it down to you. That's why when people came here their prime objective was to own a piece of property.

When my father drank, he would become very argumentative and he would get mean. I remember guys arguing about the war, the Second World War and Churchill and Stalin. I remember my father arguing and feeling very, very strong about certain things and hollering at people in his arguments. So, I think that, you know, at my age today I believe that maybe some people didn't want to be with him. Especially if he had been drinking.

My father drank but he didn't go to bars. He was drinking at home and he was not chasing the women. He didn't go out drinking but he got mean when he drank. Sometimes it was violent and I was scared and we all were scared. And that's how I grew up.

But I can recall, you know, some tender moments. Him and I walking to North Avenue and Cleveland every winter buying a Christmas tree. They had trees in St. Michael's lot. It was just like one of those Christmas cards, him and I walking down North Avenue with a tree. I'm holding the, the light end and he's carrying the heavy end. To me it was very nice. It's a good memory for me.

Another one is when I was the baby of the family and my sisters claimed he spoiled me. Being in construction as he was, I can remember him when I was a little boy, taking me on a Sunday morning. Getting on the train, and we'd go to Skokie. And we'd get off, and we'd walked around. My father always dressed up on Sunday, you know. He wore a suit and tie every Sunday. You know, unless he stayed home. But if he left the house he had a tie on and a suit. And a hat. We'd go to Skokie and we'd walk down the street and he'd show me the buildings he worked on, the houses. Nice memory for me. And did that more than once.

And of course my father did slap my mother once in a while, you know. Yeah, I saw it. And that was very scary. My father died when I was nineteen. And I wouldn't allow that when I was nineteen. But all through growing up I would see that. If he had too much wine, he'd blame her spending too much money on food. And there would be a fight, you know. Then he'd slap her a couple times and then sometimes she would want to hit him back and we'd all grab her. No, my sisters would grab her. No mom, mom no. Cause we were all afraid that it would get worse if she hit him back, you know. Well that occurred when he used to drink, almost a fifth of wine every night. But he didn't do that all the time, you know.

When I was twelve, thirteen, I walked in and he says, where ya been…whack. And I hit the floor. He had big, hard, gnarled hands. And it hurt. When I hit the floor, he kicked me. But it was the only time, you know … if he hit me one more time, it really wasn't really bad. And he wasn't above hitting my mother. That's what scared us all. Yeah, grammar school was like a long, drawn out thing. I just hated it.

And one time they were gonna split, you know. And this was just traumatic for me cause I didn't understand. I was probably seven, eight. I got older and I grabbed him one time and I threw him against the wall. I was about eighteen. You know, you just didn't do them things. You didn't grab your father. But when he slaps your mother… Anyway, boys that are exposed to shit like that usually grow up to do things like that. They're defending their mother. She didn't do nothing.

My father died of a brain tumor. There was no surgery. He had an industrial accident once. We think that might've contributed to it. Years earlier, like about 1945 or '46, he was hit on the head by a freight elevator at the Dimitriv Manufacturing Company. And ah, we think that might've had something to do with this but we're not sure. But anyhow he took a vacation in 1955 in the summer and never went back to work. He started getting dizzy and six months later he was dead.

But then he died when he was sixty and I was nineteen. And things were peaceful. Things were peaceful when he died.

Charlie Martinez

I don't recall that my father came to my grammar school, or high school graduations and he never congratulated me or made any remark about an accomplishment that I can remember. He was not involved in my school and never attended any of the sports I played but many of the boys I played with had similar experiences. I can't remember being disappointed or wondering why he wasn't there. It never entered my mind.

I seemed to have little contact with him in my late teens but one time I overheard him talking to a family member about an ordinary office job I started between college semesters. He sounded proud that I had this job and was getting paid well.

Jack Flaherty

He sent me a letter. I didn't realize it but he had written it from his hospital bed.

My father was six foot and, well, he was a laborer. He worked for the gas company. I do remember an incident where he took me to Bughouse Square. It's a park directly south of Newberry Library. Well many people gathered there. It was just a nice place to walk around. Anyways, I guess I got separated from my Dad a bit and just started running around the park, enjoying myself. Some people got annoyed and attempted to chase me out of the park or away, to which my dad observed the goings on. He went over and threatened …well whatever, he chased them away. They turned tail and ran the other way. So, my father I guess you'd say was a rather aggressive person.

Another incident I remember with him was in later years, and I was eighteen at the time. He had come home from work. It was probably a Friday evening, paycheck in hand. Well, before coming home he would stop at the liquor store. A lot of people gathered there. Cashed his check, I guess had a couple of beers. A couple of black guys literally rolled him for his money. As I said, blacks were in our area at this time. Well he went home, cleaned up a bit, went back to the bar, found the guys, and got every penny back from 'em. He was aggressive. So he was kind a, he was my hero. That bar was at Oak and Wells. It was the northwest corner of Oak and Wells.

My father's education was only eighth grade, I believe. He never had high school. He was sick when I went in the Army and I didn't realize that 'course. He sent me a letter. I didn't realize it but he had written it from his hospital bed. He didn't tell me but I found out later that's how he did it. He got out of the hospital and later he died on the job. It was first thing in the morning. He probably had his heart attack probably around 8:30, 9:00 o'clock in the morning on the job. Yeah, 1959, yeah.

Charlie Martinez

A frequent duty for all the boys was to go late at night and pick up the Racing Form. My father bet small amounts on the races at a bookie but I never saw him actually bet and I did not know the location of the bookie. I don't think I ever saw him drink alcohol. He often told the story of how he was "poisoned" in the 1920s by bad "Dago" red wine and that turned him from alcohol.

Joe Olita

On his deathbed, my father said to my sister Rose that if and when he died, she was to take the four kids and her mother and go back to Italy.

My father had come to the United States by himself in order to send money back to Italy so that they could build a house in Italy. That's my mother and he. Always with the intention that eventually he would go back. This philosophy as far as some of the neighborhood people was extremely prevalent during those days. My father never did get the opportunity to go back to Italy. Much of his earnings as a matter of fact was sent back to Italy to build a house. And as a result we really didn't have any savings here. My mother was uneducated; she never went to school a day in her life.

My father actually was a laborer and worked to build the subways of Chicago. He was a rather vain person, from what my mother tells me, in that he would not change his clothes in front of the other men. As a result of that when the weather became very inclement, especially very cold in the wintertime, rather than changing into dry clothes and warm clothes, he would make his way home with the same clothes he worked in and course they were wet, and when the weather was cold, I do believe as a result of that he might have picked up the double pneumonia.

This was in 1934. I was four years old when he became ill with the double pneumonia. He was not hospitalized actually because we could not afford to have him in the hospital. He was nursed at home. After contacting the ailment, he didn't live that long and then he died.

Prior to his death he had called on my eldest sister, Rose, who at the time was really the communicator as far as the family was concerned because she was the one who knew how to speak English rather well, and therefore he called her into the bedroom. She might have been in her early teens. He said to her that if and when he died he wanted my two sisters and my brother and I and my mother to go back to Italy. And my sister told him "I would never do that."

Yes, she told him this on his deathbed. Her relationship with my father was a very, very bad one. He was extremely mean. He didn't care for daughters, and from what my sister tells me that when my brother and I were born, there was nothing too good for us. That we were always dressed very well. He did everything he possibly could for us, and apparently there were many instances where my sister had related to me that my father thought that the sun rose and set on both my brother's and my heads.

After my father died, my mother being totally uneducated, and never had gone to school a day in her life, we fell on some pretty seriously hard times.

Charlie Martinez

In the spring of 1945, during World War II, a telegram arrived saying that my brother-in-law, Marty McDonough, was killed in action in Germany. He was wounded and died all within two weeks of the war's end. I was in fifth grade and had come home for lunch. The house was quiet except for sobbing coming from my sister Maryellen's front bedroom. My father was sitting on the top of the two steps that led out of the kitchen to the back porch. He was waving the yellow and black telegram in his hand and said, "They oughta wipe that German's ass with this." He had tears in his eyes.

A few years later, we all gathered around an open gravesite in All Saints Cemetery. Marty's body was returned from Germany and was to be buried. The sun was bright and it was in the fall with the trees having given up most of their leaves. An honor guard gave a six-gun salute and the noise was shattering. The soldiers sharply put their rifles to their side and stood at attention. Then I heard the wail of a distant locomotive flow over the mourners and the gravesite. I felt the sadness of the distant train and the sadness of the occasion as I looked at the casket being lowered into the grave.

John Owens

> *He told me that he went into the service because they would give us an allotment every month. And he says to his family, you're gonna be better off with me being in there than being here.*

My father was black. He was totally black. He was from South Carolina, my mother too. She was white. Yeah. They met in Evanston. Both were married, yeah before they met and both divorced. And then they got together. My father had a daughter. I remember when I was a kid I saw her. She had to be in her twenties, her late twenties.

My father went into the service. I want to say it's probably 1941. I was six years old. He came back in '46. Yeah. He was in the Seabees. And I think he came home once on furlough during the whole time. Yeah. And he took me to the show, to the Woods Theater to see the "Fighting Seabees."

At that time, I'm about eleven years old. We took the streetcar. The old red streetcars. He was kind of a character, you know. We were watching the movie. It was with John Wayne. And I said, Dad why don't I see you in the movie. He says, well I was at the dentist that day when they were making the movie.

He was a crane operator. He worked for I don't know if you remember 'em. Consumer Materials Company, yeah. He made good money. He wasn't a crane operator before he was in the service. He was a laborer. Okay. He learned it in the service. He was a crane operator after he came back.

The reason he told me that he went into the service is because they would give us an allotment every month. We received the stamps to get food and he says, "You're gonna be better off with me being in there than being here" 'cause what I'm making …so his income wasn't that great. So I think he just figured, hey, this is the best thing for them me going into to the service. And he was up in his thirties when he went in, I mean. Yeah. He was probably at the limit where he could join. Got in under the wire, you know.

In the service he did mostly construction. He was stationed about 200 miles off the Australian coast. It was just like an island, I guess.

He would go to work. And he was a heavy drinker. You know he'd usually stopped at a tavern before he came home. There was a tavern on the corner of Division and Halsted Streets called the Greek's. He liked to play cards too. He'd get off the streetcar on Halsted Street and he'd go in there and he'd drink. Sometimes he wouldn't come home until seven, eight o'clock, nine o'clock at night and he'd be stiff. By that time my mother was all pissed because he, you know, was drinking all night. Sometimes they'd get in to little scuffles too. They'd have their arguments. Those things kinda got touchy here and there.

My father never hit me. But when he came home from the service I remember once my mother told him that I'd been getting into fights at school and I was getting beat up. So he took me to the basement and he came home with some boxing gloves. And he was punching me. "Put your hands up," I remember his saying ... I can't forget this, you know. I was crying and he's punching me with the gloves. He says, "You gotta learn how to fight." This went on for fifteen or twenty minutes. It never happened again. I guess I did learn how to fight a little bit, you know what I mean? As I got older I kind a, I got pretty tough. I don't know if that was the turning point or not.

I think he finished grammar school. That was it. He could read and write but he was not very literate. I mean, he was very well spoken and wrote perfect. I mean his penmanship was excellent. And he wrote letters. I mean, like he used to write me letters when he was in the service from the island. We used to get letters every day. Two, three pages, I mean. I don't have 'em. I don't know what happened to 'em.

Yeah, well once in awhile he'd say, how's things going over in high school. If I told him I had a situation where something was going on, he would say, "Well why don't you try this approach." So in that way he did get involved with me, you know. But he wouldn't go to the school.

Charlie Martinez

He would hide some of his pay in the window shade and then roll it up

When I was in my late teens, I asked my older brother, Tommy, about my father because I wanted to know how my father appeared to Tommy as a young boy. "Oh yeah, Dad took me fishing and everything and was like a normal father."

My other brothers and sisters were bitter towards my father because his lack of work caused the burden of supporting the family to fall on them. Another older brother, Clem, said he would hide some of his pay in the window shade and then roll it up. "This way Ma would get the money for essentials and Pa couldn't get his hands on it."

Once, without warning, he punched my artist brother, Jerry, in the face as Jerry walked up the stairs drunk one night. But when I came home with Jack Flaherty at age twenty after we had visited several bars and could hardly walk, we both got into bed with my father. He fell on the floor and then slept on the couch. We got up in the morning and went our way with no comment from my father.

I distilled out the good things about my father when I was young. I didn't dwell on the negatives, like his temper (which was mild compared to some of my friends' fathers). I didn't think about the lack of attention because I guess I didn't expect it. But to a boy, his baseball background, interest in sports and politics, beautiful penmanship, disdain for alcohol, fix-it attitude around the house and the fact that he was always around and never left the house for taverns or to be with the guys were all points of pride. None of this was discussed with other boys, siblings or adults.

Part Three: Mother

The Song of the Old Mother

I rise in the dawn, and I kneel and blow
Till the seed of the fire flicker and glow;
And then I must scrub, bake, and sweep,
Till the stars are beginning to blink and peep;
But the young lie long and dream in their bed
Of the matching of ribbons, the blue and the red,
And their day goes over in idleness,
And they sigh if the wind but lift up a tress:
While I must work because I am old
And the seed of the fire gets feeble and cold.

William Butler Yeats

Charlie Martinez

My mother was tall and thin in my childish perception. She had high cheekbones and a narrow, sharp nose. Her smiles were scarce and when she did smile, I noticed ill-fitting dentures. Constant was the flowered house dress and apron. Her rimless glasses produced a red, painful dent in the bridge of her nose. She kept her brown hair in a bun; I never saw it down. She wrapped a black turban over her hair when she left the house.

She let me play for hours in the gangway moving dirt with a toy bulldozer when I was four or five. When my brother Clem came home from the war in 1945, he hollered "Hey Irish" from that same gangway and I saw her smile. She was born in Chicago, I believe on Sedgwick Street, near Division on the Near North Side. Her parents were Irish immigrants and they died before I was born. Her mother died in childbirth and it was rumored that the doctor killed that baby because it was too much of a burden for a widower to raise. Though she finished eighth grade at St. Dominick's grammar school, I never saw her read anything but prayer books, missals and religious tracts. All through grammar school and high school I don't remember any discussion with her. My siblings and even my friends said they knew her as patient, sad, tolerant, non-judgmental and caring -- but my only response to these comments was that I didn't really know my mother.

Since I was the tenth out of eleven kids, my older sisters and brothers frequently acted as my parents by speaking to the teachers. When I was seven, I tried to open a large jackknife by holding down one side and pulling up on the blade. The blade slipped and cut my little finger. At that time my mother was entertaining some lady friends. She stopped the bleeding and bandaged my hand. She made no comment and did not chastise me.

My mother took me to a wake on Lincoln Avenue when I was about twelve, which is the only time I remember being alone with her. We took the streetcar to a funeral parlor across from St. Alphonsus Church on Lincoln Avenue. She had on a tired tweed coat and a black turban covered her hair. I recall no hugs, kisses, or compliments. I ran away from home when I was twelve and I was gone a week. My mother questioned where I had been, but I never answered. She threatened to put me in a "home" (orphanage) if I did that again. I was not punished and I felt that the family was very worried that I had gotten sick during my absence.

Every Irish mother in that neighborhood dreamed her son would become a priest. This duty was expected of me. I went to what they called the minor seminary. This was Quigley High School at Rush Street and Pearson Street, near Loyola University. I went there for two years, never studied and flunked Latin both years. They wanted me to repeat the second year but I decided to quit instead. I quit without any discussion with my family and they never asked me for an explanation but I sensed my mother was very disappointed. When I went to the senior prom, it seemed my mother knew her dream of my ever becoming a priest was now dead. I remember some kind of argument we had about this and I ended it by saying "You never did nothing for me." I have regretted that remark all my life.

My mother died in a car crash when I was eighteen in 1953. I was at work on a Saturday, enjoying the time and half pay as usual. My sister-in-law's niece called me up and said to come over. Naturally at eighteen, I fantasized that something sexual was up but she told me about the accident and I said, "Now she is in Heaven."

Later that day, I heard my younger sister Lee screaming and crying from the second floor when she was told. "I didn't tell her I loved her," she said. My brother-in-law, Dave, was in the basement on his haunches poking at my mother's polka dot dress with a stick as it soaked in cold water to remove blood stains. That was the dress she died in and wore in her coffin.

That night at the wake I seemed to float in a perplexing haze of people. Over and over comments were offered, such as "How do you feel," "Sorry to hear," "Anything I can do?" and "It's a shame." Ike Putrus, one of the guys in my crowd, asked me if I wanted to go out for coffee. I didn't go, but I never forgot his interest.
Father Morrison, my mother's favorite priest, said the funeral mass and gave a warm, sensitive sermon. In his closing lines he likened my mother's eleven children to stars lighting up the heavens for her arrival.

In my imagination, I visited the funeral parlor before anyone had arrived.

Sullivan's Funeral Home is just a block up the street from our house at the corner of North Park Avenue and North Avenue. The door is heavy and black with smoked glass panels near the top. I am early and see no one else. The entrance hall holds a half-filled water cooler and several chairs with heavy, dark brown embroidered upholstery. On my left is a board with white plastic changeable lettering. I read "Ellen Cassia Martinez, Chapel B."

It takes a few moments for my eyes to adjust to the dim lighting in the chapel. The room is long and narrow and filled with folding chairs, their backs marked "Property of Sullivan Funeral Home."

A brass stand with an open guest book is on my right as I enter. There is a stack of funeral holy cards and I pick one up. The card's embossed lettering gives it unexpected weight as I read: "Ellen Cassia Martinez, born to Christ 11-20-96. Elevated to heaven 5-31-53." A short prayer followed. On the reverse is a picture of the Blessed Virgin ministered to by angels.

An odor of stale air mixed with leftover cigarette smoke meets me in Chapel B. As I move toward the front of the chapel, the fragrance of roses, gladiolas, and lilies of the valley refreshes the air.

At the front is a long couch with dark brown upholstery matching the dark brown walls of the parlor. Three open boxes of Kleenex are on the cushions.

I go up and kneel on a padded leather kneeler in front of the coffin. Mother is resting in an all-wood, lightly-stained coffin, just what she wanted. I reach out and pass my hand along the highly varnished surface.

I turn my gaze to my mother. Her hair is pulled back in a bun the way she always wore it. She has on a white dress decorated with small dark blue polka dots; this was the dress she was wearing when she was injured and died in the collision. She has on her rimless glasses that make a noticeable dent in the bridge of her nose. Her mouth is more prominent because of her ill-fitting dentures. A rosary, blessed by the Pope, is wrapped through her crossed hands on her abdomen. I stare at her expecting her to take a breath or open her eyes but she is as still as the coffin.

Years later, after I was in medical school, I happened upon the missal she bought me when I was starting Quigley Seminary. Inside the original box were the missal and my dried, preserved prom boutonniere exactly as she had placed it, years before.

Michael Lutazzi

She worked downtown, on a sewing machine with a lot of other immigrant Italian women doing seamstress work.

Her and I would walk down Wells Street to North Avenue and then to Sedgwick. I'd go off to St. Mike's grammar school and she'd wait on the corner of North Avenue and Sedgwick, going south to the Loop. And she'd get on a streetcar. She worked downtown, on a sewing machine with a lot of other immigrant Italian women doing seamstress work. She did that for many, many years

At home if she had time, she did repairs on anything that needed sewing, and sometimes she'd make things. Very neat. My mother was a beautiful woman and she dressed very nicely. Very nice. She always had nice stuff on. When we went out, you know. She was a good dresser. She liked to, you know, dress up.

The thing that used to get me to come home on Sunday nights was my mother's bread. Yeah. On Sundays she'd make about five loaves of bread. I would leave my friends on Sunday night and go home just so I could get warm bread with butter. We'd be out screwing around in Lincoln Park or something, stealing hubcaps, breaking things. Aw, shit, what time…I gotta go home. I'd get home at seven o'clock and that's about the time, you know. And, she didn't know that. Maybe she did, maybe she did, but it got me home and nobody had to tell me to go home. But otherwise I would have stayed out another couple of hours screwing around.

And she must've known that I'd come home because the bread was still kind a little bit warm. Butter would be out there. Glass of milk. But what does bread smell like? Fresh bread? Yeah, I got it. I got it in my head, you know.

The trouble I got into, they didn't know about. You know, I came home on time. But one time, I came home real late. My mother, father, they were both waiting up in the kitchen. And my mother had this, I'll never forget, this look even till this day. She had this sad, forlorn, disappointed look, sitting in a chair. Maybe eleven, twelve o'clock at night. And I walked in and my father gave me a whack.

I don't know if she was so sad because she knew what was coming or she was disappointed in me.

John Giovenco

And her parents immediately pulled her out of school.

My mother was born here of parents who came from the same village that my father came from. A place called Alta Villa Milicia, which is a suburb of Palermo, Sicily. She went to school here as far as the seventh grade. When she was in eighth grade some boy walked her home and her parents immediately pulled her out of school. That was the last time she'd ever gone to school. So she never went to school again but sat at home and sewed and took care of the house.

Mother did not work up until the third child was in school. She went to work eventually for Continental Illinois Bank. She worked down in the vault. She filed stocks and bonds and clipped coupons down there. She was very, very happy with her job. Very proud of the fact she worked in an office. Very proud of that. She worked there till she died.

I did not have much interaction with her. More than my father, but there was never any intellectual conversation.

Joe Olita

I never really got a hug and a kiss from my mother till I was twenty-one years old.

My mother was sixteen years old when she got married. So my father had indicated to my mother that he was going to come to the States with the idea of getting himself established and then he would send for my mother. It was pretty obvious after awhile, and I'm saying a couple years, that my father really had no intention of inviting my mother to the United States.

After a period of time had expired she decided on her own, without any notification to my father at all, that she would take her two daughters and get on a ship and come to the United States. Now she stayed in New York only long enough to contact some relatives that at the time were living in Cleveland, Ohio. She stayed in Cleveland a very short period and then from there she moved out to Chicago to surprise my father.

My mother, because she lacked an education, was the one motivator I had in making sure that I went on to school to obtain my education. I honestly believe that if it wasn't for her constantly telling me how important it was for an education and seeing what the lack of education had done to her I would not have persevered. It had really hindered her progress because, all in all, she was a rather intelligent woman. She could really add very well. I mean she would go to the store and if she gave somebody a dollar and she was expecting 73 cents change back, she knew what 73 cents…well she had to know … right. Yeah.

My mother never came to my high school graduation at all. I got dressed up for the high school graduation and when the ceremony was over, I got on the streetcar and came home. There was no celebration at home. No. None.

As a matter of fact I don't think my mother even congratulated me. I knew she was proud, you know, because she was really the motivator for my education.

After my father died, my mother wore black. Black hose, back dresses, she wore nothing but black. In mourning for I'd say ... 30 years. Which was very common with Italian women. She was matronly appearing to me when I was a teenager. She wore her hair pulled up in a bun at all times. We used to try and convince her that, you know, wearing black like that was really ridiculous. Finally she did decide that she'd had enough of black and she went to the floral patterns and things like that. Yeah.

Well, yes. She did have a male friend. His name was Horatio-Horace. Okay. Horatio was a Communist. He was very interested in marrying my mother. I think he would have been a very good provider. My understanding is that he had made a proposal to my mother, of marriage. And she turned him down. In later years, I asked her, I says, you know Mom why is it that you never got married? She said, I didn't want anybody but your father disciplining you. And since your father was no longer around, I wasn't gonna have anybody telling you what to do or how you should behave and stuff like that. Which of course was ridiculous.

Incidentally when I was twenty-one years old, I did get a car. My mother bought it for me. I remember it was a 1951 Dodge. I bought for something like $1,800. She had saved the money I didn't know she had it. Yeah.

Yes, the money from my pay that I gave her, she saved it for me. She said, "You know you're the only one who doesn't have a car and you don't know how to drive." I said, "That's all right Mom, don't worry about it." She said, "Naw, I think you should go looking for a car."

I bought a car; it was a demo. It was $1,800 and I had never driven before. And I got in the car and drove it home. No problem. I was a little leery, but no problem. Cause I had always been with

65

people who drove cars so I knew the basic things about driving but had never really sat behind the wheel.

I never really got a hug and a kiss from my mother till I was twenty-one years old, but there was no doubt in my mind that my mother loved me more than anything on Earth. This happened when she was going back to Italy to sell the building that my father had built. She had never seen it. It was her first plane ride. I took her out to Midway Airport. In those days it didn't have the ramps which you got on, you had to walk up the stairs of course. So I followed her out to the plane and she turned around and gave me my first hug and my first kiss as she was boarding the plane. And I think she did that, Charlie, and this is very emotional for me, I think she did that because she figured well if the plane crashes she is never gonna see her family again.

Ken Martinez

And my mother says…you don't feel good. I can hear her voice…you're not feeling good.

My mother was always praying and sitting in a chair. I came home from school sick. It was in the wintertime. I came in the back door and she was sitting by the stove praying. She had a blue apron on with little tiny flowers and I went in and I put my head in her lap. She put her hand on my head and she says … "You don't feel good." I can hear her voice … "You're not feeling good." I don't know what she gave me, but I didn't feel good at all. I just had my head, you know in her lap. She was sitting in the red chair with the knobs on the top of it. Pa came in and put his hand on my forehead. I don't know where I was laying down but I could see his big hand on my forehead. Like to see if I had a fever or something.

She had her galoshes on with wax paper sticking out. Well, she went to church a lot and she always had her galoshes on going to church and the wax paper was so she could slide them on and off easy, see.

She always wore a dress. She had a turban. A black turban. She always wore it. And then she had biscuits in the back of her hair. Two of them.

My mother was Irish and her parents came from Ireland that I know of. Ma's mother died when she was a baby. I think. My mother was born here.

She could talk Gaelic to Uncle Tom when he'd come over. They'd talk a funny language so you wouldn't know what they were talking about. So every once in a while as I got better, I would listen to them and I could mimic 'em. See. And Uncle Tom talked (mimics him with garbled brogue) Nellie, Nellie, you think you got a little tea?

Peter Eichel

See something happened when I was about seven or eight years old, because up until that point, we were doing fine, you know, aside from this apartment.

I didn't explain my mother's mental illness to my friends. I wasn't embarrassed by it. It was never an issue. My mother was well liked by everybody and she liked most of the kids that we knew. And without ever knowing there were any drugs in the neighborhood she singled out people who were doing drugs as not good people. She somehow was able to figure that out, I don't know how that happened. No, her being mentally ill was never an issue with my friends.

She wasn't a bad person; it's just that she was incompetent. My younger sister was the one that suffered the most because my mother had thrown my older sister out of the house. Just threw her out. Can't come home. Can't live here anymore. Who the hell knows why at that time but fortunately she was able to go live with my aunt, my mother's younger sister, who lived on LaSalle Street and North Avenue.

No one suggested or got medical help for my mother. Nobody understood at that time. We didn't think of it in terms that she was crazy; it was just that she had these problems. You know nobody knew or understood what a paranoid psychosis was.

My father and older sister Nancy weren't competent to make those kind of judgments. You know, they couldn't assess it. And of course Nancy was off on her own which is another story. See something happened when I was about seven or eight years old, because up until that point, we were doing fine, you know, aside from this apartment.

John Owens

She was a very superstitious woman, I mean, very superstitious. I mean she believed that somebody could put a hex on ya so to speak, you know

My mother was kind of a real caring person. She liked people. I mean she would be on the street and she'd talk to people, you know. She always liked the little kids. She always walked out there and say, "Don't do it. You're, you know, you're a good little kid, don't." She was always after kids, I mean, you know, to try and make 'em not do things they shouldn't do and things like that.

She used to get after me with the ironing cord she had cut off. And she'd whack me, you know. She'd beat the shit out of me if I did something wrong.

My mother never went to church regularly, but she liked to listen to these gospel programs on the radio or on television.

Yeah. She favored all religions. She'd get on streetcar and go to St. Jude's. I don't know if it was on 35th Street or something like that, on Halsted, and make candles. She'd watch the programs on television with the gospel singers. She had pictures of saints and she always had holy candles in the house. She was a very superstitious woman, I mean, *very* superstitious. I mean she believed that somebody could put a hex on ya so to speak, you know. She believed in that kind of stuff.

I don't think she ever finished grammar school. I don't think she had much of a education. She, yeah, she read but she had a lot of trouble. I don't think she read that well. And her writing, I mean, I don't think she ever was taught how to write properly, you know, any kind of penmanship or Palmer type of thing. It looked like she just picked it up on her own.

Bunny Byrnes

That was a different type of people, Charlie.

Jesus, my mother paid off everything. Just paid it. You know what happened? I'll tell ya. This is a true story. Rubloff managed the place at Delaware Avenue and State Street. When we left Delaware and State, we left because they were putting the subway through. They were afraid some of the older buildings were gonna fall in. So, ours was a wood frame building. So they were telling the people in the wood frame buildings to move.

Well, Rubloff was managing our building and he told my mother, you know, you're gonna hafta find another place to live. She was about a month behind in her rent at the time. Do you know that about 1945 she went down to Rubloff's office? He was on Grand Avenue and this is like seven years later. And she gave him the rent. That's right. She said, 'I was at 907 State, I owed ya twenty-two dollars, here it is." And he said, "Ma'm that's all right keep it." She said, "No, it's yours, you keep it." She gave him his money. The guy was a millionaire. But she says, "That bothered me for seven years. That I owed that guy's rent money." And she paid him. That was a different type of people, Charlie. Different type of people, you know. They believed in paying their bills and doing things right.

Joe Zummo

She was a consummate extrovert.

My mother was a talker. She said she graduated from high school but I am really not sure. She may have graduated from grammar school.

She was the ultimate socialite. She always did things to the extreme. She would make a huge amount of food and there was only four of us. Huge pots of different things—potatoes, carrots, pasta, steaks and chops. She loved clothes. She had an extensive wardrobe and she was pretty much wrapped up in herself.

She loved to visit her relatives and liked to go downtown and meet with her brother who had an office on Randolph Street. He was a lawyer and she would get all dolled up and take me and my sister there and go to a movie after meeting with my Uncle Tom. Then we would go eat probably at the cafeteria at Walgreens.

She was a consummate extrovert. Hair fixed every week. Around the house she just had a housedress and she didn't get dolled up when my father came home. I don't think they did get along. In February of my second semester in college, I came home and found that my father was in the Hudson Avenue police station. He had an argument with my mother and she called the police. I went over to the station and I said my mother was a very excitable woman and that's no hyperbole. I knew the sergeant didn't know what that meant. I took my father over to live with me at my grandmother's.

I got them together again for a year but that was it. My father had just had an operation for cancer and my mother just walked out on him. He was quiet and she was outgoing and I didn't have the feeling they were a team. I asked my father why did he marry ma and he said simply, I loved her.

Jack Flaherty

They were just two people getting along and going along that's all.

Well, my mother was a meek lady. A laid back woman. She just took care of all my needs. I guess I was the first thing in her life and she tended to my father, his needs also. They never argued. Nothing that I ever observed. They were just two people getting along and going along that's all.

My mother did hotel work at the Drake Hotel for a while, and also the Webster Hotel up on North Lincoln Avenue. She cleaned rooms. Cleaned hallways. Just, you know, maid work.

One time, she babysat for Nancy Davis who became Nancy Reagan in later years. When Nancy was a little girl, my mother took care of her. Her father was Loyal Davis, the chief neurosurgeon I believe at Northwestern Hospital. In fact, I believe my parents had a wedding reception at Davis's place. Yes, a small one. They were married at Holy Name Cathedral.

Then my mother and father had a more personal reception for themselves at the apartment that they had at that time over on Locust Street. Locust and Wells. Which I heard was quite a party. I believe the police had to tell them to quiet it down.

They didn't do much socializing if you mean going to parties and stuff and having company over. No there wasn't a lot of that. We had some. I don't know why. Maybe it's because of small quarters we had. I mean. I didn't realize it at the time how small they were, but later on you say, my goodness I grew up like that.

She got out of hotel work and then she went to work for a paper box company. It was the Apex Paper Box whatever they did down around Orleans and oh maybe Ontario.

When my father died she took it very rough, very rough. I can remember the day of his funeral. It was a very hot day. He was waked at Sullivan's up on North Avenue and North Park. When her and I got to the undertaker's I wanted to go do something. She like didn't want to let me out of her sight. I guess she felt she was gonna be deserted if I left to do what I wanted to do. She almost didn't want to let go of me. So, yeah, she took it very hard then. But we got through it, everybody does.

Charlie Martinez

I returned to my house on 329 West Schiller Street where I had lived till I was nine. I went in through the back door and stood in the kitchen where the dim light made all things gray.

"Ma?" I said.

I listened for a moment and heard nothing. The few rooms seemed too small to have held all my memories.

My shoes made slapping noises on the linoleum. I touched the back of my hand to the garbage burner. The iron stove was cold. In the dining room, I turned left, following the residual scent of urine, Sloan's arthritis liniment, and body powder.

I hesitated at the bedroom doorway.

"Ma?"

A double bed hugged the far wall. A beige chenille bedspread, neatly in place and tucked in under the two flat pillows, covered the bed. A tall dresser filled the rest of the room. The bed and dresser lost their details in fuzzy edges that fused with the shadows.

I reached and turned on the dresser lamp; the ivory-colored plastic shade had pink roses scattered in it. "The base is solid brass," she would say. I read the words "Made in Lima, Ohio" on its underside for the hundredth time.

St. Martin De Pores beckoned to me from the far wall and St. Jude was still there in his six-inch plaster likeness next to the lamp. Fine Tweed body powder dust covered the top of the dresser where I once wrote "Charlie" and "I love you" with my fingertip,

Where was the old black turban hair-covering she always wore outside the house? Where was her crystal rosary whose facets were rounded from use? Where were her holy cards gathered from the funerals? I thought.

I ran my finger into the dust but found I could no longer write as a child.

CHAPTER THREE: FAMILY LIFE AND ETHNICITY

Part One: Half-breeds

I had these relationships with all these different people, from all the different ethnic groups in the neighborhood. But I wasn't Italian. And I wasn't Irish. And I wasn't German. And I wasn't Assyrian. So I don't know what the hell I was.
                                                            Peter Eichel

Charlie Martinez

Ethnic activities? Huh?

Our house was devoid of any ethnic celebrations, remembrances, special parties, or ethnic activity. I never heard my mother talk of Irish culture or Ireland. We were always told we were half Irish (mother's maiden name was Lonergan and her parents emigrated from Ireland in the 1880s) and half French. Because I was not "pure" Irish, Patty Irwin nicknamed me "Half-breed." That was a subtle, gentle form of prejudice. It was almost a compliment that *at least* I was half Irish.

But there were other not-so-subtle incidents. There were no race or class distinctions in shooting dice in the Franklin School yard. This huge area, half cement and half gravel for the ballfields, was hidden from the outside world by five-story walls of brick and stone. This was our retreat. Patty Irwin, Jimmy Foley, the Russos, Nick Gallo, and I along with several others from farther west on Cleveland Avenue and Mohawk Avenue were spending some mid-teenage time on a Saturday morning trying to beat the odds and get some money. For me, it was a chance, if I won, to spend the afternoon at our candy store hangout, Third Base, and actually buy food and soda.

We were intense players. If we had only spent half this energy on schoolwork, what a bunch of scholars the neighborhood would have produced! But our attention to the details of the game kept us from hearing the number 162 squad car slowly creep up. The cops drove through a hundred yards of gravel and cement and we kept looking to make four the hard way.

There was no use in running. The dice and money were on the ground. The guilt was on our faces. They were two big Irish-looking cops, with the biggest of the two asking for IDs. An assortment of real and fake Selective Service cards was produced. I handed one cop my driver's license. At sixteen, I had this license and had never driven a car in my life.

He inspected the card as he shifted the thick leather belt holding his gun, billy club and radio around for comfort. He seemed to read it as if he was in first grade, moving his lips silently. Then he looked at me and said with a stabbing arrogance:

"What are you, a Puerto Rican?"

I blushed with shame but gave no answer.

"Alright, get the hell outta here," he bellowed.

We hesitated, not knowing if we should retrieve the dollars on the pavement but everyone wisely left it for our tormentors. I'm sure several of the guys were relieved that no personal searches were done which would have uncovered roaches, bennies, red devils and other assorted pharmaceuticals intended to stimulate and twist the psyche.

My mother's parents were born in Ireland but she never told old stories she had heard about the beauty of the land or hardships they faced causing them to emigrate. I did get the distinct impression that to her most Irish were "shanty Irish," which I took to mean low-class, prejudiced people.

I wondered, when I was older, if her marriage at eighteen to a nineteen-year-old wallpaper hanger with a Hispanic name in 1914, who might be part black caused a silent or maybe not-so-silent backlash from her family. Perhaps in response she decided to ignore or deny her own heritage.

There was no feeling of prejudice in the group itself against half-breeds. You could call the neighborhood (that part of the Near North Side that I grew up in) a half-breed neighborhood. It was peopled with mainly Irish, Italians, a few Germans, and the rest half-breeds. The Irish had a special advantage since most of the priests and nuns were Irish, the policemen and firemen were Irish and a lot of the politicians were Irish. The Italians were protected by their strong culture. The half-breeds were more rootless as far as ethnicity was concerned even when only the father was Irish and the family carried his name.

Peter Eichel

Before I went to bed at night I used to kill all the bedbugs.

My first place to live was a rear apartment, at 1526 North Wells Street. Now, the buildings to the north of us as well as to the south were residences of mostly professional people; commercial artists, attorneys, people who could walk downtown. I lived there from birth to eighth grade. So we lived there for 13 years.

We had five kids in the family. An older brother, an older sister. Younger brother and younger sister. Of course my mother lost three children, also. The first died right after birth. One was a miscarriage, I guess. The youngest was two-and-a-half I think or three years old when she died. So there were eight of us actually.

I had this old bed in the corner. And on the opposite corner, my brother and older sister slept. My mother slept with my younger sister in the bedroom, and my father had the other bedroom to himself. That was off the kitchen. It was very disgusting. It was never clean. The apartment had a living room, kitchen, two bedrooms and a bath. I remember the toilet kind of took up most of the room. And from the water flowing on the floor from the tub and from the pipes leaking, the wood underneath got all rotten. The tub sunk into the floor. And we just left if that way, you know. Rats actually came out the holes. It was just incredible. Cockroaches. Before I went to bed at night I used to kill all the bedbugs. I remember in fact, I would rub my hand and kill them all in the lining of the mattress.

My father made sure that everybody had play clothes and school clothes. We never felt like you didn't have any money. It was just that it was so embarrassing living in those conditions that you know I couldn't bring anybody home. Even for my best friends I was embarrassed. Course my mother was psychotic. Literally. She was a paranoid psychotic.

I can remember eating real well. When we sat down to eat, we'd have things like mashed potatoes and pork chops and hamburgers. We had steaks.

She cooked a lot of German meals. I remember kidney stew, how great it tasted. And the gravy and mashed potatoes and there was always bakery goods. My father would leave two, or it might have been four dollars. I remember there were stacks of quarters. He'd put 'em on the table next to his bed. She'd complain, so he gave her money at the beginning of the week, but when he did it was gone Tuesday. So he would only leave a couple of dollars each day and that kinda worked out better.

Well, he was a doorman so it was always in coins. He'd come home with his tips, and he'd leave quarters. Later when we were in high school, he'd do the same thing. He'd leave us fifty cents.

When we were younger, probably five, six, seven, it had a be that early, that my father used to take us to the park on picnics. Lincoln Park on Sundays. And every Saturday we went to the show. To the Plaza Theater with my family. My father would take us to the show. I can remember walking in front of 'em. You know, my father, my mother behind me. Yeah and they'd be talking. Sure. The other thing he used to do was take us downtown to the parades all the time. We probably walked. You know. Let's see this would of been, fact I have some pitchers, from back then, photographs. This would have been when I was five, six, years old. 1942, '43.

We had to be home to eat. By the time I was fourteen or fifteen, it didn't make any difference. I didn't have no such thing as curfew. Incidentally when we lived on Wells Street they moved and I came home and I didn't know they moved. And I didn't know where they were.

I was thirteen. Right? I'm going around asking, trying to find where the hell they were. You know and I don't remember how I found them. But you know where they moved? Remember the Mexican family that lived across the street from you? The storefront?

My father moved us for some reason from Wells Street to this *smaller* apartment. Charlie it was incredible. Okay? It had two rooms. No hot water, no bathtub and we shared a toilet with the

Mexican restaurant and that didn't have a washbasin of course, it was just a toilet. Yeah, Tio had opened a Mexican restaurant there.

I remember using the bathroom and there were people wanting to get into the fucking bathroom. It had no bathtub. My mother had this old fashioned metal tub she'd fill with water, hot water from the stove for our baths. And there was one gas space heater. Yeah, that's not so funny when I think about it.

And my younger sister, and my younger brother, and I were living there. And my brother was in eighth grade. And that's when he got addicted to heroin. I was a freshman in high school. The bedroom was actually an oversized closet. Yeah my father slept underneath and I slept on the double bunk right above him. There was maybe a foot and a half between the bed and the ceiling. It's a wonder I didn't get asphyxiated because the heat from that space heater used to kind of generate up there and it would be just suffocating. Then of course in the other room, it couldn't been nine by twelve, slept my mother, my brother Billy, and my sister. No wonder the poor kid became addicted to heroin. You talk about degenerate. Whew. It was terrible. And it wasn't because of lack of money. That's what is such a shame because my father was a doorman on Lake Shore Drive. He had to make excellent money.

When did I move out of there? Sixteen. No, I gotta think about that. I moved out and I moved back, then I moved out and I moved back and I stayed with my sister for a while. But I moved back because of my younger sister.

They couldn't get a decent apartment on their own. It wasn't that they didn't want to, but how do you explain when there's adequate funds that people are living in those conditions? I found an apartment on Evergreen Avenue. I had to be seventeen. Yeah. Walked down the street, talked to the old Italian guy there. Course I talked to my father before I went because somebody would hafta pay the rent. But I went and I found it. We moved the furniture down the street. Phil, John Owens, and a bunch of us, walked all the furniture down the street.

I never had a conversation with my father in those days. Well, sure, you know I'd ask him for fourteen dollars for a school sweater, er, you know.

My mother was not competent. There was no conversation. Poor Leon. No, my older brother and I had no relationship. I kind of ran the family. When my sister Sandy, was in high school, my mother carried on the same pattern with her that she did with my older sister. But Sandy, when she went to St. Michael's, the nuns didn't want to let her in the school because of me, but Father O'Donnel overruled 'em. Course she did very well in high school and she was very popular. She had a lot of friends and was very outgoing, very sociable. She did well academically. And my mother told her that she had to come home from school and she couldn't go out. She went to school in the morning, came home, stayed home. My mother said that her friends were all bums and she couldn't hang around with them. Yet she was so nice to all the kids I hung around with and was able to separate out the druggies. So obviously there was something psychopathic. Of course she slept in the bedroom with my mother. Same shit. My father had his bedroom, and I slept in what was the dining room.

Then I moved back to the bedroom in the back. How old woulda ia been? Eighteen? Seventeen? So I came home and my mother had nailed the windows shut in the bedroom because my sister had climbed out of the window. So I came home and I kicked all the windows out.

Charlie Martinez

Pigs' ass and cabbage.

Smoked butt of pig, cabbage, and boiled potatoes were my mother's contribution to Irish ethnicity in our home. Of course when you are growing up, your mother's cooking always tastes good and I loved it. For that meal, our sole seasoning was mustard, which to this day I enjoy on ham cuts of any type. She cooked a dish of beef chunks, with carrots and potatoes that we called "Irish stew" but I am not sure she labeled it other than just stew. American chop suey with small bits of beef, celery, and onions ladled out on rice was another pleasant but bland dish. I don't recall using any seasoning but salt and mustard. However, when she would cook a pork or beef roast for a Sunday dinner, that's when I noticed she would slip in pieces of cut-up cloves of garlic in slits she made in the meat. That added a lot of flavor to me but I realize now that the amount of garlic was minimal compared to what other ethnic groups, like Italians or Polish, were using. Fried pork chops were another common dish.

My favorite dessert dish, which she made occasionally, was pineapple upside down cake. This was a special treat. And to get one of the pineapple slices! But usually dessert, if we had one, was a portion of a can of fruit cocktail, sliced peaches, or sliced pears. I recall no fresh fruit.

All food was given out as minimal servings and there was never seconds. Shopping was done with this amount in mind and there was never enough money for excess food.

I never saw my father actually put together the ingredients for cookies but I know he baked them and they were tasty. He did this at odd times for a treat, especially I recall when I was younger than nine but after that we moved to North Park Avenue and his cookie baking seemed to stop.

My father's gumbo filet was unique for our neighborhood and much appreciated in our house. The smell of the filet, the sliminess of cooked okra, the rare taste of shrimp. All this ladled out on rice was the apex of our menu. Red beans and rice was a filling favorite but that was the extent of his Creole cooking that he brought up from New Orleans.

On some Sundays, but especially on Thanksgiving, Christmas, and Easter Sunday he would be the chief cook of the main dish of turkey, ham, pork roast, beef roast, or chicken. If turkey was the meat then he would strike up a match to light the gas burner. The barbs of the turkey feathers left in by the butcher were burnt off, sending up an unpleasant smell in the kitchen. It seemed to me the turkey was cooked for days in the oven but it did consume the whole morning.

In our house, the Sunday afternoon sit-down dinner was not an absolute ritual. We had them, but I may have missed many of them because of playing baseball or football.

John Owens

My mother used to make biscuits and molasses for breakfast. South Carolina biscuits yeah.

I was born in the Cook County Hospital in Chicago in September 5th, 1935. We lived in Evanston at the time. But they had the delivery at Cook County. I figure because they probably didn't have enough money to go to a regular hospital, you know.

I have a sister who is four years younger than I am. Her name is Betty. I'm not sure where she was born. You know that? I really don't remember. You caught me off guard on that one.

It was a house that we were renting. And we rented it from this old lady. She was an old Polish lady that lived in a house in the back. Her name was Bocchie. That's what we called her. And she wore the old babushkas. She had an oil stove. I'd bring the oil up from the basement for her and she'd give me fifteen cents or something like that, you know.

My father went in the service when we moved there. Now I want to say it's probably 1941. And ah, he came back in '46. Yeah. He was in the Seabees. And he, I think he came home once on furlough during the whole time.

I mean the apartment had two bedrooms, a kitchen, and like a living room. One floor. I had my own bedroom. My mother and father had the other one. And my sister slept on a sofa, in the living room. They used to fold it up during the day, yeah. The bathroom had just a commode. There was no hot water. We had to heat our water on the stove.

We had a little tin tub for baths and every Saturday night everybody would take a bath. You know. You'd heat up a bunch of water and get in there. My sister would go in one of the rooms and I'd have to go somewhere else when she was taking a bath. And ah, we'd heat it up and you'd get in there with your soap and water and in the tub. You will rinse off with some more water that you had in another pot. Yeah.

We heated the water on the coal stove. On the top of it. We had a potbelly stove in the kitchen which heated the whole house. We put coal in it. Yeah. Then you would have to shake and take the ashes out every day. And you shake it down to get the clinkers out of there. You know. I think we had a separate stove for cooking, but I don't remember.

It heated the whole house very well. Yeah. I mean one time I was there and I remember putting too much coal in it. The stove got red hot. Yeah. And it scared the hell out of me, you know. So I ran outside and a guy was coming by the street. I said my stove was all red. So he came in the house, he opened the bottom door, opened the top ... took the top off. He had a little hook that ya put ... you know to pick it up. He put that in the sink. Pretty soon it starting to settle down a little bit, you know. But I mean, I thought, I mean the stove, even the pipe on going up into the chimney was getting red. I thought, oh, if I burn this house down my mother's gonna kill me.

Yeah, my mother did all the cooking. My mother used to make biscuits and molasses for breakfast. South Carolina biscuits yeah. Sometimes she would make what she called a "Hoke" cake. She had a big black skillet and she made this dough-like bread and put it in the skillet and then put it in the oven. When it came out it was really good. You know it was almost like French bread but with a sweet taste to it. We'd take that and you dip it in the molasses. Black molasses. She used to buy what we call B'rer Rabbit Molasses. I guess this was a big thing in the South. You know.

I remember Sundays we always had fried chicken or mashed potatoes or macaroni and cheese. That was a big Sunday meal but nobody came over on Sundays.

When I was in grammar school I had rheumatic fever. They kept me in Children's Memorial Hospital for two months and they didn't do anything. I didn't take any medicine; I just stayed in bed all day. I must have been eight or ten years old.

Had no medical problems in the rest of grammar school or high school,

For clothes shopping, sometimes I would go with my mother and sometimes she would go alone and just bring the clothes home when she'd go downtown. She always shopped in the Loop. She would go down on the streetcar and she'd bring home stuff. But she used to get most of our stuff from Montgomery Wards. On Larrabee and Chicago Avenue. Yeah. That's where she bought most of our clothes. She'd buy us like little overalls, and things like that. I don't think I ever went shopping on my own.

Charlie Martinez

Shopping: toil and disaster.

I was in charge of the family fortune when I was seven years old. I was given the duty of going to the store each afternoon to buy goods for the evening meal. Rubin's grocery store and The Butcher Shop were a half a block away, down Schiller Street and around the corner north on Sedgwick. But *it being a duty,* the trip grew in my imagination to several miles.

A strange event occurred on a typical winter shopping trip that helped end that awful obligation. When the time came for me to begin my journey, my mother would recite to me the food she wanted purchased. No notes were given. All the items had to be memorized.

"Get one nice tomato, one nice head of lettuce and four nice pork chops," she said. She then slipped the few coins she had available each day into my pocket. Out I went into the cold with no hat, no gloves, no overshoes and only a thin Mackinaw jacket. Course, if I was going sledding, this would be fine, but doing a duty seemed to drop the temperature drastically. I slogged away to The Butcher Shop.

That's what it was called, The Butcher Shop. We called the owner and only worker I ever saw in the place, Butch. He wore a white square butcher cap and a heavy sweater under a blood-splattered full white apron. His build was thick and he spoke with a German accent. His hands were large with sausage-like fingers that were perpetually bluish-red. However, he was kindly and I was not afraid of him. He was generous at times and I know he sometimes gave us an unspoken discount on the meat. The shop had that pleasant, cool smell of freshly-cut meat. There was sawdust spread everywhere on the wooden floors. I wondered why the sawdust was also on the customer side of the meat cases.

"Four nice pork chops," I said.

He moved around several chops and finally settled on four. He placed them on a piece of butcher paper he ripped off a large roll. Onto the scale they went. Then he wrapped them in more butcher paper and sealed the package with white paper tape and quickly marked the price on the outside with a black carpenter's pencil. But now when I had to pay, I found no money in my pocket. I searched and searched but it was empty. I turned it inside out and found a hole just big enough to let the coins fall through.

I retraced my steps back to my house but found nothing and was sure the snow swallowed up the money.

Thus this heavy duty of shopping temporarily came to an end, until a few years later.

Charlie Martinez

Imagining ways to die.

"Going to the basement" meant a journey into a dark, dusty, creepy world. The key, a long, narrow instrument with a notched end, appeared to come from the Middle Ages. Why do I remember always being alone as I walked down the gangway towards the door? The gangway formed a chute that funneled a wind towards you in any season. Glancing at the basement windows in order to catch a glimpse of a possible monster or killer hiding behind some trash was of no value because the dirt-encrusted panes let in minimal light. The basement appeared to me as a separate place from the house. Once in the basement, there was no sensation of this hidden space being part of the house. It had its own sinister life. It was a junk-filled, forbidden area with unimaginable rituals occurring when no humans were present. At least that's how my twelve-year-old imagination saw it.

The door fit poorly and was obviously rescued from some former life. There was a crudely cut hole in the door to receive the key. And the key always worked!

But once the door was opened and no one charged you to slash your throat, the real test of courage was about to begin. You had to time a dash in the near darkness to the middle of the basement and reach blindly for a pull chain of the bare bulb strung from the ceiling. If you missed, and you didn't want to think of that possibility, the basement door would slam shut cutting off what little outside light had penetrated and you were in almost total darkness and alone with the thousands of potential monsters you knew were lurking in the shadows!

But if you were lucky enough to catch the chain and snap the light on, the swaying bulb created dozens of possible mass murderers and all sorts of three and four headed beasts bouncing off the walls and ceiling. When things settled down, you looked for the sandpaper or pliers or hammer your father had sent you there to retrieve. Once found, you now steadied yourself for the reverse ordeal. You had to pull the light chain and run out the door with snakes snapping at your heels. Usually I was not eaten alive.

My father's response when I handed him the tool: "What the hell took you so long? What are you hanging around the basement for?"

Charlie Martinez

Ironing: the Romans invented it; my mother perfected it.

Galley slave work, I thought. Ironing was galley slave work. Glued to a spot on the floor, pushing a heavy instrument back and forth and facing an endless stream of handkerchiefs. Square the cloth, press it, fold it, press it, fold it, press it; now it was in its final three-to-four-inch square shape. All these cloths for nose snot! Isn't that what sleeves were for?

"Yo, Charleeee!" Joe Zummo called from the front of my house. He knew better than to come to the door for fear of being gang-pressed into helping out with our chores. He and a group were on their way to the IC lot for baseball. "He can't come out yet, he's ironing," my mother replied. "Well, can I use his baseball glove?" And she threw it out the window to him! He took it, assuring a low place in hell for this traitorous act.

Now washing the front hall was something I could plan and calculate and knock off in a short time. I soon learned to get the job done in a most efficient manner. You take a large bucket of soapy water and several washrags to the top of the stairs. Wash up the landing. Then (when no one was looking, I need not add) you accidentally spill the water down the stairs. All that was left was a soaking-up drill. No one was ever the wiser and you were finished with your chore and out the door to fun.

Charlie Martinez

Monkey Wards: better to be in the stocks all day.

Monkey Wards was what we called Montgomery Wards. Catalog and retail sales departments occupied two huge white buildings running along the Chicago River on each side of Chicago Avenue. Some personal potential fame was attached to the south building. It had a spire with a statue on top perhaps fifteen stories above ground. My father claimed he painted that statue. I wanted to believe him but never fully accepted the story.

Many Saturdays were turned to drudgery by spending all day picking up a catalog order instead of playing ball. Ken and me, and whatever unfortunates we could shanghai, walked down Orleans to Chicago Avenue and west to the river. We were eleven to fourteen years old. In bad weather we took the streetcar. We got off at Orleans Street and Chicago Avenue and walked west to Wards. We encountered strong winds in that direction almost every time we went to Wards. Those two buildings must have formed a wind tunnel. First, I went up to the order placing desk and presented myself as Philly LoVecchio (The brother of the next door neighbor who worked at Wards and therefore we could get an illegal employee discount. This was also the singer Frankie Lane's family). Next I had to write up the order sheet, copying from the list my mother gave me. Usually the order consisted of a dozen items. Shoes, socks, shirts, handkerchiefs, sheets, pillowcases and other miscellaneous household items. Right before Easter and Christmas the orders were largest.

After placing the order, the waiting drudgery began. We waited in the order area watching the people, in the loading dock watching the trucks, at the river watching the bridge open and close. We wandered around the retail store. We had no money to spend for treats or food. Those three or four hours were unbearable for young boys. At a designated time written on our pick up form, we wandered over to the pick up counters. Some group of little men, hidden away from the public in the bowels of those white buildings, had selected our items and they magically showed up in certain numbered bins. When finally they called our number, I worked my way through a series of large buttocks and shoving people to find the order was usually only half filled. Numerous pages were flipped, stamped, stapled, added up and sorted. I paid the bill and we trudged home, totally exhausted from this mindless business.

Ken Martinez

I didn't go out after supper. Not until I was older. Until I was seven.

I was born in Chicago, Illinois. 329 West Schiller Street. It was a house. My mother, my father, my brothers and sisters lived there. Eventually I had six brothers and four sisters. All of us were born at home.

There was two steps to the front door, you opened that door, there was a hallway. There was fourteen steps going into the second floor. The door opened to your left was the first floor. I lived on the first floor. You walked in, you opened the door, that was the living room. There was two windows. There was a couch, a chair, and an end table with a lamp on it. And then you went through the hallway to your right. The stove was there. I believe it was an Isinglass stove when I was small. It was a coal stove. Next to it was a closet. On the opposite side was my parents' bedroom. My mother had a dresser with a great big mirror. Another dresser with doors on it. And funny cut handles to slide the doors out. There was a bed in there and also a window looking at the next house. Next to it was the girls' bedroom. And then you walked a little ways, there was a big dining room table. Then you walked and there was a closet to the left. They made it into a pantry and it was a closet later on in life. Then you went out into the big porch. It was open. There was ah, no bathroom, just an outhouse.

The kitchen was way at the end of the porch. There was a sink in there. There was a long banister on one side. And on the other side was a shed. The pantry was a flat place with glass doors; it was gray. And like the kitchen chairs, it had red knobs. Linoleum had black and red squares in it. On the floor in the kitchen. There was remodeling but I don't know exactly when that all came. I really don't.

Later my father built a bathroom right off the big room after it was partitioned off. There was a tub in it. But I don't remember using the tub. I got washed in the big pan. So did you. And mom used to heat the water, pour it in there. Uncle Paul, Aunt Nini and Grandma Teen lived upstairs.

In the dining room, right off where Dad's radio was, right under a window off of Ma and Pa's room was were Bobby and Jerry and I slept on the floor.

Before I started school, I played in the yard and played in the chicken coop. There was a tree. A tree of Heaven. You pull the leaves off and you could make a whip. And then I used to take Grandma's mint that was growing there. There was no grass. No grass. But there was a crazy thing of a sidewalk that came from our door and went all the way back to the back building where Amau lived. He was a cousin to Uncle Paul but he would give me a nickel or a dime and I would go to the L station and get him a thing of Tip Top chewing tobacco. I would get Pa a pack of Wing cigarettes. I was seven, six or seven.

The first time I went for the tobacco was in the summertime, it was warm. I heard two radios playing the same program. There was two cars parked and I heard music coming from one and as I passed the other one, music came from it. And I stood there for the longest time wondering how they both had the same music.

Always oatmeal for breakfast. It took me a long time to eat oatmeal again. I ate oatmeal twice a day with prunes and bread. And I got my hand cracked because I was eating all the brown sugar. It tasted good to me. So I used to eat it all. And I don't know if Pa hit me or if Ma cracked my hand. It took a lot to get Ma to hit me.

Had oatmeal for lunch and then sometimes I'd have a sandwich, sometimes I'd have soup. Sometimes I'd have, it looked like stew with carrots in it. And then I'd go right back to school.

Oh, yeah. We came home for supper. Then I washed my face and hands and went to bed. I didn't go out after supper. Not until I was older. Until I was seven.

I remember Thanksgiving we had the turkey and that was the first time I got the leg. I remember that.

Christmas was great. Always got a pair of shoes or shirts. I got a tank. A funny looking tank. I got some lead soldiers one time. Four or five of 'em. I got a Buck Rogers gun once. It flashed. What you would do, you cocked the handle and you pull and it would be like a little light would go on inside. Nothing came out the other end. But ah, I never got a BB gun. They wouldn't give me one.

We all got dressed up for Easter. We always had new clothes. I remember coming home and one time we had a roast. I don't know if it was a Sunday. I think I was very small but we had this big, big roast and I got a great big piece of the end. And I thought that was great. But I couldn't remember what year it was.

My mother cried an awful lot. Yeah. She was in bed. And she was crying. She didn't feel good. And in that bedroom there was a pipe that came down from upstairs. I couldn't figure what that red pipe was for till I got older and then I realized it was a toilet pipe.

Ma did the housework. And then sometimes she would let me sweep. I washed the floor for her with those red and black squares in the linoleum. Then I would stare at them and I would think of things. You know. You're imagination runs wild with ya. And I was thinking there were soldiers marching and other things. I saw the movie the Fighting 69th. It was 1935, '36 whenever they had it at the Plaza show. I saw it and I was fascinated by it. Anytime they had a, a war movie, I would go, see. But I didn't like some of the movies I went to see. But now I watch some of the old ones on television, and I say my God I saw that when I was a kid.

Ma used to do the laundry but then she used to send it out in big white bags. And big bags would come back and the laundry was wrapped up in paper. White paper inside. And then she would hang it all out.

Yeah it was wet when it came back. And then she would iron. She used to do a lot of ironing for the church. Those altar cloths. She used to iron all that. And then I dropped them one time. And I brought them back home. But I just dropped 'em taking them to church. I don't know if somebody pulled me or pushed me and I dropped 'em. I brought 'em home and she had to wash 'em again. It wasn't my fault. Lot of things were my fault though.

The only medical problem I remember was when one of my sisters took me to a doctor. For my ear. Mastoid? They thought I was having a mastoid or something. It just went away whatever the hell it was.

Yeah we had Sunday dinners. Sometimes when we were on Schiller Street Uncle Mike would come over with his wife. She was very nice, he was a crab. Yeah, they'd come over for coffee and sit and talk. And Uncle Tom used to come over all the time. Used to bring us wood.

Yeah we sat down and had a meal. There was a round table in the kitchen and there was a long table in the dining room. We had a lot of eggplant. Mainly fried in thin slices. I can't stand eggplant to this day. Sometimes it was chopped up eggplant or okra and rice. I couldn't stand okra because it looked so slimy. I don't eat it to this day. Ma cooked all the food.

I been thinking about it, we did have an Isinglass stove with a silver thing at the top. And there was one upstairs. And then we got an oil stove. And then we didn't have a tank for oil in the back; we had to go up to a gas station to get oil. That was at Schiller Street and Wells. My brother and I would bring five gallons of oil home. We went to the gas station at Schiller and Wells with a five-gallon can to get the oil. Jerry and I went then you and I used to go. In the wintertime we had it on the sled. Sometimes we took the wagon but when the wagon wheel got broke, okay? ... You know how the pin came off and the wheel went off ... and it broke, the axle we almost spilled the oil. But both of us used to carry it half way ... one on each side carrying it down from Wells Street.

But then I remember going to Burhalter's. That was a bakery and health store up on Clark Street. I had to get carrot juice for my Aunt Nini, upstairs. And bismarks. Yeah.

But never felt poor in my life.

I had quite a bit to do with my siblings. Oh, taking them to the show. Do this. Do that. I used to wash the floor with my brother, Charlie. On North Park. And wash the dishes with my little sister Lee and Charlie. She used to pretend we were always hitting her and she would cry so she wouldn't have to do it. And Pa caught her one day, pulling her act. And we didn't have to wash dishes no more. She did 'em.

It took a lot to get ma to hit me. I don't know, no matter what I did, she very seldom hit me. She used to hit me with the umbrella as I got older. You know, that crazy umbrella she had. It never hurt. Yeah. But it took a lot. She would either hit you with a little spoon on the hand. But she never hit you on the face or on the head. She never hit my head at all or slapped me. Of course, I was a pain in the ass to everybody.

Charlie Martinez

Birthdays: how to live forever.

I discovered in my late twenties that I was immortal. I realized I had had no birthdays. You see, in my house no acknowledgement of my growing older was ever made. I don't recall having a birthday party till I was twenty-seven years old. No marking of time each year on November 25 was observed. Usually, sweet sixteen means you've had sixteen birthdays. Sixteen birthday parties. A parent's shoebox of pictures. Numerous presents, all but forgotten. And you were growing older in each of those years.

I asked myself: you must be mistaken; you must have forgotten. You just have a bad memory.

Back in the corner of my mind I can recall once someone baked a six-inch pumpkin pie for me on Thanksgiving (which was always within a day or two of my birthday) and presented it in recognition of my birthday. But there were no candles, picture taking, presents, songs or doting relatives.

I asked Joe Zummo about his experience.

"Joe, what birthday parties do you remember at your house?"

"None. None for me, none for my sister, none for my father, none for my mother."

I lived at home for twenty-three years. On the average, we had thirteen people living in our two-story house and the two-story house on the back of the lot. We should have celebrated roughly three hundred birthdays during that period. Of course, I could have forgotten a few, but three hundred? I talked to my older sister Jackie.

"No. Never had any birthday parties in the house that I recall," she said. Jackie said my mother suffered from depression almost her entire life and this may have been part or all of the reason we didn't have celebrations. She also said that the next-door neighbors, the Lo Vecchios, had no birthday parties that she remembered. Matter of fact, it seemed no one in her immediate group had birthday parties. She felt terrible that there was no celebration for her, but at times there was nothing for the family to eat and no Christmas presents either.

Joe and I had just left my apartment and were on the upstairs landing when he remembered my fifteenth birthday. He reached into his pocket and gave me a handful of change. I thought that was great. Joe, himself, threw his own little party. He had certain rules—no used comic books to be given as gifts. Of course we then went out of our way to collect the crummiest used comics we could find.

There was no discussion with friends or family about this absence of birthday recognition. Boys in general didn't open up to this kind of discussion with anyone. I do recall an underlying sadness that there was no fuss made over me. Heaviness built up in me towards my birthday but disappeared when the day passed. I had developed a habit of restraining any anticipation of happiness for fear of letdown. However, I think the disappointment increased my overall confusion during growing up before and during adolescence.

Charlie Martinez

Paying the bills or getting street smart in a hurry.

Coffee and toast and off on my mission. Always alone.

"Here's your twenty cents for carfare and put the payment envelope deep in your pocket," said my mother. Nothing extra to spare for a treat. I was eleven years old.

East two short blocks to Wells Street to catch the red streetcar. In a few moments the streetcar came careening north on Wells. I got on the rear platform at Schiller Street and paid the conductor my fare. I hurried to the front of the car. The best part of early Saturday travel was the possibility that you could get the front left window to yourself. As I raced to the front, I saw that the window area was unoccupied. What glory! I was a few inches from the motorman and I stood there with my face almost touching the window and at times bouncing off the glass as the streetcar picked up speed and began its moderate careening. In summer, the window would be half-open and there was this glorious rush of warm air.

The motorman had a lever that fascinated all the kids. It had a large knob on it and he spun if with his left hand through a series of clicks to pick up speed or slow down. He also had a lever controlled by his right hand that looked like he was tapping Morse code. Each tap gave off a loud hissing sound as the brakes were applied. All the while he banged on a steel plate with his left foot that caused a bell to clang as he swore at every motorist who got too close.

The streetcar turned into Lincoln Avenue at about Seventeen Hundred North, where Wells Street ended. At Belmont, Ashland, and Lincoln I got off. Even at nine in the morning the shopping area was crowded. Everybody was rushing past me. I felt small and worried that the fat ladies would knock me down.

"Let's make him a jockey," my brothers would say. Just as others would want to turn their brother into a basketball player because he was tall, they felt I was best directed to being a jockey because I was short. That is why I was fascinated by the old man, my height or shorter, who approached me on Lincoln Avenue while on this family bill-paying mission. The only other adult short person I knew was my grandmother.

"Hi."

"Hi," I replied.

"Could you do me a favor?"

Taught to be polite and helpful to adults, I mumbled yes, and noticed he was gray-bearded and his tweed topcoat reached his ankles.

"I need to get my gas bill paid and could you do it for me?"

"Yes," I said answering as if it was a perfectly normal request from my father instead of from a total stranger.

"Are you a Catholic or a Protestant?" he asked.

"Catholic."

"Good, I don't trust Protestants."

I followed him about a block and then he entered a three-story apartment building. Then this strange feeling overcame me. My gut and streetwise background set off a feeling of unease. I didn't think specifically what I had become alert to, but instincts fastened me to the floor of the entranceway. I thought, "I'm no dummy; I'm not going up to his apartment." He motioned me to wait in the entrance hall and disappeared quickly up the steps.

After a few moments, I heard him walking back down the steps. He was holding a package the size and shape of a small loaf of bread. The outer wrapping was of newspaper tied with lengths of gray cloth.

"Do you have to pay a bill too?"

"Yes."

"Give me your bill and money and I will put them in with mine, that way you have less chance of losing them."

I complied without a thought and handed over an envelope with the $37.58 loan payment and the loan payment book. Wrap, wrap. Fumble, fumble. He handed me the bundle and we walked out of the building. He stopped on the sidewalk.

"Thank you," he said. "Would you like to stop for a hamburger?"

"No."

"There will be a little change left over. That's for you."

I walked away thinking the gas company was only a block further and why didn't he pay it himself?

The Household Finance office was at the top of a steep, long flight of stairs. Half way up, I thought … what if he swiped my money? I untied the bundle and searched through it. I held a handful of newspaper clippings.

No one at home scolded me. The police were called and I was driven around the Lincoln-Belmont-Ashland shopping area looking for a very short old man with a tweed topcoat reaching to his ankles. I saw no one fitting that description. He had vanished with our $37.58.

Part Two: Irish

Charlie Martinez

"Oh, my name is McNamara, I'm the leader of the band.
Although we're few in number, we're the finest in the land."

Irish ethnicity did not run deep in the Near North Side. The density of the Irish in our ghetto was far less than the almost one hundred percent density of the Italians in their ghetto. The Irish were predominant, but there was a plentiful mixture of Germans, half-breeds, hillbillies, Italians, a few Greeks, Japanese and some Mexicans. I don't recall any Jews or Polish in our area and certainly no Black, French, Scandinavian or other Eastern Europeans that were involved in our childhood.

The only Irish store was Mary Joyce's candy store. There were no other Irish businesses except a few taverns on the fringe of the neighborhood and the Lowery Heating Oil Company.

When entering an Irish home, you got the impression that it was just another nondescript lower-class American home. No obvious ethnic signs like flags, vegetable gardens, wine presses, smell of pasta, odor of garlic or relatives speaking a foreign language. Occasionally you would hear some Gaelic but usually it was in whispers so the kids couldn't hear. My own mother talked to my father and her brothers in this way. But I recall no heated discussion in Gaelic. Some displayed an Irish brogue and this was considered interesting as opposed to broken English spoken by new and not so new Italian immigrants.

There were no Irish ethnic gangs in our area. There were loose combinations of several ethnicities with the Irish predominating. We assumed, and were usually right, that all firemen, cops and most postmen were Irish and that most politicians of any power were Irish. Four of the six priests in our parish were Irish.

And yet the biggest feast day of the year for us was St. Patrick's Day. Each spring the students at Immaculate Conception Parish School were conscripted to put on a variety show with the Irish flavor predominating.

The verse at the beginning of this entry is from "McNamara's Band." This was one of a dozen Irish songs we learned for the show. There were no pageants for Easter or Christmas. Why St. Patrick's Day? Part of the reason was that the parish saw itself as being Irish in the sense it was founded as an Irish parish in an Irish ghetto many years before. This concept never changed during my childhood although the Irish ghetto by then was diluted markedly by other types of people.

Bunny Byrnes

> *We were there a year and got thrown out. And the people downstairs were deaf and dumb and the noise was driving 'em nuts.*

When I was born I lived at Ohio and State. Maybe 5 West Ohio. In an apartment building. I was about four when I left Ohio Street. It was on the ground floor. Bars on all the windows. It was a back apartment and it faced the alley. And all the windows were barred 'cause it was ground floor. It had maybe two bedrooms, living room, and a kitchen. We had four kids and we moved when my younger sister was born. Two boys. Two girls. I was second and my sister Madge was the oldest.

I lived there about three years and then moved to Delaware and State. That was a two flat. It's still there at 907 North State. Then I moved to 324 Concord. Sedgwick and Concord.

I was there a year. Got thrown out in a year. Too much noise. Landlord threw us out. Then we moved to 1551 Wieland. I was there a year and got thrown out. And the people downstairs were deaf and dumb and the noise was driving 'em nuts. Yes. They were deaf and dumb.

Then we went to 1505 North Wells. We were there almost ten years. After supper in third, fourth, fifth grade, I would eat and go back out. I had a curfew to a fashion, yeah. About the time it got dark, we'd come home. 'Cause don't forget I was on Wieland street in third grade yet. And by the time we got over to Wells Street I was in fourth grade and by then everybody was out in them days. People were sitting on their porches. So, you know, specially in the summertime, you know, nobody stayed in the house. So it was nothing to be out to eight, nine, ten o'clock at night.

Yeah, we spent ten years on Wells Street. Third floor apartment. Right. Seven rooms. Big. Me and my brother were in one bedroom. My two sisters were in another bedroom, my mother and father in another bedroom and the rest were just a, a living room, and a dining room and eating room and a kitchen. That was like in a row. A big place. It's still there. And the guy that owned it was Italian. He lived on the first floor. He had eighteen children. Veverito's were their names. Eighteen children.

I had no duties around the house. My mother was from Ireland and she did everything. All the cooking, all the housework and everything. That's right. Our only duties were to take the garbage down, and we usually threw that over the rail from the third floor. She was a good cook. Supper. Roasts, you know. Fish.

My dad used to wire money home from Michigan, but you know about that time you know, we're talking now into the '40s, my dad was here. It was only when he was building the locks in the thirties he was up there. That's when we were like two, three, four, five years old. Then when that job was finished he came here and he worked in Chicago the rest of the time.

Mother was the disciplinarian. She threw a horseshoe at me. She thought it was a rubber horseshoe but it was steel. She almost killed me with it.

By the time I was a junior in high school, nobody in my family had any control over me anymore. No. I came and went when I pleased, you know. No hours. I go to school then if I went to the Lake Shore Club to work as a bellboy that night, I came out, I go to the Cloverleaf Lounge you know, or somewhere and come home when I felt like it, you know. They had no control over us. After like I say, from about sophomore in high school that was about it. There was no such thing as reporting to your parents. Well, you know, it was a different life then, Charlie. It was so different, you know. They weren't worried about us and we weren't worried about them. You know.

We did take vacations. We went to Lake Geneva. My mother worked for wealthy people for the first ten years she was in the country before she got married. She worked for wealthy people up in Lake Forest. And they had a home on the lake in Lake Geneva. And what they had was servants' quarters in town. They were little shacks, little cottages like. And they were 'in four or five blocks from the beach. So, my aunt, who still worked for those people, would tell my mother when they weren't up at the lake and she'd get permission to use the cottages. So we went up there probably three or four summers anyway and used those cottages when they were empty. Yeah, it was nice. It really was nice. 'Cause we had the beach an everything.

Part Three: Italian

The culture from our neighborhood to your neighborhood was a hundred degrees, Charlie. Totally different. Yeah. 'Cause your neighborhood was a dukes mixture of Irish and German and everything in between. But in our neighborhood if you weren't Sicilian you were rather bizarre.

            Jack LaBrasca

Charlie Martinez

 I did not enter the domestic Italian culture through the front door. There were many frame houses, neatly attended to, that were owned by Italian families. But I made contact through back doors or along narrow, dimly-lit hallways in apartment buildings. Except for my friends, Johnny Nicolini and Joe Zummo, I never entered into a social situation in an Italian home. My main contact was to deliver newspapers and especially to collect the weekly payment for those newspapers. My route was mainly on Sedgwick, Evergreen and Scott Streets, which were densely Italian in those days.

 I guess the hallways were dim because the landlord wanted to save money. There was usually a bare bulb, probably 30 watts, hanging down to light up an entire hundred-foot hallway. And this was during the daytime. Strange, but I don't recall meeting an adult or kid on those excursions into the hallways. The hallways were narrow in these old buildings. The stairs and floors creaked as I lumbered up carrying my Saturday load of papers. But they were clean and after the landings and stairs were scrubbed, old newspapers were placed on the linoleum or wood to protect them from dirty shoes for a while longer. "Capelli, three south" my collection ticket read. There were no numbers or names on the doors. Those indicators were in the front entrance hallway on the mailboxes.

 I knocked on the door and said, "Paper boy." The response through the closed door bounced back, "Whosesa dere?"

 "Paper boy," I repeated.

 There was shuffling of feet and sometimes soft mumbling of two parties could be made out. Locks were thrown and I was presented with a short, thick-bodied woman with her black hair in a bun and wearing a print housedress. Frequently the smell of simmering tomato sauce and garlic was released when she opened the door. As I looked in, I noted that the apartments were painfully neat and clean. Holy pictures were scattered about with St. Anthony on the wall next to a St. Phillip Church calendar. Linoleum covered the floors. It all seemed foreign to me compared to the openness, noise and clutter of my house. Sometimes if the door opened into the kitchen, a man was sitting at a chrome and Formica table hunched over a newspaper. He never looked up. The woman worked her purse, mumbled something in Italian, the man nodding with a similar mumble. I was impressed by the neatness and order of the kitchen and its shiny chrome and enamel gas stove and refrigerator. She counted out the money to me in English with a strong Italian accent. I ripped off a receipt and handed it to her. I recall no tips.

"Danka you," she said.

And the business transaction was over.

Jake Pistone

Well, St. Joseph's table, it's a wish. If somebody in your family is sick, you make a wish to St. Joseph.

We had relatives on the whole block. You know. My grandmother lived next door, in the basement. My mother's sister lived two doors down. My dad's cousin lived another door down. So the whole block was relatives. On the same side of the street. You know. I say there was five homes from 1147 to 1137 Orleans Street and there were all relatives.

In our building, there was just us. My dad rented three apartments. But in the next building there were three flats, all relatives. The following building, there was three flats, all relatives, and the next building was two flats, all relatives. So that's two, five, eight, about ten flats of relatives.

Ya, mean? But we were the last to leave. My mother died so, as the World War II ended, the boys came home. The old people were dying off. The young people didn't want to stay in that area. They were buying in the suburbs. Or farther west. And uh, all our relatives left. So we were the last ones to move. Moved outta there in 1955. So at that time we were the only white people on the block. All right. It was a different environment.

Well, we had a pretty happy childhood. Me and my brothers. My oldest brother we didn't see him that often cause he was ten years older. We had a back porch. On the hot nights we slept on the back porch. You know what I mean? There was no air conditioning, you know, so when it got hot we just slept on our back porch

Mother did the laundry every Monday. That's what the thing was in those days; you did the laundry on Monday. You know she'd wash everything in the tub. They had the old machine where you know, in the old wringer machine, and you had the tub full a water and ah you rinsed the clothes into the cold water. My mother didn't work you know. She took care of the house and me and my kid brother.

Yeah, we always had a big Sunday dinner. Yeah, all relatives, aunts and uncles, with the family about nine or ten people. Well, my grandmother on my mother's side always came to our house. She lived downstairs. My grandmother and grandfather and her brother, they always came to our house every Sunday cause they lived, you know, in the basement, next building. We didn't go somewhere else. The old man liked staying home.

That Sunday big meal was wit da spaghetti, with da meatballs, the baslego. There always was fruit. You know. All kinds a fruit, all kinds. Nuts. My mother would do the cooking and my Dad would help her. You put the baslego in sausage. But they used to chop it up, put it in your sauce. It was like a mint, you know. It gives it flavor. Yeah, my Dad grew it himself on the back porch. A lot of Italians did in those days.

Well, they used to start the sauce about five in the morning. They used to put chunks of meat, hamburger, you know, meatballs. Garlic. Oh a lot of garlic. That was the thing. Then they would cook a big pot of spaghetti. There was always salad and fruit afterwards. Always fruit. And maybe some cookies, you know. They weren't much for coffee. My mother did the cooking and maybe my grandmother'd come up and help. My dad wasn't afraid to cook. He was a very good cook. Yeah. But the sauce had to be started at least about six in the morning, you know. So it gets done well.

Oh, the smell was beautiful. It smelled terrific. You open the front door and you know, you would smell it. See, the longer it cooks, the thicker it gets. You know what I mean? And the meat gets done better and everything. And then they used to bake bread. On Sunday, yeah. Fresh bread. Oh, the bread was terrific. Terrific.

Well, we had a St. Joseph's table. It's a wish. If somebody in your family is sick, you make a wish to St. Joseph. If he gets well then you have a table with all kinds of food and fruit. Anybody could come in and eat off that table. You know.

We had it 'cause my brother was very ill. My mother and dad made a wish and he got well. So one year they had a table wit all kinds of fish, bread and Italian cake. There was no meat on the table 'cause it was Lent.

My dad and my mother made the table about 1940, '39. Just before World War II. It was a big display, all kinds of fishes, flowers, fruit, cookies. And all the neighbors would bring a dish here, a dish there. They would have an old man playing St. Joseph and a little boy playing Jesus and an old woman playing Blessed Mary. Just sitting there. But in those days it was a big thing. It was costly too. But they promised and then when they could afford it, they fulfilled their promise.

Jack LaBrasca

It seemed like every year it was like a new movie. Yeah. It kept evolving, that neighborhood. It kept changing.

I lived at 1122 North Sedgwick from 1935 through almost 1955. Almost twenty years. Same place, which is now Cabrini Green. It was a two-flat with the basement being my dad's barbershop. These were nice residences. My grandfather bought this building in 1902 from a French-Canadian named Baudette.

In those days a traditional breakfast might be toast, and a glass of milk. If it was a real special occasion, your dad would go out and get a bag of sweet rolls. If they went to a wedding and there was wedding cake, they would bring it home. You would have that for breakfast on Monday morning. And my mother and father would have coffee and toast. Then my father'd go down to his barber shop.

Lunch could be anything from Italian bread with lunchmeat or Ricotta cheese on it. Or, something from dinner from the night before, or it was catch as catch can but usually it was a remnant from a previous dinner. And then, you know, traditionally, supper was like spaghetti and sauce on Sunday and sometimes on Monday too. And Tuesday might be like chop suey. That was like a fad in the old neighborhood where everybody made chop suey or someone learned how to make chili and then everyone did it. Friday was always fish. Saturday was always steak or some kind of a meat.

We had a telephone. Which came right around '44. No telephone before that.

My mother cooked on a gas range. Yeah. Very old. Very old. She had a icebox and then we got our first refrigerator in 1940. They put a box in and you put a quarter a day and that's how it kept going. And when you got to a certain number, then it was paid off. But you had to put a quarter in every day. Otherwise it wouldn't run.

And I can also remember a toaster. I mean all it was wires with an element and you perched the four slices on the outside, then you had to hand-turn them. And it was a simple heating element with wire that you placed on the kitchen stove.

My mother would wash the clothes by hand and then would wring them out with a hand wringer. My mother washed clothes every week.

Well, the pants that we wore to school as I remember, we would change twice a week. Underwear we would change like every other day. We took one bath a week. That was Saturday night. You took your bath. We had a bathtub. There were no showers. Sunday you wore your best clothes to go to church.

You had one outfit for church on Sundays. Blue suit, black shoes, and white shirt. You got home after Mass, took 'em off. Had dinner. Headed for the movies. That was traditional.

Sunday nights were interesting. They had the same radio shows on. They would listen to ah, 'the *Inner Sanctum*, or *The Hermit*. All the old radio shows, you know what I mean? And you didn't miss

Horace Hight. And you didn't miss any of those famous shows. The Lux Theater.

I didn't notice problems with money.

I mean, by today's standards they were probably in a poverty stage but they had a home, which was paid for. So theirs was not one of fear and desperation. They didn't have any money but they were comfortable.

St. Joe's Church was on Orleans Street, which was on the east side, the Irish side, and from Sedgwick to Larrabee on the west was the Italian side. My grandfather was head of the Holy Name Sodality at St. Phillip's for the old Sicilian guys and you know they had all these societies and they ran the feasts. You know, the street feasts. And each of these villages from Sicily had their own separate Holy Name Sodality. The church was deeply ingrained in us and everybody got married at St. Phillip's. And if you were Sicilian, that's where you belonged. St. Joseph was strictly for Americans not Italians. If you were Irish or German, you were considered non-Italian.

St. Phillip Benizi was at 336 W. Oak. That neighborhood was purely old world Sicilian. The stores, the shops. Everything. It was like transporting an entire Sicilian village right into the neighborhood. As you crossed over, for example to North Avenue, in 1940, most of the shops only spoke German, because it was a German community. St. Michael's community. And you went into some of the shops and they only spoke German. So there was this dichotomy. I mean neighborhoods changed dramatically from one block to another and that's what my impressions were. We had really sharp contrasts. If you went to Wells Street, if you got as far as Franklin going east, going toward the Merchandise Mart, there was a whole Tuscany neighborhood, I mean they were all from Tuscany. And they were an entirely different breed of cat. A whole different flavor, a whole different world. We had nothing to do with them. So as you went from block to block, in that neighborhood it changed.

My parents spoke English. They would speak Italian to their parents in hushed tones. Yeah they were both born here, really. Yeah. St. Joseph's feast day was huge. I'm glad you brought that up. Almost every fifth house had a table. And in fact I've got a picture, I'm gonna let you have it, of the granddaddy of the St. Joseph's tables, which was prepared by my mother's aunt. The Tribune came and took a shot of it every year. They would work for two months preceding it to fill it up.

Then of course in late August and September was the street feast. What would happen is like if they were from a particular town in Sicily, say a town called Alta Villa Milicia in Sicily. And the people who emanated from that village would have a feast. It'd be three days in honor of the Blessed Mother. And all the proceeds from that would go into charities that they deemed worthy. I mean if there was an Italian orphanage that money would go to the Italian orphanage. Well, there were maybe four societies that each have their own feast. There'd be Holy Name, Sodality Societies. They were usually three or four days. They were always somewhere just before Labor Day or slightly after Labor Day, but it was always Labor Day.

The saints started at St. Phillip's and went around and collected money. They would pin money on the saint and wind up back at St. Phillip's. Then they'd put the statue away for another year. And that would generate a huge amount of cash for the parish and for the schools. I mean, even people that moved out of the neighborhood, which was rare 'cause you didn't move out of the neighborhood, they would come back for the feast. A fiesta. That was a major, major event.

We had St. Joseph's Day, we had the feast, we had St. Lucy's Day. I mean there were all these different little highlights were part of our culture that were something to look forward too. And then of course we had the American traditions, which were Thanksgiving and Halloween and Christmas and New Year's. And so we had something going all the time. Our life was enriched. I mean truly enriched.

But if you lived around St. Phillip Benizi, I mean your life centered around that church. Everything was going on there. Everything. That was the center of the entire structure of the Sicilians. I mean, anybody that you know from the old neighborhood mostly, even Cleveland Avenue, all got married at St. Phillips. I mean, if you go today to San Francisco or New York and you say you're from the old neighborhood, Near North Side of Chicago, they'd say, "Oh, St. Phillip's."

My dad and my mom were, you know, married there and we were baptized there. So that was, that was the hub. Father Louis Giambastiani, who was a Tuscan, was the pastor. And here he was this guy who studied in Bologna, was from a wealthy, aristocratic family and he was suddenly tossed in with these tough Sicilians. I mean this guy was going in half-goofy.

Shopping for food was usually, up until about 1950 or '51; it was all done at Paul Davies grandma's store. Mrs. Krapa, she had a little grocery store. There were little neighborhood grocery stores. That's the way it was done normally. Then about '50 or '51, we got our first supermarket, which was National Tea on La Salle and Elm. And we started going there for larger baskets of food.

They had no great aspirations. They read the comic strips on Sunday. You know, and went to the movies and their heroes were Cary Grant and Bing Crosby. My mother, sometimes on Fridays, she would get on the streetcar and go downtown. She'd go to St. Peter's church and then she'd stop at Stop and Shop and get an apple pie and come home. I mean they had little traditions. My mom and dad would go to the bank once a month, downtown. First National Bank. And then they would stop at Walgreen's at the counter and have lunch. I mean it was like a thing they did. It was a big thing for them. In grammar school and high school I never went anywhere with my mother or father except to a show or to a relative's wedding.

Well, Sunday dinner was an automatic for us being in a Sicilian-American household. At the dinner was always my brother and I and my mom and dad. Relatives would be there now and again but not often. But that would not be the norm. No. The meal was traditionally tomato sauce with neck bones and of course pasta. You know, theirs is usually a long pasta as opposed to mostaccioli or your short cuts. We did not make the pasta. That was done on a rare occasion. That was always store bought. And then about four o'clock my mom and dad would take me to the Plaza or 152. My brother never went. Then we'd get home around seven. And then we'd probably feast on the, you know, meatballs and the neck bones from the sauce. And with a salad and then listen to the radio. That was life. That was our social life. I mean, it wasn't like you had tickets to see an Irving Berlin show.

Across the street from our grammar school, was Morreale's fish store. You know you would buy the fish to go. He would cook it on a coke fire. And he had a coke fire burning all day long and he would take orders on roasted fish. I mean it was grilled outside. That would be summer, winter and he would take orders.

That was excellent. Most of the families would give him an order and then you went and picked it up. Maybe you wanted a nice mackerel. Nice. A beautiful mackerel. And then he would put it on the coke fire. Yeah. And then he would wrap it for you. You went home and heated it up and you would have it on a Friday evening.

And it would smell so good. I mean, he put oregano and lemon on there and you know, the aroma. You'd be out there as a patrol boy, and I was stationed right in front of that and you can smell all the aromas.

See that was a culture south of Division Street. That was a true Sicilian culture. If you walked down Oak Street when you were kid, it would not be a lot different than in Palermo. The merchants only spoke Italian. You could hear the radios blasting in the houses playing Sicilian music. The guys would come by peddling fruits and vegetables. They would chant in almost Arabic because most of those towns in Sicily had an Arabic influence. So as kids we would depart from Oak Street, which was a world of Sicilian culture, go to North Avenue during the '40s, which was all German. All German merchants. So we saw different societies. All in one space. And everything outside. Then there was the Loop. Which was Disney World! I mean you had theaters, and restaurants. And you walked and it was safe. And we walked to the Loop or we took the Taylor and Western streetcar. Right in front of my house.

It seemed like every year it was like a new movie. Yeah. It kept evolving, that neighborhood. It kept changing. The culture kept changing and changing and changing.

I had lived right where Cabrini Green was built. Right in the middle of it. 1122 North Sedgwick. They tore down the house. I was across the street from Seward Park. My house was the house where all the ice skates, and the baseball bats, footballs were stored in my hallway. 'Cause I was across the street. So everything was in my hallway. Everything. So if the guys wanted to play ball, they came in my hallway. That's the way it was. And they played ball in the summer every day. Every day. Maybe six, seven games and then you went to the beach. Went to the lake. Made a loaf 'an sandwich, a Pepsi and you finally got home at five o'clock. You'd leave at eight in the morning and got home around five. And your mother always said the same thing. Where you been? Out. Out. What do you mean where ya been? Out, just out. Whatja do? Nothing.

Joe Zummo

We didn't get involved in any Italian stuff.

The only thing Italian about us, even though my mother was born here, she could speak fluent Italian and when she got together with the Italian people she spoke fluently with them. My father spoke Italian too. Of course we had a lot of pasta but other than that I didn't see us as being especially Italian, I thought we were pretty Anglo-Saxonized as a family in our customs, our clothing, our social habits. We didn't get involved in any Italian stuff. But my grandmother went to an Italian church—St. Phillip Benizi at Oak and Larrabee and that whole neighborhood was considered Italian. They had the Italian feast there, the clergy were all Italian.

Michael Lutazzi

Always on Sunday, the smell of sauce, garlic, onions was in the house. Ah, those smells again.

I was born on Mobile Street, which was out around Division Street and Harlem. At that time it was like near the country. It was a very nice area. Before that they had lived, you know, in, on Hill Street. Italian neighborhood. And then they saved some money, moved out and they bought a two-flat together. They came back to Hill Street. Around Hill and Cambridge. I was just a baby then. Cambridge would be a couple of blocks south of Division. Later they built Cabrini housing, around in there. That was an Italian neighborhood. Very much so, back in the twenties.

And then my father started his climb out. We moved to 1422 Wells Street. I remember being nine because President Roosevelt died in 1945 on my birthday.

The apartment on Wells Street was three bedrooms, a front room, a living room, and a kitchen. A big ass kitchen, bigger than the one I got today. My brother and I slept together. And my two sisters slept together.

For our meals, first of all, Sunday was spaghetti. And I continue to do that today. Fridays was fish. Mondays was something called, spicidado, which is a meat stew with tomato sauce.

Spicidado is a Sicilian word that may or may not exist anymore. I believe it would be a slang word. I can't translate it literally for you. Spicidado. It meant pieces of meat maybe, you know and string beans and carrots and tomato sauce. But the sauce would be different sauce than the sauce you would put on spaghetti. 'Cause the sauce you put on spaghetti is made with meat. Meatballs and neck bones. And that cooks and simmers for hours, three hours. And then you put that on your spaghetti. So there's no little chunks of meat, you know. But some people like it that way. They take the ground meat and break it all up and spread it around in their sauce. We don't do it that way. But when you make tomato sauce for spicidado, there's no meat because you already have beef. It's a different kind of sauce. But it's still made with tomatoes.

Mom did the cooking, always. My father, he did no cooking. My sisters helped my mother. In the early days, you know, my mother wasn't working. But as the kids grew older and I was the last one around and my grandmother was living with me, she went back to work. So she didn't work all the time, you know. But when she was at home, you know, she did the cooking, the cleaning, the baking and everything and then she did the dinners.

We had banilatte for breakfast. Bani is bread. Latte's milk. Banilatte. We'd have these bowls and my mother made her own bread every week. And you'd take this bread and put it in a bowl, and for the kids, she would put coffee and milk. But a lot of milk. Banilatte was wonderful. I enjoyed it very much.

It was a bowl of bread soaked in milk and hot coffee. And you'd put sugar on it. But very little coffee, you know. My father for breakfast, every morning, the first thing he did was ah, break an egg in a cup of coffee and stir it and drink it. My mom made sandwiches that we took to school.

Always on Sunday, the smell of sauce, garlic, onions was in the house. When you first start sauce, you fry the onions in a little oil. And then you throw the garlic in and then they blend and it goes in the neighborhood. Yeah. Every Sunday, I still do that. Ah, those smells again. The sauce on Sunday.

October. Grapes, wine. Every October, you walk through an Italian neighborhood; you could smell who's making wine. You could smell the grapes. My father bought the grape for his wine. So we used to go with my brother; my brother had a car. So when October came, the three of us would go. My father, my brother, me. And my brother would take the back seat out of the car, empty the trunk, you know. He made every square inch of space available for grapes. Then we'd go to the railroad yard where they came in from California. My father would negotiate; buy eighteen cases, twenty cases of grapes. Two bucks a case. Two fifty a case. And load 'em up in the car and bring 'em home and then we'd carry 'em in the basement. This is on Wieland Street. My friends, Sal, and Mikey, and Johnny Dempster and guys were there. My father says, come on, help carry them in. So they would help carry the grapes in and then when we were done he would give 'em each a couple of pounds of grapes. "For your mother," you know. Take 'em home.

After my father opened the grape cases he cleaned off any leaves. He had a 55-gallon wooden barrel with an open top. It was a used whiskey barrel. The whiskey makers would char the inside and the old Italian guys valued these barrels. He had a crusher. This was a box shaped like a V. It was mounted on two-by-fours holding it up. This was placed on top of the barrel. A series of teeth in a cylinder was attached to a handle from the crusher. He would throw a case of grapes in the crusher and start turning the handle. This crushed the grapes and let the juice, skin, and vines fall into the barrel. When the barrel was three-quarters full, he would cover the barrel with blankets to keep in the heat of the fermenting. This keeps the gases inside also. The rule of thumb was that after a week, the barrel was inspected. The barrel was now almost full with foam and the gases from the fermentation were intense. He transferred this mush into a wine press. This manual press squeezes this stuff and juice runs out as the skin and vines and seeds stay behind. This juice still has sugar in it and needs to cook some more.

Now they took this juice and put it in a waiting barrel, which is clean and sealed except for one hole. When the barrel is almost full but not completely full because of further fermentation, a cork is placed in the hole and the barrel sits there until all the sugar is fermented. It is tasted three months later, about Christmas. But no drinking till Easter when the cooking is ended and the fruity taste is minimal. Now it is considered wine.

Took six months since the grapes were bought. He ended up with about 60 gallons of wine to last a year. There's a strong smell and it goes all over the neighborhood. You could walk by some house and, oops, that guy's making wine. You could smell that. It just comes through the bricks and little basement windows. And I still got my father's wine press, crushing box, and wine barrel.

My father always had a garden. That was like his little postage stamp of ownership. The house, the lot. He lived to own a house. He didn't get his house till after the war and up till then he was a renter. Then they were able to buy a two-flat on Wells Street and that was in 1945.

Everybody had a garden. It was like that's what they did in Italy. They farmed but they didn't own nottin'. My view of all this was they finally got here and all they wanted was a patch of land they could call their own. Campinelli had the biggest space of all. He had grapes. My father didn't have grapes. My father was not one for the atmosphere of things, he was all business. Campinelli was a romantic maybe. My father tried to grow figs. What he did was in the fall he would dig a ditch next to the fig tree and he'd bend it over and bury it. In the next spring, he'd unearth it, bring it back up. You can only do that for a few years. The tree gets too big. But figs are the staple of Sicily.

My father and three other guys from their hometown in Sicily, Monteleone, started a club here in Chicago about eighty-five, ninety years ago. There's a lot of clubs like this with immigrants. You paid dues, bought a little life insurance from them. The club is still big, powerful. There's very few young people joining these clubs today. They don't need to.

Frank De Monte

> *Other than the feast, my parents weren't involved in much Italian stuff. You know St. Phillip's feast, cause they were from that neighborhood. My father was a shill at the feast.*

My mother was not a good cook. She became a good cook after my grandmother died. But the deal was she would do the cleaning and my grandmother do the cooking. So my grandmother ... you talking about a cook. Man, she'd cook your ears off. That's how good she was. Like constantly cooking. Constantly cooking. My father never cooked. He could, but he never did.

But for supper we had the basic staples of an Italian family. Pasta. Meatballs. Chicken. 'Cause you can bread or deep-fry the chicken. And for the longest time, even when I was a kid, I drank coffee. Not a lot of milk 'cause I was not a big milk fan but lot of coffee. That's what we used to drink. This was my supper.

And what did you have on Friday because you couldn't eat meat? Fish. We used to eat a lot of baccala fish. Dried fish. Yeah. My brother was born later and he doesn't like fish, so my mother had to make him scrambled eggs. He says, "I'm not eating that fish." And there was all kind of fish that they would eat. I just can't remember most of it.

There were fourteen steep front steps to go into my house. Those fourteen steps were the meeting place for everybody on the street. They wandered to our steps and my father had built a bench. People would come and we loved to eat. Pumpkin seeds and lupines and chichis. Then we would get fish at the fish store in little containers. Then come to the steps and talk. One of the things we talked about was boxing. At that time the boxers were Joe Louis, Rocky Marciano, Rocky Graziano. And of course the guy who was from our area was Tony Zale.

We had ansalada. Yes we used to have salads. But I don't remember salad as much as the other stuff. But salads we had like during the week. The other stuff was on the weekends.

You know I think there may have been wine but I didn't drink any. I think they had wine but it wasn't a big deal. Oh, my grandfather on my mother's side, yes there were wine there because he had the press. He used to make his own wine. Yeah.

John Giovenco

> *After World War II, we had a lot of relatives come and go through our house. They would come over from Italy; the next day they would have a job.*

My parents lived at 1315 North Orleans Street at the time I was born. That was the house my mother was born in, 'cause her parents had owned that house. My grandparents had left the house to their children but my father bought all of those children out and therefore my mother and father owned the house. I was brought home as a baby and lived there too.

Lived there until I was twenty-two years old. My brother and my two sisters were born there. I was the oldest son, second child. My sister is seven years older than I am but my second sister is nine years younger and my brother is eleven years younger.

We lived there with lots of different families. It was a fourflat apartment building. They were a lot of immigrants who came in after World War II, stayed with us and then moved on. After World War II we had a lot of relatives come and go through our house. These were people who were unable to leave Italy during World War II, and were very poor and came to the United States. A son would come, make enough money to send for the father who would then send for his wife and other children. We had going through our house dozens of families.

Some slept with me. I slept with some of the children and men. They slept in the living room on the floor. We only had a kitchen, a living room, and two bedrooms and one toilet. Sometimes we'd have twelve, thirteen people in the house. But my father's relatives from Italy came over; we were kind of like a stopping place. They would come; the next day they would have a job. They would work, save money, send it to Italy. And other people would come. They were all legal immigrants.

My sister was seven years older than me, and by the time I was in first grade or second grade she was in high school. So my mom was home, sometimes. I remember a lot of times my mom not being home. I don't know if she was working or what.

Just walked in the house made a sandwich. Brushed the cockroaches off the table. I used to surprise them by turning the lights on. And if you turn the lights on you can see all the cockroaches running around. And if you left crumbs on the table, the cockroaches were all over the table. So we used to put the bread in the refrigerator. It keeps cockroaches away from them. And then of course you just brushed them off if you see the cockroaches running around. You make your sandwich, eat it and go back to school.

Yeah, it was a very independent lifestyle as compared to today, I think. I just functioned. I didn't expect my parents to really participate in anything. As they never did in high school or college. Never knew what high school I went to.

I also remember going downtown. Taking the streetcar downtown when I was in third or fourth grade. We used to have to raise money for the school all the time. Either through subscriptions or chances. My friend and I took a streetcar and went downtown and we stood in Marshall Field's and sold chances. I was in fourth or fifth grade. I didn't ask my parent's permission. They never knew where I was. They never asked.

Sunday was the big meal. No breakfast as I remember. We go to church. Go to Communion and I would come home and we'd have dinner around one o'clock. It was a big deal dinner. My father had been making spaghetti. Started it Saturday night making the sauce and so forth. Then Sunday morning I remember all the pots going because the meatballs were being cooked and everything. I remember the smells. It was mainly spaghetti and basil. And my father had his basil plant in the backyard. Yeah. He would grow fresh basil. He was the one who usually made Sunday spaghetti sauce. Yeah. He did most of the cooking. My mother was not a very good cook.

We had lots of company always in the house. My uncles would come over. My aunts would come over. My mother had seven brothers and sisters so they would come and visit us all the time because this is the house that they were raised in and they always felt it was it was kind of like their house. So we always had people come over. My father would make a big spaghetti dinner. We all sit around on Sunday, eat spaghetti and then each go off to where he was going.

Went to the Italian feasts all the time. Sure. It's a tradition brought over from Alta Villa Milicia where my mother's parents were born and my father lived. There were a lot of people in Chicago who came from Alta Villa Milicia. There seems to be an awful lot, hundreds, many thousands of people who were from that small village congregated together here. It's a feast in honor of a saint. Lorantona is the Italian name of the saint. They carried this statue around and everybody goes up and kisses the statue, puts some money on the thing. It's a lodge kind of thing. Yeah once a year.

Joe Olita

Before I went to school, life was extremely, extremely trying.

We had to move all the time. My mother was a recent widow, an Italian immigrant with four young kids, no education, no job. If we could find an apartment that was fifty cents a month less, we would move. Okay. So you gotta realize that this is all in a period of probably no more than six or seven years and we moved six times, usually only a block away. Because it was economic necessity more than anything else. I recall terrible summers and terrible winters as far as being cold and being very, very warm.

At the time what we got was not called welfare it was called relief. It was during the Depression. My recollection is that my mother got something like seven dollars a month for a family of five. Our sustenance was food that my sister would have to go to the relief agency to pick up in a couple of shopping bags. What my mother did pick up at the relief agency was script. They never gave her money. They gave her script. What the script was used for is to go to buy shoes, or to buy clothing if we needed it. Similar to food stamps now.

We lived a very tight neighborhood. People really relied on each other and sort of were more or less in the same boat. We were fatherless and really no one had any jobs and most of the men that were there were peddlers. They would go to the market and buy fruits and vegetables and then they usually had push carts or something like that or they would have a horse and a wagon. And then we had one individual who really we considered the wealthy person of the community. He had an old pickup truck that he used selling his wares.

But my mother always ran a credit with a local grocery store owner. He was Nick Nitti, and he had a store on the corner of Grand and Racine Avenue. And they used to keep the chickens out in front of the store in these little wooden cages. Live chickens, yes. People would select a chicken, but before they had the chicken slaughtered they would always feel the "gullet" to make sure there wasn't a lot of food there because that would increase the weight.

We couldn't afford to buy chickens. Now the chicken we ate were the chicken heads and the chicken feet after the chickens were slaughtered. They would take the chickens to the back, slaughter the chicken. Then cut the head off without the neck. Then they would cut the feet off below the thighs.

Well they took everything, the feathers and everything else and all the guts they cut out of the chickens and they would throw them in a big barrel along with the heads and the feet. About every other day, Nitti would allow us in the back room where the slaughtering took place and then we would go and dig into the barrels to pull out the chicken heads and the chicken feet.

Every one of us would do it. My two sisters, my brother and I. We had to do it because it was the only source of meat we had. We never told our friends about chicken heads.

This was something Mr. Nitti gave us for nothing. Now people will think about eating chicken heads and chicken feet and they will be grossed out by this. But we were absolutely elated when we got a chicken that had a big crown and the large jowls. It was absolutely the best find that we could have in the barrel. Yeah.

Oh, the other thing about the chicken heads, not only did we want the one with the biggest crown, but we'd also eat the eyeballs, and we ate the brains by breaking the skull open. There was like a little bit of an indentation on the skull of the chicken, which I believe, is the same with humans, I'm not sure. But we would get a fork and stick the fork in there after it was cooked. It would soften the skull a little bit. And then we would tear it open and we would suck that brain out. Yeah, we'd suck it out. Yeah. Yeah.

The eyeballs were inserted in the socket of the skull. And there were two ways of eating 'em. If you wanted to irritate each other, you would take and suck the eyeball out or you would break the skull and then suck it out. But we always tried to suck it out without having to break the bones to see how much power we had to suck this thing out. And the one thing that I remember about this there was a little bit of a hard thing that was always in the eye. It might a been the lens. See and I never knew what it was. But whatever was there we just sucked that thing out and it would go down and it was fine. We would enjoy it.

My mother would take the head and she would cut the beak off. She would turn on the burner on the stove and she would singe off all of the feathers. Okay? And then she would remove the lower jaw of the head, because that was nothing but bone, okay. She would take the chicken feet, cut all the nails off, take the leg with the foot itself and hold it over the gas burner. The outside tough skin would bubble and start to peel. And she would remove it from it there, pull that tough layer of skin off, then take the feet and the heads and make her pasta sauce.

Well, basically she would have her tomatoes and maybe if she was lucky to have a little can of tomato paste. She would put em all together and whatever herbs were available, maybe some basil. In other words, if the basil at the store was starting to spoil, we were able to get that basil. And the same thing with fruits. If there was some fruits ... like there was a banana that was really turning, really brown and they knew they weren't gonna be able to sell it, they would hold it on the side for us. And then we would go in and we would be able to pick these, these pieces of fruit up and then we would bring it home.

I honestly don't know how that was established with the Nitti's. But what I think was that there were no secrets in our neighborhood.

He was extremely nice to mother. I asked one day, did you ever pay the bill off? And she said to me, "I don't ever recall that I did." Then I said, "Are you telling me that at some point that he forgave whatever you had owed him?" And she said," I believe he did."

We had breakfast. Ah, it probably was bread because my mother made her own bread. As a child I would sit there and watch her rolling the dough out. When she made bread she would make seven loaves of bread at a time. One loaf of bread for each day. Since she didn't really know how to put her name on the bread, she had a mark that she would put on a piece of paper, and she would take this little piece of paper and embed it on one end of the bread. And she would take the seven loaves of dough to the local baker who had an open-hearth oven there, and he would bake it for her.

I think he charged about a penny or two a loaf. As the bread was finished, he would take it and put it in a bread rack and my mother like all the other neighbors that were having this done would go there and she'd just look for her mark, on the bread and she would take the seven loaves and bring the seven loaves home.

During those days there were no preservatives put in the bread. The bread was fantastic the first day, and the second day. Well when you got to the seventh day, it was like a piece of rock trying to cut through this thing because of the fact that it hardened. And now whatta ya do with the bread? So my mother used to make a pepper and tomato concoction. Which to this day I absolutely adore.

And if I ever wanted anything sweet, well we couldn't afford to buy candy, I mean candy was something that you never got. Ice cream. Forget about that. My candy was to take a piece of bread soak it in water and put sugar on it.

My older sister went to work for the government. She worked for the Army at quartermasters. I believe it was on Pershing Road at the time. With her first paycheck, she stopped and bought a candy bar. And what we did, we measured that candy bar precisely and cut it in four exact portions. It would be for my two sisters, my brother and myself. And I'll tell, my piece of candy lasted me a good hour and half. Cause all I would do was just nibble on it a little bit. I might have been ten. Yep, and that's what I would do, just nibble it and keep it because it was such a treat, that I wanted that treat to last for a long time.

When my father was living we had a six-room apartment. We had a kitchen, a dining room, a living room. We also had our own bathroom facility. And there were three bedrooms. And once we moved out of there when my father died, we shared a bathroom with all of the other tenants. All it was a toilet facility. With the tank above the toilet, remember those? And there were no tubs or anything like that. No showers. We shared the bathroom with three other tenants on each floor. So there were three floors to the building, so were three bathrooms for the entire building complex of which approximately nine families lived.

The apartments were extremely small. We didn't have any hot water. My brother and I always slept together. My two sisters slept together. It might 'ev been that maybe they slept in the bedroom, my mother slept on the couch. But my oldest sister of course was anxious to find her own way. Because obviously the situation we were in was not very pleasant. She was fourteen years older than me.

How did we take a bath? Okay. Saturday was always bath night. And my mother had a very large metal tub. And what she would do is she would take the water, heat the water up on the stove and then the water would be poured in this particular tub. And all four of us had to use the water. Because here again we had the cost of the gas to heat the water so my mother was very frugal and said well as long as the water was rather warm, it doesn't make any difference how much soap scum was on the water, we'd just brush it away. And if you were the last one to get in you were very unfortunate. There were many times when I was the youngest who was usually the last one in, but at the time frankly, it didn't bother me. I used to play with the soap scum while I was in there see. I do recall that it was rather comfortable being in the warm water, but when you had to stand up, getting out of the water, you immediately were hit with a cold blast because we had no central heating. I think there was only one stove, and I think it was coal-fired. I believe it was in the kitchen. The bedrooms were very cold. We would let the coals burn down. Because we would not keep fire up, cause my mother said she had to conserve on the coal, see.

I told you my mother did a lot of baking. She made her own pasta and made her own bread. Now when she baked, she never made any cake. Because the ingredients in a cake would be too expensive -- eggs and butter, you know, was not something that she was ever going to be able to afford. And she used to get the Cerasota flour in these big sacks. And when the sacks where empty, she used to use the flour sacks as pillowcases and then she would sew them together for sheets for the bed.

She filled the pillowcases with old cloths that she had around. But I'll tell you this, you never want to lie on a Cerasota sack that has not been washed at least twenty five times. Because it is so rough and itchy and scratchy.

Covers, again whatever was available. If there was somebody that had a blanket and they would say to my mother we are getting a new blanket and we have one available, and I'd like to give it to you, she would accept that. And I think this is usually the major way that we got things.

The other thing that I recall very distinctly was a form of punishment. My brother and I slept in the same bed. And the bed was an old iron bed that stood pretty high. And my brother and I would get in bed and it wouldn't be long after we get in bed and I'd say to him, "You're on my side." And he'd say, "No you're on my side." And I'd say, "You're on my side." And we'd go through this several times. And then the next thing I would know, I would pick my hand up and I'd say, "Now if you're not on my side then you won't get hit by this arm," and bam I would come down and hit 'em. And then he say, "Is that right? Well it's the same thing for you, you're on my side." Well it didn't take very long to hear my mother saying, "Shut up you a sommabitch. I'll be in there." And, you know, we kept this up and then she had a broom handle that she had cut for herself. That I would say would be about two feet long. Talk about being dexterous. Within a matter of a split second the door would fly open and the hand without the broom handle would grab whatever covers we had on us. Those covers would go off in one sweeping motion and the broom handle would come down after those covers were removed. And as soon as we would feel those covers off, we would dive under the bed and she started poking with the broom handle. And of course we yelled, "Ow, ow." Now if we were getting out of line, before we went to bed, my mother always threatened to send us to Montifiore.

Montifiore was the school for misbehaving children. And in our neighborhood it was maybe two steps less than being imprisoned. We would be threatened with this all the time. She loved the word "sommabitch." And she always said, "Sommabitch you're gonna go Montifiore." But if we missed behaved during the daytime, and she saw it, ah, she would take my brother and I and she would tie us to the legs of the potbelly stove. And we would stay tied to this potbelly stove till she felt ready to release us. And it got to the point where we used to play a game about being tied, it was like cowboys and Indians. Hey, hey we'll get tied to the potbelly stove tonight. Oh, yeah, we would goad her into it many times.

And the potbelly stove had four large flying buttresses that came out of the corners of the stove. They were the greatest foot warmers you ever had in your life. What we would do is bring a chair up and we would put our feet right up on these buttresses there, and they would warm up and become so nice and toasty warm. When we really got cold that was the first place that we would try to go. And the four, the two girls, my brother and I would get up and put our feet up on these flying buttresses.

Well my mother washed the laundry in that metal tub that we took the bath in, with ah, Fels Naptha soap or something like that. She had a scrub board. Yeah, it had to be done by hand, yeah. I don't think we owned an iron.

Well I know we didn't have a refrigerator. We had an icebox. I remember the icemen coming down the street during the summertime. And they'd be calling about ice and the people would put their little signs in the window. And they would indicate how big a piece of ice you wanted and then the iceman would come up with his tongs and bring 'em up. Incidentally one time my brother had an accident with this and really blinded him in one eye. Where he was riding in a wagon and somebody had loaded a large piece of ice in there, and the wagon was being pulled and he was sitting in the wagon, the piece of ice toppled down and hit him right above the eye. And that blinded him, yeah, yeah.

We also had a neighbor who gave us haircuts because we could not go to the barber. He also had a little shoe repair shop that he kept in the back room of his house. And he had all kind of scraps of leather and then what he would fix our shoes for us. He would put soles on our shoes. And we always had a tendency to scuff the toes up, and what he would do he would take a small piece of leather and he would put the small piece of leather over the toes of the shoes when they were worn out. And this way we wouldn't have our toes sticking out.

For supper we ate whatever was available. Ah, dandelion greens many times with eggs. We used to and pick them up off the side of the road. You got to get 'em before the flowers are on 'em because otherwise they're too tough. Once in a while we'd have some cabbage. A lot of neck bones. Because neck bones were very cheap and sometimes if they had an overage they would give them to my mother for nothing too. But that didn't happen very often. So you might be able to buy a pound of neck bones for three cents or something like that. When we were done with the neck bones, there was no meat on 'em. We would suck 'em dry.

We didn't have any telephones. When my sister got older, she was the only one in the neighborhood who had a telephone. That was the one you put a nickel in. Right in their house. Yeah, you put the nickel right in the house. And they would come up and collect the money, sure. Her brother-in-law would take horse race bets on the phone.

I'll tell you what the girls did. They helped clean the house. The steps in the place where we lived were scrubbed every week. And my sisters and I and my brother scrubbed them all the time because my mother would not have dirty steps. They were scrubbed so much that they would turn white 'cause they were never coated with paint or anything. They were just raw wood. We had to hang all the laundry out on the, on the porch, you know. The girls generally they just hung out together sitting on front steps and stuff like that talking to, you know, some of the younger men who would be their age and things like that.

My mother did most of the shopping; the kids never did. She would buy a "brajola." Okay. A brajola is a piece of flank steak that is split down the center in two whole slices so that you have two thin slices. Then you put spices in it. Garlic, parsley, a little bit of Romano cheese and maybe a little bit of oregano if you want it. Occasionally a little bit of basil. And salt and pepper of course. Then you would roll this up and you would close it up with toothpicks and you would take this brajola and put it in your pasta sauce. We don't call it sauce. We call it gravy. In any authentic Italian community, pasta sauce is not sauce it is gravy. It's always known as gravy.

Part Four: Blacks

Charlie Martinez

"And who is my neighbor?"

Pressure. A mass was present, exerting itself constantly against our collective space.

The resulting force pushed in strongly from Division Street and with lesser intensity from pockets on Wells Street. When walking west within a block of Division Street the pressure was felt on your left, going north on Sedgwick Street, on your back, and in your face when walking south on Wells Street. We didn't name or discuss the sociological aspects of the pressure but we were aware of the consequences if the pressure became too strong ... fear, fights, and displacement.

No parent sat down and gave us insight and wisdom on what the pressure was or how to deal with it. No teacher ever mentioned it. No priest or nun advised on specific applications of the Christian principles they taught in school or church concerning the pressure. "And who is my neighbor?" was never a question answered at the local level. To us, the children who existed in the actual world of sidewalks, streets, candy stores, pick up sports and hangouts, this pressure was real but not discussed and only realized with outbursts of fights or tolerance for an athlete.

This was the black pressure.

A forbidden zone began in the alley under the L at Evergreen Street and extended south, diffusing like an amorphous film east and west past Division Street. There were no signals warning us of the dangers or telling us that to venture further south would chance a fall into the racial divide. What was this divide? No one could describe it except that when you began looking over your shoulder for familiar objects or places and mentally judged distances and escape routes to busy intersections, you knew you had passed over the divide.

We knew that to enter the zone, you must be with a group. No white youth went into the zone to loiter; it was always that we were passing through. If possible, we went in groups of five to fifteen, which seemed to give us a defense in that any attack on us could be costly. This zone was the realm of the black youth. We had no discussions with the black youth and did not officially mark out territories but both sides knew that going north was dangerous for blacks and going south was dangerous for whites. Encounters were frequent but usually nonviolent.

Peter Eichel

> *Later on when we joined the National Guard in 1958, they rejected John because he was black.*

John Owens? You, you remember John Owens? John Owens was half Italian and half black. He's a big guy ... about six two, maybe weighed two hundred twenty pounds. He actually was light skinned and he had brown kinky hair. But anyhow, otherwise he was white. When he was introduced to white girls, who suspected he was black, we used to tell them he had all his hair burned off when he was a kid and it grew back that way. It was light brown, but it was obviously Negro hair. Um, is that okay to say Negro now?

Later on when we joined the National Guard in 1958, they rejected John because he was black. Course they said it was 'cause he had a heart murmur when he was a child. The Illinois National Guard was segregated back then. And I remember how everybody copped out. I got all pissed off.

Well, you remember how we were. We had this closeness and we protected each other. So I thought we should make a stink out of that. John Giovenco and Ike Putrus and Phil Irwin didn't want any part of it. I said, "What the fuck are ya talking about? They're not letting him in because he's black." Well, that was the end of that. They didn't want any part of that stuff, and John, didn't either. And John said to me, "Pete you're fighting something you can't win, so don't even bother." But I don't know if that was true, I think that, you know, we could've.

Joe Olita

> *We called him nigger Johnny, but I think that he knew that we weren't being derogatory when we called him that.*

We did have one black family that literally lived across the tracks which was about half a block away. They had a son whose name was Johnny that we referred to as nigger Johnny. But I think that he knew that we weren't being derogatory when we called him that. At least that's what the assumption was. He never really said anything about the fact that he didn't like to be called by the "n" word.

The one thing that I do recall more vividly than anything else is when we were in the Boy Scouts we would go out camping. I'm gonna say that we probably were thirteen, fourteen years old. Including Johnny, yes. Including Johnny.

Yes, he was the only black one. Did we treat Johnny equally? No. What do I mean we didn't? Well, I'll give you an example. We went out on this camping trip one time, and it was raining. So nobody wanted to be at the flap where the doorway was at, entering the tent. So guess who lied down at the tent flap? Johnny.

I was walking to work one day when I was working at Imperial Japanning. And course now I was probably eighteen years old and as I was walking west on Hubbard Street. This black fella comes walking east on Hubbard Street. When we got a few yards away from each other, it was really nigger Johnny and he recognized me. And we went up to each other and hugged each other. Oh God, you know, we were so happy to see each other.

And I said, "How ya doing Johnny?" And he said, "Not too good." And I said, what do ya mean?" And he said, "Ah, well you know I got married when I was pretty young, and had to get married because I had a child." And he said, "I'm no longer married because I have a really severe drug problem."

It really hit me rather emotionally because he was always really a real nice guy and I hated to see that happen to him. I said, you know I asked him, "How did you do that?" He says, "I can't tell you about it. I don't want to talk about it." So, but that was really the last time I saw him. Yeah.

Charlie Martinez

But I understood instantly that I had to give up my money.

By two o'clock in the afternoon, under a broiling summer sun, I half-carried and half-dragged my newspapers in a canvas sack that was ripping at my shoulder. I counted and recounted the change in my pocket, trying desperately to arrive at just enough left over from my collections to buy a Pepsi and Hostess Cup Cake when this torture was finished.

I was about eleven years old. I had just placed two copies of the Herald American in the lobby of a three-story hotel on La Salle Street and then cut through the alley to finish up my route on Wells Street. Five or six blacks about my age confronted me in the alley. They blocked me by forming a semi-circle. I am not sure if I was even verbally threatened but I understood instantly that I had to give up my money. I gave up my money and they ran away without touching me but carried my hope for a Pepsi and Hostess Cup Cake with them. On neutral ground, downtown, I was standing in line with my movie money in my hand when a smaller black boy hit my hand sending the money flying. I was instantly enraged. I chased him away and gathered up all my money.

Pat Rogers

And when every one of the white kids was hurt and four or five of the blacks were standing I said, "You center me the ball, I ain't quitting."

As a young man, I met a young black fellow whose last name was Prince. Or was his first name Prince? I can't remember. Anyway he was Prince and he was invited into our home at the time. He was always nattily dressed and we were scrubby kids. His mom and dad lived on Franklin Street between Wendell and Hill in a basement apartment. And when you went to their home you were treated normally. You know. If you were hungry, you could eat. Prince came into our house and was accepted. I think it was at least one summer we were pretty good buddies. Yeah.

We didn't have any racial fights per say but I can remember the black kids that came in over on Locust and Wells. Just around the area where the Fergusons were living in at that time. Some of these kids were pretty big and we were young. I can't remember the age frame, maybe eleven. But I can remember Richie Barnes, myself, Donnie Albanese, and Ronnie Luster and a couple of 'em. It was white on black and they were bigger kids. I was kind of dumb and stupid. We were playing tackle on Institute Street on concrete. And when every one of the white kids was hurt and four or five of them were standing I said, "You center me the ball, I ain't quitting." And I wouldn't quit. They kind of laughed and said, well, the game was over. Was it antagonistic? Yes.

I went to the Audie Home (for juvenile delinquents) and it was there that I encountered a lot of racial hatred. I was told by my brother that a group of black kids would come and try to accost me at that time. My brother said find the loudest mouth guy and challenge him to go into the ring and face you and that happened. I fought the guy and I beat him. Well you could go one on one, it wasn't necessarily a gang thing you know. It was a power thing. So I kicked this guy's butt and they left me alone and I got out and after about three weeks or so with the court time.

Jay Pistone

What they did at Seward Park is when we played basketball; they had built a barbed wire fence in the balcony. Ya know I mean? So they couldn't jump down on ya there.

Oh, yeah, they would jump down on ya and you know we're playing against black teams, ya know I mean? Now if they were winning or something, those apes would come down, jump on ya. You didn't have a chance. Then they put barbed wire in the balcony all the way up to the ceiling. So they couldn't jump down on the players. The only thing they could do was spit on ya.

There was some colored guys that loved trouble. You know. But there were some other guys, like a kid by the name a Booker T. Washington. He went to Wells High School. He was about six eight. In those days six eight was big. He didn't like when a little black guy would pick on a big white guy because he knew the white guy hadda take it. You know I mean? That's what usually causes your trouble. A little black guy, you know, feeling his cheerios, cause he knows he got thirty black guys behind him. But Booker would go and grab the little punk and say "listen, you know, straighten your act."

You know. I remember one time my buddy, Nick, was a being a godfather for a guy. And it was right in front of St. Joseph's School on Orleans Street. A couple colored guys came by and they wanted to rob him. Nick lives in the building his dad had, which had seventeen apartments. Sixteen were black and him. That was on Franklin Street. He wasn't afraid of nobody. Ya know I mean? I mean he was the only white guy in that seventeen-apartment building. He grabbed those two colored guys and threw 'em over a car. He was so strong. And then we went in and the guy was confirmed. Nick was being the godfather.

But you never knew what's gonna happen. You know. Me and my brother used to go to the show and they'd say gimme your show money. Well you just didn't let them do that. Because once they knew that they can take your show money without an effort, you were a target. So you just hadda stand up for your rights, you know. And fight 'em and you know.

It wasn't as violent as they are today. You know. They didn't have guns in those days. They would have maybe a baseball bat, all right or a knife. But there was no guns. Today you got guns. Guns. And there was no dope in those days. Most of those ah black kids I grew up with they died of the bad liquor and marijuana. There was marijuana in those days. They had marijuana. But there was no cocaine, no shots and all that crap. You know. But we got along with most of the black guys in those days. They accepted us. We were there so long. And we didn't cause any problems. You know. We played sports with them. Softball. Touch football. You know.

My dad taught us to treat people right. To treat the tenants right. He was always checking on their homes, you know, of his tenants. And make sure they kept everything clean. For Christmas time he always would buy them like you know, a gift. The case workers never came around to check the tenants because at first a few caseworkers, college girls, they did come around but they got raped, beat up, you know I mean? So, everything was done on the phone because they were not gonna go into those areas.

So, what my dad did, said okay, ya make the rent let's see for a hunnert and sixty for ya. But you give me eighty, but I'll only charge you eighty. So they would get eighty dollars more from the system. For food and stuff. So, when he made up his income tax, of course he put down the eighty, but the receipt he gave them was for a hunnert and sixty and the caseworker got the receipt for a hunnert and sixty. That gave them eighty dollars more to live with, you know I mean? Our house had four flats. There were two flats in the basement, and the flat above. And we lived in the middle floor. There was two Negro families below us and one above us. We lived in the middle. Never had no problem.

The tenants in the other building hadda pick the tenants. The ones who were still there. They'd have to live with 'em. Right. Now they can't came back to my dad and say wait, listen John this guy's a dope head. He says, okay, you know, what type of people live here so when the guy comes over here to rent, he has to rent off you. You tell him what the rent is, and you can't kick back to me. An they would tell him, John, we got a guy. Or we got a person or a lady, you know. They would always pick the tenant. Yeah, he says you live there, I don't live there, I don't have to put up with any shit.

Charlie Martinez

One of the stops on my paper route was a black beauty shop on Wells Street. I dreaded to go in there to collect. When I opened the door in the cold weather the blast of hot air actually pushed me back. Past the entrance hall the air was a superheated sickening mixture of hair dye chemicals, hair straightening chemicals and perfumes. The shop was always full with black ladies sticking their heads in dryers and others getting chemicals or whatever put into their hair. They were all talking loudly in a language I barely understood. The owner greeted me and immediately paid the bill. She paid me correctly and with a small tip.

Frank DeMonte

My parents or grandparents didn't think too much about black people. The black people, they were not like us and that was it.

Yeah. I had contact with one black. One. Charlie Tousant, he was in our class in eighth grade. He was the only black guy in our class. He didn't come into our class until seventh or eighth grade, but he was a great guy. And a good athlete. He wanted it that way. He went to school with us but didn't socialize with us. He even went to high school with us. Social connections? Not at all. Talked about them? No.

We had a fight with the blacks when I was maybe, twelve, thirteen. Well what happened was there was a dividing line between black people and white people. And the dividing line to me was Division Street. If you went downtown on the bus for example, you hadda be with ten guys. Because what they would do, since I believe they were so poor, get on the bus and take the money from the white kids. The white kids would always be scared. And so they would come up and say give me a quarter or a dime or whatever and then take it. So we hadda go in groups so they wouldn't bother us. When we were smaller, you know, it was easier but then as we got older then we started to not particularly care for that type of procedure from black people. So we had more encounters with them fighting than we did in the past when we were younger.

My parents or grandparents didn't think too much about black people. I mean that wasn't the topic of conversation. The black people, they were not like us and that was it.

Jack LaBrasca

Her name was Fanny. And she was a gentle, lovely, black young bride with her husband.

The frightful thing was that, kitty corner from St. Phillip's Shool, was Jenner School which was 99.9% black. That was a scary scene walking through their schoolyard, especially when it was snowing, 'cause they would heave snow on you and they would jump you.

We would cut through there, yeah. On days when the snow was "packy," you went around the school. Jenner School to me was a frightening place. These were African-American kids that to me were very frightening. I was scared to death of them. I don't know why I was so fearful ... there was something about them that really scared me.

When we hit about like ten, Seward Park was across the street and there you had basketball and you had athletic programs. We would do that after school and there again that was another frightening thing because we were in the minority. It was primarily ... it was about 80% black. Each year from the time I was about five years old, our neighborhood was becoming overwhelmed in terms of black.

In fact, when I was about ten years old we went to the movies at Christmas. They had a free movie at the Windsor Theater on a Saturday afternoon where you went ... got a free movie and you got a orange and a little box of hard candy. We went into the show and we got there it was dark. And they turned the lights on to give out these gifts. I was with my brother and a guy by the name of Rigerio, Cyril Rigerio. We were the only white guys in the whole theater. We were scared to death. I wouldn't go into the bathrooms. I would always hold it. 'Cause I was scared I would have to go in there with a black person. I mean I was that frightened of black people. I just thought they were horrible.

You know, you knew the 152 Theater was segregated. You knew it instinctively but you never put it in vocal terms. Well you always knew that on the right side of the theater the white people sat and blacks would be on the left. You knew that the blacks went to the left of the candy counter and the whites went to the right. Yeah. Right. That would be the norm.

You also knew that they did not go to the Windsor Theater which was more east on Division when we were kids. They normally did not go to the Plaza Theater. They just didn't go to the Windsor or the Plaza. They went to the 152 because of the proximity of the blacks to Division Street as opposed to the proximity of the blacks to North Avenue. There was too wide a gap.

There were no blacks in my school until I was in seventh or eighth grade. Then there were two. They were practically, in their demeanor, almost Caucasian. There were only two. There were one boy and one girl. The one boy, his name was Lorenzo Jones. Truly. The girl's name was Geraldine Holt. I have no idea where they lived. I had no idea of their circumstances. I only knew that they were there. But then, when we were that age, we never knew anything about who kids' parents were, where they came from. It was never an issue.

Well, you know, in high school, we always called 'em malojohns. And we always thought of them as being eggplants. Eggplants or malojohns were black. I mean we were very unsophisticated.

There was a single family that lived next door to us in the basement of Mr. Bonifedi's building. Her name was Fanny. And she was a gentle, lovely, black young bride with her husband. The two of them were very quiet. They seemed to understand that they were in a white community and seemed to be very respectful and quiet and not very involved. They may as well have been on Mars; you know, they were there, but they weren't there. My contact with them was only to say hello. Only to say hello.

No kids. Then she stepped on a nail, a rusty nail, and got lockjaw and died in about eight hours. Yeah. And she was really a neat lady. But nobody knew who they were. Her name was Fanny. And I don't remember her last name.

But the crowd from Jenner School, we always considered them as being screwballs, crazy people. You know. I mean they were rough. They were you know, mostly up from Mississippi and they weren't used to urban life. So, you know, it wasn't like if you were living in Wilmette and you had a black family next door to you. I mean, if you considered them less than you are in that structure, obviously you're a redneck. But in our environment where it was a huge culture clash between Sicilian and Mississippi Blacks, they just didn't fit. So whenever we went to Seward Park to play ball, basketball, we'd be the only white team in the tournament. There'd be seven black teams. They would be up in the rafters and they would be spitting on us and calling us names. So we were the underdogs. It was just the reverse. We were the abused. So, you know, you basically considered they were a roughneck crowd. Nothing personal.

Yeah we had fights with them, but mostly we got chased. They'd freeze the Seward Park pond in the winter and we'd go ice-skating or play hockey. One night they chased us all the way home. We just made it to my house and locked the door. My dad was sleeping watching TV. He had his two feet tucked into the chair and the commotion was so sudden that he got up and forgets where his feet were and he fell flat on his face. There were a few incidents. They would jump us. But it didn't happen all the time.

Well, my parents never said anything about the blacks in so many words. But, you know, they knew that there was a cultural difference. I mean these were people from a different culture. From a farm culture in Mississippi, probably Baptists, non-Catholic, ah, black and not white, living in probably in impoverished standards. Not a European culture, but an African-American culture. So, I mean, they were considered like they're there, and we're here. Yeah, we don't want to bother them, but we're not gonna hook up.

Charlie Martinez

I noticed that each of the floors in the other rooms of the apartment was filled with men sleeping on mattresses.

I had learned that Sunday mornings was the best time to catch several young black men who owed me for newspaper delivery. Although I could leave the papers in the hallway of an apartment building during the week, to collect I had to go to a second floor apartment. This was about 9 a.m. on a Sunday morning. My knock was answered by a long silence then mumbling, then shuffling of feet slowly toward the door.

"What's it?" a hoarse voice asked through the door.

"Paperboy. I gotta collect from Albert Whiteside and Theodore Brooks."

A black man opened the door and pointed to a room without a door. The apartment was hot, smelled of sweaty socks mixed with the odor of vomit and alcohol.

The first time I collected, the man at the door pointed out my customers. As I walked toward the correct room, I noticed that each of the other rooms in the apartment was filled with men asleep on mattresses. No beds, just mattresses on the floor. They had on just undershorts with their clothes piled in a corner. Their bodies glistened with sweat. The mattresses had no cover sheets and I saw no blankets. I went over, woke each customer up, presented the bill and amazingly they fumbled for their wallet through the pile of clothes, found it, and paid me with a tip! I had no fear of going into this building as a lone eleven- or twelve-year-old white boy on an early Sunday morning. It never occurred to me that I was in danger and of course my family never accompanied me or asked where I was going so early on a Sunday morning.

Michael Lutazzi

And Mr. Brown died. Yeah. I was twelve. I went into his house when he died. We went into his house because he was loved.

Any blacks on my street? On Wells street? Yeah. Mister Brown. He was a mailman. And everyone liked him. An he knew us as, "Hi kids." "Hello, kids."

Did Mr. Brown have kids? We didn't ever see 'em. I don't remember seeing 'em. They were nice people. Him and his wife. But we didn't play with any black people. Toward Schiller Street, on Wieland there was a big empty lot and there was apartment buildings on Wells Street. And the back of the apartment buildings face the empty lots on Wieland Street. A lot of blacks lived in there. And they barbecued and stuff, you know. But they didn't mess with us and we didn't mess with them. We lived on the same block.

Yeah. I went into his house when he died. Only when he died. He was laid out in his house. On Wells Street. Yeah. I would think that was the first time I ever seen that. Black people do it a little different, you know. We didn't put dead people in houses. I found out much, much later on in life, that in the early days the whites did that. Yeah. We went into his house because he was loved. And Mr. Brown died. I was twelve. We went there. Went with Sal Bury. It was kids. We went over with the guys. No parents. Comb your hair. Go see Mr. Brown. Pay your respects.

I don't remember any personal interaction with blacks in grammar school. There were none. Oh, ah, yeah. Playing ball. But nothing personal. Only contact with blacks was in baseball. We had a guy, it was funny, he was on our team and, but we didn't see the black, we saw that he could play ball. But after the game was over, he could not hang around with us. You know something like that. There was a definite split. There was no mixing. Except for baseball. As you got older, when the marijuana started coming around, then we started sharing pot with some black guys. They'd come to Magrini's tavern, one or two guys, not too many and they knew in them days too, you know, they couldn't come around.

But John Owens was special. I met John in high school. He was a great mechanic and he was a racer and he just was a nice guy. He was half black and half white and, and, it, it didn't seem to matter to us. Ah, we even didn't care if he went out with a white girl. He was one of us. How did it happen?

Oh, yeah. I remember a fight and there was more than one where the black kid was outnumbered. And there were a lot of those. But there was one fight, a black kid at Washburn Trade School, and we just beat the fuck out of him just 'cause he was a nigger, you know, 'cause he was black. And that's been with me all my life. Guilt. I mean he was a nice guy. We just pounded the shit out of him in the school. He was a shine.

There's an insurance company in Elgin, Illinois and one day I was passing through and I seen it. When I occasionally go to the casino in Elgin and you go down the street to get there and then there's Leroy Cox's Insurance Agency. I don't know if it's him, but that was the kid's name we beat up at Washburn High School. And I don't know if I want to stop, 'cause he might punch me or he might think that just 'cause we're sixty-seven, you know, bygones be bygones. So that's in my mind, you know. I would love to stop in let bygones be bygones but he might not feel that way.

After high school, Charlie, there was guys on Wells Street, we'd smoke pot together. Me and a black guy. I can't remember the guy's name. You know, we were like brothers in pot, brothers in music. Other than that, no.

An incident happened at Magrini's Tavern that has bothered me. I was sitting there by myself and it was during the daytime. I usually didn't go there on Saturdays and Sundays during the day. A lot of guys did. The beer drinkers. And I had nothing going on and I didn't live too far. At that time I lived on Armitage, out west. I came in. I took a ride to the neighborhood. I was sitting in the bar there and two stools over a black guy walks in, sits down. And he orders a Budweiser. Old man Magrini took about five minutes to serve this guy a bottle of Bud. Then he finally brought it over. And I was uncomfortable. You know, almost fifty years ago and he wasn't serving him. You know, and I'm thinking, get him a beer. Mac was his name, Mac the bartender, yeah.

He brings the guy a bottle of beer and then when the guy finishes his beer, and I heard that this happened a lot, not just at Magrini's, lot of other places but this is only time I ever saw it. The guy finishes his beer. Mac was watching him. Soon as he finished his beer, Mac didn't give him a chance to order another one, Mac just came by, he grabbed the bottle and he threw it in the garbage can and broke it. I don't remember them doing that in them days. They used to put the bottles someplace. But he took this bottle and broke it, you know. In the garbage can ... right in front of the guy. And I was standing there. I was embarrassed. The guy got up and he left. That was the old man Magrini.

Charlie Martinez

> *We were playing tackle football in the fenced-off lawn of the Franklin School when a black group started to harass us.*

There were no blacks in grammar school with me. I don't remember any discussion or derogatory remarks from my parents or siblings concerning blacks. It was like they didn't exist. Nobody warned me about them although some lived in the neighborhood and my oldest brother Tommy lived within a block of the black ghetto forming south of Division Street. On one occasion, we were playing tackle football in the fencedoff lawn of the Franklin School when a black group started to harass us. They wanted money and were interfering with our game. One of our guys became upset and began to cry, but nothing was given to the blacks and they left.

Jim Sullivan

> *Race was never discussed at home that I remember. Never, never really discussed 'cause it was always like pretty much like taken for granted. It was a pain in the ass.*

You know and I can probably honestly say that eight years of grammar school and four years of high school, I always had a black or mixed class for every class I ever went to. You know, I never went to an all-white school. You know, Chinese, Japanese, and others they used to call Assyrians. You know, it was always an integrated school. So there was never a problem, you know, as far as like kids are concerned.

I can recall as a group playing you know, the black guys at Cabrini Green. And almost winning the game but Herman Mitchell deliberately dropped a double play ball so they could win and we could get out of there with our skin. So he was pretty smart that way. But ah, they were pretty aggressive. I mean, blacks even in those days when they got together in gangs, they were much more vocal and aggressive than let's say their white counterparts. You know, that's, that's just the nature of the way they were.

You know, if you had a school outing. Like we'd have like say go to the circus in Medinah Temple. All the schools would like walk, you know, their children to the Temple. There was no busing and stuff like that so. Like if you had to walk like six or seven blocks, and across the street or behind you was a black school, there'd be fights. The black kids would tear into the white kids and you know, go like a feeding frenzy. So the black schools were always much more physically aggressive and tougher than say, white schools, you know.

Inside the schools, like say Franklin, even though there was a fairly decent size black population, there was never a problem. But if you went up against a school that was let's say all blacks, the demeanor changed as far the students attitudes were concerned about everything, you know.

There was a couple of blacks guys in our group at Muzzie's Candy Store. Acey was a big brute, eighteen or nineteen years old, you know. At that time I was younger, maybe I was fifteen or sixteen and they were like older. But Acey made a remark to Bob Klein. I think it was. Klein was not the kind of guy that you'd expect to get into a fight, but you know, something Acey said set him off. He lived right next to Auda Mion. But he just got discharged from the Marine Corps. In those days they used to all wear these belts with large buckles. They used to file the edges of 'em and they would wrap the belt around their hand and fight with 'em so that you could like nick or cut with the buckle edge. Acey made some remark to this guy and there was one hell of a fight that lasted like a half hour and they were just a bloody pulp. And Acey stopped coming around after that. The other guy was pretty well torn up too, so it was a fight that broke up the neighborhood as far as those two guys were concerned.

There were a lot of guys like Herman Mitchell, Pete Montana, Joe Mendoza. They all graduated and went to the tech school at that time which was Wells. And once they got there they lasted like a year and they all dropped out. 'Cause it was basically a black school at that time and it was kind of rough.

The other black guy was William Sommerville. He was a real nice friend, a real nice you know, companion. I played baseball, football, with him year in, year out until we were in our almost like midteens. He finally stopped you know, coming around the neighborhood because he realized he couldn't date a white girl. Oh, yeah. He told us that. That was why he never showed up because he was seeing a black girl at that time and of course she was like from Cabrini Green or you know, someplace around there. So, we sort of lost contact then I went in the service and we lost all contact.

After I got out of service in 1955 I ran across Sommerville on ah Division and Wells. I was driving at that time '53 Mercury. It was a hot car. I loved that car. It had leather and stuff like that. And he was like non-working or working in his uncle's shop. His uncle had a shoe shine shop just north of Division Street on Wells Street. And I used to always get my shoes shined there. Great shop. Great, great shoe shines. But, you know, he was you know, nice guy. Never had an argument with him.

Race was never discussed at home that I remember. Never, never really discussed 'cause it was always like pretty much like taken for granted. It was a pain in the ass.

Bunny Byrne

We had no contact with blacks. None of 'em were in our group. No blacks.

Well, yeah, picked up junk and sold it ... for show money. You'd start about Thursday, Thursday and Friday and by Saturday you had enough to go to the 152 theater down on Division Street. It was about a nickel to get in. Nickel for popcorn. Yeah, we went there every Saturday.

All cowboy movies. And believe it or not, at the time we were there, it was, the left aisle was for blacks and the middle aisle and the right aisle was for whites. Yes. And there was a sign. Oh, it was during the war. Yes. Yes. They were blacks on the left side, whites in the middle and on the right. Never a problem. Yeah.

Well they just didn't want them mingling, see. And they just wanted the white kids. When you came in the show, the candy counter was in the middle, the white kids got what they wanted and they went to the right and the black kids went to the left. And there was never a problem. 'Cause they were on the left and we were on the right.

We had no contact with blacks. None of 'em were in our group. No blacks. We never had any at grammar school. We had about three black girls in high school. No black fellas. We used to hafta go in high school and play black schools. And we had a go to a black neighborhood, Corpus Christi, which was down at 49th and South Park or something. So you hadda be damn careful, you know. But to be honest we never, never had a confrontation ever with a black.

Ken Martinez

> *I was in Camp McCoy and they pulled us all back after the first week. Back to Chicago and went to Maywood to put down a race riot. A black doctor moved into a white neighborhood and they had riots.*

Oh, yeah we had a black kid in our class in grammar school. Eugene, was it Eugene? His mother worked in the laundry of the convent. And Eugene was in my class. But we always used to play on Wieland Street with the … what the hell was their name? There were two brothers … their father died. They were white. They were Irish kids. Walshes! Yeah, there was two of 'em and their father died. And his mother, his mother used to work cooking. She used to cook for the nuns. Yeah. Eugene was quiet … we never thought anything of it that he was a different color. He lived on Wieland Street. We didn't think anything of it.

Yeah he hung around with us. Sometimes he would come over when we lived on Schiller Street. He would come over and go over to see Mr. Miller who was a chauffeur on Lake Shore Drive. He used to make little trains. He lived on Evergreen. He was black. Very nice man. His wife was real nice. Yeah. And I knew his son for the longest time then he became a detective in Chicago police department. I saw him a couple a times. When I had my business, Mr. Miller still lived there. Retired. I used to fix his television set. Had no black or race problems in high school. I didn't know anything about races until I was in Camp McCoy and they pulled us all back after the first week. Went to Maywood to put down a race riot. A black doctor moved into a white neighborhood and they had riots. Yeah. And we went down and we had to walk the streets. With a rifle. I was sixteen going on seventeen. The rifle had no bullets but we had bayonets and we just walked down the street. Okay. And we just walked the streets for two nights. And they gave us coffee and sandwiches. They gave us a place to sleep. Ah, it was a school. But I have no idea what the name of the school was. Then ah, they took us back up to ah, Camp McCoy after it was all settled down. It was in '47, '48.

Charlie Martinez

> *"They won't let the colored girls swim so we're leaving the park."*

There may have been blacks at Quigley High School, but I never saw one in my two years. However, when I transferred to Mundelein Cathedral High School two blocks away at Chicago Avenue and State Street, my class had three or four black girls but no black boys. The other classes at Mundelein were similar. I don't recall any personal contact with those few girls and I thought little about them till my Senior Class Picnic. We went to Potawatomi Park, a state park in suburban Chicago.

In the early afternoon, several of us were walking toward the outdoor swimming pool at Potawatomi Park. The year was 1952. As we approached the doors to the pool area, a priest from our school was briskly walking toward us. He was surrounded by a group of students. "Go back, we are not going swimming in there," he said. Several of us asked why not. "They won't let the colored girls swim so we're leaving the park." I was shocked and confused at something I didn't believe existed. I was also proud of the priest and the school for reacting that way.

John Owens

My father was black but he was probably more prejudiced than white people, I mean.

My father was black. He was totally black. He was from South Carolina, my mother too. She was white. Yeah. They met in Evanston. Both were married, yeah before they met and both divorced. And then they got together.
My mother was born in South Carolina. She was born there and she came to Evanston I guess in the '20s or, yes probably the '20s. No, I never went back and visited her relatives. All of her relatives eventually came here from the South. They all came to, seems like they all came to Evanston.

She was, I want to say ah, Irish, mixture of Irish. Truit. Rachel Truit. Yeah, that was her maiden name. Maybe Scotch-Irish.

They knew people in South Carolina who knew each other, yeah. But I mean, she always used to tell us she was black. I mean there was nothing that looked like black in her. She looked like I mean that she was white, you know. But she told us that she had relatives, some of them were black. You know. I don't know if she was adopted or what the hell happened. I didn't look into her background. I was thinking about that. I shoulda probably checked it to see, you know, what was going on there.

In Evanston she lived basically with black people. She was included in the black community. Right. But she mixed well with white people because I mean when she went downtown nobody knew whether she was black or had black blood in her. You know. So she would socially go out and if she wanted to go out to a restaurant in those days where they wouldn't serve black people ... I mean she walked in, sat down and that was it. No. No. No. No. She didn't go with my father. I guess that caused a lot of trouble, you know, for them.

My father was a crane operator. They wouldn't let him join the union because he was black. I think he told me he went down there once or twice and they would tell him Okay, ah, let's check on this and have a seat. Stall. He'd sit there. He said one day he sat there for two hours. And finally, you know, he just got up and left. They stalled him.

So one day he was telling one of the business agents of the union about the problem he was having. He used to come around the yard a lot. So he knew my father, my mother. He had seen my mother. He says, wantcha do this: wantcha tell your wife to go down to the Union Hall with the fifty dollars or whatever it is and, tell 'em you want to join the union. And she went down there and they put him in the union.

And they didn't know he was black. I mean, I tell this story to people and they just crack up. I mean she went down there, walked in, said, here I want to sign up my husband, he's at work. He wanted to join the union and here's his dues. The form didn't ask for race. Not in those days. They wouldn't take any blacks in the union 'cause 150 was a tough union. Nothing happened. I guess they were afraid to kick him out because it would cause a stink. But after that he had his union card, he started getting union scale at work, you know. He got a raise.

Probably when I was like six, seven years old. I saw him. I saw him and realized he was black. Yeah, I was confused, yeah, 'cause I was white. Right. I mean, like he would take me places and the people would be staring at us, you know. Here's this little white boy with this black guy. Cause in those days I wore kinky hair. I straighten it now you know. He would always tell my mother when she'd take me downtown, he always say, "Put a cap on that kid's head so they don't see that he's a nigger." He was black but he was probably more prejudiced than white people, I mean.

I played with a bunch of white kids down on the block. The Kuhn brothers. Yeah. I mean there was like five of 'em. And ah, l used to play with them after school. There was a black kid, John Swope. I used to play with him sometimes. He wasn't accepted with the white kids, no. Naw. He was a real black kid. Real black.

But everybody seemed to just take an affection to me. I mean, just accept me, you know. Just like when I started hanging around with the guys at Third Base, I mean, I was just John. That's all they would say.

This black father and white mother thing, I guess, I got a lot of hard times because of it. The fact that people would look at me and say hey, this guy's half and half and mixed and things like that. Just mainly over remarks and stuff like that. Every once in awhile I'd get in a fight because somebody would say something to me, you know, you half-breed or something like that. I'd punch the guy or something, you know. More in high school.

There was just a handful of blacks in high school. I think there was Harry Meyers, I can just about count 'em there was only, I think there was only about three black guys in our whole school.

Yeah. Yeah, I had arguments with black guys. More in grammar school than high school. Well, they'd say, you look like you're white and all this kind of stuff. You know. Real stupid things.

In Chicago, when we moved and needed to rent a house, usually I think my mother used to go. Yeah. And all of a sudden we all used to show up, you know. Yeah. I don't think they had any trouble with the renting of the houses.

My sister, is you know, very white and she has real straight hair, so you wouldn't know she was black if you saw her on the street. She's a bookkeeper in a manufacturing plant in Evanston. She does the books and does all the purchasing down there. She's married. Her husband is like real black. Yeah. He's, you know, he's not a real educated guy. I mean … rough.

He's a janitor. He's got a good job; he's a janitor in the School District 65 in Evanston. I guess he's gonna try and retire next year.

My wife is black. She knew I was black when we met and we had a long discussion. When we got married I was probably about twenty-six. Yeah.

Charlie Martinez

He received one black ball in the voting, meaning he could not join.

I was about eighteen when several of us decided to go to a Knights of Columbus meeting. The Knights of Columbus was a benevolent Catholic men's group. My brother Tom was an officer in the Daniel O'Connell Council and my brother-in-law Dave as well as my brothers Clement and Bernie were members. We were really not interested in becoming members but on certain meeting nights you could drink free beer and get to watch movies of the Chicago Bears football games. What a treat for a bunch of underage guys!

However, as things moved along, we sort of got suckered into joining the council. I believe the group consisted of John Owens, Patty Irwin, Joe Zummo, my brother Ken, several others and I. Each new member was voted on in a secret ballot. We all passed easily except for John Owens. He received one black ball in the voting, meaning he could not join. The cause of the black ball vote of course was never revealed but we all knew the reason: John Owens was half black. None of the others joined after that except my brother Ken and myself. We knew it was unfair, did not discuss it and joined the group because that's where our people were.

The blacks did not realize how rarely the whites thought about them and the whites did not realize how frequently the blacks thought about them.

And so the blacks went on seething in near silence and the whites continued with deadening indifference.

CHAPTER FOUR: PREPARATION

Part One: Grammar School

> "An' as it blowed an' blowed
> I often looked up at the sky
> An' assed meself the question,
> What is the stars, what is the stars?"
>
> Juno and the Paycock
> Sean O'Casey

Charlie Martinez

Smell of starch with gentleness and smiles. All I remember of first grade. Thick frowning eyebrows, orders, and a crack on the knuckles from a ruler. All I remember of second grade. Nothing of third. Nothing of fourth. Fifth was the world made clear to me through geography illustrated with colored maps showing stacks of wheat, steel wheels, smoke stacked factories, bananas, wine bottles, cattle, pigs, chickens, milk and cheese, olives, lumber, cotton, clothes, furniture, people … symbols whose size reflected output were all meted out to different countries so we could know where they fit in the world's economy. I was fascinated. Fractions. Don't remember literature or any language. There was no gym or lunchroom. Was religion actually taught as a class? Can't remember.

Seventh grade. At first, big tough nun. "Never clean your patrol belt in bleach!" she bellowed. Of course that is exactly what I did and it became shreds of white string. I could not face her. Jackie, my older sister brought me to school to defend me. "Why didn't he come and tell me himself?" the nun asked.

"He was afraid of you," Jackie said.

The nun turned to the class and asked, "Is anyone in this class afraid of me?"

Silence.

I survived. That nun left after a month or so, but before she left an incident occurred which restored our faith in the theory of revenge. The seventh grade boys were allowed to leave class and clean up the bingo hall on Monday mornings. What a treat! All the pop you could drink, stale popcorn you could eat, all the half-empty bottles of beer you could take a sip of, plenty of ice cream, and occasionally finding a few coins or even a dollar bill and all this while being out of class. Mr. Coyne, the huge Irish Hercules janitor was there to guide us as we gladly swept the floors, stacked the chairs, and washed the counters and tables. On one particular Monday morning, the big seventh grade nun came down and pounded on the door. Mr. Coyne opened the door halfway and was greeted with an angry red face outlined by a white and black headpiece. The nun demanded that Mr. Coyne hand over the boys for further torture in the classroom. He listened politely and then slammed the door in her face. O heavenly joy!

Pat Rogers

And here comes her nude second grader home with his clothes in his hand.

One time, when I was at St. Joe in second grade, I had asked repeatedly to go to the washroom. And this nun wouldn't let me go to the washroom. Well after about an hour, I'm sure she could smell me, you know. She said, "Go down to the bathroom." And I went down to the bathroom and I must have had diarrhea. I had crap all over my body including my ears. I took all my clothes off and I ran from the school a half a block down to the alley on Hill. And then a block south to 219 Wendell, where we lived. I ran upstairs and my mother was washing clothes and here comes her nude second grader home with his clothes in his hand. Well, that nun listened to me in the future. When I said I had to go to the washroom, I had to go to the washroom.

Charlie Martinez

New nun in seventh grade. Sister Seraphia. Very smart. Very academically demanding. I loved it. "Go to the board and on that map and find Chicago," she told a girl who was a year or two older than us.

The girl was lost. My parents and siblings had told me I was a brain many times but now I knew then that there were smart kids and there were dumb kids.

Seemed to find it easy to do rhetoric. Diagramming sentences. Like a mystery story to solve. Eighth grade. Pleasant nun but learned nothing. That grade was for fun and fooling around. Sat in front of class with the smartest kids.

Jack La Brasca

We were a mission school for impoverished people.

I started first grade at St. Phillip Benizi grammar school. And the nuns were Dominicans, from Sinsinawa, Wisconsin. Dominicans were not Italians. The Servites, the Sicilian nuns, could not speak English; consequently they couldn't be teaching, so Father Louis went to the order of Dominicans and got them to teach at St. Phillip's. We learned years later that it was a mission school for impoverished people. But we didn't perceive ourselves as impoverished because we had excellent gourmet foods at home, a clean home, a mother always home. We had a rich life. But by standards that we weren't acquainted with we were labeled as living in a ghetto.

Charlie Martinez

Sister Ann Marie was the principal and eighth grade nun and our teacher. But how could this be? She was so simple minded and pleasant. I remember nothing academic from eighth grade except that the smarter kids sat in the front rows. I sat in a front row next to the bookshelves. I was then able to pass appropriate textbooks back to Jimmy Foley, Tommy Mauro and Patty Irwin if they needed extra help on a test.

Sister Ann Marie placed a terrible burden on the class one day. She told us that Tommy Mauro and Marty McDonough were caught constantly causing trouble and skipping school. One of them had to be expelled. She asked the class to decide! Well, it was almost unanimous for Tommy Mauro. A totally accidental fateful turn in the road for Marty McDonough.

Joe Olita

Getting slapped in the face was humiliating.

If we would get out of hand and the teacher couldn't handle us any more, she'd go down to the principal. The principal would come up and he'd line us against the wall and he would go right down the line slapping our faces as he went. Oh yeah, bam, bam, bam, bam, bam, bam. We knew we deserved it. But it was just the fact that you know, being punched in the face is different than getting slapped in the face. It was humiliating. Because I always looked at a slap as being feminine. And the last thing I would ever do is go home and tell my mother, because then I would get it again. Because I was never right, I was always wrong regardless. My mother always thought that the teachers were always right just like the doctors were always right, see. The professional people were always right.

But as far as any particular moment in grammar school that I can remember was the happiest, no, every day was more or less the same as the previous day. If we had a sports figure that came in ... but none of that stuff ever occurred. If that of happened would've it been great? Because you know, you look at people like that as people you want to emulate when you get older.

Charlie Martinez

Power. One time we had power. Sister Ann Marie instructed a group of eighth grade patrol boys to place wooden horses in the street on North Park Avenue at Schiller Street blocking access to North Park Avenue. This was to cut automobile traffic on the street as kids were coming to school. This was right in front of Mary Joyce's store. This order we obeyed with ruthless enthusiasm.

But why would such a foolish order be given? Didn't Sister Ann Marie by then know how twisted these early adolescent male minds were?

Tommy Mauro was the natural leader of the group. He was the same age as us but he was socially more advanced, thought through the group dynamics and knew that what he said was the last word. He also could and would beat the shit out of anybody who pushed a point too far. He arrived at 8 a.m. Paul Marconi and Tommy Walsh, who were sitting on the curb eating Twinkies, were ordered to place the barrier. Patty Irwin, and Jimmy Foley, who were leaders themselves, allowed Tommy Mauro to take command. Johnny Nicolini and I were stationed as sentries to warn of any approaching cars. With everything in place we waited.

Soon a poor soul turned his car into North Park Avenue and stopped abruptly at the wooden barriers.

"Move the horse," he shouted through his open window.

No response.

"Move the god damn horse."

Just what we wanted, an escalation.

"We got our orders. Sister said …"

"I don't give a shit what the sister said, move the horse. I live on North Park Avenue."

This terrible language burned our tender ears. Jimmy Foley responded in his most gentlemanly manner. "Fuck you."

Well, now things were heating up.

The guy got out of his car and moved the horse but by the time he was back in his car the horse had been replaced. He went through this several times, appearing more flustered and angry each time. Then out of the blue, the men in blue appeared.

"He's trying to run us down and Sister said …"

"I'm coming home from work and I live on North Park Avenue."

"Sister said …"

But glory be! The man was ordered to park his car and get into the squad car. We were told to follow on foot to the Hudson Avenue Police Station.

At the station, we were all brought into a warm room. The man (we never knew his name) was sitting on a chair in the middle. He looked lost with his tie untied and face full of sweat. What happened next was beyond all comprehension. The policeman asked us, seven snot nosed young teens, if the man should be put in jail!

We hemmed and hawed, savoring this delicious power stew for a few minutes. Then we all nodded in agreement that he should be let go. The man smiled in relief. So ended our taste of Gestapo power.

Joe Zummo

My folks not being practicing Catholics, they sent me to Franklin public school.

That's where I started kindergarten and then I of course went to first grade the next year. I never really liked Franklin public school. When you went into recess in the schoolyard it was actually dangerous. The older students were very aggressive and they were extremely threatening, pushed you around and beat you up. So I put up with that for three more years and then when I got to fourth grade I borrowed some money from my aunt Ann who had a job in a factory and I borrowed nine dollars from her and went over to Immaculate Conception school on my own. The first time I went I took a test to get a double promotion because I flunked in first grade. I took the test and passed and I could go right from third grade to fourth. I went home and asked my parents for money to go to school and my mother said we're sorry we don't have it. So I went back to Franklin and flunked another grade and the following year went to a different nun and I passed the test and she said I could skip a grade. I went this time to my aunt to get the money. And I remember it was nine dollars I got from her. I think I only needed eight dollars and I stole a dollar from her. And years later I paid her back the nine dollars with compound interest and it came to a hundred and fifty-five dollars. No one at the school asked to talk to my parents. Thank God! I would have been totally out of luck. Of course all my friends were at Immaculate Conception and they were my entire life---my friends and their families. I was just an average student. Didn't flunk anymore. One teacher in particular that I thought was outstanding. A nun named

Sister Seraphia. I got pretty good study habits from her. I came home from school, change my clothes, go to work at the Upton Super Market and come home a little after six and study for three hours a night. She was a tough hard taskmaster and she also ran the altar boys. She was a double contribution to my life—education and being on the altar boys. I graduated in 1950. I don't think my mother and father came to the graduation. I don't recall any party, or celebration or presents or relatives. After the graduation mass I went to Schiller street at the lake, and went for a swim.

Jay Pistone

Well my dad gave me a crack right there, y'mean? Right in front a the nun. I hit the ground.

My mother didn't like the public school system and she got me transferred into the Catholic school system. It was much closer, and with the Catholic school system, half the people on the block were going there. We would just walk together.

I had the same nun from fourth, for five years. Sister Mary Stanislaus. As I got promoted, she got promoted. Third, fourth, fifth, sixth, seventh and eighth. There wasn't more than fourteen kids in a class. That's all. In a grade. My grade was fourteen kids. We had seven boys and seven girls in my class.

Oh I liked it. I liked the Catholic school system. They was always had games, you know. You had times tables, you have speed tests. The nun would say, "What's seven times seven?" Now whoever said it first, 49, she would continue to the next person. Now the minute you got beat on the speed, then the following person would stand up and guess the number. And the same thing, everything in spelling, everything. Everything was competitive. You know, which made the class interesting. It wasn't boring at all. Y'mean? Cause they made games out of the class. You know. They had spelling bees. Whoever spelled it the first and fastest, continuing, you know, that's how the nun did it.

And then my mother died so the nun, Sister Mary Stanislaus, sort of adopted me because she was worried about me getting in trouble. So she was actually my teacher and my guardian, you know.

Every time the Cubs would play an opening day series, I'd be gone. I'd ditch school. See, I could sign my Dad's name in grammar school. I'd be at Wrigley Field. And then the guys would say where's Jay? And guys would tease her and say , "Well I think we could sing ah 'Take me out to the ballgame' and we'll know were Jay's at."

Well one year she caught me. Yeah. She called me in and she called my Dad in and my Dad didn't know. You see my Dad was working nights, and, you know, my mother was deceased, and he didn't know I missed school, you know. Ah, so she said ah, "Did you write this note Mr. Pistone?" My Dad couldn't read an write. Y'mean? He said, "No, I didn't know he was outta school." Well he gave me a crack right there.

Oh, yea, right in front a the nun. I hit the ground. I had it coming, you know. I hit the floor. Boom. You know. He says, "Well any time he's bad, you just give him the stick." Yeah. That's all you have to tell a nun. There was a guy by the name a Al Perchachio, his dad told her the same thing; if he's bad give him the stick. And we got quite a bit. She, she just wanted to keep us straight.

My grammar school graduation was held at the St. Joseph Church. Ah, my mother was deceased. My dad and my grandmother were there. They didn't say nothing. I guess we had a party. I can't remember. See, my dad took my mother's death pretty hard.

Bunny Byrnes

I made it through fourteen years of school and never did homework once.

I went to grammar school at the Cathedral. I was living at 907 State. Yeah I went there till third grade. Then I went to St. Michael's. And that was a total disaster. They wanted me to write with my right hand. I was left-handed. I refused. See, the nuns there were like German nuns. It was a German school. And it was just the time the war was breaking out. It was a bad time. So then they sent me home. They told my mother to bring me back when I learned to write with my right hand. My mother was unfortunately so unworldly. Immaculate Conception grammar school was right down the street. All I had to do was to go down to the end of Concord and I'm on North Park. It's at the end of my block. It's about two hundred feet further than St. Michael's. And she's got us over at St. Michael's where it was so strict. I finished third grade there. But I didn't pass. So I started again at third grade at IC. We moved to Wieland. And that's how I got to IC. And Wieland to Concord is three hundred feet. Three hundred feet from Concord to Wieland! Now I'm in third grade.

IC was hundred percent different. Hundred percent! It was just an easier way of life. Didn't learn too much. I can say one thing; I never took homework home in my whole life. I made it through fourteen years of school and never did homework once. I know that!

The first grade nun was a young, cute nun. Sister Mary Apaulos, and maybe the eighth grade nun's name might have been Ida. Yeah. And then we had a seventh grade nun. She was a great nun. She suffered from ah, allergies something awful. She was a big round-faced nun with real high cheeks. She was probably the smartest nun in that school. Yeah. She put plants under glass, you know. And grew things. I mean she was almost like Eustella at Cathedral. You know what I mean. Just a notch above the rest. You could tell. As young as you were, you could tell. This nun is smart. Lot of them nuns in IC were like being pensioned off. You know. Really bad.

John Owens

I was kind of like always in trouble in school.

When I moved to Hudson Avenue, I went to Schiller School. That was on Scott and Burling. At the corner of Blackhawk, actually at the end of the street where we lived on Burling. The school was like to the north and there was a big empty lot. And in those days they had the Victory Gardens out there. For the war, yeah.

I was kind of like always in trouble in school. You know, I mean. I always had to go to the principal's office. You know, talking in class or doing something screwed up, you know.

We ate lunch at school. Yeah. Man they used to have some good lunches. They had these women, these old women, you know. They would cook in the cafeteria. Yeah. Right there. Mashed potatoes. Aw. There were real good … meat loaf. Yeah. I mean nice soup, like chicken noodle soup. I don't know if there was a charge but if they charged you it was very little.

Yeah. I remember ah, Mrs. Savage was one of our teachers. Probably about, I would say, fourth, fifth. And Mrs. O'Leary was the principal. Mrs. Savage's husband worked for Boeing Aircraft. She used to bring me these nice photographs of these airplanes. Boeing aircraft, you know. She said, you should probably go into something like either mechanical repair or something like that. I guess she had a lot of faith in me. She wanted me to get involved with the aircraft industry, and I was only a kid. You know her husband would bring pictures home for her and she'd give 'em to me, you know. Later on I started to build aircraft, miniature. In those days you'd buy these kits and as I got older, I started putting these airplane kits together. So I did quite a bit of that. I always liked planes. I don't know how I got interested in planes. I think maybe because of her.

You know I was really good at reading. But as far as math, I had a lot of trouble. 'Cause, I remember the teacher used to put me and this kid Joe Lombardo out in the hall. This guy was another piece of work, I don't know if you know him or not. But he, ah, yeah he used to come to Third Base too. He turned out to be a junkie, was in the Army or the Air Force. When he came home, he got strung out on smack. But anyway, she put me and Joe in the hall and he was real good in math and I was real good in reading. So we would sit there and exchange ideas on how to do this. I mean he would tell me how to do the math and I would tell him how to read. They were pretty good for that in those days. She says, you know Joe's pretty good with this and you are good at that, at the reading so I want you guys to sit out there, maybe half an hour or so a day and ah, you go over what you know. Exchange ideas on how to do things. It helped. You know. I mean 'cause after awhile Joe started reading better and I started learning how to do a little math.

Charlie Martinez

Sister Ann Marie, the eighth grade teacher and principal, was pleasant but clueless. Well, she appointed Thomas Flynn to ring the bell for the start of school, lunch period, and the end of school. Of course, we immediately corrupted him. One of us would set the clock, *which was directly above her desk*, about ten to fifteen minutes ahead almost every day. The bell would ring and she would stand up abruptly as we all tried to suppress our snickers. So we were let out a little early as many times as we could get away with it.

This was the era of the atomic bomb and the Communist scare, neither of which any of the boys took seriously. All was fun. One day, Sister Anna Maria noticed that across the street from the school and almost directly in front of my house, two men had set up a camera on a tripod and were peering at the church and rectory. She became alarmed and asked if anyone knew what was going on. This was too good to be true. Naturally we used our imaginations to the fullest. These were Communist spies we told the nun. They were taking pictures to be used in future attacks. She swallowed it and called the pastor at the rectory to warn him. The police came and questioned the men who actually were hired by the priest to take a new picture of the church and rectory for the Sunday parish bulletin. We laughed on and off for hours retelling the story to each other and the hangers-on at Mary Joyce's store. What silly fun!

We were nasty too. A lay teacher sometimes filled in for Sister Anna Maria. One time the boys noticed that there was a puddle of urine on a hallway landing right after she came to class. We immediately passed the rumor around the class that this was her accident. She sensed that we noticed her embarrassment.

Ken Martinez

I think after I dropped the fire bell, I think they lost patience with me.

I went to Immaculate Conception grammar school. I was a very bad student.

The first day there, Tommy Sholenberger kept hitting me. Kept punching me. And I got sent to the principal's office because I turned around and I punched him right in the mouth and broke his nose. In first grade. They sent me to the principal's office and they used to ah, they send me over by the ugly sister.

The ugly nun went to slap me and I hit her hand. She made me stand in the corner for the longest time. All the kids were going home. And that's when I started to rebel. I rebelled against everything. I wouldn't do anything. I refused. Then they sent me back to first grade. They sent me way in the back of the classroom. I spent two days in her office then she sent me back to the room. And Tommy Sholenberger came with a tape across his nose. And she scolded me something terrible.

My mother and father found out about this. I don't know how they found out but they found out. My father kept hitting me. He kept hitting me, hitting me. He was bigger, a little bigger than me. Heavier.

I used to go by Father Fleming and sit there. He was half blind, the poor man. And would tell me, start telling all about the church and everything. I got sent over there 'cause I was a pain in ass in the school. Yeah. Then I would have to rake leaves.

The tall one. Father McDonald. He says, you know you gotta straighten up. He always said you have to straighten up and be a good citizen and a good man. And I was the opposite. I was the opposite.

Yeah, they had a cake for me for graduation from grammar school. Ma had a cake. I got the picture with a pin on me. Somewhere. A ribbon. She was so happy. She wanted me to be a brother. Yeah. She wanted me to be a brother. And I said, 'Naw, naw.' She said, 'Your brother's gonna be a priest, why don't you be a brother." I says, "Huh?" You know. "No." I used to carry the laundry when Ma used to iron the altar clothes and stuff. I used to carry those over. She used to do some of that. She used to iron the black ... what did they call those things? ... cassocks. And the white thing that went over the top of it.

There was a lady teacher in fourth grade, as I said before. And ... I don't know what I did, but she sent me, sent me over to the convent and I met the sweetest person, Sister Ada. She was as round as a barrel. And she was the cleaning lady, sister. Cleaning the convent. And she said, "Oh, you're over here to help me?" I said, "Yeah, they sent me over here." And she says, "Oh, will you wash the windows?" So I said, "Okay." So I was supposed to wash the windows on the inside only. So I decided to wash the windows on the second floor on the outside. So, right across from the windows I was standing on was the fourth grade classroom. So I got out on the ledge and I was washing the windows and I was making monkeyshines ... didn't realize how high I was. And I washed the windows. I washed the four windows and the poor nun almost had a heart attack. And the lady teacher, she had a fit. And I couldn't wash windows on the outside no more.

And there was a teacher in there that taught music. There was a ... she used to look at my hands and she says, "Your fingers could just hold a violin just right." You know. And she says, "Would your father and mother like you to learn to play the violin." And I says, "Oh ... I don't know, I'll ask." And I asked and they couldn't afford it. So ...

Yeah, I had a lot of problems. I wouldn't do what they told me. I had to sit in the back of the room because I was the tallest kid in the room. 'Cause I was sitting up in front and one of the girls complained 'cause she couldn't see the blackboard over me. So then they moved me to the back. Then that's when I really got teed off. Why should I sit in the back? I was just as smart as the rest of the kids.

And then I got to fifth grade, sixth grade. I think after I dropped the fire bell, I think they lost patience with me. They sent me to Mr. Coyne who was the janitor. And there was two other guys we were doing stuff, mopping, helping him mop and stuff. We used to help him mop the church. Or they would send me over by Father Fleming. I'm just a bad kid. Wouldn't do what I was told. They had me polishing the fire extinguishers. They were big cans, the old type, full of water. And some had water, some had chemicals. And we'd polish 'em. They were brass. And I had to get up and polish this bell. There was a nut. I turned the nut too far and the bell fell and everybody evacuated the school. That was the end. Then I went up to Lourdes.

Lourdes was a Catholic grammar school. I did very good there. They understood my problem there. Got on the North Avenue streetcar, got off at Ashland and went up north on Ashland all the way to Lourdes. It was a church they turned around to make Ashland Avenue wider. It was a big, beautiful church. I still got the prayer book the nun gave me. Sister Leo. I finished grammar school then they put me into the high school end of it.

Peter Eichel

They put the kids in the dummy room that were retarded or whatever and they stayed there until they were thirteen.

I went to kindergarten at Franklin public school. Didn't have a very good start in life in public school. Ya know I think the teacher's name was McGuilacuddy. A huge woman. She was this odd-shaped huge woman. And I remember my older sister had taught us how to write. So at least you know, we knew how to write our name and some other things. This McGuilacuddy person told me I was writing my name wrong. That I was being inappropriate using something my sister had taught me to do. So it really was kind of an attack on my sister. And I can remember really strong family ties back there among our siblings. I mean we really were like very close and very protective of each other.

Well anyhow this little black kid and me, my buddy, we hid in the … do you remember in the Franklin School there was a on the east end, right behind Zummo's building, there was that iron fence and there was like a gangway? We hid back there and we threw rocks at her. Me and this little black kid. So we stoned her and we got caught. Well Franklin School had a dummy room. The dummy room at Franklin School was where they put the kids in there that were retarded or whatever and they stayed there until they were thirteen.

Yeah. It was terrible, terrible situation. It was a lucky thing for me because my mother took me out of there and brought me over to IC.

She wasn't going to let me stay in this dummy room. So she went over and talked to Father Fleming. We didn't pay any tuition. Anyhow we could afford to pay a quarter a month, cause she give us a quarter each to put in the box for church on Sunday. And I'd take it and I'd go buy a package of cigarettes at Mary's on the corner. You know I was in grammar school. Yeah.

Remember Sister Mildred second grade? I really loved her. She was a real phony at being mean. Well she'd take a ruler and hit you on the back of the hand. That hurt like hell. Try it. But the girls, ha, she would take them to the cloakroom, lift their dress and pull their panties down and slap 'em on the behind with the ruler. Now you remember there were two doors to the cloakroom in that building. One door was from the classroom, and the other door was from the outside hall. And they had these old fashioned keyholes with these huge keys. So whenever one of the girls was bad, and she took her in to slap her, we'd all fight to get to look in the keyhole. You know with all the noise and the scrambling, you wonder that she didn't know. But I remember seeing those little behinds; I think that's why I was a sex maniac before I got out of grammar school. Yeah. Yeah, I would've become a nun if I'd known I could'a.

I did real well in grammar school, you know. I liked school in those days. But I guess I had what would've been called today a behavior problem. Course I didn't think so. But I was always in trouble in school. And uh, I wasn't always wrong, you know.

Frank DeMonte

And my father, who was going to the play that night, said to her, "Sister you're mean."

The first grade teacher at Immaculate Conception was an angel. Her name was Sister Sulpice. And she was gorgeous. We loved to come to school because she was so pleasant. She was about 18, 19 years old.

Now we went from heaven to hell. Sister Mildred who used to hit our knuckles with the ruler. Now the third grade teacher I don't remember. But I remember the fourth grade teacher. Sister Mary Kalen I think her name was. And the reason I remember her so clearly is that she really tried to be nice but couldn't. And at that time when we were in fourth grade, we had a play *'Jiminy Cricket.'* I can never forget it. *'Jiminy Cricket.'* They had a Mr. Rooney. He came in there, was teaching everybody how to do plays. And *'Jiminy Cricket'* was the play. Anthony Rini was Jiminy. And I was in there someplace; I don't know what I played. But we were going down the steps of the school, to go into to do the play and ah, and she wasn't tussling me but she tussled somebody, hurrying them up to get moving. And my father, who was going to the play that night, said to her, "Sister you're mean." And I never forgot that. I never, ever, forgot it.

She took it to heart. So during the school year she came up to my father and she apologized. My father felt so badly that he had told her that. He worked like I said for the paper box company. So he would bring, free of charge, the paper that they made, you know, in, in the paper box company. He would bring rolls and pads of paper. She loved him.

Michael Lutazzi

I didn't become civilized until my third year in high school.

No, in grammar school I didn't do very well. I had trouble concentrating. I was afraid to ask questions 'cause I didn't want to feel stupid.

Asking questions was something that I didn't do. And ah, to this day I'll ask a question no matter how stupid it is of anybody, because of that. 'Member a teacher saying one time to my mother I was a smart kid but he doesn't apply himself, you know. And I'd get in trouble. I'd rather not be in school but I had to be there. Grammar school. There wasn't too much that I really liked about it.

I didn't pay a lot of attention in school. I would change my grades on the report card when I took it home. I didn't become civilized until my third year in high school.

Of course my mother and father came to my grammar school graduation. What do you mean? Naw you're getting … I'm not getting through to you. Ah, naw, we were a tight family. Now, there's something wrong here. Did they come to my graduation? Of course they did. That's the pictures, you know. They bought me a suit. They were very proud. There's pictures I have at home of my mother and father and me, when I was fourteen. You know, the day I graduated, a very nice picture. Wonderful parents. You know. My father had a rough time in life and he passed it on to a few other people.

Charlie Martinez

"Where did you go those last two weeks of Christmas vacation? To the King's Castle? To the King's Castle?" (he implied I went to a magic land) the priest said. He looked around the classroom with a half smile waiting for an answer that did not come. I felt sweat dripping down my armpits, causing dark stains to develop on my blue shirt. My heavy corduroys were too warm for this early spring day.

"Where is the King's Castle, Charles?" he asked again. He sat in the principal's chair with his heavy black cassock open at the top without a Roman collar and tracks of his breakfast trailing down the front. I noticed the starchy odor that all nuns and priests gave off. Sister Anna Maria, the principal, stood near him like a Buddha with a silly smile. I glanced around at my classmates hoping they would answer my unspoken appeal for help. Jimmy Foley and Patty Irwin continued reading comic books hidden in their desks.

Father Fleming called on Mary Condon but did not dismiss me. He put my report card down and picked hers up. He complimented her on her grades, attendance, and attitude. She thanked him and gave a half curtsy.

Still I stood mute. I never would tell the priest about the King's Castle. With a little effort I could turn my head and look out the classroom window directly across North Park Avenue to my house. I imagined myself running out of the classroom, down the steps of the school, straight out through the schoolyard and across the street to tell my mother and father about this awful experience.

To the priest, the idea of a boy of twelve running away from home the year before was a tempting tale to explore. But he had never called me over to the rectory to talk in private. He always asked me about it in front of the class.

Visions of that runaway time began to flash through my mind. I saw myself sleeping on back porches. The first night I was hiding behind a garage trying to get shelter from the December wind. This was in back of a house across the alley from Jimmy Foley's. I heard my brother Jerry calling Jimmy and asking if I was with him. "No," said Jimmy, "I ain't seen him all day." My brother shuffled away through the snow making it give off crisp cracking noises in the bitter cold. I came out from the side of the garage and went up to the second floor landing and curled up on a step to try and sleep. Soon a back door opened above me and a dog was let out. It approached me and began growling and barking. I heard a man and woman argue between them about the dog's strange behavior. Eventually they called the dog back in without finding out why he made a fuss. After a few moments I went down to the first floor and crawled blindly into a pile of newspapers and junk and fell asleep.

The priest finished giving out the report cards to the other kids. He turned back toward me. "Well, Charles are you ready to tell me about the King's Castle?"

My feet were soaked and my face was burning with embarrassment.

"Why should I tell him," I thought. "It's none of his business." I hadn't even told my friends or parents, and they did not push me about it at all. My mother did warn me not to do it again or she would put me in a home. My father never mentioned it. I wasn't sure why I had run away. I only thought of actions in those days. My mind became muddled when I tried to construct motives or explanations. I was in awe of adults who seemed to have logical explanations for everything they did. Maybe the reason I ran away had to do with money.

I had a job downtown selling the Daily News at a newsstand at Dearborn and Madison streets. Being downtown was exciting but I never sold many papers. I found myself daydreaming and watching the lights as the people hurried by, going home from their jobs. I imagined they were doing things that were marvelously important. In my job I would buy papers for five cents each from the man who owned two newsstands and try to sell them for ten cents each. But many days I made no profit and felt embarrassed to tell my parents although they never demanded I give an accounting of my earnings. But I had told my brother Ken that I would buy two tickets to the Shriner's Circus and I would take him. I did not have enough money. I desperately tried to sell metal clothes hangers at the cleaners to raise more money. I did get enough, but by then it was too late to go to the circus. I hated to disappoint him. That Saturday I ran away.

The tapping of my report card against the priest's thumbnail drew my attention back to the classroom.

"Everyone would like to hear about your trip," the priest said. The priest's face and hair were red just like the Irish setter dog he owned. All the students looked straight ahead. I thought of myself being larger and striking that red smiling face with a giant fist again and again. The students would cheer me. I dreamed of going home and relating this disaster to my parents and sisters. They were not afraid of this priest. They would storm the rectory and demand an explanation and apology.

"All right Charles, here is your report card. I can't waste any more time with you," said the priest. He initialed the card, handed it to me and I hurried to my desk. I sat down and my sweaty pants and shirt stuck to the wooden seat.

Father Fleming rose and blessed the class and left the room just as the bell rang. I rushed out of the school and ran across the street to my house. I ran up the stairs and into my apartment. My father was sitting on the top step of the two that led into the kitchen from the half finished back porch. He was reading the newspaper and listening to the White Sox baseball game on the radio. My mother was standing at the kitchen table wiping with a wet rag at the oilcloth covering. I hesitated, said nothing and went into my bedroom. I sat silently for a few moments and then moved over to a cage by the window. I started talking gently to my hamsters.

Part Two: High School

Charlie Martinez

I floated through the day in a dull dream-like state. All through childhood I had no clear-cut idea on how you were supposed to act as a child. I responded to the outside world as it demanded but I also kept inside a secret world that I could not articulate. It did not contain the wishes that others imposed on me but I could not clearly see what it was I was hiding from adults and where it was leading me. I thought of adults as having this magical life where they had answers for everything, acted in meaningful ways and talked about important topics all day. How did they do this? I was quiet around them but searched their faces and noted their actions for clues to their secret. And more important, was I finally to achieve that state of mind when I grew up, probably somewhere in the early twenties? I was happy and had fun with my friends, but around adults the instant intuition I thought they possessed frightened me and made me hold back.

Throughout this period and well into my adult life, I had only one real wish. That was to be a writer and probably an English teacher. I never spoke to anyone about this dream. The only active thing I did about this ambition was to enroll in a correspondence course for writing when I was in third year high school. I was involved in maybe two lessons, but then dropped it.

And so I was to go to a high school already selected for me. Not by direct order but by the snowball effect. It was assumed, but not discussed with me, that I would be a priest, so each day that passed allowed the snowball to roll a little farther and get a little bigger. Soon, there was no turning back the snowball and I ended up at Quigley Preparatory Seminary. But first there were certain administrative details to clarify. A letter of recommendation from my pastor was required.

There was no hesitation by my mother or older sister Patsy when I handed over the letter I had brought home from eighth grade. They set the gas fire under the teakettle to high and waited. Sister Anna Maria had handed the letter to me. The front of the envelope read "Father Schmidt, Rector, Quigley Preparatory Seminary.

Chestnut and Rush Streets Chicago, Ill." When the teakettle started to wail and vent steam, Patsy began to pass the sealed side of the envelope back and forth through the steam. The glue softened and the envelope was violated. Patsy did the honors: "Charles J. Martinez certainly has the intelligence to be admitted to Quigley but he is prone to foolishness." Signed: Reverend T. Fleming, Pastor, Immaculate Conception Church. So short a letter.

My family saw these comments as complimentary. The envelope was resealed and I later presented it to the admissions office at Quigley.

"You now are embarking on a new adventure," said Mrs. Turk. She sat in a pew directly behind Jim Turk and me at our eighth grade graduation held in the Immaculate Conception Church directly across the street from my house. We both were enrolled in Quigley. That is all I remember about my eighth grade graduation. I remember no party, but my brother Bernie gave me a check made out to me for five dollars. I was impressed.

Charlie Martinez

The Catholic Church was in its heyday in 1948. The two hundred fifty freshmen I entered Quigley Preparatory Seminary with that fall were the cream of the male intellectual crop from all the Catholic grammar schools in the Chicago area. I was about to enter an elite, college prep-type school with my peers and I had never studied a day in my life -- nor had I ever done any homework.

Ten question quiz every day in every subject. We were seated alphabetically in class. Father Kluszinski (he smoked a cigar in class, likely to try and cover up the whiskey breath, but he was a great teacher and very pleasant), "Martinez, translate the first four lines of 'Caesar's *Gallic Wars*." "Ah, Omnes Galli tres parties ..." "Sit down." He couldn't compliment me on my knowledge of Latin, but did say I was a good dresser. But by the end of that year and into my second year, that suit's elbow areas were worn through and not repaired. My daily Latin tests were a series of 30s and 40s. I flunked.

English rhetoric. "Martinez, take sentence six and discuss its structure and meaning. Identify each word's usage." I loved this class. Father Bennet used a workbook in which all the sentences were from the Great Books, mainly Shakespeare. He walked up and down the aisles with the book open and draped over his hand. He never reprimanded anyone. His total interest was in showing the beauty of the English language. I passed.

I loved to write the alphabet in my Greek class. It was like artwork. I guess because I liked it, some of it stuck each day in class and even though I did no homework ... I passed.

Father Basehart, a smooth, handsome priest, taught basic science and the class was just average but ... I passed.

Other classes in those two years were Algebra, Geometry, Ancient History, Bible History, and Medieval History. Pretty good education of which I took no advantage.

Michael Lutazzi

> *I walked up there, stood in front of him, and he hauled off and he whacked me.*

I had a hero in my first year at Washburn Trade School when I was fifteen. His name was Nucio. He was a math teacher. And he didn't take no shit from me. And I loved him. I walked into high school my first year as if I was a big shot. On the first day of high school at Washburn, he's got us sitting in our desks and he tells us he wants us to bring this, this and this tomorrow. And he's a little short, tiny guy. The next day I come in. I didn't bring nothin' and I was making a fool of the guy. Everybody brought their stuff; I didn't bring shit. I laughed it off. He says, "Lutazzi come up here to the front of the room." I walked up there, stood in front of him, and he hauled off and he whacked me. Yeah. He slapped me hard. It's the second day of school. And I was totally embarrassed and humiliated. Wasn't so tough. He says, "Go back and sit down."

For the next four years we were buddies. He'd invite me into his office. We'd smoke. He'd tell me about his family. He tells me, he smokes three, four cigarettes after lunch 'cause he can't smoke the rest of the day. We became friends. But it took awhile. And when I went into his class, I behaved myself. I respected him. He was my hero. Yeah. He taught me somethin'. My father would have done that, but he didn't know. He didn't know how nasty I was. If I got in trouble, my mother says "that's the friends you hang around with," you know. I'm telling you stuff that, you know, this is almost like heart leveling or something.

Joe Olita

And then from that point on I was like the rest of 'em, like scum.

I went to Crane Tech because I really at that point didn't know what I wanted to do. When we were introduced to the homeroom teacher it was first time that I heard a teacher use profanity in the classroom. It shocked the hell out of me. I mean he called us sob's and f'ers and, oh yeah. "One thing you better learn you sonofabitchs is if you step out of fucking line we'll come down hard on ya."

When I was in my sophomore year, my homeroom teacher was Miss Hansen. Miss Hansen and I were buddies. I could do anything I wanted. I would sit there and I would eat a sandwich. I would get up, and walk to the window. If I wanted to go out in the hallway, I could walk into the hallway without even asking Miss Hansen for a hall pass. And all the guys in the class were saying to me, "What the hell is going on with you and Miss Hansen?" And I said, "Hey guys you know, let's face it, she likes me. I got it made." They said, "Well there's something wrong here."

But then I made the biggest mistake. I got my course book. It has my name spelled O'Lita. And I said, wait a minute she spelled my name wrong. I went up to the front of the class and I said to her, "Miss Hansen you misspelled my name." She says, "Well isn't it Olita?" And I says, "Yes it is but it's not capital O apostrophe capital L." She says, "Aren't you Irish?" I said, "No I'm Italian." "You go back and have your seat!" And then from that point on I was like the rest of 'em, like scum.

My mother never came to my high school graduation. I got dressed up for the high school graduation and when the ceremony was over I got on the streetcar and came home. There was no celebration at home. None.

The purpose of high school in my culture was to get your education and get the hell out and get a job.

Charlie Martinez

A teenage boy is like a young child; everything is interesting and fooling around was a way of life.

There were no religious classes as such at Quigley, but we were required to attend Mass each morning in our parish church. Father Bracken, one of the administrators/professors from Quigley, lived at our priest house because our parish was so close geographically. He was a stern person and distant. Forty years later when he was the Cardinal's chief administrator, I argued with him rather severely over the phone concerning racial justice.

I didn't comprehend or accept the personal God aspect of religion. It just made no sense that this God was so involved in our life. I went through all the motions of going to Mass, serving at Mass, listening to sermons but I only enjoyed the philosophical parts of the teachings. At times I would get taken up with a guilty conscience or feel emotional reading some of the parables in the New Testament but I was never into the praying part of religion. The artwork, the Latin Mass, the Gothic chapel, all these were wonders to me and I enjoyed them.

Each day at school was total fun. A young teenage boy is like a young child, everything is interesting and fooling around was a way of life. I had a friend, Bob Mariner, who was in my class and my constant companion at school. He was also my protector.

"Bob, Jim Boyle is after me because I hit him in the face with a piece of chalk and broke his glasses." Down the hall comes bulky Boyle after me. Mariner was slightly larger than me but afraid of nobody. Bob steps up, wrestles him to the ground and punches him a few times. Of course this was all done while we were wearing the required suit or sport jacket and tie. Bob and Boyle became stinking bags of sweat.

Bob and I set up an underground betting syndicate on the World Series the fall of our second year. I can't remember how much money we skimmed, but it reflected our streetwise background compared to the other students. We also set up a newspaper in second year for our room. It was called the 2C (for our classroom) for 2 Cians. We published two or three editions of school gossip and nonsense. We handwrote all the copies and passed them out free.

Somehow, I got involved in the photography laboratory. I wasn't officially in any kind of after school photo club and it wasn't a course offered by the school. The door was always unlocked, so I just helped myself. It fascinated me and I proceeded to develop my family's and friend's film and I made many prints and enlargements. I just used all of the material that was in the lab. I don't recall anyone questioning my use of the lab or chasing me out.

Lunch bell. One hour and forty-five minutes of free time! It amazes me that I ate lunch in the cafeteria every day for two years and yet I remember no particulars of the meals or of even being in a lunchroom! But wait. Some of us had been conscripted into the choir. One hour of this precious time was thrown away on choir practice. Each freshman was required to report to Father Meter for voice testing. Beyond all expectations, I was chosen for the choir. I couldn't carry a note.

We would sing at the Cardinal's Mass at the Cathedral on Sundays. After Mass, each kid was given a quarter to take the streetcar back home. Of course I walked and saved the quarter. I was even on television twice at Easter and once when they consecrated three bishops. The consecration of the bishops was a grand affair. A special platform was built out over the church space from the choir loft. Father Meter took this position high over the congregation and led a large part of the Chicago Symphony Orchestra in the music. At no time did I utter a sound during any song except during choir practice. I was short and in the front of the group near Father Meter. And on Sunday, to avoid his wrath at a mistake, I only mouthed the songs.

Frank DeMonte

He was funny, could crack jokes but he caught Brother Noonan on a bad day and the Brother beat the living crap out of him.

My mother and father had no input into what high school I was gonna go to. Whatever I said was it. And St. Michael's was the closest Catholic high school we could walk to.

St. Michael's was a eye opener as far as I was concerned. They had some nasty brothers in that school. But there were some good ones too. Brother Dorack was very nice. He was the brother who also coached the basketball team. But then there was Brother Noonan who looked like a bowling ball. I don't think he was more than five-eight, five-nine. But he was five-eight, five-nine width-wide too. Good teacher, but a nasty guy. You remember Anthony Rinatti? He was in our class with Dickey Azzaro and Joe Lendino. Anthony Rinatti was a wise guy. He was funny, could crack jokes but caught the brother on a bad day and the brother beat the living crap out of him. I mean he beat him up. Anthony didn't have a father. Had a mother. His father was in jail. He's a notorious burglar in the area so he spent almost his entire life in the state prison at Joliet. So there was no father figure. There was his mother who was a lovely lady.

I went to DePaul Academy for my last three years. They were tough guys. Lay teachers. Toughest bunch of psychopaths I ever found. There were two in particular. One was Tommy O'Brien, the football coach, and the other one was the basketball coach, Frank McGrath, who became a really a great guy when we got out of school. Frank McGrath was the assistant coach to ah, to Ray Meyer and he taught Latin. I had four years of Latin. Four years of Latin!

I was a very good student. And the reason I was a good student I think in high school was I did it by fear. If I didn't know my classes, those guys would beat the crap out of you. Frank McGrath took Mike Benadetto and beat the living crap out of him 'cause he didn't remember his lesson. Mike's father, for some reason he never knew what happened to his son. I loved Mike Benadetto. He was one of the nicest people, but he was a psychopath. I seen him beat the crap out of somebody, that's why I know. Big time. He almost killed him. And he owned Benadetto's Funeral Parlor. It was on North Avenue.

But I don't think the son told his father and I'll tell ya the reason why, Charlie. He caught a beating so badly that he was bleeding. I couldn't stand to even look at him. And his dad would've, if he would've known he would have went over there and did something to Frank McGrath cause that's who beat him up. I think he told his dad that he got in a fight with us. I hit him and he hit me and that's it. And that was the end of the story. Cause if he told his father, who was a tough hombre. his father would go nuts if he knew that.

Ken Martinez

My best teacher in high school was my history teacher. What the hell was his name? He would take his time and explain all the history. That's where I got to like history so much. Well, you know, a lot of teachers talk real fast and go through subjects real quick. He would take his time and explain to us. The thing he would like to spend a lot of time on was the Civil War. But I barely passed everything. Just made it.

Charlie Martinez

My mother said nothing. I knew my mother was heartbroken.

Quigley gave out no corporal punishment but they did have a system of demerits and you carried a demerit card at all times. Father Tuchislawski was the Dean of Discipline. He tried to be tough, but was really only average at the game. After you had accumulated twenty demerits, you were liable for conscription. Since we were off school on Thursday and went to school on Saturday (so as to break up any gang affiliations), those who acquired twenty demerits had to spend the whole Thursday doing clean up chores around school.

Father Tuchislawski gave me the assignment of opening and cleaning lockers. A dreary business. But one locker held a treasure. There was a three-foot high stack of cardboard boxes, each holding a square tile. On the tile was an engraving of the Saint James Chapel at the school, which was modeled after a Medieval masterpiece in France. The tile was given each quarter to the smartest kid in each class. I slipped one under my shirt and later presented it to my mother. She proudly hung it on the wall of our dining room next to a picture of St. Martin De Pores, her favorite saint.

All of this high school activity, at Quigley and for my last two years at Cathedral High, took place in the area of Chicago and State streets. This was an area of nightclubs, crooked cops, mob types, prostitutes, apartment buildings, hotels, flop houses, fancy restaurants and some upscale stores. The corner of Chicago and Michigan was a block or two away. Sometimes on our lunch hour, when there was no choir practice, we would wander the four or five blocks to the lakefront. But at the end of the second year all of this was to end. Without any contact with my parents for the two years, the priests at Quigley asked me to repeat second year because of my poor grades. Actually this was a kind of compliment; it meant I was the right stuff for making a priest, but I had to work harder at school. I sensed that some of the smarter guys who where asked to leave were more sophisticated sex-wise than I was and the priests saw this as a future problem, I guess.

"I quit Quigley."

"Why?" my mother asked.

"They wanted me to repeat second year."

My mother said nothing. She probably prayed twice as long after daily Mass and went to extra Novenas asking God to turn me around. I knew my mother was heartbroken.

The horn honked at 7:30 a.m. I had on a white shirt, tan slacks, brown shoes and a knit tan tie. I wore a tan cardigan with dark brown leather buttons down the front. As I ran down the outside stairs, the guys in the car whistled. I jumped into my cousin Pat Kennedy's car to start my first day at Mundelein Cathedral High School at Chicago and State streets, only two blocks from Quigley. Thus began two years of fun and silliness. with no knowledge passed on to me.

Jay Pistone

I used to like civics and, ah, that was my best course cause in our neighborhood the politicians ran the neighborhood.

At Waller High School, actually I was just sort of a stranger cause I didn't live in the area. Ya know wha I mean? But because my brother was living on Sheffield, in one of my dad's buildings, I was able to get that address. I liked Waller. It was all right. Well, Waller was ah, one guy, twelve girls.

I used to like civics and ah that was my best course 'cause I used to argue about civics. See in our neighborhood the politicians ran the neighborhood. Like my dad one time, he had to drive all the Italians on Election Day to the poll. Ya know I mean? Cause he had a car, he could drive. So he had to drive all the Italians 'cause the precinct captain said so.

Peter Eichel

No teacher stood out in grammar school or high school that I had any admiration for. They all screwed me over.

Well, after one year at Washburn High School, where I learned nothing, I just went home and told my father that I didn't want to go to school anymore. He said, "Do you have a job?" I said, "Yeah." And he said. "Okay."

From there, you and Giovenco right about that time talked me into going back to school. To Cathedral. They let me in and I made a real effort. And did I ever tell why I left there? You had to go to Mass and Communion for every First Friday. I couldn't go because if you were in mortal sin and you received Communion … you couldn't get absolution.

No. Wouldn't do that. It was a sacrilege. I would play it safe. I didn't believe in any a that bullshit but I wasn't going to defy, you know, what they said. It would cause me to burn forever and ever in the pains of hell. You risk that, you're crazy. I don't believe today I would risk it.

I got through one semester. I quit. I went to night school at the Central YMCA. I took a language and math and business writing, then accounting. I actually had a good, probably a better high school education.

The important thing in my life back then was that I went back and got that high school thing. I joined the National Guard in '58. Right? We were down in Fort Leonard Wood and they offered that GED thing. At that time they were giving you a diploma in the high school district that you lived in. So I got a diploma from Lakeview High School.

My mother or father never had any contact with the grammar or high school. Well, I think one conversation with my mother or father would've made it obvious that it ... served no purpose.
No teacher stood out in grammar school or high school that I had any admiration for. They all screwed me over.

Charlie Martinez

Days and months went by where not one new fact or bit of learning got into my head.

Mundelein Cathedral High School was a Central Catholic coed high school which meant anybody could come from anywhere in the city to attend. In reality, the students came from the Near North Side, Near West Side and a few farther away. The quality of the education was average at best and taught totally by nuns. It was really a school for children from financially lower-class Catholic families. Tuition was two dollars a month. The shocking thing is that later on we became aware that this mediocre education was still better than what the local public schools offered. I spent another two years doing no homework, no studying and learning nothing. One nun stood out above all the others. Sister Eustella. She taught English classes.

"I am going to read the two short stories that I think were the best that were handed in," she said.

"The car headlights caught a fleeing figure in the road. He is my brother and I am going to kill him." So started my story. I had no idea she was going to read it. She suggested I send it in for publication. Of course I didn't.

Sometime in junior year at Cathedral High, I received a letter from the University of Chicago. It was unopened and left for me on my bed.

"You have been selected to continue your high school education at the University of Chicago Lab School. Please respond ... "

Here was a letter out of the blue requesting that I transfer out of Cathedral High to a prestigious, expensive, private college prep school. How could this happen? I never showed it to my parents. I threw it away. Why I threw it away, I do not know. Maybe it was because we were brought up to suspect the university of being really a nest full of Communists. But more likely, I didn't feel adequate, was very unsophisticated and had no guidance. Why didn't I turn to my older brothers and sisters? I don't know. One of the many non-choices of an accidental life.

Of all the classes I had in those two years at Cathedral, the one that impacted my later life the most was the typing class. Learning to type in those days was like learning to use the computer today. Every employer wanted someone who could type and they would pay relatively well. And Sister Monica taught us to type whether we wanted to learn the skill or not. She was proud of the fact that the downtown offices were standing in line to hire her typists as part-timers from a school only a few blocks away.

She ran the class like a master sergeant. She taught us typing rhythm to the tune of *"Tea for Two"* played on an old Victrola record player. We had constant speed tests with subtractions of words per minute for each mistake. So if you could type seventy or up to a hundred words a minute and made ten mistakes, that was still great. Speed was the thing; mistakes would decrease later. And she was right. In one typing class, I was the only boy. At times, she would ask if there was a gentleman in the class who would open the windows. Of course, I was it. The pole was heavy and six feet long for those huge old windows. It was a struggle and I was smaller than most of the girls.

We did have a religion class taught by a priest. What a difference from Quigley! Father McAvoy was boring, recited from a book and had us write it down verbatim.

"And God the Father knowing Himself resulted in God the Son and the Father and the Son loving each other, there was the Holy Ghost."

What the hell did that mean? However he was movie star handsome and a nice person. The girls swooned in class. He was a heavy cigarette smoker and died rather young from cancer.

Days and months went by where not one new fact or bit of learning got into my head. But it was fun and silly.

The nuns made a terrible mistake and placed a small bathroom in the library. Now that wasn't terrible by itself, but someone had put a sliding lock on the *outside* of the door. Poor Sister John. We'd read studiously until she went into the bathroom. Then we'd lock her in. We could hear her pounding on the door and saying, "Let me out of here, let me out of here" as we walked out of the library and down the hall trying to hold in our laughter.

Carmen Costa, who was short but stocky and shaved, put on a hat and tie and announced to Sister John that he was from the FBI. She did not recognize him!

"Sister, I've been sent to inspect magazines for lewd material and remove any that I find."

He merrily went through Life and Look, tearing out pages. Sister nodded in agreement as we practically peed in our pants.

John Owens

I graduated. I don't know how that happened.

Mrs. Savage, the one I told you about who gave me the pictures of the Boeing aircraft planes, called my mother and had my mother come in. And she said that rather than him going to a regular school, like to Waller High School or something like that, I think he'd be better off at a vocational school. So she suggested I go to Washburn. That's how that came about.

I think at that point I was just starting to get interested in cars. And I thought, yeah, I know they got an auto shop at Washburn and that'll be something I like to do rather than go into Waller and have to sit in class all day.

Washburn was a trip! That's were I met Ike and Frank Delarosa. I kinda got in a lot of fights when I was in there. Ike and I were always up to something that was mischievous so to speak, I guess. You know I had a lot of fun when I was in high school. We got thrown outa one class, the physics class because we didn't show up. Ike and I didn't show up for two months to the guy's class and we walked in one day and we said, "Are you gonna pass us" and he said "No." We had the nerve to walk in and ask him if he was gonna pass us after we hadn't shown up for two months.

At Washburn I probably learned just how to repair cars. That's what I really liked to do and I worked on cars all the time and I learned a lot about cars. As far as the academics, I don't know if I got anything much ought of that, Charlie. History and English and things like that I just … I didn't do well in them. I graduated. I don't know how that happened.

Once in awhile my father'd say, "How's things going over in school." If I told him something like I had a situation where something was going on, he would say, "Well why don't you try this approach to it, you know." He always had a kinda solution, you know. So he was kind of in that way he did get involved with me, you know. But he wouldn't go to the school.

Joe Zummo

Some of the guys I knew went to DePaul Academy and I liked the idea of playing football. But I decided to go to Quigley because a friend of mine, Chuckie Martinez was a student there and a good friend of mine and I really had the thought of happiness because we would have Thursdays off and we would play basketball. When I was about to go there, Chuckie transferred out. So I was more or less stuck for that year. It was a good school with a good academic program.

But a lot of my friends were going to DePaul so I went to DePaul. I never asked my parents about changing schools and I am not sure if they knew where I was going to school. They gave me the money for tuition so somebody knew something. I played football there and then I ran into a little difficulty and they asked me to leave. I missed classes and by the end of the year it caught up with me and they asked me to leave. I transferred myself over to Cathedral High School.

I liked Cathedral, the kids and the fact it was co-educational. They had a football team and I got on the basketball team which I enjoyed even though I wasn't that good. Frankly, Cathedral High School was two of the happiest years of my life. That's where I met my wife, Winnie. The teachers were mediocre at best but I wasn't interested in education: I was interested in having a good time. The buildings reminded of a condemned warehouse. The bathrooms were outhouses. I went there for two years and never sat on the commode because I was afraid my flesh would adhere to it. I graduated on time. Sister Eustella was a no nonsense person, never smiled but I learned a great deal from her. Cathedral had no labs, gyms, or cafeteria.

Charlie Martinez

"You know, those guys would steal a red hot stove if they thought they could carry it."

I signed up for advanced algebra but Sister John of the Cross thought I was undeserving to attend because she had decided I was of the hoodlum element. So my spiral downward in math continued and limits me to this day.

How silly was the day? Sister Daniels also monitored a study class. Ephraim Abraham, of debating fame, would, *every day,* walk up to the front of the room, right next to Sister, to sharpen his pencil. As he fumbled around, he flipped on the typing class Victrola that was stored next to the pencil sharpener. It was an old instrument and took about two minutes to warm up. By this time Ephraim was safely in his seat at the back of the room. We all became very quiet, trying to hold in our laughter. Softly, the melody of *"Tea for Two"* filled the air. It always took Sister Daniels a minute to notice the music but then she would jump up from her chair staring through her pince-nez glasses and demand to know who turned on the Victrola. Of course, no one answered. But from the back of the room, Ephraim stood up and very politely offered to turn off the disturbing instrument. She assented. He did. She thanked him. More suppressed guffaws.

And yet the nuns tried. We had an art class. An art class for a bunch of juvenile delinquents! Patrick DiVinci and James Michael DeAngelo visited us one day. (AKA Patti Irwin and Jimmie Foley, our buddies and high school students at DePaul Academy.)

They claimed they were college art students at DePaul University and wanted to look into the quality of her students' work. She was naïve and said sure go ahead. They wandered around making nonsensical comments and then left. After school we all laughed till we were in pain recalling the episode with the two "artists."

You see, most of the silliness was not malicious. However one time, and I always felt bad about this, several of us placed a ladder against the Art room door. When sister returned, she opened the door and the ladder fell hitting her. Nothing serious, but she must have felt terrible to think that after all the effort on her behalf to teach us art (and she was very good) that we would do such a thing.

In the spring of the third year, I was called to the principal's office. I did not know why I had to present myself. When I arrived, two detectives were sitting in her office. They told me that the stored-up money for the yearbook was stolen from the safe the night before.

"Did you know anything about it?'
"No."
"Do you know guys in your neighborhood by the names of James Connors and Michael Platt?"
"Yes."
"Did you know anything about the theft?"
"No."
"You know, those guys would steal a red hot stove if they thought they could carry it."
"Yes, sir."
"Alright, you can leave."

High school became a nuisance distraction between first period and our after-school jobs. We tolerated it because it was so much fun. I was never proposed for student offices. Fact is I didn't even know who the officers were ... and this in a class of only eighty! I was not on the student newspaper. My only citations in the yearbook were for football and basketball.

Stars and Stripes Forever. I was shocked. Never had I heard anything so rich, so beautiful. I listened suspended in a dream state. I said nothing to my fellow students. Members of the Chicago Symphony Orchestra had come to our small auditorium and played several pieces. This is the only one I remember. I had never heard orchestra music in such an intimate setting. I had heard a few pieces when in the choir at Quigley, but I was a church-length away in the Cathedral. But now I was ten feet away in a small hall. I did not want it to end. If only the teachers had asked us our impression. What they could have learned! I was grateful for the exposure, however.

John Giovenco

But now all of a sudden people were reading things and teachers were reading things; so I felt so much better.

I wanted to go to a high school called Lane Tech, which was a long streetcar ride away. But I just didn't like Lane Tech. In my second year, I went to Washburn High, which was two blocks away from the house. It was a trade school. It really was populated by MRs ... mental retards. English class was Life magazine, math class was how many board feet would it take to build a house, you know, shop kind of thing. I was very unhappy there, so with my parents' urging, decided to quit school. They asked, "Just when are you going to quit?" They figured I'd reached the age, which was sixteen at that time, and I could quit.

Then I ran into you, Charlie Martinez, and you said, "You know you oughta go to school to Mundelein." I said, "I probably can't get in because it's full." You told me to tell the nun I was losing my faith at Washburn High School. Tears ran down her face and she let me start Mundelein High School.

My life took a dramatic turn 'cause all of a sudden I was associating with at the time I thought were a bunch of higher caliber persons and teachers and educational concepts. I began getting interested again in offices now instead of print shops. Typing instead of lathes. Working as a filing clerk instead of a machine shop person. So I came out of the laboring group and more into the office worker group kind of thing. And also back to reading, although I always read even though I wasn't associated with people who read. But now all of sudden people were reading things and teachers were reading things so I felt so much better. Then there was a priest there named Father Ragen. Father Ragen took an interest in me. And him taking an interest in me made a big difference although I was very nervous about his taking an interest in me. I had a wonderful teacher in my senior year, Sister Sharon.

My mother and father knew nothing of this. They made no comment on my graduation that I remember. Education was not a big deal with them. Work was a big deal with them. They were more impressed about the fact that I was working in an office downtown than I was going to school. It was more concrete. There was, you know, no money in school. But there was money in going to work. And if you worked in an office you were somebody.

I don't remember conversations like that with my parents; I just remember attitudes.

Charlie Martinez

"Kid, get an education, then nobody can take that away from you."

My father held my Quigley report card in his hand. I was uncomfortable sitting on a chair opposite him. I supposed my mother had put him up to it. I remember him asking me about my poor grades. I said nothing. There was no further discussion. That was the only time he or anyone in my family asked me about schoolwork in my entire life. My father seemed educated to me. He was articulate, read the newspapers, listened to the news on the radio and I heard him comment on politics many times. I never saw him read a book.

His frequent advice to me, and really to any of my brothers or sisters, was, "Kid, get an education, then nobody can take that away from you." Or "Get paid for what you know, not for what you do." This was pretty good advice from a man who painted walls and hung wallpaper for a living—when he worked.

Bunny Byrne

If I couldn't copy Pat Kennedy's homework on my way to school, mine wasn't done.

A whole slew of us went from Immaculate Conception grammar school to Mundelein High. Yeah. I don't know, you know, what triggered it. But of the guys, Eddie Randazzo went, Frank Corbett went, Vince went, my brother went, I went, Terry McGovern went. I betcha there was about, at least ten of us went.
You know. And I don't know how that came about. Well first of all, it was cheap. You know, I mean, let's face it. It was a buck a month or something. So, that may have had a lot to do with it. You know, my mother probably said, "Your sister's going down there, and she's only paying a dollar a month. I'm not sending you to DePaul," it's six bucks a month there or eight bucks, whatever it was. So, you know, so that's probably it. She wanted us to go to a parochial school.

Naw, I didn't learn anything in high school. Probably not. I would even threaten the nuns. In my last year, I would just say to the nuns, "Look, ah, I don't have my homework and I'm not bringing any homework and if you wanna throw me out, you're welcome to do so because my cousin across the street is making thirty bucks a day working on the Greyhound Bus Station right now, and I should be over there with him not here."

A few of the nuns impressed me. I thought Sister Monica was a great teacher, I really do. She was putting girls out of that class. Offices had contracts with 'em to come and work for 'em before they ever graduated. They knew what they were gonna get before they were done. You know. They were doing hunnert words a minute in shorthand, ninety words a minute in typing. You know. A whole class of thirty, forty girls. They were all had jobs downtown by the time they walked out of high school they walked into a job. My sister, same way. That Lake Shore Club came to the school and got her. She didn't go looking for a job. The Lake Shore Club came to the school and said we need a girl. But naw, they didn't come for me. Yeah, my mother and father came to my graduation but they didn't say nothin' or congratulate me.

I had a car from the time I was about a sophomore. Yep. And that's another thing the nun was saying, "Don't bring the car to school." She used to see me parking it. She'd call me aside. And she'd say, "Mr. Byrne, I saw you getting out of your car down there." I says, "So throw me outta school. What can I tell ya, I'm caught. I'm busted. Throw me out, I'll go to work." "Go sit down," she says. She just nursed me right through the senior year. Sure, she wanted me to just get through with everybody else. When they'd be having a test, she say, "Mr. Byrne come up here. I don't want you disrupting the class, go into the newspaper office." It was right outside our classroom door. The Phoenix. I'd go into the Phoenix and sit around, bullshit with the kids in there, you know. She was a hell of nice nun.

I never wanted to miss school 'cause school was great. We'd meet all the guys every day. Sometimes me and Vince'd skip school and go right down to the Chicago Theater, see a movie. Go to a movie, see Lou Breese. The band. Catch the movie. You know. We'd be just on the streetcar, an going along and I'd say, "What ya say we go downtown for a movie Vince?" "Why not? Let's go." So everybody'd get off at Chicago and State and we'd keep going.

They didn't seem to keep track. You know what? It was like, they didn't bother. Now Vince was a pretty good student. . And Vince was involved in stuff in school and sang in the school play. But Vince did his homework, let's put it that way. I never did. If I couldn't copy Pat's on my way to school, it wasn't done.

Pat Kennedy was a whiz in math. So they'd give us math problems see. And he'd get on the streetcar and he'd just hand us the paper. And we'd all scribble the damn things down. See. And if I was half done, you know, I'd go in and she'd say, "Well Mr. Byrne this is incomplete." I'd say, "I fell asleep. I was up late." They never did anything.

I don't even remember if I got marks or anything, Charlie. I just waltzed through senior year. I really did. I just waltzed through it. I did nothing. I don't ever remember doing homework at home in my whole life.

Well my mother and father didn't say nothin' 'cause they weren't into that, see. My mother went to third grade, my dad went to second grade. They figured if you knew how to read and write, you were doing great.

Pat Rogers

Being a sophomore, I always had an erection looking at the pretty girls.

In my first year at Cathedral High I had A's in everything. I can remember Rita was in that class and probably Priola and Rosie Ventura. And Kay Keane. And all the guys from the neighborhood. I was infatuated with Tubby because she had such large breasts at the time. Course you couldn't see anything because the girls were covered from their throat to their ankles half the time. I did quite well in ancient history and ah, algebra. My grades were good my freshman year. They were good my second year except for geometry.

Sr. John of the Cross taught the geometry class. I was president of the class; Rita was vice president. We were sitting in her geometry class and Sister was constantly asking me to get up and discuss the Pythagoras theorem or something which I probably didn't know anything about. But I always had an erection. Being a sophomore, I always had an erection looking at the pretty girls. I can remember Mike Hennessy and all the guys making fun of me. So Sister thought I was obnoxious at the time because I wouldn't get up and answer the question. She said she was gonna report me to Father Brett, the basketball coach, that I was not to play basketball. Well I did play basketball and I didn't tell Father Brett. And when she found out she was furious. So Father Brett kicked me off the basketball team. And

I lost my presidency also. She failed me and Jim McDonough, and Jimmy Carpenter in geometry. But that was about the only bad grade I ever had in high school at Cathedral.

Charlie Martinez

"Your mother lied to me, didn't she?"

"He is on his way, Sister." My mother lied. I was still at home, desperate for a solution to my problem. An important religious event was taking place that evening at Holy Name Cathedral. It might have been the beginning of Forty Hours Devotion. Every student was required to attend and the boys were expected to wear a coat and tie.

I had no sport coat or suit coat. I tried on my brother-in-law Dave's coat. He was six feet one and I was five foot seven. It didn't work. My brother Ken was just as tall. Bobby and Jerry weren't around. In desperation, Joe Zummo brought over his sport jacket. It hung on me and I was humiliated to wear it but I went down to the Cathedral anyway.

I was late and all the students were in church after marching there from the school next door. Sister met me at the church door. She said she called my house, looking for me. Without thinking, I said, "Yeah, I know."

"Your mother lied to me, didn't she? You hadn't left home yet when I called!"

I mumbled something in a weak defense of my mother and started up the aisle to my seat. There was no way to sneak in unnoticed. The lights were all lit and everyone was standing. I was sure all eyes were on me as I walked toward the middle of the church. By the time I arrived at my place, Joe's sports jacket was soaked with sweat.

And eventually high school ended with a ... I don't remember. I don't recall walking the aisle in the Cathedral and receiving a diploma. No party at home. No crush of relatives patting me on the back. Where was that graduation watch or electric shaver? Was it possible I just forgot all that? Not likely. But more likely there was no celebration at home and the ceremony at church was minimal.

John Giovenco

And he said what if you get in trouble with some girl? He says here's another twenty.

One day Sister Sharon walked up to me. I'll always remember this. She said, "You know you got a pretty good head on your shoulders." Now that's the first time anybody had ever told me anything like that. "You oughta go to college." I said, "I don't know anything about college." I never met anybody that had ever gone to college.

Nobody in my family ever went to college. I said, "No, I got to go and get a job. My mother and father want me to go to work." She said, "Well you oughta go to college, think about it." So next thing I knew, they had a contest in Chicago as to who could sell the most subscriptions to the New World Catholic newspaper and win a scholarship to college. And what Sister Sharon did was take all of the newspaper subscriptions for the entire school, sent them in under my name, and I won a scholarship to college. To the last scholarship given. Christian Brothers College, Memphis Tennessee. Went home and told my parents.

My father said, "Enough! You been going to school enough. You really don't want to go to school any more. It's bad for your eyes. Where is this place? How are you gonna get there? How are you gonna pay for it." Etc. So I said, "Well, it's a one-year scholarship. I'll go." It was worth six hundred dollars. Room and board! And tuition.

'Course I went down there with my Aunt Fran's suitcase because we'd never gone anyplace and we didn't have any suitcases. She loaned me her suitcase which had a rope around it. Everything I had fit into one suitcase. It didn't lock. So we put the rope around it.

I was going to the train station, and my Uncle Brazi said to me, "You're going away to school, how much money you got?" I said, "I've got twenty bucks." He says, "Twenty bucks? You're never gonna do anything with twenty dollars." I said, "Well they've paid for everything, you know." I didn't know I needed books. And he said, "Ah, what if you get in trouble with some girl?" He says, "Here's another twenty."

At school, they asked me to declare a major. I didn't know what a major was. They said pre-medicine, pre-law, business. I said, "Okay, pre-med." They said that would be fifty bucks for labs. I didn't have fifty bucks. I said, what doesn't have lab. Business. So I became a business major.

Jim Sullivan

I never, never gave college a thought. My father offered, you know, wanted to know if I wanted to go to college and they would pay. But I knew they weren't in a position to pay for my college education. There was just no money, you know. So I told them "No. I didn't want to go." And then I went into service about six months later. Went into the Navy.

I never discussed those things with my parents cause in those days high school education was considered pretty good for you know, the average guy. Nobody that I knew that we hung around with had parents that were, say college graduates.

Jack Flaherty

So how you gonna pay for college?

Well I gave college a thought. I didn't have anybody pushing me toward it or directing me. 'Course there was the thought of how do you pay for college. You know your parents don't have that kind of money. So how you gonna pay for college? You know you have to work. But guys were being drafted at that point and were only six months out of high school. To fight the Korean War. I thought, well heck, I don't want to go to school for six months or a year and then get drafted and pulled out and be missing for two or three and then come back and start all over again. I'll just wait this out, get drafted, come back and go to school. But it did not happen. I didn't get drafted 'til about six years later. In the meantime my friend got me a job so I was gainfully employed all that time.

Jack LaBrasca

I drove a Redtop cab and went to school when I could.

I do remember that when I came out of the service in 1960, and I said to my dad, "Dad I'd like to go to De Paul University. Can you help me." And he says, "No I can't'."

Well, he says it just wasn't financially feasible. So, I did what I call my Redtop education. I drove a Redtop cab and went to school when I could. Took up a course here and a course there, you know, patchwork. But I had this strong desire to go to De Paul University. I really wanted to go. It would have been nice.

Charlie Martinez

I had had little discussion with my parents or older siblings about school and I suppose to them, my high school graduation was an anti-climax. What to do next? There was no discussion at home about college. Not that I was discouraged, but it just wasn't brought up by anyone, including me. I asked no one's opinion, received no counseling from the nuns, and was given no college catalogs to review. There was no "college days" at the high school. I never inquired about or knew anyone who talked about going to college.

However, I held this kernel deep in my mind and acted on it without help or encouragement. In fact, I never wanted people to know my mind. My method was to act, and that was really what life was all about. I wasn't very articulate or sophisticated but had a bulldog determination in pursuit of a goal. And I never thought ahead, fortunately, of how difficult it would be to get through college. I only had this unconstructed idea that through college I would continue to be stimulated and exposed to knowledge and could somehow get to my goal of writing.

Money was not a factor because I had none, my parents had none and my siblings had none. So a college degree had to be obtained by the usual neighborhood means, that is, by dogged pursuit and the total cost would only come from my willingness to work full time to pay all my expenses as I went to college. This I did without hesitation. I never thought in detail where the money would come from and so I walked the two blocks to Loyola University Lewis Towers Campus and signed up as an English major. Through all of college and the rest of my life, I had a secret weapon. I never spent any emotional energy on the possibility of not having enough money. It just never got into my consciousness. What value this blissful ignorance!

CHAPTER FIVE: WORK

Part One: Paperboys

Charlie Martinez

Delivering or selling newspapers was the entry-level job for a preteen in my neighborhood.

October into November is the darkest time of the year. The switch from Daylight Savings Time immediately brought the night upon us at the end of the school day. There is rain and wind in those weeks. And the cold seeps in with the rain, wind, and dark giving a foretaste of what was to come in December. I sold newspapers from a newsstand downtown in those months.

Although many of us took a tour of shoe shining with our homemade shoe shine boxes, delivering or selling newspapers was the entry-level job for a preteen in my neighborhood. Like my friends, I held a series of newspaper jobs, probably passed to me by word of mouth.

I was in the fifth grade when I began selling newspapers from a newsstand. How I got the job, I don't remember. I'm sure my parents and older siblings knew nothing about this job. For many of us in the neighborhood, there was this compulsion to work. People would think you did it for spending money. I don't remember having any spending money of my own. I gave all my newspaper pay to my parents and I did not get an allowance. I told them I sold newspapers but shared no details. They never questioned me further.

I walked downtown after school and walked home after the crowds of office workers had faded. This was about two miles each way. I walked alone.

A short, thick Sicilian man, Guy Maniscalo's father, ran a newsstand at Dearborn and Madison. He sold the Daily News and the Herald American as well as Life, Look, Time and other magazines. He sold the Daily Racing Form and the Abenpost, a German language newspaper. Directly across the street was another newsstand he owned. I never saw it, but everyone suspected he did some bookie work at that newsstand.

When I arrived for work he stacked that stand with material to sell to workers going in the opposite direction and not crossing Madison towards his other stand. I did not hustle or try to sell the papers; people just asked me for a certain paper and essentially I made change. I was paid by the amount of newspapers I sold. I don't remember how much I made but I would always come home with a pocket full of change, always less than one dollar for two hours work.

I was cold and totally confused and bored by this job. I think it was too simple. The crowds were a huge dark sinister mass to me. The rain made the car headlights and streetlights larger and star shaped. The background noise of people talking, walking, streetcars clanging, and auto tires slapping the wet pavement was a terrible distraction. I was cold and wet with no rubbers or galoshes and no hat or gloves. All was confusion. At times I felt I was lost in a strange world with all these people a blur moving past me. I always made it home. I knew no one. I talked to no one. I don't remember being happily greeted at home like the wild dogs of Africa when they return to their den.

Peter Eichel

I witnessed incest.

I don't know if you remember those apartment buildings that ran from Schiller Street maybe a block and a half and they were three- and four-story brownstones? Up La Salle Street? Remember when the Appalachian whites, the hillbillies, moved in there? Yeah, well I delivered newspapers in there at twelve, thirteen years old. I was in grammar school, so I had to be eleven, twelve, thirteen. And, uh, that was incredible, you know.

I witnessed incest. The kids would run around with no clothes on. It wasn't unusual for me to be walking down a hall and see incest. It wasn't frightening 'cause we kinda were used to that kind of stuff, weren't we? 'Course, if I walked from my house when I was eleven or twelve years old, south on La Salle street, I was at risk from being assaulted by the hillbillies. Ya go a couple more blocks and you're close to where the black people lived in the projects. Then you were at risk for Cabrini Green. But even before Cabrini Green, there were black people on Wells Street at Wells and Division. But when I delivered newspapers in there, and you can't put this in a book cause it's discrimination, but none of the black people paid their bills. So I didn't want to deliver the newspapers, cause I could never collect.

And the bastard Harry. Do you remember Harry? Harry was the guy that had the newspaper distribution agency in the basement. Right on La Salle Street. Well, you used to collect all the money for the subscriptions. Right? And your pay you had to take out of what you collected. So if you didn't collect from everybody you didn't get paid. So these black families never paid their bill. I wasn't getting paid.

John Kennedy

> *It was not unusual for me to come home around the holidays with three hundred dollars.*

Well, actually I started working at nine years of age, delivering newspapers. Worked for a fellow named Paul Gordon, who owned Gordon's News Service or actually it was called Dearborn Parkway News Service. When I started he had a little storefront at Goethe and Dearborn. And he had a morning group and an afternoon group of delivery boys. Irv Gordon was the one who did the morning group and Paul Gordon did the afternoon group. And Paul was also a musician. He was a piano player. 'Cause I could remember at times I'd come to work after school and he'd be dressed in his normal casual outfit. But when I returned from doing my route to bring back the wagon, he would be dressed in a business suit or tuxedo, very fancy 'cause he was going to play the piano at some nightclub or something.

I probably delivered three hundred newspapers a day. But I had a lot of hotels. I could remember going to a hotel for example 1309 North Astor where I'd give the doorman maybe twenty Daily News and ten Herald Americans and he would take 'em to the various floors and distribute them.

I worked six days a week after school. Started at nine and worked until I was thirteen. Every day. Never missed. Five, six days a week. Rain and snow. Whatever.

At Christmas time Mr. Gordon would get yearly calendars that he would sell to us for a nickel a piece. And then we would take them around to the people we delivered the newspapers to and ring the bell and say season greetings from your newspaper deliverer, or news carrier. And many of 'em gave us an envelope with cash in it. So at Christmas time it was not unusual for me to come home after doing that a couple of days around the holidays with three hundred dollars. Remember getting a twenty-dollar bill in an envelope from a guy by the name of John Knight. And he got the Daily News. And he was the publisher of the Daily News!

But all that money went to my parents. The only thing I remember I asked my mother for a baseball glove. And she took me downtown someplace to a sporting goods store and bought me a baseball glove with some of that money one year. But you know that money went to the family. I never put that away.

Joe Zummo

I was a newspaper delivery boy. I had a hell of lot of paper routes. I had the largest paper route in the city of Chicago. I inherited it from Jimmy Foley. It was 399 papers and my boss was a guy named Gordon. I started at the Drake Towers at Lake Shore Drive at Oak Street. There was a whole line of hotels on that stretch and I think I got rid of most of my papers on that first block. I used to deliver to the 33rd floor of the Palmolive building to the people who use to advertise for Milky Way and Mars Candy bars. They gave me all my Boy Scout equipment. They liked me and I belonged to Troop 142. Two of the best newspaper delivery boys I knew were Joe and Steve Russo. They had a few routes and you would get premiums at getting new customers. Great premiums—softballs and stuff like that. I was never good at getting new customers. I had a friend of mine—Chuckie Martinez—he had a paper route where you did the collections over on Wells Street crossing over on Oak Street. I used to go with him and the first month I collected from everybody but one and the boss thought that was terrific.

Jim Sullivan

So I started dumping the papers in a coal chute.

I had the paper routes, you know, a number of different paper routes. I did the advertising paper route for a couple of years. I forget the name. North Town Economist or something like that. I had one for a long while. And one winter, you know it was exceptionally severe weather. My route was on the lakefront. And I got frostbite. So I started dumping the papers in a coal chute. And the people who owned the building called up the company and they fired me, you know. Later on I had a route a number of years with the Sun Times. On you know, Hudson, Mohawk, Cleveland. You know, the old Cleveland Aces territory. Yeah, collected for the paper too. I was probably, ten or eleven. I used to give the money to my mother.

Bunny Byrne

And what you couldn't get rid of you opened the sewer and threw 'em down the sewer.

We delivered the Shopping News. Me and my brother. Oh, that was terrible. We had a route. And they would drop off about maybe a thousand papers in front of our house. And then we recruited different kids in the neighborhood to get a wagon or a cart and them gave 'em routes. The routes were all east of us in the Gold Coast district. And it went from about Bellevue on the south, which was way past Division. To North Avenue on the north and then from about Dearborn over to the lake.

You just threw one in every hallway. You know, and what you couldn't get rid of you opened the sewer and threw 'em down the sewer. Or threw 'em all in somebody's basement window.

Charlie Martinez

There was no joy, only boring repetition.

Down a few steps to the half storefront on the westside of La Salle Street just south of Division you entered into the world of the newspaper agency. This was a ma and pop type business usually handling the morning or the afternoon papers, in this case the Daily News and Herald American. The room was about ten by twenty feet but it was crowded with delivery boys, thousands of newspapers stacked against its north wall and large tables for sorting up against its south wall. Harry, the owner and sole employee of the agency, was everywhere telling kids where they screwed up on deliveries, how their collections didn't jibe with their expenses and to get to work a little earlier. Harry was a stocky, black-haired, nervous fellow who I thought was Jewish. Our only contact with Jewish people was with these proprietors of small businesses.

He counted out each route's allotted papers by grabbing about fifty at a time and walking his ink-stained fingers quickly through them saying out loud the count in fives. He never hesitated or recounted. Once finished with the count, he grabbed our route "ring" from the wall, saw that we took it in our hand and pointed us to the door. The route ring was the most valuable piece of equipment Harry owned. It held playing card size thick pieces of cardboard imprinted with the name, address, type of newspaper, charges, and time preferred for us to collect. They were color-coded for streets. A double of the ring was kept safely in his office.

I delivered about one hundred papers at that time. I quickly learned to fold the paper so that it would not open up as I threw it onto a porch. For some reason I was very good at folding a tight paper but some guys never mastered this skill. We loaded the papers into heavy canvas bags. Carrying the papers was absolute drudgery. The straps of the bags cut into my shoulder almost instantly, forcing me to change location of the bag from shoulder to shoulder for relief. We stumbled out into the bright, hot sunshine. This same sun that we would expose ourselves to all day long at the lakefront was now a torturing beast.

From Chicago Avenue north to North Avenue, I delivered on both sides of La Salle Street and a few addresses on Wells Street. La Salle Street in that area was very different from where I lived on Schiller Street a few blocks away. On both sides of La Salle Street were what I would now call townhouses, small apartment buildings, a few large apartment buildings and a few small hotels. There were no free-standing houses like on my street. Some of the townhouses were really mansions, especially just north of Schiller Street. Although the street was very different from mine, I realized that the quality of construction with mostly brick structures with plenty of stone trim and occasional stained glass windows was definitely higher. There were few trees and no lawns.

But in doing the job there was no joy, only boring repetition. The boredom doubled the actual effort demanded by the job and the hot sun and lack of money for pop added a further burden. Using a bike was only partially helpful because the heavy bag at first made steering the bike difficult. I rarely was given a wagon. Time dragged and relief came only as the load lightened.

Collecting my money was a bewildering process, which I never mastered. I put in time, went around to people twice, tracked them down on Sunday, but when I had to pay Harry for the papers each week I sometimes was short or had little left over to show for my effort.

Harry explained to me over and over the mechanics of collecting, and how to make change as if I was retarded. I just did not understand what he was talking about which was ridiculous because I was one of the smartest kids in my class and my family kept calling me the "brain." I never did catch on and made little money on that job.

I remember two high points of that daily struggle. I delivered to Tokyo Rose's mother. Tokyo Rose was an American-born Japanese who went to Japan and broadcast propaganda to the American troops during World War II. And still in my mind's eye I can see the front page of the Herald American showing the Empire State building and the crash site on its 79th floor where a B 26 bomber struck it in the fog. That fascinated me.

Jack LaBrasca

Pretty soon I was making some real serious money.

I started selling newspapers. But what happened is I bought two routes. A kid named Whitey Blake had a couple routes and Lenny LaPaglia had a couple of routes. I bought two from him and two from Whitey.

Well, the routes were really large office buildings on Orleans Street. Ah, Orleans and Superior, Orleans and Ohio. They were large office buildings with either office or light industry, and you go right to the main floor or lobby of the building and you put your newspapers there. When the office workers came out you would sell them a newspaper. That was your spot. Your route.

I sold the Herald, the Daily News. That is what you got late in the afternoon. It was usually the Daily News or the Herald. Because they would sell the Times in the morning and the Tribune late at night. But it was usually the, the daily Herald.

Yeah. I would pay like five bucks, something like that for the route. And ah, I had four. But I thought that it might be a little extra touch to actually deliver these newspapers to their offices. So I started a new thing. I started go into the office and delivering them and they were tipping me. Pretty soon I was making some real serious money. And I had built a reputation. Then I bought another route.

Joe Olita

Nobody in my neighborhood delivered newspapers. If I had to rely on subscriptions from the neighborhood I might as well forget about it. Yeah. Yeah. Ah, nobody could read English.

Charlie Martinez

Chunks of gray tissue and blood clots were being swept into the gutter and then down the sewer.

I went on to somewhat better newspaper delivery jobs. First I delivered the Daily News in the Gold Coast for Mr. Gordon. This was a cleaner, neater job and there was no collecting or Sunday delivery. I don't know if my route was peculiar, but I never saw any of the people who subscribed to the paper, just their hallways. One Saturday Mr. Gordon disputed the amount of pay he owed me and refused to give me what I thought was the correct amount. I went home and returned with my older brother Bernie who was a short, muscular ex-Marine. I got my full pay.

I moved on to a job I liked even more. There was a newspaper agency in a building at La Salle and Lake Street, downtown. The building was not kept up and had dreary halls, freight elevators and rooms that looked like they hadn't had a paint job since before the war. The paperboys delivered the newspapers to customers in their downtown offices. I handed the papers to the office workers personally or put it on their desk. The pay was three dollars and seventy-five cents a week. When I told my mother the amount and that I wanted to take the job, she commented that it was awful good pay. All my pay I gave to my mother. I knew she needed the money for household expenses. It was not demanded and I felt good knowing I was helping out.

The people greeted me with smiles and sometimes candy bars and you could get out of the weather for a while. I felt proud when I discovered one of my customers was the "Nancy" of the "Shopping With Nancy" column in the very paper I delivered. The business of offices fascinated me. People were always talking, typing, mimeographing, drinking coffee, talking on the phone and running around with sheets of paper in their hands looking very deliberate and important.

Once, in my wanderings in and out these office buildings, I came upon a patch of people huddled together talking quietly at the entrance to a ground level parking lot. As I got closer, I noticed a parking lot attendant hosing down the sidewalk by the entrance to the subway stairs. Chunks of gray tissue and blood clots were being swept into the gutter and then down the sewer. With no prompting, I was drawn towards the group of people huddled together. No one seemed to take notice of or bother with young boys.

"Your car went into gear on its own, lady," the attendant said to a middle-aged woman. A grey Oldsmobile with Hydromatic Drive was parked at the entrance to the parking lot; the car sat there silent but dignified, looking like a scolded dog to me.

"Oh…was anyone hurt?"

The man put his hand on her shoulder. "Yes, an older gentleman…he died."

"Oh! Oh!" Sobs.

I then heard the attendant tell a passerby that as the car dragged the victim, his head was smashed against the granite structure of the subway stairs. As a boy, I was near a dead body or saw the aftermath of an accident several times. Every time I felt that somehow the world had stopped and an amazing truth was being presented to me. I didn't know how to respond but just buried this treasure in my heart and eventually went about my business.

This job ended my newspaper delivery career.

Part Two: First Jobs and Other Jobs

So that's what you say...you never had a job. You can't imagine how many jobs you had, you know. Odd jobs, yeah. You're always doing something, you know.

--Bunny Byrne

These were the jobs culled from the group's memories. Jobs they had up until graduating from high school. Almost all were within walking distance of our neighborhood.

    Butcher shop clean up boy
    Carpet peddler helper
    Electric condenser waxer
    Tool and die apprentice
    Clothing store clerk
    Drugstore stock boy
    Photo studio delivery boy
    Department store inventory control
    Tavern and burlesque cleanup
    Shoeshine boy
    Dock and truck unloader
    Construction worker
    Soda jerk
    Transformer company messenger
    Post office mail delivery
    Order picker
    Liquor store delivery boy
    Auto mechanic helper
    Vegetable peddler helper
    Billing clerk
    Drugstore delivery boy
    Advertising agency file clerk
    Milkman delivery helper
    Auto shop worker
    Tool boy
    Mosaic tile packer

Supermarket stock boy
Typesetting helper
Meat company truck loader
Drafting intern
Junking
Horse stable cleaner
Tailor shop delivery boy
Print shop helper
Art supplies delivery boy
Banquet worker
Parking lot attendant
Roofing worker
Machinery mover
Bakery pan scraper
Stock mover
Traveling companion
Artist model
Plastic factory caster
Typist
Park district paper picker
Candy store clerk
Coffee filter plant floor sweeper
Mailroom clerk
Library page
Plastic ashtray and knob finisher
Cloakroom attendant
Floor painter
Laundry shop delivery boy
Garbage horse attendant
Bowling alley pinsetter
School sweeper and classroom cleaner
Bakery shop cleanup
Electric pump cleaner
Elevator operator
Movie house usher
Busboy
Plastic factory shop and toilet clean up boy

Metal finishing paint shop sprayer
Book publisher stock boy
Newspaper subscription filer
Photocopy delivery boy
Butcher-block scraper
Caddy
Snow shoveler
Office typist
Railroad switch cleaner
Tax and law book combiner

We all worked cause, you know, if you didn't work, you know, you had no spending money, you know.
                                    Jay Pistone

Charlie Martinez

The pressure for these jobs as we left grammar school did not come from the family but from yourself. No one goaded you into finding a job. To get a decent allowance was a dream and so in order to buy the clothes you wanted and pay for a certain amount of entertainment—you had to have a job.

Jobs were everywhere and everyone wanted a job. However not all jobs were created equal. Most were boring and underpaid. Underpaid because boredom on a job made the work ten times harder and made the clock run much slower. Therefore you actually put in a lot of hard time. The boring job's day started off with apathy, rose to ennui and listlessness and then collapsed into fatigue. Throughout those days we were given to much daydreaming. This daydreaming consisted of baseball, sitting at the lake, sex, and especially the other jobs that we thought were a miracle and only given to some of the guys by a cruel, fickle God.

A construction job was much sought after because it combined good pay and a chance to grow muscle and get a tan. But these were confined to people who knew someone in the business. A job at the Park District picking up papers at the lakefront and looking at the girls was another desirable type of employment. This paid well too.

However you had to be born into a connected family. Other jobs like elevator operator or parking lot attendant were appealing. But the job I lusted after, unbeknownst to my family, was that of a companion to the son of a family relative. He was a comedian and did one night stands all over the country. The job brought travel, money, and adventure. Jerry, an older brother, had had his turn and traveled all over the United States. Ken was next and spent three full summers on the road. My turn came but the gods, instead of smiling, spit on me because the son was no longer in need of a companion.

The Uptown Supermarket was located on the northeast corner of Clark and Scott Streets. The store was not in Uptown and was not a supermarket. A large grocery store with a butcher section would better describe it. My brother Ken and Joe Zummo had worked there, so I went there for a job. I can't remember what I said to apply, but I imagine I asked if a job was open. The butcher probably asked me my age and I lied like everyone else and said I was sixteen when I was fourteen.

To me it was a dreary place with old or second-hand fixtures and counters. The lighting was poor. The job they offered was in the butcher department. The butchers were friendly guys, always dressed in white with blood stained aprons. They joked with each other and kidded with the customers. They were thick men with sausage like fingers that were reddened from handling the cold meats.

I had to empty out the display cases and clean them, washing the pans and using Windex on the glass. This was difficult because I was short and I had to stretch to clean the glass. Scrubbing the maple chopping blocks with a wire brush and then hot water was tedious. Leftover scraps of fat, chicken heads, intestines, and meat that had gone bad had to be carried to the garbage cans in the alley. To get to the garbage cans, I had to run through swarming frenzied flies and stomp my feet to scare away the rats. I worked there only one Saturday for ten hours. My pay came to $2.50 for the day. A quarter an hour! I never went back.

Peter Eichel

I just went home and told my father that I didn't want to go to school anymore.
He said, "Do you have a job?" "Yeah." "Okay." I was fifteen.

And I went to work for this Jewish guy that sold carpets. So I'd ride around in his truck with him all day long and he made me do all this dirty work for him. And I'd get a couple bucks a week or something, you know. It wasn't really a job. I think the guy wanted me around more just to have some company. He told me one day to make the lights. Well I'd never heard the phrase "make the lights." We turned the lights on and off, so if somebody wanted the lights turned on you said, "Turn on the lights" or "Turn it off." And he kept saying, "Make the lights. Make the lights." And I said what the hell ya talking about? He got mad at me. He fired me. "Kinda stupid person are you?" he said. "Make the lights!" I said, "I don't want to make the lights. I don't make lights. You old asshole."

I went to work at Automatic Electric as a messenger. I worked for the market research and display department. Whenever they needed models, or they were designing new models, they'd send me to their maybe seven, eight, nine, factory locations on Green Street and Halsted Street. I ended up in the tool and die department. The guy there that influenced me, you know, was Steve Hogan. Hogan saved me probably in that time I lived in those terrible conditions.

Rudy Verbski was the manager of the tool and die department, and he said if I went back to school and got a high school diploma, that he'd make me an apprentice tool and die maker. And these guys, they made good money, you know, back then. It's not all that big a deal today I guess because the industry has changed.

When I was eighteen years old I worked for Ric Imburgia. Ric had a clothing store on Division Street.

Ric Imburgia was really a nice man. His wife was nice and they had a beautiful daughter. And she was maybe a year younger than me. She used to come in the store and she was always very happy. I didn't think very much of myself. And I always felt inferior. I mean I grew up in this shit apartment, you know, with all those cockroaches and rats. I *was* socially inferior. I think I was pretty goddamned realistic about it, but I didn't need to stay that way. All right?

Ric Imburgia kinda took me under his wing. He said to me one day. "You're never gonna get anywhere" I said, "Why not?" He said "'Cause you can't even speak English." He said, "You should hear yourself talk, you sound like an, an immigrant." Well I grew up around all these Italian people; maybe I was talking like them.

But one day in comes this con artist and fast-talks me. Now he did this quick shuffle and gave me a twenty, then ten change, five take this back and the guy left. I went to Sam and said, "You know, I think I just got taken," and Ric didn't believe me. Didn't believe me. Now his wife did. Fortunately right while he's being pissed off at me, in walks the cashier from a drug store on Division.

Yeah. In she walks and she's all out of her mind. She just got shilled out of twenty dollars. She describes the guy, and it's same guy I describe. So now Ric's wife says to him, "You son of a bitch you." Then she tried to fix me up with her daughter, and that was too much for me to handle. I did do something with her; I went to the Windsor show with her or something. But I'll never forget how much that meant. It just never dawned on me that she would think I was good enough, you know.

John Kennedy

> *So I took the mail, went and delivered the mail and I came back to the station. The guy says, "What are you doing? How come you're back so soon?"*

I worked for the Postal Service at Christmas time for a couple of years. The funny thing is they assigned me to the Chestnut Street station and the route that they gave me was the same route I had delivered newspapers on Division and Astor and State and Ritchie Court. The same streets that I knew. Lake Shore Drive. They gave me a bag of mail, gave me money. Said take the Clark streetcar.

So I took the mail, went and delivered the mail and I came back to the station. The guy says, "What are you doing? How come you're back so soon?" I says, "I delivered all the mail." He says, "Did you get the drop?" They had dropped off mail in one of these storage boxes. They gave me the key and I took it out and delivered all that. I says, "I know all the streets, I know the houses." He says, well you're back too early. You shouldn't be coming back so soon, he says. So they put me on sorting some mail until I guess my eight hours were up or whatever it was. So I got the hint. The next days after that when I finished delivering the mail, I went home. And when my eight hours were up I went back to the postal station and said I'm through. "Okay."

Charlie Martinez

"You're fired."

I didn't argue with the boss. He caught me sleeping in a cozy corner that I had walled in with boxes in a vain attempt at concealment. This was a job as an order-filler in a company on Ohio Street. It was a summer job but only lasted a month. I was fifteen. It was overwhelmingly boring.

The building was huge, running almost a block long. But it must have been built before 1900. There were huge timbers, twelve by twelve inches, for inside support. The walls, ceiling, and floors were dark and dusty. You were given an order slip and a canvas framed cart and had to wander around the building putting the appropriate items in the cart. I soon learned from Jim, a fellow worker, about secret places for taking a nap. Jim was older, maybe eighteen, and a regular full-time employee. At lunchtime, we sat outside in the shade of the loading dock. He always had two baloney sandwiches. As he maneuvered the white bread sandwich to his mouth I noted that he had long fingernails with almost a quarter inch of dirt under each nail.

Pat Rogers

> *Coming back from a delivery after I collected money for prescriptions, I was turning the money over to the druggist and the rubbers fell out of my wallet. I got fired.*

North of the Chicago River on Clark Street there were a number of burlesque houses and restaurants and we could pick up pennies by sweeping up the store and helping out. Sweeping the burlesque was infrequent. Some drunk didn't show up for a job so they pulled you in off the street. You made a nickel or a dime.

Actually I saved that money. I'm sure I turned some over to the house. Everybody had to turn some portion of their money to the house to help support the family. But at age six I bought my first pea coat and I spent the princely sum of twenty dollars. And I delivered papers at night. I don't know how long I saved; maybe it was six months, maybe a year. At age six, ah 1943. Yeah. So I had my little pea coat.

When I was living down on Ohio Street, me and my brother Frank used to shine shoes down on Clark Street. Maybe half of the businesses on Clark from Grand up on to Chicago were taverns and burlesque houses. So that's how we picked up a little change. We went shining shoes and looking for tips and so on.

I didn't have to work in summer until I was say twelve. Then at twelve we would get a job as a delivery boy. At that time I think it was the Elm Street prescription drug store at Elm and State Streets. We would actually deliver prescriptions and drugs to the people all over Lake Shore Boulevard and Astor Street.

Marty Barnes and some of the older boys asked me to get some Trojans, some rubber johnnies. I didn't even know what they were for. So I went in there and I picked some up. Coming back from a delivery after I collected money for prescriptions, I was turning the money over to the druggist and the rubbers fell out of my wallet. I got fired.

Between eighth grade and high school I worked at Rexall Drug Store. I got fired from Rexall's for giving away all the whipped cream and the cherries and nuts to pretty girls. So my soda jerk days ended.

At thirteen or fourteen you could probably pass for sixteen and get a job on the docks unloading, you know, cargo from trucks and bringing it into the warehouse. This was at the McClurg Book Company. With some of the cartage I brought into the building I built my own little place where I could sleep down in the valley of my own city. And of course I got found out. I got fired.

I was working construction at the end of my sophomore year. My cousin, Jill Rogers, his brother-in-law was a foreman of this one group. Jill Rogers, myself, Don Cummings. We were working construction out at Glenview. I think it was Carmeny and Crate Construction Company. We were building homes. Our job was to build carports. You learned a little something about the trades then. If they skimmed a little they made a lot. We were told not to lay four inches of peat gravel or four inches of cement. It was generally three and half inches of peat gravel and three and half of cement. I mean if you're in a huge housing development, this meant a lot of money. So I worked in construction then. I think it was $2.12 an hour then. This was the summer of '54. Yeah. That was big money then.

John Giovenco

I quit school. I mean you didn't have to tell anybody you were not going back, you just don't go. Just don't show up.

I built myself a shoeshine box and I used to go up and down Sedgwick Street and all the way to North Avenue. Going into the taverns with the shoeshine box asking people if they want a shine. They would give me whatever, quarter, nickel. One time I got a half dollar for a shine. I'd stand by the bus stops as people were there and I'd ask 'em if they wanted a shine.

I remember I was pretty experienced at it when I was nine years old because my sister Mary was born then and my mother and father didn't have enough money to buy her a Christening outfit. I was shining shoes and made enough money to buy her Christening outfit, so I went North Avenue and actually bought the outfit as well as shoes myself.

I usually gave most of the money I made to my parents. I didn't get an allowance. They were always broke so I didn't expect anything from them. In fact I always figured it was my responsibility to contribute. So I'd work and contribute the money.

I worked at Solomon's drugs as a delivery boy between eighth grade and first year high school. State and Delaware someplace around there. I worked as a delivery boy there delivering drugs and liquor. I don't remember how we could deliver liquor because we were only fourteen years old, but we delivered liquor.

My uncle, Rossi was a peddler and he lived with us. He peddled fruits and vegetables from the back of a truck. So I worked with him peddling fruits and vegetables. I asked him if I could go to work for him.

I worked with my other uncle. He was a mechanic, an automobile mechanic so I worked with him for a while, but that was not my cup of tea.

I finished my sophomore year and got a job. I got a job in a print shop. I quit school. I was not going back to school. I mean you didn't have to tell anybody you were not going back, you just don't go. Just don't show up. So I got the job and I was making pretty good money. Bringing it home and my parents were enjoying that.

I worked as a billing clerk when I learned to type after I went back to high school. School was a mile and quarter from my house and my job downtown was another mile, mile and a quarter from the school. I walked there and back because, you know, it was what, twenty cents for the bus. You saved the twenty cents, which was a pretty good amount of money. I mean it wasn't the world but you certainly didn't want to piss it away.

I also worked for an advertising executive one summer as his cost accountant. Figuring out just how many responses per dollar of advertising was received. I thought it was a great job working with all these guys who were college educated, and I could walk around the advertising agency because as a file clerk I had to get correspondence. You got to see all the different guys working, all the pretty girls working. Rooth, Roth, and Ryan. Early Times was one of their clients; Shakespeare Rod was another, Beltone Hearing Aid. Very creative people, fun people. Pretty girls. They let me work there during the summer. Find things for me to do. Which was really nice. And they were very nice to me.

Joe Zummo

It was like a public service.

One job that I had that I liked an awfully lot that was working at the Uptown Super Market. I got it through Ken Martinez and he was the butcher shop boy. I was able to work my way up to stock boy to produce boy and eventually Ken left and I became the butcher boy. I was in seventh grade about thirteen years old. I don't remember anyone asking you for proof of your age.

When I left that job I went to work at Solomon's Liquors for fifty cents and hour. You had to be sixteen and I got a fake baptismal certificate from the undertaker that showed my age as two years older than what I was. We went to the undertaker and he had those forms for baptism. It was like a public service. And they filled it out. I worked with Jimmy Foley and Patti Irwin. I tried to get my friend Chuckie Martinez a job there but he wouldn't lie about his age. There were guys that were stealing from the liquor department. They would find out who was getting married and would sell a case of whiskey for a third of its retail cost. The thieves were sixteen and they used the truck drivers for delivery. I did not participate in that part of the job.

The following summer I went to work on construction at fifteen years old and it was a wonderful job and it paid a dollar twenty five cents an hour. We would bring the cement and sandbags and bring the scaffolding. I worked that job six summers in a row. It was one of the best jobs I ever had in my life. You would dig a hole and pour cement and then you had a house. I also worked at Commerce Clearing House combining tax law books. One of the worst jobs I ever had was when I worked for the Rock Island Railroad keeping the switches free of snow and ice and the danger was if the track would close on your foot or hand you'd lose it.

I never discussed my jobs with my parents. There really wasn't much I could discuss with my parents. I gave no money at home. No never. I stole money at home. What was mine was mine and what was theirs was mine. I remember finding out where my mother hid her money and took two dollars and spent the day with Ken and Gus Johns at Riverview Park.

Charlie Martinez

My job at the drugstore in the Ambassador Hotel was to deliver filled prescriptions to customers in the neighborhood and to people in the hotels. Also, I delivered some medicines to doctors' offices. I have no idea what the medicines would have been in those days.

Taking medicines to a doctor on LaSalle Street downtown was my favorite chore. The drug store was at 1300 north on Dearborn Street. I walked straight south to around Washington Boulevard to the doctor's office. I always pocketed the carfare unless it was raining or horribly cold. In good weather this walk was not a chore. Boys are like dogs. They have a natural liking to walking and wandering.

Dearborn Street was mainly residential for almost the entire distance until you approached the river. As I walked, I dreamed of living in one of the large apartments in the three-flats or small hotels. All the movies showed Fred Astaire or Clark Gable living in huge apartments, never in houses. Near Division Street on the east side was a grocery store where a woman could call in her order and have it delivered without leaving the house. And I was going to the corner grocer one to two times a day for my family!

Trees grew along the parkway and birds, mainly sparrows, were busy in their branches. There were small lawns in front of the buildings and at the curb, both protected from the dogs' leavings by a two-foot wrought iron fence. The Dearborn Theater was on the west side near Division. This was a small place but seemed luxurious compared to the Plaza or 152. I went there several times but only remember seeing Laurence Olivier in *Richard the Third*. I crossed Division Street noticing a sudden increase in people, cars and noise. Then came Elm, Cedar, and Oak Streets. The Newberry Library, a great stone building, was on the west directly across from Bughouse Square. The Scottish Rite Cathedral was kitty-corner. I often wanted to go inside it but never did.

Down to Chicago Avenue were again mainly three-flats with the Lawson YMCA on the northeast corner of Chicago and Dearborn. To us this was peopled with homosexuals although my sisters, Patsy and Jackie worked, danced, and dated there in the Second World War. A tavern across the street, The Haig, was the place where they went after hours with the sailors and marines.

Once Grand Avenue was passed, the street was lined with commercial establishments with a few surviving three-flats scattered about.

At the river, a pleasure awaited you that outdid any inconvenience and washed away any feeling of being cheated out of playing ball instead of working. If at that time you heard the bells ring and the lights blink and the guardrails descend, you were thrilled. I ran up to the bridge that crossed the river. Of course the motorists were mad about being delayed. Now the bridge would show itself off to the world. The half span on your side rose slowly, ponderously. Its gigantic weight moving smoothly and delicately as if one man were slowing raising a flagstaff to the upright position. Finally the span was totally perpendicular and you marveled at its height. In that upright position it appeared several times longer than when horizontal. Then when the business on the river was past, it began its elegant, unhurried descent to a perfect connection with its mate. The bells stopped, the lights went out and the guardrails bounced upright. Another miracle for a teenage boy.

Across the river were all the skyscrapers in which we actually played, at times running up twenty, thirty stories on the outside fire escapes for the joy of it. I knew the names and heights of several of the taller ones. That was our "Emerald City."

When I arrived at the doctor's office he was pleasant to me but his body bulged out of his shirt and pants as if another person was inside trying to escape. His cheeks filled his face and overflowed, narrowing his eyes, which almost disappeared behind his glasses. There was sweat seen on his arms and above his upper lip. He wore short sleeve white shirts winter and summer.

His hands trembled and his glasses were thick making his eyes seem tiny. His face was constantly flushed and the red scalp showed through his sparse white hair. He sat at a large cluttered roll top desk. I never saw him out of the chair in all my visits. In my recollections the office and examining room were one. I don't recall a waiting room.

I took advantage of his poor eyesight. You see, when he counted out the payment, he always had new, crisp dollar bills. Well, with his tremor and poor eyesight, he didn't separate the bills out well and overpaid me a dollar or two each time. I pocketed this amount, never correcting the doctor.

John Owens

The milkman give me milk and butter to take home for my mother. In those days you know, it's like gold, yeah.

The first job I had was working with the milkman. I don't think it was too long. Probably couple three months or something like that. I was probably twelve, thirteen years old.

On the weekend. Yeah. He'd pick me up like six o'clock and he would take me to a restaurant on Larrabee Street just before you got to Montgomery Wards. All the drivers would be in there and he'd buy me breakfast. Bacon and eggs, you know. It was a big deal, you know. I think he'd give me a buck and a half a day. Plus he'd give me milk and butter to take home for my mother. In those days you know, it's like gold, yeah. I think I just did that on the weekend.

If there was a woman up on the third floor and she wanted two quarts of milk, I'd run the milk up to her. You know. Save him steps. He was like I say he was good to me. Buck and half I guess wasn't much money. I mean it was probably a lot then, you know.

They had night courses in Washburn High School there that they had brought in teachers that were in the automobile business and they would teach these students auto repair. I was given the job of tool boy. Lot of the guys were from like the CTA bus company, places like that where they wanted to get brushed up on their repair skills. I think I worked three or four nights a week. You know from like six to nine or something like that. They mailed me a nice little check every week from the Board of Education.

Well the guy who ran the place was a guy by the name of Rudy Janu. And he owned Janu Brothers, an auto repair shop at 1810 N. Wells right where Lincoln Avenue starts. So he says, "You know, when you get out for the summer you can come over work in the shop." So I says, "Yeah, sounds like a good idea." So I started working for him in the summer. Then I would do work at the school at night during the school season. So after I got outa high school, I went to work for him full time. Yeah. I worked all through high school there. I used to give my mother money. I used to give her something every week. 'Cause my father used to tell me, give your mother something, you know, for room and board. And I used to give her, you know, twenty bucks or whatever it was a week outa my paychecks.

Michael Lutazzi

I had quite a bit of experience on a typesetting machine. By the time I was twenty, I was dreamin'.

I played baseball for Washburn Trade School and when I was sixteen my father, you know, said "Maybe you ought to get a job." But up until then I was working in A&P, Jewel. The Jewel in the Gold Coast on Oak Street. Yeah, I was not sixteen when I was doing that. They were paying me sixty cents, sixty two cents an hour. I used to work for Illinois Condenser. That's another job I had as a kid before typesetting. On North Avenue and Throop, which is near Elston. They made condensers and then I was sixteen and I started to learn something about printing, I got a part time job in a print shop.

I gave some of my pay to my mother and my father. Everybody did, in my house. There was no argument about it. It was just expected. And there was no hurt feelings. You paid your share. You know, if I made twenty-five bucks, I give five to my mother. If I made fifty, I gave her ten.

And then after high school I went to a typesetting shop and went to work because I had been setting type for two years, part time, in a print shop. My goal at the age of eighteen, nineteen, was to get out of the print shop and go to work for a trade typesetting shop. That would allow you to make more money and would allow you to learn more. In time I would become a union man, which was a hard thing to do. It would take you six years to become a journeyman in typesetting. At that age I thought that union typesetters were God's chosen people. But I found out that that's not true. The open shop typesetters are just as good as union shop typesetters and many times, better. Just because you're in the union doesn't mean you're a very good typesetter. But that was my thinking when I was eighteen, nineteen. So that was my goal.

McGinty was a union man, you know, my teacher. But he didn't care where I went to work, but he said, if you go to a union shop make them promise you when you're gonna start your apprenticeship. He was a tough old crabby Irishman. He says, "If you go to a union shop and they say, yeah, we'll start your apprenticeship in a while, you know." He says, "They may forget about you. You won't start you're apprenticeship for three or four years, you won't become a journeyman for ten years." So I tried that. I made 'em tell, when will I start my apprenticeship. One guy says, "I don't know, you know." I went to another place, when do I start my apprenticeship. Two years. Aw, piss on 'em, you know. I already had some talent as a typesetter. I was already working part time, two years on a machine. I was eighteen, nineteen years old and I had quite a bit of experience on a typesetting machine. I was really rather lucky that anyone would let me on at that age. On a very expensive machine, you know. By the time I was twenty, I was dreamin'.

Jim Sullivan

But as far as the pay was concerned, it was a turnover to my mother.

The earliest job was at Oscar Mayer on Scott Street. They used to like load up the trucks for the day's run to all the different stores, you know. The baloneys and the salamis and the cheeses and the stuff like that. And the driver would have to carry all the stuff out from the inside of the building to the truck. So I used to go over there and just offer to help. I was probably around nine or ten maybe. They would give you like a quarter or a dime. Never asked my mother if I could do that job.

Then I had a job at a grocery store when I was like fourteen or fifteen and I was making like seventy-five cents an hour, which was a lot of money, you know. I'd bring like home thirty-six dollars every week. After school and in the summertime it was all summer long. Then somebody came in the store and squealed on us. You know. Well somebody said under age workers. With the child labor laws I had to be sixteen and they fired me because I was fourteen or fifteen at the time. But you know, I was probably one of the better workers that they had. I just, you know, I gravitated toward the money. Hard work is like my nature, you know, so.

I didn't get an allowance at home but whenever I wanted money for whatever reason, I would say that I needed two dollars, or a dollar or fifty cents or a quarter or whatever, and then I would always get it. But as far as the money was concerned, it was a turnover.

Sometimes I worked during the school year. I worked at Wurlitzer with Louis Provenzano one year. So we had a job for like nine months. It was a pretty nice job, Downtown. But that was a job we got through the school. They evidently put out a call or ran an ad to the schools looking for people and we went and they hired us.

So I took a job with Western Electric, where I was a draftsman. I worked for them for twenty-three years. I was with them when I went into the service. So when I came outta service, I went right back to the same job that I left, you know.

Bunny Byrne

I mean we were street-smart Charlie. We were street-smart. They had no clue. See, they were raised in a cocoon. They had no clue.

To get money in grammar school we did junking. Up alleys. Pick up beer bottles, scrape the labels off 'em, made Dad's Root Beer bottles outta 'em, take 'em in for deposits. Yeah. Paper, pick up paper, take it to the junkyard. That's all. That's how we spent our time. Well, yeah, for show money. You'd start about Thursday. Thursday and Friday and by Saturday you had enough to go to the 152 down on Division Street. It was about a nickel to get in. Nickel for popcorn.

I was probably about ten at the time. Then we worked over in the horse stable, you know, on Clark Street there, Clark and Burton. You know, cleaned out the barn, the stalls and yeah, wiped the horses down. You know they used to ride 'em in the park. They had a big brush. You'd rub 'em down.

I also had a job like you say, did you have a job. I had a job over on Orleans Street. It was garbage horses we had in the neighborhood at that time, during the war.

They would pull a gondola. Two big Belgian horses. For the garbage. They had no garbage trucks during the war. So they used ta barn 'em over there on Orleans and North Avenue. It was like a quarter a horse you'd get or somethin' to wipe 'em down. They'd be all sweaty when they come in, see, so you hadda wipe 'em down. Keep 'em from getting pneumonia. So, you'd go over there and you could make a buck in a couple a hours wiping them horses.

I also swept the school out in grammar school. Coyne, Bill Coyne was the janitor. I went in every day when school let out. I went back in when everyone went home and I swept all the big stuff off the classroom floors. I'd go like I'd start in first grade and I'd, I had this broom and a dust pan and I would just sweep crayons, newspapers, whatever all to the front of the room and then sweep it into a pile, throw it into the garbage and go to the next room. Go all eight. I did that. I got a couple bucks for that. Every day.

When I was in grammar school, probably in eighth grade, I worked at Jays Liquors at North Avenue and Sedgwick Street.. Had the bike with the little front tire and the big basket. You know what? That's not an easy bike to ride. I guarantee it, Charlie, if I fill that bike up with cases of beer you couldn't drive it. You couldn't drive it, couldn't ride it. You know why? It throws your equilibrium off so bad when you get that weight on it that you can't steer right. You gotta practice. I hadda go over under the L and practice with that bike before he would let me go anywhere on deliveries with it cause he must of known kids fell off it.

He says, go in there, he threw a case of beer in it, and he says, just go through the L posts until you get used to it. And ah, I did. I went in there and he was right. I ran into about four posts before I finally figured it out. Jesus, this is top heavy here, I gotta … and I finally learned. All the business was Marshal Field apartments. That was ninety percent of his business.

I had one last delivery to the L station at Schiller Street. I'd deliver to the guys. They'd all be waiting. And one of the guys'd make the call. "Yeah, would you deliver four quarts of Atlas Prager beer to ah … it was Billy Ellis' house address we used to use next to the L. "Deliver four bottles of Atlas"… "Okay, four Atlas Prager" … and the boss 'id say, "Okay kid, four Atlas Prager." I'd take 'em over there. This 'id be like the last delivery. 'Cause as soon as I was through working, we'd all go down to the beach, drink the beer.

Yeah. I worked for that liquor store, man I hated to quit there. You know. It was such a great job.

I had a job between eighth grade and high school. I worked for a tailor over on Division and State delivering laundry.

That was probably between eighth grade and high school. Because then, when I went to high school I got a job over where Jerry, your brother, worked. At the Near North Guild that sold artists supplies. Yeah. I don't now if Jerry took my place. That was right next door to the Cloverleaf Tavern. On 50 East Chicago Avenue. Just east of, between Rush and Wabash on Chicago.

I didn't work long at the Guild, not long. Maybe the first year of high school or something. Maybe not even that long because then I got a job over at the Lake Shore Athletic Club. Right across from Lake Shore Park on Pearson and Lake Shore Drive. My sister worked there. She graduated from Cathedral and she went to work for the secretary to the manager of the Lake Shore Athletic Club. The woman that she worked for had big connections there. So she got us a job over there on the elevators, see. My brother John and me. Well, me first. Me first and then, and then there was just a progression. John was working somewhere else. He was still at Solomon's probably.

I was probably fifteen when I got the job there. And then we just moved up see. Fact is, you know who we worked with was Father Smythe. His dad was the manager there. They were so naïve it was unbelievable. His brother Joe and him, they were two of the most naïve guys. I mean we were street-smart, Charlie. We were street-smart. They had no clue. See, they were raised in a cocoon. They had no clue. When they saw us, this Smyth used to shake his head, you know. He'd go, "You guys." Like even going home at night. We're supposed to observe the curfews. They'd have somebody pick them up. See. We'd just go out the back door. Just walk out. And they'd go … "How can you guys go out at this hour of the night?"

We used to work banquets and stuff as checkouts and things like that and it was supposed to be free. Free checking for coats. So we made up a little sign. "Donations twenty five cents." Put a cigar box there. See it was against the rules of the hotel, but who cares at that hour of the night. Who in management's around?

Well they would be beside themselves, the two brothers, because they were like as honest as the day. Well they had one brother in the priesthood at the time and he was killed playing touch football. But when we put the sign up and John Smyth would say, "You can't do that." And I say, "Don't tell us we can't do that." I says, "It's a donation." "But they don't allow that." I says, "Who's here? It's midnight. There's no management people around." In the cigar box we had four quarters. These guests were all gassed up. They're coming out of these parties. "Hi, ah, kid," throwing quarters, half a dollars, everything into that cigar box. See, we'd be handing out coats. There'd be maybe five of us in there handing out coats. Well Joe and John, when we'd get all done, we'd say come into the locker room. They'd go, "Why?" I says, "Come on we'll cut this up, you know." And he goes, "We're not taking that." I said, "These are tips!" "Naw, naw, we can't take it, you know."

Well then eventually what they did is, make another big mistake with us. When we get through with a party real late, we'd have to stay overnight. See somebody got caught out about two o'clock in the morning and said they were coming from work. The police got after the management; so then they give us a room. So what we'd do then as the waiters we were pulling the gurneys out of the banquet hall, loaded with bottles of beer and glasses that people didn't drink, we'd run up there, you know. Guys, late in the evening they, they'd order a bottle of beer don't even drink it. You know. Manhattans, martinis … full ones! So we'd get trays and we'd load it up, and up to our room. Yeah. Drink all night!

Well, that Lake Shore Club took us right through high school, yeah. Because I worked there then I became a bellboy there. Then from a bellboy, because I could drive, I was put out in the lot because the guy in the lot couldn't drive to park cars. They were getting into a new phase where they wanted to take the cars and go park 'em for the people and the old man, Walsh, you knew him. He lived on North Park. The old Irishman. He was in the lot for thirty years but he couldn't drive. So he would sit in the shack and I would take the cars in. So, I mean that job took me right, right up through high school just about 'cause ah, it was a good money job. Good money. And Johnny worked there too. Yeah, we had a lot of guys that ended up there.

I started roofing when we finished high school. I was going roofing 'cause roofing was paying good money. Then I got with the machinery movers, see. My dad had a friend who had ulcers in his toes and he was a foreman. He was a big shot foreman. But he couldn't drive. He lived at Diversey and Halsted, I was at Belmont. So he got a hold of my dad and says what's the boy doing. And my dad says, he's working with the roofers. And the guy says, tell him to come on to Penauer. He says, I'll get a nice job there. Now they paid more than the roofers. Yeah. Machinery movers. Yeah. It was a hard job. Oh, it was hard Charlie. Moving machinery. I mean, nothing was light, Charlie. Nothing. You go to put a jack under something, the jack was the size of that little fridge, you know. It weighed about a hundred and fifty pounds.

Charlie Martinez

Miss Mundy, the pharmacist at the Ambassador West Hotel, was an overweight single woman in her early thirties who also was naïve. She had a pleasant face and her brown hair was cut short. She trusted me completely. She asked me if I would paint the living and dining room floors of her apartment while she was on vacation. I discussed this with my associate, Joe Zummo. We decided between ourselves that, yes we would do her the favor of painting the floors for a certain amount of money. She agreed to this. What she didn't know was that we also planned to throw a party in the flat on Delaware Street just east of Michigan Avenue, across the street from the Northwestern Ratskellar Inn. The Ratskellar was a hangout for the college types from mainly Northwestern University. They became extras in our drama later in the evening of the party.

We went with Miss Mundy one day to inspect the flat and to size it up for the party.

We also discussed another topic several times between the two of us.

"What ja think?"

"It's worth a try."

"Okay, let's ask when the time seems right."

In our brazen but unsophisticated style, we had decided to ask Miss Mundy if we could sleep with her. After looking over the apartment, Joe approached Miss Mundy.

"Charlie and I wondered if we could do something with you."

"Huh, what?"

"You know, go to bed."

She seemed shocked but kept her composure and politely turned down our, for us, perfectly straightforward, normal request.

Well Joe and I painted the floors an ugly dark, almost black, brown color. Unfortunately, the party took place before the paint had a chance to completely dry. There was a noticeable tackiness wherever you stepped. Course this didn't bother the thirty to forty teenagers having a good time. The party was breaking up around twelve and I left with Tubby Priola to take her home on the L. After I had left, Zummo and several others from the party walked down Delaware Street towards Michigan Avenue. They passed over in front of the Ratskellar Inn. Now you have two groups of young males from totally different socioeconomic classes and both groups having had their share of beer and other drugs and with testosterone levels at their peak sharing a narrow sidewalk passage. Did our crowd make fun of their kakis, saddle shoes, and neat haircuts or did the college boys poke jabs at the greased-back hair and cool walk of our heroes? No one will ever know. However (the way it was told to me), our boys beat up several of their men and left before the police arrived.

What a wonderful night! Our friends thanked Joe and me for the cool party. However Miss Mundy, on returning from her trip, didn't see it that way. She went berserk after she saw the destroyed paint job and asked us what right we had to throw a party without her permission, etc. etc. etc. What right? What right? There were no rights involved at all. She again was a naïve adult attempting to control a bunch of streetwise teenagers.

P.S. She fired me from the delivery job.

Ken Martinez

I got ah, seven dollars. Plus if I walked real fast I could save the carfare. See. They would give you carfare to deliver it.

We learned to climb up on the L tracks' storage area and get the rails and stuff and take it over to the junkyard that was on Larrabee and Division during the war. We used to sell it to them. At that time you didn't think of it as stealing. Well, you see, it was rusting stuff, so we figured they weren't gonna use it. It wasn't new. We were eleven or twelve.

I worked for Butch the German butcher for four weekends or five weekends. I scraped the maple cutting blocks. It was on Sedgwick Street. He gave me a quarter to come and scrub the blocks.

The Cardinal's house was over on Astor Street. Fifth grade we went over there. A whole bunch of boys had to go over there. Mr. Coyne, the school janitor, took us over. And we had to take coal up to these little fireplaces that they had, see. Or wood or something and then we got milk and cookies. It was a day off, but we all had to be there for that. A day off. I remember going up there. I used to shovel snow all along on Astor Street for extra money. In grammar school, yeah. Shovel snow and get a quarter, seventy-five cents.

Then probably the first job I had was scraping pans at Mueller's Bakery on Sedgwick and Schiller for twenty-five cents and carry two buckets of coal up and two buckets of ashes out. That was my job. After school I'd go over there. I don't remember how old I was but I was in grammar school.

One summer, we had three or four weeks of working at the riding stable. Cause we were small, they wouldn't let us handle the horses. But we'd sweep and clean. Christensen riding stable. Next to the pool hall, on Clark Street.

They would run the horses up the ramp. Okay and then up there if they did any crapping or stuff before they went to their stall, that's what we would sweep. But there was another guy who used to go in and clean the stalls. We just swept out there and then he would fill up the basket and we would empty it in wooden wheelbarrel and take it to this place and just dump it. There was a big wagon outside. Looked like a big steel box and all this manure would go in it. I think we got twenty-five, thirty cents. It didn't last long cause you get tired of that. You smelled terrible.

I worked downtown. I got the job at Lamberty's. I was the delivery boy. They were in the Chicago Temple building. That just flashed in my head. They were photocopies that I used to deliver to the different lawyer's offices. I would get there at ah, three thirty. Three thirty, quarter to four. And then I had two hours to deliver all the stuff. Because most of all the offices would be closing by six thirty. And they needed the stuff and you'd get it out.

always told Ma where I was … sometimes, not all the time. I didn't tell her everything I was doing. I got ah, seven dollars. Plus if I walked real fast I could save the carfare. See. They would give you carfare to deliver it.

The first real job I had was working over at Welch's putting stock in cubbyholes. At Welch's Manufacturing on Orleans Street and on Sedgwick Street. The building had ends on both streets. Yeah. That was a nice job. Yeah. I worked at Yeoman Pump in the summertime. Ah, scraping, the rust and stuff off these pumps that would come in. Or they'd have me put stock up on the shelf.

Ken Martinez

You think this is an ugly thing to play with, well I know some people who play with uglier things.

Then Archie and his wife Goldie wanted me to travel with them as a companion for their son, little Jimmie. Archie was a relative to Uncle Paul. Jimmie was two or three years younger than me or four years younger than me. Archie was a comedian and would play gigs in nightclubs. He did a whole month in St. Louis. At the nightclub in the hotel. That's when Goldie used to introduce me to girls and the girls'd go, "Oh, he's so cute with those long eyelashes, good looks." And they'd pinch my cheek. 'Cause I was taller than Goldie, almost as tall as Archie.

Yeah, he gave me money. But I kept all my money, I didn't spend it. If I wanted to buy something, he would buy it. There was a tour to the zoo. The brewery. Meister Brau brewery we went through. And then we went to Reno. Yeah we were there a long time. That's where Goldie lost five thousand dollars in the crap table. He was gonna kill her. "You Christ killers, they didn't kill enough of yas. They should get the rest of youse." And he would start in. She was Jewish.

He had a comedian act. He had a saw and he would say "You think this is an ugly thing to play with, well I know some people play with uglier things." That was his line and he would make the saw sing. I think it was almost three years that I went with them.

Charlie Martinez

Sister Eustella, my homeroom nun in my senior year at Mundelein High found out that I had a chance to be a bellboy at the Ambassador West Hotel. I was confused as she called me to the front of the room to her desk for a conference. This job meant a neat suit, big tips, meeting celebrities, probably given money to keep my mouth shut on stuff I shouldn't of seen, perhaps some sexual adventure, envy of the guys and just a great fun job. She put thumbs down on the job and said that if I took it she would call the hotel and demand I be

Because he'd send them down and they'd kill the cats. I mean, these rats were big. I always remember going down there being scared to death. He had like supplies down in the basement. You'd run down and get something and you're looking around. You'd get down there as quick as you could and get the hell out of there, you know.

He was a great man. That's something that's gone from our lifestyle. You'll probably never see again. He did an awful lot of good for a lot of people in the old neighborhood.

Charlie Martinez

Wandering through the stacks at Newberry Library could be a spooky, lonely journey. At times I had to recover a book from the rare book room. This room was in the corner of one of the upper floors. By the time you got to its locked doors, you were past shouting distance for any help. I was always looking over my shoulder when I had to go there. The thick walls of the building and the numerous books lining the stacks absorbed all the outside noise. I unlocked the door and as I walked in, I had the sensation of entering a chamber purposely made to be quiet. I *knew* a thief or bum was hiding behind a chair or stack waiting to cut my throat. I entered a baroque world of heavy drapes with pastoral scenes, ridiculously thick carpeting, and ornately carved furniture. Hundreds of books stared down on me from their imprisonment on the stacks. It reminded me of scenes from *Phantom of the Opera* and *Great Expectations* movies. I hurried to the correct case and of course fumbled with the key in my haste which added to buildup of terror thinking of an ax murderer hidden behind the drapes. I did not loiter and incidentally never saw anyone else in the rare book room.

Invariably, a teenager has friends visit him on the job. Once Joe Zummo was with me and I ditched him in the stacks. He wandered around calling my name. I saw him coming down a row, removed some books and stuck my head in their place. When he got to me, I screamed and he was terrified. What fun for a teenage boy!

There was a four-passenger elevator in the building and at that time an elevator man ran it. He was middle aged with gray streaked hair. His use of English seemed above what you would expect from someone on that type of job. I suspected he had some higher education. One day as we were talking, he produced a card showing that he belonged to the Communist Party. In that McCarthy witch hunt era, exposing yourself as a Communist was a risky thing. He engaged me in talking about capitalism and the economy. He told me that economics were everything and Communism was the future. I responded with quiet interest, a technique I have used all my life when I am unsure of a response but am skeptical.

Jack Flaherty

I worked at this Harry Davies place for a while. Plastics.

Early on I tried to get little odd jobs in grocery stores. On Division and State I worked one summer in a grocery store there. Yeah, I can't remember the name of it. It's on State Street. Worked in the back. You cleaned off the fruit. Ya keep everything clean back there. I didn't do any counter work. I probably was in seventh grade. Summer of my seventh grade, maybe. '47. I put in probably two months or a little more. But I didn't like it. It was kinda, it was messy work. I don't remember what I got paid. Later I caddied a few times to make a few bucks.

I believe I kept the money. My mother didn't ask for any, she just let me keep it and do whatever I wanted with it. I had an early savings habit. That helped as I went along. I always had money to pay for anything I wanted to do or wanted to get. If I wanted to get something and didn't have the money, I just didn't get it. Pretty much. Yeah, I bought my own clothes and spent the money.

After second year high school in 1950, I worked at the McClurg factory over at McClurg Court near Lake Shore Drive. It was a book publisher or something but we used to go there and stack books. Then there was the New World, a Catholic newspaper. I worked a summer for them in downtown Chicago. I guess we'd take subscriptions and file 'em. These were written. I suppose we had to recopy 'em and make some sort of a filing system out of them. We had to count newspapers, get 'em ready for deliveries to different churches. I guess that paper was only found in churches.

I worked at this Harry Davies place on Wells Street south of North Avenue for a while. Plastics, between third and fourth year. I did a lot of buffing. They had us polishing ashtrays and knobs for well, you know any type of control. These were all just knobs that were gonna be screwed on to something. But for the most part we were buffing them and polishing them. The same with the ashtrays. Taking the rough edges off of 'em. I was probably seventeen, sixteen, seventeen. We had some part time employment, and then some full time summer employment.

Popular Mechanics Magazines was another place of employment. Popular Mechanics was located east of Michigan Avenue and probably around Superior or Ohio. We did a lot of typing in there. Must have been some sort of filing things. I know there were a lot of metal stamping plates in there. Only lasted a few months I believe. Wasn't there too long.

I didn't have a job right out of high school. I don't think I was working when I graduated. Charlie, if you remember but you got me my first legitimate full time job out of high school. You were working at the place already. You came calling me one day and telling me there were job openings, whatever. You were I guess really part-time and going to college but you told me they were looking for full-time openings. And ah, so I went and applied and I got the job. The company was Terminal Freight. Remember Randolph and Wells? The 188 West Randolph building.

Charlie Martinez

Phil Gentry walked with a shuffling, awkward gait, always seeming ready to fall to one side but he would slam a foot down and then lean to the opposite side. By duplicating this strange gait he made his way around the office at Terminal Freight Forwarding Company at 188 West Randolph Street. This was a company owned by Sears Roebuck. I was seventeen and working part time as a billing clerk.

Phil was the billing office boss. A saliva-soaked cigarette hung from his mouth, his tie was loose around his neck and his shirt appeared several sizes too big. His black, horn-rimmed glasses were continuously ready to fall off the tip of his nose. His pants hung on him below his waist and appeared ready to fall to the floor despite his suspenders. He half mumbled when he talked, never taking the cigarette out of his mouth.

My career as a biller started in my senior year in high school and continued on into medical school. A biller (a job typing up bills of lading at transportation companies) was much in demand and so one could have varied hours, overtime, and a higher hourly wage compared to other office jobs but not as well paid as the envied construction job.

The worst time for that job was coming to work on Sunday morning about 9 a.m. We wanted to come because we were paid at the overtime rate for Sunday. It was like free money. However, getting up at eight o'clock with a hangover and having to sit for eight hours at a billing machine was horrific torture to a teenager. The letters and numbers I typed were a blur and how many wrong items, charges and destinations I created, I will never know.

Frank knew how many bills on the average we would type an hour, and since the bills were numbered, he checked up on us on Monday. However we beat him at that by simply ripping out half a day's work from the roll when we first arrived on Sunday morning and throwing it away. Never try to outsmart a teenager!

Frank Demonte

Mike worked on the police boat on Montrose Harbor. When somebody jumps in the water and they're in for a long time they would pick up the stiffs.

The first remembrance I have was working delivering groceries. If I was gonna guess, I was six or seven. I worked for the A & P. on Sedgwick Street. And then I went up big in the world and went to work for Truers. You know Truers was next to the grocery store just north of that. I was delivering groceries to the Town & Garden Apartments. I did that after school.

You know, I gave all my money to my mother. I think she saved it for me. I don't know what I made a week, but say I made five bucks with tips.

In the summer when I was sixteen years old I worked for the Park District. I was a paper picker. Picked up papers from Oak Street Beach to Fullerton Avenue. Yeah, I dragged a bag around. I was making big money then. That job alone put me through high school. I paid my own tuition. I didn't expect my parents to pay. Yeah, I gave the money to them, sure. I didn't have any reason to keep any money. I kept virtually nothing. I mean she would give me a buck or two. She either put it in my bank account or she would pay the tuition.

I got that paper-picking job from my uncle Tony who knew the superintendent of the Park District at the time. His name was Anthony Pecarro. Never forgot him. The nicest man.

Anthony Pecarro was just a prince. He would help anybody that needed it. Uncle Tony and him were friends. All those jobs with the city and the Park District in all municipalities, they got through patronage. And that was my first job. Great job. But you know what though? Everybody says ya didn't do much, but I worked my tail off. I picked papers from Oak Street Beach to Fullerton Avenue. And of course all that was picked with a stick. Yeah, a pointy stick.

Well the full day was, maybe six thirty to two o'clock. We had lunch right around ten thirty, eleven o'clock. But it was, yeah it was a sweet job. When I was finished I used to walk to Montrose Avenue from Fullerton Avenue. Fullerton Avenue was where we had the shack. You know, where we would get all our stuff, and they would drop us off. I went to Montrose Avenue to see Mike Bonifedi who worked on the police boat on Montrose Harbor. Then we would go on the boat with Mike for an hour or so. You see, when somebody jumps or falls or is pushed or dumped into the lake and they're in for a long time, Mike's boat would pick up the stiffs. Of course the view from over there was gorgeous, so when we went on the boat we would see all of the lakefront. And it was fun.

Charlie Martinez

Phil Gentry walked into the billing room where a dozen high school kids and a sprinkling of full-timers pounded away on electric typewriters with blank bills of lading feeding into the machines from a seemingly endless roll. His entrance broke up the monotony and tedium momentarily.

He would walk up to a biller, expose a piece of densely folded paper that was in his hand. He then carefully unfolded the paper. On the piece of paper was written the amount of the biller's raise in pay. The raise was usually five cents an hour. There was no paper work for evaluation of the biller. How Phil arrived at the number was a mystery to us all. But the real reason Phil was so personal with this information which could easily been sent out on a memo was that while he showed you the little note his other hand rubbed your back and neck. He only did this to the boys and we were instinctively repulsed by him.

Jack La Brasca

> *Him and a couple of the other neighborhood hooligans brought some girl in there and she went to the police and said she was raped.*

Between eighth grade and first year high school I worked at Tony the Wop's. The candy store and poolroom. I worked until they closed him down. They closed him down because him and a couple of the other neighborhood hooligans brought some girl in there and she went to the police and said she was raped. So they put a padlock on the door, so I lost my job.

I was a clerk. I would you know, make ice cream cones, sell candy. On Sedgwick and Hobby streets. There was a grocery store, which was Paul Davies' grandma and next door was the candy store, which we called Tony the Wop's. And Tony the Wop had the candy store and the poolroom in the back. And I worked there seven days a week. Right.

It was kind of musty smelling in there. Although, what you

would smell more than anything was the fresh packs of playing cards.

Also like you been around a lot of dry goods like, like cartons of candy. The cigars would leave an aroma because there was no air conditioning in those stores. The doors were open, so, whatever products were in that store, candy, cigars, playing cards that sort of thing, all made a bouquet of smells that we didn't pay attention to but you could recognize them if you were looking for it. Yeah.

There was a building where they were making badges over on Erie. It was called Hansen Manufacturing. They made the badges for the cops and for the firemen. And I started delivering newspapers in that building. Then I got friendly with a guy I was delivering papers to, a Jewish family. They were making cotton coffee filters for commercial coffee urns. They asked me to come in on Saturdays to sweep the floor. They were paying me cash. I was going to Cathedral at the time. About 1950 in my sophomore year. It was a good life. However, you know, it was always a tough time to get home. When you got through, you know, with your paper route it was dark in the winter. And then you had to go through the neighborhood to get home and lot of times the brothers would mug you.

I had no curfew or hours at that time. My parents had a great deal of confidence that, you know, whatever I was doing it was okay. After school I was working. In fact in my junior year at Holy Name, I was working at Stop and Shop Hillman's. It was at Washington Street, off of State. I was a clerk, grocery clerk. Stacking shelves. On Saturdays I bagged. We worked from three thirty until ten every night and all day on Saturday. That was during my school year. I probably got about 45 cents an hour. They paid you cash in a little brown envelope. Kept it all. Paid my tuition, bought clothes, bought schoolbooks. I worked like this in sophomore, junior, and senior year. My parents never commented on whether I should be studying or working. They just didn't get involved.

No. No. But they knew I was buying my peg pants. They knew that you were going to Smokey Joe's on Maxwell Street to buy a suit. You'd look like something out of a cartoon now, but that's what you did. We were accountable. We took care of ourselves. We were like little men. We didn't know it. But we were. They perceived us as being grown up.

In the summer I worked. I worked for Time and Life magazine at 666 North Michigan in the mailroom. Yeah. Full time. I thought that was quite a good job too. You got paid every two weeks on Friday nights. You got a paycheck. And you went to Uno's or Duo's for a pizza. Big night. You know. Or Papa Milano's.

Charlie Martinez

Then one day Phil Gentry, the boss of the billing department at Terminal Freight, said to me, "Charlie, you didn't sign your loyalty oath agreement."

Phil was right. I didn't sign it. This was the time of the McCarthy Communist scare era and right at the ending of the Korean War, about spring of 1952. Some misguided idiot thought that a loyalty oath would help defend the U.S. against a nuclear attack. I never thought too deeply about it, but just decided I wasn't going to sign. I was the only one, adults or teenagers, in this large office that didn't sign. I was a senior in high school.

"That's right," I said.

"You're gonna have to see the big boss."

"Okay with me."

The big boss had his own office, which signified his importance. I walked in and he didn't invite me to sit. He sat behind a large desk that was piled with I guess important papers.

"Why didn't you sign the loyalty oath?" he said.

"I think it is un-American."

To my surprise, all he said was all right go back to work. And that was the end of it.

There was no rule that a worker had to deliver a part of his pay to the household. I paid my high school tuition, bought my clothes, and took care of my entertainment out of my pay. I did give my mother a portion of my pay but I don't recall the amount.

Once I received a special request.

"Chuckie," my mother said. She had just finished washing the dishes and turned to me as I sat on a kitchen chair. She demanded nothing but only asked with her sad and weary face. "Could you help Jerry with some money?"

I instantly understood what she meant. Jerry, my brother, was four years older than me. He was an artist, enrolled in the Art Institute, and barely getting by on odd jobs. Jerry was gracious, friendly and non-judgmental. Everyone loved Jerry. So it was not difficult for me to help support him. Just like giving money to my mother for family support, I felt great satisfaction in helping Jerry rather than seeing it as a put-upon burden.

CHAPTER SIX: TIME EATERS

Part one: Draggin' the Street, Junkin' and Games

Charlie Martinez

> *Goin' out again to drag the street? Ain't ya got anything better to do?*
>
> My father

That's what it was to adults: draggin' the street. Just purposeless shuffling along the sidewalks. But that's not what we thought we were doing. To us, every minute of every day held the potential for adventure. Alleys, empty lots, school yards, abandoned buildings, riverfront, lakefront, at times churches, hardware stores, grocery stores, war surplus stores, garbage dumps, back areas of factories, roofs of garages, roofs of factories, loading docks, abandoned cars, public parks, under the L: all these were to our imaginations possible places of buried treasure.

We found dead rats, dead cats, dead dogs, even a dead horse. There were pieces of steel from the L, piles of plastic buttons and ash trays, rotten fruit and decaying chickens behind grocery stores, broken knives, axes and hundreds of miscellaneous nuts and bolts, old clothing, some new clothing, bags of newborn kittens, fires, rocks, old tires and inner tubes, cigarette rolling machines, chunks of roofing tar, odd broken pieces of lumber, bullets, marbles, bricks, cement slabs, neon signs, car doors, newspapers, magazines, parts of bicycles, bundles of burnt out light bulbs, cases of old radio tubes, empty wooden crates, half empty paint cans, pieces of aluminum blinds, sections of rope, and lengths of wire. These hundreds of odd things were magnified in use tenfold by our fantasies and resourcefulness.

Summer was the high season for draggin' the street. Long days, no school, no curfew, some minimal time delivering newspapers, and always left to our own interests. No organized play from adults, no mandatory museum visits, no television, no computer games. Just 'draggin' the street and inventing fun.

Exploring the neighborhood and finding these gems was what occupied a large portion of our day up to the end of grammar school. Sports and games were okay, but did not compare to the thrill of finding a rusting jackknife or a World War II trenching shovel in the alley. With either one in our possession, we were a squad of marines in the jungles of the Pacific fighting for honor and glory. We dug trenches in IC lot. A broken brick was a hand grenade, a piece of two by four a machine gun. These wanderings were never planned out in detail. They were an instinctive part of our childhood. No one said, "Let's go under the L and look around." It was a natural thing we did unless interrupted by school, work, sports, or meals. We just followed our noses and wherever we went and whatever showed up was fine with us and this was called draggin' the streets.

John Owens

We were just always in some kind of mischievous stuff.

We used to, you know we'd go outside and play. In the summer we'd play in the middle of the street. We'd play ball or cops and robbers. Right around the house. Yeah. Cops and robbers and hide and go seek and that type of thing.

Otherwise, right after breakfast I would leave the house. I would take off and go over by Tony Petito and sometimes we would go down to a factory down there that made guns. You know, not real guns. Guns, but they were wooden. You know. Yeah. And we'd go over there to scramble through those things, their garbage.

Yeah. If we didn't do that we would be over by the National Tea which was on Division Street. The railroad cars used to come in there and we would go back there and get fuckin' watermelons outta the fuckin' cars and tomatoes. And we'd end up throwin' 'em, getting in fights with 'em on the street. We'd throw the tomatoes at the streetcar conductors. You know. We were just always in some kind of mischievous stuff. We didn't have any set pattern. It was like, well what are we gonna do … well let's walk over here. That's basically, you know, the summer day. Otherwise we'd go play, like I said, play baseball. But you know, going that far back, I can't remember all the things that went on.

In the summertime we used to go down and play on the banks of the Chicago River. We used to make these slingshots out of the end of a grape box. We'd cut a "u" out of the grape box. Get an inner tube tire and cut the rubber off, you know, and make a strip of rubber and go to the hardware store and buy these big staples. And we'd go shoot these river rats. These river rats were like, you know, they were like cats. They were so big. And we'd shoot 'em and they would have five or six staples in 'em and they'd still be running around, you know.

There was an old boat that was sunk on Division Street by the river and we were always going over there and playing around there. So, that was kind of our summer activities, you know.

Between that and Stanton Park and you know, on the Ogden Avenue bridge when it was real hot and we'd throw balloons full of water at the cars. That was our activities you know. You know, like you say, I was thinking about all the things, you know, I think this fucking booze has got my brain. I can't remember things. You know, I'm trying, but I can't really think of it. I know we used to play in the street. But I can't remember exactly everything we did, you know.

Bunny Byrne

Run across a bunch a garage rooftops

God knows what I did with my time in third, fourth, and fifth grade. Don't know. Don't know what we did. Run across a bunch a garage rooftops. Playing different games, you know. Kick the can. Just kick the can around. It was a milk can or something. I have no idea what the point of that game was Charlie. I can't remember.

We'd jumped the railroad cars and throw the beans off. Beans. Yeah. 'Cause we only wanted them for the bean blowers. In sixth, seventh, eighth grade. It was summertime and ya got the bean blowers and tortured everybody with bean blowers. It was so dangerous.

When we weren't doing that, we were also involved with the cart. We had a cart that we'd go up the alleys picking up the bottles and junk and yeah, pick up the iron and newspapers and whatever we could get. Then we'd store it and when the guy came by with the horse and buggy, we'd sell it to him. Well, he'd only give ya a fraction of what it was worth. But I mean, we weren't looking for big money. We were looking for show money. We needed a total for all of us of about a buck. You know. If we had a huge pile of paper and a lot of iron you know, he'd give ya a buck.

Charlie Martinez

The adults were on the porches or in the houses sweating from the humidity and heat of a July evening. What heat? What humidity? We never discussed it. Our running blew away some of the heat and sweat.

All we knew was running, doing, jumping, tagging, arguing, and competing. We played for hours without resort to a drink of water. We might divide a Pepsi among six of us but usually we did without. The idea was to play games till some of the crowd went home. I was never called in by my mother or father nor were most of the other kids. We played kick the can, buck buck how many fingers up, some combination of tag and prison using King's hallway as the prison, and relievio. Marbles was a simple, cheap game to play, as was a game of territory with a knife.

Every evening after supper the crowd gathered around the fireplug in front of Mary Joyce's store.

What'll we do? asked Johnny Nicolini.

Buck buck? Someone said.

Naw, lets play prison tag.

There was a round of okays and let's pick sides.

Then, like a canola, a delicious, fun filled, exciting three to five hours was eaten down to the last crumb.

Peter Eichel

The other game was relievio we used to play. That was really fun. I'd like to play it again. You drew a circle. Drew a circle that was the jail. Then you'd have sides. Okay? Then one group would go out and hide and the other side would have to go out and find 'em and if they caught 'em they'd have to hold on to them long enough to say "one, two, three, relievio." And if they did, course there were no referees and almost no one could hold on to ya long enough. To say "one, two, three, relevio." Right? And then you had to go back and you're in a circle and then we left a guard at the circle. So you could free your prisoners from your team by running and getting into the circle and hollering "one two three relevio" before the guard got ya and was able to hold you and say one two three relevio. Do you remember that? In another version, we actually had a jail, next to Mary Joyce's. Kings hallway. That's right I remember that. But we also would draw a circle. I remember Kings hallway. Wasn't that kind of a nicer building?

Paul Temple

We wandered around a lot with no set purpose.

We had a lot right across from us between the Pistone building and the Lacascio building. They finally made it into a playground. It was a political thing. The damn thing was about three feet wide but it was long. We played there constantly as kids. We played marbles in there a lot.

Like, we played kick the can and buck buck. I mean all those things. Red rover, red rover let Charlie come over. You know, you were out on the street till dark. You know. I mean there was always something to do. I remember ice-skating in the streets down there. I don't know if it was Meniere. One of the schools flooded down there one winter. They had a fire. In fact they had to rebuild it. That was on Hudson Avenue. I don't know how, again maybe its exaggeration, but it seemed like for weeks it was like an ice pond. So we're out there skating every day. I couldn't skate. We used to wear galoshes and go back and forth. You'd play hockey. Marbles.

We wandered around a lot with no set purpose. To Lincoln Park, walk around the neighborhood, go down to the lake. Hanging out together, nothing else to do. We didn't look for trouble or anything. You'd hang out. You know go to someone's house for an hour or two. Maybe listen to the radio. *Red Ryder, Straight Arrow, Burns and Allen*, the news with Paul Harvey. Krank shave cream. J. B. Kaltenborn.

Charlie Martinez

One sled, two boys, fresh snow. That's all it took for a game. We devised the rules on the spot. Nine o'clock at night. Streets empty. The soft snow muffled the distant traffic noise. The air still and cold but pleasant. Bright stars and moon. The cold not uncomfortable with all our activity and besides, when it snowed the temperature was usually in the twenties and comfortable. I had no gloves or overshoes. My partner, Frank Corbett, had gloves and galoshes. The game consisted of "belly flopping" the longest distance to achieve one point. Belly flopping was about the only way to sled with any speed if only for a short distance. There were no hills nearby and a walk to Lincoln Park to slide down the "hill" by Grant's Tomb was done only with a group. Our course was the sidewalk going north from Mary Joyce's store to the alley by Abba Kennedy's house. We never made the whole distance. Each would take a turn by holding the sled in front at a slight angle and running as fast as possible.

"Go ahead, Charlie."

As I ran, the sled moved slightly in and out against my chest and I let out a quiet grunting noise with each breath. Each step increased my speed and you realized your feet were barely touching the ground. I hoped to attain maximum speed by the time I reached the "No parking to corner" traffic sign. Then I threw the sled out in front towards the ground while holding it firmly and diving onto it with my belly. The sensation of cold wind, pure wet snow in my face, speed, and intensity in stretching the distance all combined to make each flop a glorious attempt at some kind of world record for belly flopping. During the slide I made some adjustments with the steering wings that bent the steel runners and helped me stay in the previous paths to help my speed.

We would then mark the farthest reach and declare the winner for that heat. This went on until, without any discussion, one of us, usually Frank, decided he had enough and went home. I lived a hundred feet away but when I arrived home there was no warm towel and a cup of hot chocolate with cookies. There was only bed and memories of that holy night.

Joe Olita

The object of the whole game was to jump on the weakest player.

The game that we really liked was buck, buck how many fingers up?

Well, the first strategy in the game was to pick the strongest kid that you could possibly pick for your team. You had one of your team members stand up against a brick wall, generally. Generally there would be maybe four or five on each team. So we would put that fellow up against the wall and the first person would lean over with his head against the individual in front of him and grab him around the waist. He would make himself like a horse and then the next individual would grab the first person who was bent over the same way and then it would run all the way to the back.

The object of the whole game was to jump on the weakest player. Because if as many guys as possible could get on the weakest player, it be too much weight for him and he would collapse and then we would win the game. You weren't supposed to move once you jumped. See, once you made the leap you were not supposed to move. Okay. But we always moved a little because we wanted to get as much weight up there as we possibly could.

Once our team all got on, we would have to count. Yeah. One guy on top would say, "Buck, buck how many fingers up" as he held his hand out of sight. That's right. And if the bottom guys guessed the number of fingers, then you got down and they jumped on you. And if they guessed wrong, you'd keep going till they collapsed.

Joe Zummo

I feel badly to this day that I pushed him that much.

I spent the lion's share of my life on the street. In the dead of winter in grammar school eating dinner, washing up—I was sort of a Lysol king—bundling myself up and going out to the streets to see if any of the guys were out. And the hub was Mary Joyce's grocery store. And she had that oil stove in the middle of the store which we would gather round and get warm. It was such a disappointment when nobody was around because I didn't figure out you could knock on their door and get in their house—I was too young. I was about ten years old when I did this. I didn't ask my parents permission and nobody asked me where I was going.

I do remember hanging out at Christianson Stables. I spent most of that winter there when I was in fourth grade. I was a voluntary stable boy—that was really exciting being around the horses and feeding them. I remember my father telling me to come home early—I would get home around ten o'clock. I was about ten years old. I figured what the heck is he gonna do—he isn't gonna do anything to me. So I came home late again and walked into the house and the first thing he did he punched me in the mouth. He was a perfectly sane pleasant guy that I drove crazy. He knocked me down and started kicking me and took off his belt and whipped me. I am not sure it stopped me from going to the stables to work but I saw a different side of my father—I knew now he wasn't the total pacifist that I imagined him to be. I feel badly to this day that I pushed him that much.

I used to love to go through the alleys and load up my pockets with stones and pieces of glass. Sometimes you might find a discarded yo-yo or top but going through the alleys was everything. That was exciting.

Jim Sullivan

I was just like a schoolyard rat. You know, because I always played after school, either before school or after school. I was never the kid that had to go home like right after school. I could stay and play an hour or two and then go home because my mother was busy with the other part of the family. In those days, nobody had any problems with kids not reporting home right away. 'Cause there wasn't like, you know, the hysteria that you have with kids missing, amber alerts and stuff like that, that you have today. I could get out of school and shoot marbles until you know, four or five o'clock and then go home.

Yeah. Right. In third or fourth grade, when I was going through grammar school. Coming home and reporting was never a problem.

Joe Zummo

We would climb up the L to get a free ride…

I remember playing hopscotch believe it or not. Touch football we played and if we didn't have a football we used a Carnation milk can. We played some kind of softball under the elevated where the elevated posts were bases—this was behind the elevated station behind Gus Johns house, Pat Kennedy's house and Chuckie Martinez's house. That was a big place to play. Then when the Martinezes moved to North Park we used to play in IC lot. We started a fire with venetian blinds and caught the L on fire and we all ran. We would climb up the L to get a free ride but I was afraid to go through the tracks. Usually we snuck under the cage where the ticket taker was and run up the stairs to catch the train and it was too late for them to catch you. We would ride all the way to Science and Industry.

We used to play Capture the Flag and we played that for hours. Matter of fact the game was played so long that at times I would go home and eat and wash up. Everyone was frustrated looking for me. We played hockey with broomsticks.

Ken Martinez

Yeah. I didn't go out after supper. No. Not until I was older. Until I was seven. Then I'd go out.

I played under the L. That's where I dug up an old fireman's helmet. I used to go over to Mr. Bartali's barn. That was behind the house. A big old red barn. Next to it was a tar company. They did roofing. I was in there a lot. I played with the sticky tar and always came home with tar on my hands. We used to chew it. Take it off the thing when it was cooling down and put it in your mouth and chew on it.

We went to the corner. All of us would go to the corner. We had to come home before the money car for the L came to collect fares from the station. It was nine o'clock in the summer. In the winter nobody stayed out too long. The money car would come, make the turn at Sedgwick and Orleans Street and come down to Schiller Street L. And Pa says you be home before that car gets there.

We played on the corner of North Park and Schiller. We played there. We used to play hide and seek and then we used to play on Orleans Street at the corner, right there by the Temple Art Glass and play ah, what the hell did we call it? Run across back and forth. From one side of the street to the other. Yeah, something like "ocean free."

And then Pa caught me up on the Temple Art building roof running around. I could see why he was worried. I didn't realize at that time that one of the fellows came down that utility pole, fell and crushed his head. Bushalaki. Right at Schiller Street and Orleans. I was running around up there.

Then I got my foot burnt 'cause we was jumping. We built a bonfire in the alley and I was jumping over it. We were jumping to see who could jump over it and my foot landing in there and got all burnt.

I was at the Temple Art Glass building. I came home and I musta been sitting in acid. And I had acid all over my hands. They had big bottles of these things sitting on the dock. They used to clean buildings and I finally got one of the big spoon caps off. I was sitting in this stuff. I didn't realize what it was.

During the war there was a place that took in scrap metal. And we went and picked up everything we could and then we remembered up on the elevated platform there was barrels of pieces of iron. Gus Johns and I shimmied up there, got up there and we threw a whole bunch of it down. Walter Gibbons had his wagon and we threw it all in the wagon and took it over to Clybourn Avenue and the guy gave us a dollar for a whole wagon. He gave us a dollar! And if the railroad people ever found out they'd of come after me.

We also learned to climb up on the elevated and get the rails and stuff and take it over to the junkyard that was on Larrabee and Division during the war. We used to sell it to them.

Was it stealing? Just about. But at that time you didn't think of it as stealing. Well, you see, it was rusting stuff, so we figured they weren't gonna use it. It wasn't new.

Oh, God, I don't know how old I was, maybe ten or eleven. It was during the war. '43? Gus knew all the places. And I just went along.

Charlie Martinez

Hockey was played occasionally in winter but not as a sport but more as a game. None of us knew the real rules of hockey so we improvised. We did buy hockey sticks and used black electrical tape on the blade to prevent wear. I don't recall any real pucks but we used flattened tin cans or Mason jar covers and goals were set as a line running from curb to curb. We never played on ice; it was street snow, packed down by the car traffic. Not all of us had ice skates, but players used either shoes or skates.

Winter into spring was wet shoes, rivers carved into ice at the curbs, ancient dog shit piles and debris entombed for months now uncovered by melting snow, mud, "packy" snow perfect for snowballs, longer daylight, and like wolf puppies we tasted the coming summer in the breeze.

In spring and summer, roller skating was a common pastime. Those skates were hooked onto the sides of the soles of our shoes and eventually the soles were ripped off. We would lay out a course with chalk in the street and speed skate or play a form of hockey on roller skates.

In April the warm breezes from the south stirred us to additional adventures. The ice was just about gone from the lake. The three-inch green crabs were moving about and we went hunting. At this time the water temperature was probably not much above freezing but we ran and hopped from one slippery chunk of cement to the next, occasionally slipping and soaking ourselves to the waist. But the crabs were no match for our quick hands. The captured crabs were thrown as far as possible out into the lake.

We wondered how they could find their way back into the safety of the broken cement and rotting wooden piles.

Our lake wandering began at Schiller Street, working our way south to Oak Street Beach and then north again to North Avenue beach. We inspected the Boat House at North Avenue and found swimming goggles, caps, tops of girls bathing suits, jock straps, used condoms, tubes of suntan lotion, and occasionally a few coins -- the debris from summer fun but sometimes a treasure for us. We then began the trek back through Lincoln Park. This journey was roughly a mile in length as measured to Mary Joyce's store, but to a twelve-year-old the length was decided with a different type of measure. Hunger, cold from the wet clothes, and visions of a Pepsi and Hostess Cup Cake increased the distance markedly.

Crossing Lake Shore Drive on what we called the North Avenue Bridge was the first leg. Midway across the bridge we broke the monotony by pausing to spit on passing cars. This was more fun in the summer when occasionally a convertible was presented to our spitting skill. Next the "football field" was an open windy trail but when we reached the water fountain we knew we could get some shelter beyond in the stone viaduct. Up the paved walk we came to a mausoleum. We made countless attempts to crack this fortress for a glimpse of its treasure of rotting corpses. The mausoleum was left over from the time Lincoln Park was a cemetery. To our continued disappointment, we never did see or smell a corpse.

A hundred yards away was Lincoln's statue. We didn't climb it in the winter but moved on to the warmth of the Chicago Historical Society building at North Avenue and Clark Street.

The attendants let us into the building despite noting some of us had frozen pants, dirty clothes, wet shoes with holes in the sides and soles, snotty noses, unkempt hair and mismatched clothes. We wandered about, getting warmed up. The sculpture of the massacre at Ft. Dearborn fascinated us. The Indians were strong, virile types and the white settlers defiant but sad in their losing battle. Lincoln artifacts were visited. We never had money to settle into the cafeteria but continued on after a decent amount of wandering and exited through the front door facing Clark Street.

This next leg of the journey was first south on Clark Street past shops and the Gold Coast Theater. The band of boys started to stretch out and each was left with his own thoughts and eye for treasure or distraction. But we stayed close to Joe Zummo because he, of all the group, held the key to food and drink when we reached Mary Joyce's store. He could charge food on his mother's bill! What power! Of course we had the difficult job of conning him out of part of the food.

Across Burton Place to Wells Street then south to Schiller Street and west to Mary Joyce's store was how we finished the journey. Five to ten of us entering the store immediately created a crowd. We huddled around the oil stove in the middle of the store and warmed up keeping one eye on Joe as he "shared" his Pepsi and Hostess Cup Cakes. This ended another glorious day of adventure or as our parents called it, draggin' the street.

Part Two: Sports

Charlie Martinez

No tennis or golf was ever played. They were for "rich" kids.

Playing ball.

That was the generic term for sports and almost all our free time was allotted to any type of sport or game played with a ball all the way through high school and beyond. In addition, in high school some of us played varsity sports but also kept up with neighborhood games.

Ledge ball, stickball (fast pitching), handball, softball, hardball, basketball, touch football, tackle football, hockey or just playing catch. These took up most of our time. No tennis or golf was ever played. They were for "rich" kids who lived north or on the Gold Coast. We swam for fun but not sport. Track and gymnastics were read about in the newspapers. Wrestling was fighting. Boxing was either for fighting or sport.

At the basic level, all sports were pickup games without any equipment or with the minimum in order to play the game. Numbers of players on a team usually related to how many of us showed up at the time rather than what the rules of the game dictated. No umpires, no written records, no spectators and no parental involvement.

We required at the minimum a ball, stick or bat, hoop or goal, a space designated as a field, and at least two players, rarely needing baseball gloves, to form sides and create competition. The decision on what to play was driven more by the season and our interests that day rather than being forced on us by any rules. For most of the games the field of play could be the street, alley, empty lot, schoolyard or public park.

Ledge ball was the most uncluttered sport of all. All that was needed was the street or schoolyard cement, a ledge or angled stone a foot or two up a building wall and a hollow pink, rubber ball.

Paul Temple

No adults were involved. They wouldn't even understand what you were doing.

I think of the joys of growing up in that neighborhood. The differences in the neighborhood and the people and the kids and everything were incredible. There were a lot of old buildings down there. And if you remember, a lot of them had ledges along the side of the old buildings. They were built in the 1800s. And the street that we lived on again was a little side street, Evergreen Street. We used to play ledge ball. You remember the Spaulding pink ball? You'd buy 'em and we'd go and we play ledge ball. Probably the greatest game ever invented for city kids. It was so sophisticated. There were cracks in the ledge that you could either spin the ball backwards, forwards, line drive it. The batter slammed the ball against the ledge and then ran the bases.

First, you had to choose up sides. I think there were four to a side. You had first base, second base, third base and home run. I mean this is in the street, actually there were no bases; it was all made up. We played off the ledge of Henry Heimsoth's drug store at Sedgwick and Evergreen. We used to chip in to buy the Spaulding balls. We used to get 'em at a store up on Sedgwick that was like a candy store and school supplies.

Everybody knew the rules. They were unwritten but you knew 'em. Remember Peter Nicalberri. The tall thin guy, lived up on the third floor? He was probably the greatest ledge ball player I ever saw. You know, the guy was like Babe Ruth. Opposite Heimsoth's was the Town and Garden Apartments wall. If you caught it off the wall it was an out. If it got by, it depended on high it went off the wall, how far you could get around the bases. It'd be a single, double, triple or a home run. We'd be playing there for hours and hours until it got dark out. And of course you had street traffic. I mean you had to watch that. We had like tournaments, World Series, and you'd have elimination teams. I mean this sounds strange.

No adults were involved. They wouldn't even understand what you were doing. We had our reunion a couple a years ago and a kid by the name of Alcini Mastasio was there. He lived across the street from us and he was a tremendous ledge ball player. Most of the times we were on opposite sides. We used to get in arguments obviously a lot of times. But we always knew the rules. And eventually you would abide by the rules. I mean you knew what they were. But if there was an argument it was settled by consensus. Never remember a fight. Like ten to twelve hours we'd be going around. It's probably one of the most vivid memories I really have, honestly. It was an exciting time.

Charlie Martinez

"Here comes that asshole with the dog."

Stickball, or what we usually called fast pitching, was a more sophisticated game than ledge ball. The same pink ball was used, although a tennis ball would do. A rectangular box, "the strike zone" was drawn or painted on a wall in the Franklin schoolyard. The batter used a broomstick. The pitcher stood maybe twenty feet away and threw the ball at any speed he wanted. With fast pitching, it was difficult to hit the ball from such a short distance but baseball rules were used. You ran the bases depending on where the ball hit off the opposite wall without being caught. The "fielder" would throw the ball at the "strike zone" and if he hit that area while you were between bases, you were out.

Peter Eichel

You know my father did come out and see one game. I couldn't believe it.

I was never good at anything, but I played everything. We had a football team called the Lincoln Park Rams. I don't know what the caliber or quality of the teams that we played were, but we went three seasons unscored on. We had all these little guys. I weighed 120 pounds I was a guard and we played both defense and offense. Joe Russo weighed 125 pounds. You weighed about the same. Ptac maybe weighed 140 pounds. Uh, Vic Faraci weighed maybe 200 pounds.

We took the sport very seriously. We'd start in August and I think the reason we were good was that we worked real hard to get into physical shape. We were very aware of the basics, you know at that time, nothing like it is today. But there were certain techniques that you used in the line that you used on offense and defense and we kinda knew that kinda stuff. And I don't remember who taught all that to us.

You know my father did come out and see one game. I couldn't believe it. But he actually came out and he took pictures of us. And I actually found out that he was showing them to everybody at his job. Which amazed me because he had never indicated any interest. And of course I don't ever remember being bothered by that though. But I kinda of felt that I coulda used a little help here and there from somebody. You know I was growing up and there just was nobody.

Charlie Martinez

And then there were eight.

Like everyone in my neighborhood, I played very little basketball in grammar school. We occasionally played in St. Chrysostom's gym, which was on Dearborn Street in the Gold Coast. They sort of let the lower class kids use the gym. We just threw the ball around and shot baskets but there were no organized games that I remember. But that gym stuck in my mind for another reason. One afternoon, the gym was crowded with kids shooting baskets. Everyone was bumping into one another and balls were flying all over the place. I made the mistake of running after my ball just as John Sotos, a handsome, older, Greek thug was about to shoot his ball. I bumped into him and he missed his shot. He grabbed my ball, and after he screamed the usual swear words, slammed it into my head from about two feet away. There was no way I could respond except to walk away.

At Quigley High School during the two years I spent there, there was an intense intramural program but no interscholastic sports.

It was great. Everyone could organize a team and tournaments were put together on some kind of ability scheme. The basketball games were played at lunch hour on a slippery, linoleum-covered floor wearing our school pants, gym shoes and tee shirt. At Mundelein High School, the varsity basketball was divided into the Lights (also called Juniors) who were five eight or under, and the Heavies (also called Seniors) who could be any height but usually were the better ballplayers. This way shorter boys could play varsity basketball. I don't recall ever practicing except right before the game and of course our school had no gym. We won a few games in our Parish League. I enjoyed those two years of basketball. At five seven and a half, I was one of the tallest players on the Lights and actually played center. Some of the guys who were five nine or so tried desperately to get on the Lights so they could be stars. There were all kinds of stories of guys staying up all night, dehydrating, practicing slight knee bending and chest sinking to make the height.

At the end of my senior year season, we all went into the tiny auditorium for the presentation of the Varsity letters. We stood on the stage with the basketball coach, Father Brett. The audience was maybe forty students and nuns. The nine letter "C"s were on a table in front of us. Suddenly the lights went out! After a few moments they came back on. But now there were only eight monograms on the table. The mystery of the missing monogram was never solved.

Jay Pistone

Ya pushed the button down, the clock was stopped. Okay. You pushed the button up, the clock is started again. You know, it was no big deal. I won a lot of games that way.

I was the timekeeper at the Waller High basketball games. We had a little clock and Chapel was our coach and he picked me to take care of the clock. We didn't have a clock on the wall. The other coach would always keep an eye on me. Well they got interested in the game, you know, if the game is close. So I would stop the clock when we were losing a close game, you know. And we'd have another minute, minute and a half. We won city that year, you know.

Oh I won a lot a games. We had Jesse White and Danny Mogan. Jesse White led the city in scoring. In those days they had juniors and seniors. So if ya five eight you were a junior and anything above that you were a senior. So it didn't mean the grades, just the size. So we won junior city that year. Jesse White was the man who invented the jump shot. And Dan Mogan was the dribbler and the shooter, you know. We were the top team in the city in the fifties. Every year our junior team would be right there. But my job was making sure on a close game they won. Yeah, close game that we got the extra minutes. "How much time left?" "Two minutes and twenty seconds." "Okay." And then before ya know it they're asking me "How much time left?" "Two minutes and ten seconds." And then eventually you know we would get the lead and I let the clock run out.

Yeah well right, I made the breaks. Well they didn't watch me that well. Ya pushed the button down, the clock was stopped. Okay. You pushed the button up, the clock is started again. You know, it was no big deal.

We played softball for money. We would play a team from another neighborhood. You know, another area. Maybe four blocks away. You collect money from your team or the people watching from your neighborhood and they would do the same. You know whatever the amount was, the lesser amount, that's what you played for. Maybe one team would collect a hundred and fifty and the other a hundred. We were about sixteen, seventeen. Yeah, well we would divide it up if we won and you'd get whatever you put up. You put up five dollars, you got ten back, you know. You put ten dollars, you got twenty back. We used to have umpires. They would draw two from each neighborhood. You know what I mean? Yeah. Four guys would umpire the game.

But the Cleveland Aces, they were little tough guys. But they could never beat us guys in softball. We were the Hawks and we played 'em in softball from twelve years old, till seventeen. Then we played 'em for money, you know, two hundred dollars a game, three hundred dollars a game. We beat 'em cause they would always play favoritism.

Instead of the best players, the guy they hung with, they'd put him right field. Or ah behind the plate. You know. We didn't do that. Ya know I mean? If you weren't the best ten guys, you know, you sat on the bench. Almost every one of our guys could hit to right field and if you had a weak link hanging in right field, you know, he'd get murdered. Jack has all kinds of trophies. I didn't know what I did wit mine. But we won. Every year we won tournaments.

Charlie Martinez

We took nothing for granted, especially the honesty of our friends.

Horns of a dilemma. Empathy or justice?

"Hello, Mrs. Walsh? This is Patti Irwin. I was calling everyone just to be sure they got home with their trophies. Did Tommy get his home all right? He did? Fine. Thanks Mrs. Walsh."

We were the Atoms and we had just won the Midget softball tournament for twelve and under boys at Seward Park in the summer of 1947. Memories of the championship game and the games leading up to it are lost in the swirling dust of the infield of that park. Probably our uniforms were just tee shirts with Seward Park stenciled across the chest. I can't relate to you a miraculous catch in the outfield by Joe Filpi or a terrific stop at third base by John Giovenco. The pitching may have been superb by Johnny Byrnes but I don't recall if the score was 10-0 or 20-19.

But even at that age, we took nothing for granted, especially the honesty of our friends. Everyone showed his trophy to the group after the game. It was about nine inches high with a three-inch wood base topped with a young man getting ready to hit a pitch. But wait, one trophy was missing. Johnny Nicolini could not find his trophy. The possible thief was narrowed down quickly. Ooner Irwin concocted a plan. He had a pleasant, mature manner about him and we eagerly followed his idea. We walked as a group to the Schiller Street L station and Patti Irwin was selected to make the call because he could make his words seem so sincere. Several of us jammed the phone booth and the rest filled the space of the little station.

"Hello, Mrs. Walsh?" he began. "Did Tommy bring his trophy home? He did? Well we were just checking to make sure thanks."

Triumph. Tommy Walsh was not on the team. Why would he have a trophy? Our instincts were correct. A courier was sent, possibly Paul Marconi, to tell Tommy Walsh his scam was over. The trophy was returned and a group of pre-adolescent streetwise kids had their justice without any involvement of adults.

Jack La Brasca

You'd find, the beer bellies, the guys from the taverns. Older men. They would pony up sixty or seventy dollars and we would play 'em.

The neighborhood was all guys. Primarily, all guys. There was Jack Flaherty, Willie Foley and myself. There was about twenty of us. And we played a lot 'cause you know softball was our life. We had championship teams. Our team was the Hawks.

I remember we joined the Herald American tournament, which was at Grant Park. We won it and then we went on to what apparently was a divisional championship. We showed up on a Saturday night at Grant Park in September. We were playing a black team from 37th and Lake Park. They were called the Metro Wizards. This was supposed to be sixteen and under, right? They came with their wives and children in buggies. They were grown men. They destroyed us. I mean we thought we were a good ball club.

We played a lot of money games on Sundays. We were fifteen, sixteen, seventeen years old. Whatever you had in your pocket, you ponied up and between the ten guys on the club plus the manager; you probably wind up with maybe sixty, seventy dollars. And you'd find the beer bellies, the guys from the taverns. Older men. They would pony up sixty or seventy dollars and we would play 'em. It was not entirely a sucker game for them because you know, you don't always win 'cause when you were playing grown men, sometimes they were not bad.

That's what you did on Sundays. And you did the tournaments during the week. You know, there was Seward Park tournament, the

Hanson Park tournament, Olivet Tournament. We were involved in all of those. And we played ball of course. Heavy, heavy softball. Usually between ages of twelve and eighteen were the big softball years. That's what we did best, we played softball. And no parents were involved or ever came to a game. Unheard of. Unheard of. Not an issue.

They were a couple of guys from the neighborhood who hung out at the Olivet with the Cleveland Aces. But most of us stayed south of Division Street. We considered them "hot dogs." They wore jackets. You remember it. They were, you know, supposed to be tough guys. And we always thought that they were "hot dogs," you know, flashy.

Charlie Martinez

The glove had to be baptized into the Holy Order of Baseball.

The first Mass we called it. The 7 a.m. Mass on Sunday. We argued, threatened, and shoved to be scheduled to serve as altar boys at that Mass. The nuns beamed, the parents were proud. They thought the spiritual spark was activated at last.

But, again, adults were blind to our motivation and led by their wishful thinking. What was the real motivation for preteen boys to get out of bed at 6:30 a.m. on a Sunday morning? Catch. It was to play catch. Nothing more complicated than throwing a hardball back and forth in the street in front of my house.

The basis for our ability to enjoy playing catch on Sunday morning grew out of another religious experience. Weddings. There was a pecking order to serve at weddings. Usually eighth grade boys had first choice but as frequently happened some of them were on the wrong side of the nuns and the seventh graders and even sixth graders were given this privilege.

Keeping a holy demeanor, we stalled in the sacristy after serving the wedding. We snuffed out the candles on the altar, secured the wine and water cruets, and helped the priest with his vestments. At last, into the sacristy comes the best man. He smiles and thanks the priest and at the same time slips him an envelope. His sweaty nervousness makes one think it was a political bribe rather than a personal gift. But then he turns to us and doles out crisp ones or a five. Looking at the bills, I didn't see Washington's or Lincoln's portrait, I saw Joe Gordon's smiling face. Now I could buy my Joe Gordon second baseman's glove made of genuine cowhide and with his personal signature burned into the thumb. Down to Chicago Avenue and the river I went to the Montgomery Ward catalogue sales office.

But before I could actually use my glove on Sunday mornings, a solemn initiating ceremony had to be undertaken. The glove had to be baptized into the Holy Order of Baseball. Patti Irwin had his glove brought through this holy ritual and wasn't he the coolest and most admired ball player as far as style if not ability? My glove must also be correctly indoctrinated or what was the use of living.

Gus Johns was the high priest who instructed and guided the neophytes and presided over the induction rituals.

I brought my glove, a Mason jar half full of virgin olive oil, and a hardball to the back porch of Gus's grandma's house. First, he ordered me to thoroughly apply the holy oil generously to all parts of the glove, but especially to the palm area. When he was satisfied that a complete penetration of the holy oil had occurred, I was told to place the hardball in the palm of the glove. Gus then supplied me with half-inch wide strips cut from a car tire inner tube. I used these to tightly force the fingers of the glove around the hardball. Now the most solemn part of the ritual was upon me. This was a supreme act of faith. Gus produced a bucket, half filled with water. Testing my faith, he pointed to the bucket. I put my glove into the bucket, submerging it. Gus, with cosmic insight, assured me that a perfect "pocket" would be formed overnight. I ran to his grandma's back porch the next morning. My faith was rewarded! I had the sweetest, most perfect pocket formed in my Joe Gordon second baseman's glove.

And so, all rituals were accomplished and I spent glorious hours throwing and catching a hardball with my anointed glove right in front of my house early on Sunday mornings.

Joe Zummo

I played sports in grammar and high school but I would have liked to play more.

We played a lot of softball and sandlot football. I loved all of it especially football—going out knocking people down and getting knocked down. Some the happiest times was playing football in high school and also I played with a neighborhood team called the Lincoln Park Rams.

The Rams were a highly organized neighborhood team—well disciplined. Nobody was that outstanding but the teamwork was terrific. For the first two years we didn't lose a game and I don't think anyone scored on us. I went away to college and played football but came home at times and played with the Rams. A sad memory was when we lost our first game. I think we lost it 13 to 12 and I had the flu and I was very listless, operating at half capacity. That was a tough thing to lose and I still carry that in my memory. I remember how competent and hard working we were and this was all self directed. No parents were involved except my father would show up and take pictures. No other parents came. But I was amazed that he was there.

Charlie Martinez

When standing at home plate, the L came straight east at you but abruptly turned south.

I played sports the same way I went to school or wandered through the day. By instinct. I mean, I never consciously analyzed anything. Never dug for deeper meaning, motivations. Never thought through a play in football or how to anticipate a double play ball in softball. Basketball was shoot, fight for the rebound and run or pass. That's all I knew. You can see I was never considered a star or top player. But the beauty of it all was that *I played*. I played every sport as much as I wanted. I never felt left out.

At times, when the half block walk to IC lot proved too much for our teenage legs or there were too few to play a game, we had alternatives to playing in that almost regular field. At the intersection of Schiller Street and North Park Avenue, in front of Mary Joyce's store, were four "corners." Each corner contained a sewer cover in the street abutting the curb. Thus home plate, first base, second base and third base could be ascribed to these sewer covers. The game required at the least two players -- one on each side. The batter stood next to the home plate sewer cover and threw the ball at the sewer cover as hard as he could. You learned to angle the ball and twist it in your hand and aim for the inch steel protrusions on the cover. To the only fielder, the ball could go off at any angle with either a low or high trajectory. If caught on the fly off the sewer cover you had one out. If the fielder got the ball on the ground before you reached first base you were out. Of course balls that went over his head or past him were "fair" balls and you ran until he picked it up. Simple, but for a teenage boy it became an enjoyable, competitive pastime.

  We also played softball under the L. This was on the west side of Ellison's building, just south of the Schiller Street L station. The field was about fifty feet wide and maybe seventy-five feet deep. The L structure was only about twenty or twenty five feet above us. The playing field itself was all broken glass and rocks with some dog crap mixed in. But we played there for hours trying desperately to hit line drives in this way avoiding the L structure. But we hit the steel many times and a new softball deteriorated fast from this punishment. Fly balls that hit the structure of the L were frequently caught for an out on the rebound. The worst-case scenario occurred when a fly ball got stuck in the structure. Then the batter had to climb the steel supports and watch for trains and the third rail as he freed the ball and then climbed down. Running to first base could be dangerous. If you tripped as you got there, there was a good chance you would crash into the steel supporting pillars of the L.]

Pat Rogers

And sometimes it was the American kids against the Japanese kids.

We played in the old basketball area in between Mundelein and the Propagation of the Faith buildings. Do you remember that, Charles? Yeah. We were probably getting introduced to basketball just about that time. And of course there would be a carry-over effect to Lake Shore Park where we participated down there in that and also ah, softball. Organized sports as such, not much. Pick-up games. There was some hardball. It was very typical to get a ball and play till it fell apart, and we'd tape it up and retape it, and retape it, and play forever. But ah, football was not yet introduced I don't even think until maybe eighth grade.

No, they did not have a football team at Cathedral grammar school. These were pick up-games and generally with the older guys. Maybe you remember Tommy Spears from Wells, and Tommy Atkins who played with the Rams too. We'd play with those guys and the Buddhaheads. Jimmy Omura was one. These were Japanese kids and they were really tough kids. They joined us in some of our neighborhood team sports and sometimes we'd played against them. We played touch football. And sometimes it was the American kids against the Japanese kids. I can recall that the Japanese kids were pretty well outstanding. They were good athletes. Now ah, of course we held our own.

They were from Tokyo Rose's area on Oak and Clark. And they would have gone to Ogden Public School and when they went to high school, they went to Wells, by and large. Yeah.

But not much organized sports at school in grammar school. No. If we were introduced to anything, it was the Lawson YMCA. It was called the outpost. Between the Cosmopolitan Bank and the Hague Tavern on Chicago Avenue. We were introduced to games over there, marbles, chess, checkers, ping-pong. There was a gymnasium. We probably had lay-ups. There was ah, a gym teacher who tried to introduce you to some rudimentary tumbling.

Now you have to understand and I think you remember, we played football with the Rams for a couple of years too. Besides playing football and basketball at Cathedral high there. You played that one year. I have a picture down at Lake Shore Park. You and Guy and myself and that whole freshman team of Stan Gould.

We also were playing in the CYO basketball. Gosh, I think we were eighteen, nineteen. And we were playing B'nai B'rith. So that side is calling Ben Beamon, who sponsored our teams, "Niggi, Niggi, come on, come on over here" they called. He says "fuck you Jews." Monsignor Campbell says, "Niggi, say a prayer for the boys." "Beat these fucking Jews." He was the funniest guy in the world and he loved the Jews of course. He was with us for forty or fifty years. This guy just died. He was so close. A father to all of us.

Charlie Martinez

"Aw shit, look at his face!"

We slid along the street and destroyed our pants and shoes. We crashed into parked cars and damaged doors and lights. This was touch football.

Touch football was one of the simplest and most enjoyable games we could play and in almost any weather except when there was snow on the ground. The game required no equipment except a football although at times we made do with a softball, hardball or even a Campbell soup can. The light poles became the goal lines and we marked the imaginary scrimmage line with our spit and spread it out with the soles of our shoe. Two to five players usually made up a side. The game was a passing game but occasionally we ran if there was an open field or everyone was covered. We purposely forbid blocking but I can't remember why. I think this allowed more passing and produced a faster game. The opposing linemen were required to count to three or five out loud before rushing.

There was no punting or first downs. We just used our downs up and handed the ball over if we didn't score.\

At times we played on a smaller space. This was the wide, concrete sidewalk in front of Franklin School where North Park

Avenue ended at Evergreen Street. This was right next to Guerney's new hamburger shop. Mr. Guerney had set up a small hamburger joint in the basement of his three-flat and it became popular for awhile. Sal, one of the Madonia boys, was holding court there one day and in his own dumb but blustering way was telling everybody about the real truth on masturbation.

"I kin take any of youse to a doctor and he can tell if you ever jagged off!"

Of course, we had no idea if he was telling the truth, but he was so loud and bullying in his style that some of us slinked off lest he would look at us and find out our secret.

Anyway, we played touch football on the concrete next to Guerney's. These games were tighter and required more skill. There was a need for quick acceleration, hard, accurate throws and fast, agile receivers who could cut and fake and catch the ball.

Boys get to know the sensation of getting hit on the head. Round stones thrown at close range or falling and hitting your head against the cement. There is a sharp noise and burst of light like you're seeing stars. You feel some nausea for a few moments and slight confusion. A nugget is raised on the scalp and sometimes warm sweet blood is tasted as it trickles down. I had experienced this hard head knock several times.

As I ran my prescribed route, my gym shoes seemed to barely touch the cement. I flew past Giovenco and left him standing still with a head feint. I cut diagonally to the opposite corner just as planned. The ball sought out my outstretched hands. I tucked it in and took a step or two, turned toward the goal and ... stars, nausea, and confusion.

"Charlie, how do ya feel?"

"Aw shit, look at his face!"

I rose to my feet, turned at once to go home and wobbled north on North Park Avenue. Joe Zummo stayed with me. I guess he was afraid I would fall. I heard Joe explain to my mother and sister that just as I caught the ball, I turned and ran into the seven-foot steel fence with one inch bars. I hit the fence with my head and face while in full stride. I figure I was going ten, maybe fifteen miles an hour. They took me to St. Elizabeth's Hospital where Dr. Schmehil, the family doctor, practiced. I stayed for observation for three days. I enjoyed the attention. Clean new sheets every day, good food, and pretty nurses. For some reason, on the second day, I released a full bladder into the bed. None of the attendants made any comment.

I felt guilty about being in the hospital because I knew my parents could barely keep their household together -- let alone pay for a hospital stay. We had no insurance.

Charlie Martinez

"Shall we prick him with the rest?" - Julius Caesar, Shakespeare

Our selection was not meant to choose those who would be assassinated, but the outcome for those who did not make the list was an emotional assassination.

We were in Frank Corbett's apartment on the third floor. This was in Montelone's red three-flat just across the street from Mary Joyce's store. The business was to select who would be given the privilege of buying a Rams team jacket, at the time the most coveted jacket in the neighborhood. This jacket with its blue cloth body, yellowish leather sleeves, and a large R on the left front with the word RAMS sewed in and a small football along side was a signal to the world that the owner belonged to a special fellowship.

There were about eight of us in Frank's apartment. Why these eight were picked for this momentous task, I can't tell. The decisions made were brutal. No actual discussion of the merits of a candidate was done, only a yes or no. We individually sized up the prospect and applied our own secret criteria. Most were active players on the football team but a few others also were selected who didn't play. Patti Irwin? Yes. Charlie Martinez? Yes. Don Slattery? No. And so on till about twenty or twenty-five were picked. There was some lobbying for borderline friends and some of these were selected.

Satisfied with our work, we went out and had the older-looking guys buy some beer for a quiet celebration.

Bunny Byrne

Well, he dipped into the church money for a lot of our equipment and he got into big trouble.

We didn't play much sports until about sixth grade when Father Sullivan came to Immaculate Conception parish.

He was the new priest in the parish. And he came and he was like amazed that we weren't doing anything but just hanging around the streets. And so, he started buying football equipment, baseball equipment, and basketballs. And things like that. And got things going. Got us into stuff. And he got us into tournaments. Played other grammar schools. So it worked out good for about the last three years of grammar school that's what we did. Our seasons got a little more defined. We'd play football in the fall and winter. And then baseball in the spring and summer, so. Unfortunately we were never too good.

He'd get older guys to come out, like Frank Corbett's brother Bob who worked for the Tribune. And a lot of the guys returning from the service. They knew a little bit about football and baseball and they'd teach us. Unfortunately we did not have many good baseball players 'cause we were all into softball, sixteen inch. Nobody could really interest us too much in league ball. Number one, it cost too much. You hadda buy a glove. No parent would give you money for a glove. And believe it or not, even back then a decent glove was ten bucks. Couldn't really afford 'em. Then ya needed baseballs, and bats, and ya break a bat and it's no good. No aluminum bats, you know. So, we just never got into baseball much. The only reason we were into football was that Father Sullivan bought us all the equipment. He bought everything. Well, he dipped into the church money for a lot of it and he got into big trouble. Yeah, we thought he had wealthy parents. I guess he was juggling the books.

Oh, Father Fleming, the pastor had a fit. They found out that he had spent thousands of dollars. I mean that's back when money was hard to come by. People were still putting dimes and quarters in the collection box and he's out spending big, big money on football and baseball equipment, so. Then he started that young men's club down in the hall of the grammar school. He bought pool tables and really made it nice. We never were allowed in there. See, it was for the older guys, like the guys that came out of service. Yeah, he was great. It's just too bad he didn't have a little backing or have any skills in getting people to sponsor things like this 'cause he did a great job. He just had no money and he was dipping into church funds. I think that's how they ended up drumming him out.

Paul Temple

The team was your own, you controlled everything.

"Ya go down to the red Chevy, I want you to cut in front of the right fender and I'll throw you a pass." I mean those were the kind of plays that you always had then playing touch football. There was no place to play except the street. And then your own imagination.

One of my memories down there is always playing sports. And we played softball. Do you know about the Cleveland Aces? Olivet Institute? Well, then they had the Junior Aces. They were our age and we started to play in high school. In fact we even played CYO ball. We had a softball team. We had some pretty good ball clubs. And we used to play the Aces. Yeah, I remember finally beating them. The Junior Aces now not the Cleveland Aces. The neighborhood was divided as you remember. I mean if you walked two blocks out of your way it was not unusual to get your butt kicked depended on who you ran into. But I remember playing 'em and couple a fights. And ah, it's like anything else you gain respect.

You know, adults were never involved. I never remember anybody, anything interfering like that. Almost everything was always the kids, you know. I mean you knew the rules. There were adults like in the league. I mean they had adults who supervised the league. There were older guys that would ump. And in fact as we got better I think they had uniformed umpires.

The team was your own, you controlled everything. You know, ya chipped in and bought uniforms.

I'm trying to remember the name of our team. And it's funny I can remember you guys were the Rams. But we had uniforms. You know, remember going to Maxwell Street? Buying uniforms. Shirts and everything. And we used to do that. You'd chip in your money, and the guys, couple of guys'd go down and get your uniform.

Charlie Martinez

They were one glob of humanity, shoving, eating, buying, and cheating, all on a pleasant Sunday morning.

"It stinks like dog shit down here!"

So spoke Joe Russo, giving us his official impression of the Maxwell Street Market. For Joe, this was a rather mild conclusion. And we were still on the streetcar.

We were here on a mission. Sent by the Lincoln Park Rams football team hierarchy for the purpose of buying uniforms.

The second you stepped off the Clark Street streetcar at Twelfth and Canal the place began oozing into your pores. You were immediately enveloped and became part of a mass of people with foreign smells, foreign accents. Some were hustlers, thieves, street kids, hoodlums, merchants and many just lower-class bargain hunters out to buy mostly the necessities of life. They were one glob of humanity, shoving, eating, buying, and cheating and all on a pleasant Sunday morning.

The hot grease garlic smell of the Polish sausage roasting on a fifty-gallon drum converted into a barbecue pit dragged you by the nose toward it. The sight of hot beef sandwiches with green peppers and onions made you lust for them.

Outside each small store entrance stood a hustler. He actually grabbed at and took hold of your coat or shirt.

"Two suits for twenty-five dollars. No? How much you got? Look, five shirts for five bucks."

Part of the allure of buying here was the rumor freely passed around that all the goods were stolen and that's why everything was so cheap.

Finally the crowd deposited us at Herman's Sports Goods. The store was poorly lit (the better to fool you on the cut and color of the clothes) and had a strong, musky odor from the goods having been sitting on a railroad siding or in somebody's basement for several years while they "cooled" off.

We inspect the goods. Yellowish-gold football pants. These were cheap goods with minimal knee padding and a small "kidney" pad at the top of the waist. How much we think. As if reading our minds a salesman says, three-fifty each.

We look up and to our surprise we see a thin, average height, black man with a dark vest on and wearing a straw hat.

We mumble "too much," acting like we are real experienced bargain-hunters.

The black man calls out to the back room—in Yiddish! Out comes a shorter, gray-haired white man. They converse a few moments in Yiddish with much arm and hand waving.

The black man says, three twenty-five. We buy.

We go through the same routine for the purple football jerseys.

We leave, proud of ourselves. We feel we didn't get taken like Abba Kennedy whose "blue" suit was two different shades of blue in the sunlight in front of Mary Joyce's store the day after he bought it.

Jim Sullivan

So that's gotta be like two and a half miles.

No sports in grammar school. They used to have a gym period but you know, there was no gym. So they used to march us up to the top floor where they had like a small auditorium, and they like tried to teach you how to broad jump, or long jump or high jump. There wasn't enough room like for races. There was no athletic equipment in the gym. You know, no baskets or anything like that. So, it was just a place where you could run around. Some mats. You could wrestle maybe.

I played basketball at Waller High School on what was probably the best lightweight basketball team in the city at the time. Had Dan Mogan and Jesse White. Both averaged over 30 points a game. We got eliminated in the city, in the city finals 'cause Dan Mogan in the quarterfinals tore the ligaments in his leg and couldn't play. So Lenny Hughes from the Cleveland Aces played. He was a good guy but not the player that Dan Mogan was, you know. And Dan Mogan was better than Jesse White and Jesse White was like one of the stars of our team.

I played two years of football there. Course in those days everybody walked whenever you were gonna go someplace. Nobody drove. Nobody had cars. Like when we practiced football. Let's say, we'd practice at Lincoln Park and Lake Shore Drive. So that's gotta be like two and a half miles. We'd used to walk there with our equipment and walk the equipment home to Division Street and then take it on the bus the next day to bring it back to school. That was a job in itself.

Charlie Martinez

His left lower leg faced south and his left foot pointed north.

"Remember, if ya hit them hard, they fall just like everybody else."

Johnny Byrnes delivered that encouragement as he went up and down our line before we received the opening kickoff. He took no training as a coach. He was our quarterback and a natural leader. We were totally overmatched by size and experience in that tackle football game -- and we won. We were the Lincoln Park Rams and we played pickup tackle football games. We were in our late teens, all out of high school.

When the Chicago Tribune started its publicity for the annual August All Star Football game, our juices got going, signaling us to begin summer practice for the coming pickup football season. About the end of July we began conditioning. In those early years we had no coach, never elected a captain, chose our positions ourselves, had no distinct uniform except painted rams' horns on our helmets and played offense and defense. And we were unscored on and undefeated for two years.

We just wanted to knock somebody down to allow Patti Irwin or Pat Rodgers to run off left guard or to tackle the opposing halfback with no gain. This was our glory. Our practices could be brutal and were unsupervised. Bad things happened. Joe Zummo, Jim Ptac, Marty McDonough and Bob Ferguson carried Joe Filpi off the scrimmage field and placed him gently on the grass in the little shade that was available. His left lower leg faced south and his left foot pointed north. Joe Filpi had blocked on his last play for the Lincoln Park Rams. Joe was stoic. Even when a few minutes later Vic Feraci, blocking for Guy Maniscalo in a practice play, tripped over Joe' ankle, he only cursed moderately loud. Joe was loaded into Vic's car and taken home and then to Henrotin Hospital. We had no insurance and no trainers.

The games were all pickup games against four or five other teams. Many teams had players much bigger than us who had played varsity at the larger high schools but didn't go on to college. We beat them, anyway.

In some games there were differences of opinion on certain plays, blocks or tackles. We had no umpires or referees to clarify where the fault should lie. This problem was solved in a direct fashion. For example, Joe Zummo was about to tackle an opposing halfback at the line of scrimmage. However, Joe was blocked from behind. Clearly this was illegal. Joe, trying to be nonjudgmental, thought the player was not being malicious but perhaps didn't understand the basic rules as well as we did. So Joe, wanting to always improve the quality of the game, sought out the attention of the offending player by lifting the player's helmet and punching him in the mouth. Joe was not blocked from behind again.

There were not many spectators at the games but we did have several dozen enthusiastic supporters who came to some games. At times they became emotional on our behalf. If they felt the game was not going as expected, meaning the Rams were losing or if they decided that an opposing player was playing dirty, in their enthusiasm they would rush onto the field to lend their support. This support consisted of punching, kicking, and stomping opponents. With this action the game was mutually declared officially over.

The attraction of football for us was not the well-executed play, nice uniforms, or willingness to give our all for coach or school. It was the sweetness, the high of throwing your padded body at your opponent as you could in no other sport.

The open field tackle, the break-your-nose stiff-arm, the smash-face forearm and the low block that knocked the guy down -- these were the enjoyable parts of the game. And if we won, so much the better.

Adults eventually did get involved but to their detriment. Joe Rossi somehow from somewhere became our coach. We didn't need a coach and did no better with or without him. But he made the mistake of over-estimating our maturity. He was a stocky, Italian man of maybe thirty-five or forty with sad eyes and hardly smiled. Way too serious for us.

At the end of a successful season he decided to throw a banquet and pass out an award to the player of the year. About twenty-five players were invited. Joe Rossi set up the whole thing at a local restaurant and was to pick up the tab. The dinner was scheduled to start at 7 p.m. At 8 p.m., Patti Irwin and I, feeling very guilty, decided to go to the banquet instead of going to the movies. Joe and his wife were the only people present. Patti got the award and we ate the meal.

Adults just didn't read us well.

CHAPTER SEVEN: THE SOFT WALL

Part One: Girls, Sex, and Social Life

Charlie Martinez

Open the fly, free your instrument, think bad thoughts (frequently not necessary to induce required tumescence), and then begin the masturbatory sequence.

We were quiet in the back house on Schiller Street. That dark, cool, smelly, wonderfully spooky place especially when Mr. Bartali's big red barn cast its shadow as the sun set. Any parent or older sister or brother looking toward the back house would be pleased with the quiet of our group. Some days we played ghosts in the back house but today we played a game of spin the bottle. We were all eight or nine years old at the most because I moved from Schiller Street to North Park Avenue at age nine. Who was in the spin the bottle group? I remember my brother Ken, my cousin Nancy Kennedy who lived next door, likely Gus Johns, Walter Gibbons, the Cullerton brothers and their sister. Spin the bottle as you sat in a circle. Kiss the one of the opposite sex the bottle points to. The strange, new rubbing together of lips and taste of spit.

Forward. Nine or ten. Yes! Must have been first half of sixth grade. We had a beautiful young nun. Can't remember her name. She told us a joke. "Mary had a little lamb and also had a bear. We often saw her little lamb but never saw her bear." Did the nun understand what she said? Must have. We all knew instantly the point of the joke.

The big nun in seventh grade looked across the room at me. What did she want? She stared at me and then pounded down the aisle. "Bring your hands out from under the desk to the top at once." Of course I complied. She probably weighed three times what I did, was a nun, had the cross hanging from her belt, had the backing of my parents, pastor, other priests, old ladies of the parish, the alderman, precinct captain, Knights of Columbus, Mayor Kennelly, and the Vatican. But why was she so mad? I knew. I knew. I could have articulated it, but never to her. I brought my hands up that incidentally were not engaged in anything more evil than slapping at my knees.

Down in the dark place where nuns could not venture, Jimmy Foley invited us to partake of the fruit of good and evil. He held a class in manual dexterity in the boys' bathroom. His instructions were clear. Irwin, Nicolini, Turk, Zummo and I listened and watched his demonstration. Open the fly, free your instrument, think bad thoughts (frequently not necessary to induce required tumescence), and then begin the masturbatory sequence. This may have been our earliest sex instruction, probably fifth or sixth grade.

Jimmy Foley not only demonstrated first-hand application of his knowledge, he also acquired textbooks to supplement the course, as you will see.

One Friday afternoon we were lined up for what today you would call a field trip. Sister Anna Marie scrutinized the eighth grade student line through her thick glasses, which exaggerated the size of her eyes.

The nun tried to look serious but we knew her as a softy with a plumpness to go with it. The line formed up in twos with the girls leading and the boys to the rear. She observed our behavior with her hands hidden beneath the outer part of her habit. Her heavy rosary hung on her side attached to a thick, black belt. The starched chalk white of the habit encircling her face and upper chest was set off against the loose ink black of the rest of the habit. When she perceived that we were under control and could be trusted to walk two blocks down a city street without bringing scandal upon our families, our school, our church, our country and ourselves, she took one hand out from under the front of her habit and raised it with the second and third fingers pointing at us.

She then signaled with a slight waggle of the hand to begin our march out of the schoolyard and north up North Park Avenue towards North Avenue and the Plaza Theater. We were about to undergo a religious experience by being exposed to a special showing of *Song of Bernadette* starring Jennifer Jones. It was fall, 1947.

We first passed the two-story brick convent that housed all the nuns, the inside of which I never saw yet I had lived directly across from it for thirteen years. Johnny Nicolini lived in a red three-flat next to the convent. I imagined his mother's fat face pressed against the third floor window, watching our progress and looking for Johnny to make sure he was in absolute obedience and pleased that he was to undergo a religious exposure. Hanging in a first-floor window was a small cloth, bordered in gold with a single gold star on a field of white. This signified Mrs. Johnson as a Gold Star Mother because of the loss of her son in the Second World War.

We passed a dreary storefront building where Pete Eichel spent several miserable years living with rats and roaches in the back apartment. Nick "Fuzz" Gullo lived a few doors away. He was the terror of the street and people ran from him in fright but the reasons were never clear. They claimed he had a "plate" in his head from an accident and that had damaged his brain. Only my brother Ken could match him punch for punch and did not back down.

Across the street, next to my house, were two three-flat brick buildings that held the Irish ghetto of North Park Avenue. Then came Mary McCarter's frame two-flat. She was an old friend of my sister Maryellen. I stood in her dining room one evening when I was eight. I was with my sister, Maryellen. They were discussing some neighbor, and the fact that the neighbor had cancer was revealed. Mary McCarter pointed her finger at me and said I was never to reveal this to anyone. I was accidentally entrusted with this astonishing secret of which I understood nothing. The fact that a priest lived in that house intrigued my young mind. How could this be? I only knew of priests living in the rectory. Why would he be there? I never learned the reason and not even viable rumors were ever forthcoming.

The next few buildings, on the west side of the street before you got to IC lot, were an outpost of hillbillies. They just didn't fit in. I don't think anyone talked to them, let alone socialized with them. For a while they opened a grocery store in the three-story brick of the group with a storefront but the shelves were almost bare. I was sent to get a loaf of bread there once and ran out after the purchase because of the oil and urine odors in the place. Later, as a runaway, I would spend a night trying to sleep in the hallway of that building. Once a fight between two women from that building caught my attention. They were in front of the store. They slapped, scratched and wrestled each other, but the best part for a young boy occurred when a blouse was ripped exposing a breast.

Jimmy Foley, who was always thinking ahead and looking out for our welfare, decided we should not waste this religious experience. He wanted us in the proper frame of mind to sit through the solemn, nonsensical and unbelievable piece of moviemaking we would be forced to endure.

He began to distribute religious texts, which we reverently called eight-page bibles. These were what you might call sex manuals consisting of eight pages in the format of a two-by-four-inch comic book. This illustrated book approach helped those who did not yet read at grade level. To ensure variety and avoid boredom, each bible featured a familiar cartoon character of the day in the title role. There was Popeye, Wimpy, Superman, The Phantom, Smilin' Jack and so on. The eight-page bibles would enlighten the reader to the most prolific sexual exploits of the main character, all with exaggerated prowess and genitalia. The bibles were passed back and forth through the line from girls to boys and back again. The nuns did notice a quieting of the group but likely attributed this to each student being lost in his own religious thoughts concerning the oncoming experience at the Plaza Theater.

There was a danger for the students in enjoying and handling the bibles. If one was found out, all would be punished no matter who introduced them to the group. There could be excommunication, perhaps some burning at the stake, castration (boys), forced into a nunnery (girls), brought before a committee of the old ladies of the parish, heads shaved (girls and boys), and worst of all, the parents would be informed.

A likely penance after we would be forced to have our confessions heard by the priest was three Hail Marys, three Our Fathers, and three Glory Be to Gods. (The more pious boys would willingly add several ejaculations—if they had not already done so on the way to the movie.)

But Sister Ann Marie never gave an indication that she knew we were practicing religious indifferentism; that is, reading a different bible. Jimmy Foley had triumphed again and our religious education continued to be a strange mixture of sex and non-sex.

Still the burning question remained uppermost in our twelve- and thirteen-year-old male minds: What was it like? What *was* it like? Softball, ledge ball, kick the can, football, serving as altar boys, school ... all these activities kept us distracted but when we were in our secret places, that one thought pushed aside all others.

On a summer night, sweating and stinking from playing touch football in the street, we moved toward a favorite and convenient secret place, which we called King's Hallway. It was the entranceway to the artists' building next to Mary Joyce's store. First to enter was the great one, Gus Johns. He sat on the inner doorstep and we disciples arranged ourselves pushing and shoving on the floor in front of him. Latecomers had to stand at the doorway. Gus was thin, past gaunt, almost at the level of emaciated. He was a walking anatomy lesson for human muscles. Every muscle was outlined. There was no fat anywhere on his body. He had a distinct resemblance to Boris Karloff. But Gus had qualities we all envied. He was a superb softball player and also a good basketball and football player. In addition, there was an aura around him that spoke of his role as *the caretaker of knowledge gained from experience.*

Exactly how he acquired this knowledge, we could not tell. However, we felt that part of his talent related to his grandmother. She was said to be Greek Orthodox but her darkened house with holy statues, many doilies on never-used, overstuffed furniture that crowded the tiny rooms; the strung beads at doorways instead of doors; and the faint odor of incense convinced us that a gypsy element was present somewhere in Gus's background.

After the group had quieted down, the great one decided it was time to give us knowledge that none of us in our wildest dreams thought he could discover on his own. Gus sat slightly elevated, seen dimly in the shadows with legs crossed under him. He surveyed the group and then spoke:

"It is like putting your dork in warm dough."

We were dumbstruck. What glorious information and he selflessly shared it with us! Gus, the high priest of forbidden experience had taken us into his confidence and we were richer for it.

Frank De Monte as told by Charlie Martinez

Somebody says, here comes this girl. I jumped into line, not sure what the hell I was getting in line for.

Frank DeMonte was driving his body as fast as its legs would work west on Evergreen Street. I crossed over and met up with him under the L.

"Frankie," I says. "Where ya goin'?"

Frankie was a couple years younger than me: but a likable guy always laughing and telling jokes. At this time he was about eleven. "I'm goin' home for supper," he says.

As we walked he related a pathetic story, which was interspersed with almost asphyxiating spasms of laughter.

"We had just got done playing ledge ball in Franklin School yard. Somebody says, here comes this girl. Everybody started getting in line. I jumped into line, not sure what the hell I was getting in line for. And I was the last guy in line. So you would figure there were like twenty guys ahead of me, right? I couldn't see the front part of the line and when they did what they did with her, they didn't say nothing when they came by. They would wave, and then they were gone. The line is movin' slow and I know I gotta be home by 5:30. I have no idea of what or how I'm gonna do anything. I figure maybe I'd get a blowjob, but I didn't know what to expect. But 5:30 comes, the line is still long, and I says, 'I gotta go home for supper.' I never did get to do anything. I went home."

Funny thing is we never seemed to have one of those other twenty guys in our group.

Jack La Brasca

Our social life consisted of getting dressed up on a Saturday night and go to Tony the Wop's place which was the candy store.

In seventh and eighth grade we were dating. We would go downtown, three guys with three girls and go to a movie. The United

Artists, or to the Woods Theater. We'd stop somewhere for a milkshake, then get on the streetcar and come home. Sometimes the girls would have parties at their house in the projects over south of Oak Street. Girls didn't form part of our group. No they did not. When I was in high school I was a pretty good dresser. Yeah, 'cause I worked after school and I bought my own clothes and I'd go to Smokey Joe's on Maxwell Street or at Litton's. I mean I always had, you know, a pair of pegged pants with outer seams and suede box shoes.

We used to go to the dances at St. Andrew's. Of course, usually, nobody danced. It was usually a brawl. You know, you walked in and all of a sudden there'd be a Joe Russo throwing punches somewhere.

Our social life consisted of getting dressed up on a Saturday night and go to the candy store. Tony the Wop's place was the candy store, which was owned by a guy, named Ben after Tony the Wop was incarcerated for rape. They raped somebody in the place and a guy by the name of Ben, an Italian guy who had a severe handicap, bought it. We would hang out there. We had our own jukebox and put our own records in there, which was usually jazz. We would meet there and get a couple a bottles and have a few drinks. Or we wind up going downtown to the show. You know, one guy would pay then they'd open the side door, everybody would slide in.

Or, we'd you know, go down to the clubhouse. The older guys, the veterans from World War II, had a place where they usually went down and gambled on Friday, Saturday and Sunday. It was a room in a three-flat. But they let us use it during the weekday if we wanted it. It was on Sedgwick Street about two doors from Mrs. Crapa, Paul Davies' grandma's place. On Sedgwick, between Locust and Hill.

Maybe one guy in our neighborhood was going steady in those days. We thought that was cool. That was like a daydream. To find some woman that was easy. That is what people talked about. Constantly. It was probably the same thing in the neighborhoods of San Diego and San Francisco and, Bronx, New York. We would get an occasional date. I remember Cookie Marcela and I would scrub up a date one way or another to go to the Harvest Moon Festival at the

Stadium. That was every November. They had dance contests. That was a big event for us.

Michael Lutazzi

Yeah, we went to wedding receptions uninvited. You gotta go late.

You know I went to St. Michael's High School. Lot of nicely dressed girls. As far as interacting with them ah, socially … I mean like doing things in school … naw I don't remember none of that. It was always with the guys. There was some times we'd get together at somebody's house where the parents were not home and we just sit around and neck. Oh, if you were lucky, you know, one time some girl would let you feel her tit. But screwing was rare. It just happens, like I say, to the girls who, those poor kids who didn't have any friends. That was later.

Girls were attractive, you know. Everybody was a potential girlfriend. But did I have steady girls? No, no, no. That was a waste of time.

Before Third Base, there was a joint on Sedgwick Street. Marie's. A Puerto Rican lady owned it. We used to go there. Sedgwick and Evergreen. We also hung around St. Michael's schoolyard. Used to go to Trio's Pizza on North Avenue. Olivette Institute a lot. There's nowhere else to go, you know that's why it was there.

You get a few guys, a few girls, you go to the park, you hang around, you know. As far as the pot ah, that wasn't such a big deal at that age. That came later, really. But mostly hanging around with girls and guys and maybe once in a while having a bottle of beer on the sneak. You got a few pennies, buy a hamburger. Kissing girls, that was a big target area.

And then high school, we used to sometimes skip a couple a classes, go over to Russo's house, take a girl over there from high school. The mother and father both worked. We used to go over there and smoke pot and listen to jazz. Joe and I went to Washburn. Steve did too. Steve was ah, a year or two ahead of us.

Washburn was close to Joe's house. Sedgwick and Division and Joe lived on Scott Street, which was right there … you know, near Oscar Mayer's. We'd take a girl there an have a little sex.

She wasn't like when we were younger, like the kids in the neighborhood where everybody would bang her, you know. Just a couple of guys. She liked sex and she liked to experiment, and not a lot of people knew about this stuff, you know. She wasn't screwing everybody. But there were a couple of girls in the neighborhood who were. So and so's here, let's get the car. And you get a car and you go park it somewhere and it's like a fucking line. It was awful. I mean looking back … that night it was great.

Yeah, we went to wedding receptions uninvited. You gotta go late. You'd just go and kinda hang around the bar. And everybody knew you were uninvited, you know. Try and meet girls. Drink. Everybody gets served at a wedding, right. I don't khow old we were but we'd go to a wedding and you're seventeen, eighteen. You're gonna get a drink.

Later at eighteen and for a few years we hung around a tavern called Magrini's at Wells and Schiller streets. All guys mostly. Very few girls came in there. I don't know why. Half of the guys smoked pot, the other half were drinkers. But it was, it was comfortable in there. And there was all these older Irish guys from North Park Avenue. It was a fun place. And then yeah, you'd venture out to other places, you know. As a young man I heard a lot of jazz all over the city. It was always usually with two or three or four guys.

I dated. You know. Ya get a date. Not often. Once in a while you'd meet a girl and you'd take her out, you know. But we were always looking for women. But we always went to Magrini's. We wasn't using our heads. And you could go to Lincoln Park and find women.

And these guys from the Olivet. You know, these fucking guys, they were going where there was broads, you know. Lot of girls and we wasn't. We were happy with each other. I was hanging around with a lot of guys who loved football. That was their life.

Joe Zummo

You had sort of a sterile existence in the sex area

My experience with sex in grammar school with girls was very limited. The sex part was almost non-existent. I remember playing spin the bottle and doing some smooching at the parties. One of my girlfriends was Bonnie Pauline. That was a classic puppy love and we were sort of sweet on each other in grammar school but once we got out of grammar school she dumped me for some more sophisticated guys I think.

Going to Cathedral High that was coeducational, that was a lot better. The only place that you could meet a girl was at a party. Rarely did you take anybody out. So you went to parties and may have done a little dancing although that took a lot of courage. In high school is where I met my wife Winnie. I didn't take her out till February of my senior year because for the first time in the history of the school it had an evening dance.

That was a hell of a night because my friend Chuckie Martinez's brother got married that night. I didn't have a car so I don't know how I did it but I picked her up at her house and then went to Cathedral's dance. I ended up by dating her which was mainly going to the movies by bus and then took her to the prom. That summer I dated her till I went away to college. You had sort of a sterile existence in the sex area.

Jay Pistone

Our life was real different because we didn't have much of a social life.

When I went to Waller High I didn't get involved with the girls. No, cause I didn't live in the area. I went out with a few. Ya know I mean? In our neighborhood there weren't that many white girls, so there wasn't that much social things. We had no dances or anything.

We used to jump in the car and go to Indiana. There was houses out there, you know, house of prostitution? I was ah, sixteen, fifteen. It cost five dollars, six dollars. And you know you pick out the girl. They didn't check your age. You know. As long you had the money. Gary, Indiana had a lot ah houses of ill repute. We'd jump in the car five, six guys. And go to Gary. That was our big deal. Our life was real different because we didn't have much of a social life. We were involved in sports a lot. Very competitive. We played the black kids, the Polish kids. And we all worked. But socially there wasn't that much. Then I got in the service and I came back, and all was a little different.

Pat Rogers

I took a vow of chastity for seven years.

One of my first interests was Marlene Inchon. I think she was in eighth grade and I was in seventh grade. We used to play post office over at her dad's place on Division at Lake Shore Drive. He was the janitor over there. I can still remember the searing lips upon lips at that time. There weren't groups of guys and girls hanging around together. Not at twelve. No. A little later.

One winter night we were walking out on Lake Michigan at Division Street, as far out as the first ladder. And I broke through the ice. Yeah, broke through the ice. I went down. This was like late January or February. And by time I got across Lake Shore Drive into her dad's apartment my entire pants leg was frozen. You know. I was very lucky I didn't drown right at that point in time. Why do you walk out there? It's there. You know. Somebody dared you so you did it.

Of course as Marlene went over to Wells High School, she forgot about little old me. You know. But that was kind of my first crush. I understand she left Wells High School with that black singer, that French singer who is still around to this day. Eartha Kitt! That was what Pat Fitzgerald told me.

Actually Marlene went with Ernie Taylor if you remember Ernie Taylor. And I think that would have turned her against men.

Yeah, he was crazy. He was run over by a streetcar as a young kid. Very beautiful body, great swimmer. He was just a malicious kid. He gave me a crack and Frankie, my older brother, found out about it. I was in eighth grade. We were at a party at Billie Boyle's house and Ernie was there. Frankie just beat the hell out of him and threw him down the stairs. I was about thirteen and Ernie was about sixteen at the time, and he was a bully. There were some of those.

No, nothing happened in high school. I mean if you were looking to score really, you weren't gonna score there. You'd go down to the Chicago Theater and you could score.

Girls galore at the Chicago Theater. They were just looking to find somebody to hold hands and kiss and neck. It was very common for ten or fifteen of us to go down to the Chicago Theater. One guy would buy a ticket, go in and open the side door and everybody would go in. Yeah. We saw Sinatra.

I don't recall much sexual activity when I was a senior. I actually met my first wife then and I took a vow of chastity for seven years. Even when I was in the Marine Corps I wouldn't have any sexual activity at all till I got married.

Yeah I took a vow of chastity. I did, because I loved her. That's not to say I always kept it. We did break up occasionally. Let me tell you honestly, you know at that age all the gaming that goes on, I really walked away from a lot of relationships in the Marine Corps and here in Chicago area.

Charlie Martinez

The guy did imply he had a gun but in no way was he going to give it to a imitation Al Capone.

The Rams' Dance. What a sweet sound but what an incongruous reality it represented. With this dance, the Rams now completed the mission of their title as a social-athletic club. But how could this be? How could twenty or thirty guys, all underage at eighteen to twenty, meet with businessmen who owned the Belmont Hotel and rent their ballroom for a dance serving liquor? Did these men have no sense? Who cares? Certainly not the Rams. And can you imagine that one of us that met with the manager was Joe Russo? He was five feet five, had black greased-back hair with a ducktail. He wore Frankenstein box-toed shoes, billowy tapered gabardine pants, open collar shirt, and a black raincoat that came to his ankles and past his wrists. He talked liked a gangster from a movie and had immense self-confidence.

We sold hundreds of tickets at about five dollars each. What we did with the excess money, I never knew. The place was packed. Besides beer and liquor sold openly, there was an underground market of marijuana, red devils, probably some shooting up of heroin in the bathrooms and of course some adventurous people mixed liquor and drugs.

Many people came without dates and some with dates. I brought Monica. This was I think in the early spring of 1955. It was one of our first dates. Somehow, we ended up at a table sitting across from a girl named Mary. It might have been because Steve Russo was dating Mary's sister. I can't remember her last name but I had taken her home several times from the tavern on Sedgwick Street near Armitage Avenue.

That tavern was our local hangout for a while. All of us were underage for drinking, but the owner didn't care. He wanted the sales. One glorious night, the police raided the place. As they came in the front door, we dove out the windows and ran out the back door. The cops didn't chase us. They probably stopped for a free beer.

This Mary lived a block away on the third floor. We had necked in the hallway each time and once I left my athletic bag with my college books and notebooks on the stairs. The next time I took her home, her father opened the door and gave me the bag. He smiled and said, "What kind of college guy forgets his books." I always thought he was proud that his daughter was going out with a college type. Actually I never did take her out on a date. Well anyway, she must have thought I was going to ask her to the Rams' dance. All night she glared across the table at us. Of course, we didn't talk. But what amazed me, Monica later made comments about Mary as if she could have read my mind.

Now the evening became well lubricated with alcohol and drugs and some minimal pushing and shoving was beginning between the guys. We didn't really expect trouble because we were all essentially from the same neighborhood and gang. For some reason the manager of the hotel started getting anxious. Joe Russo, Patti Irwin and I went to his office to talk things out. Evidently about eighty percent of the guys at the dance looked like extras in a gangster movie and this made him very nervous. He was worried about handling several thousand dollars in cash.

Joe Russo had a solution. Why not get the gun Joe was sure the guy had in his desk and give it to Joe? Joe would then police the place and prevent any robbery. This seemed like a logical solution if you had a cheese pizza for a brain. The guy did imply he had a gun but in no way was he going to give it to an imitation Al Capone.

Well, things went along all right and the dance broke up at about midnight. Again, greedy adults ignored their common sense and allowed hundreds of underage teenagers to have a wonderful time and make some money too.

John Giovenco

Sports was the biggest part of my activity. Very little dating. Didn't have a car.

There was a girl next door that I liked in grammar school. Her name was Cookie. But I never had a girl friend. There was always the guys. I remember one party over at Paula's house. There were some cute girls there. Barbara Galluzo, Alice Kuhn. I remember walking around that party with a hard-on all night long. I could not sit up or stand up. That was in seventh or eighth grade.

In third and fourth year of high school there was parties. Sports was the biggest part of my activity. Very little dating. Didn't have a car.

Yeah. Went to movies. Same place. 152, Plaza. Occasionally went downtown. Sometimes went all the way as far as Clark Street. It was all within the neighborhood. Same circle of friends, same groups.

We'd hang out at the local drugstore. You're doing nothing, hanging out.

I never had a curfew. Nope. No discussion with my mother or father about that. I had no rules or restrictions like that.

At the lake, I remember there were a couple girls there, but never did anything. Never talked to them or anything. Just knew there were a couple of girls there.

Peter Eichel

Aw, shit. Well, you know, no we didn't have friends who were girls. And that's terrible. We did have girlfriends. We were hanging around Wally's, which was on Sedgwick Street, right around the corner from Evergreen. Next to Wally there was a tavern. The shoemaker shop was on the other side. But the tavern was north, okay? And the Rangusos lived there.

There were two daughters. And one was younger, and the older one was very attractive and had fully developed breasts at age fifteen or sixteen. Yeah, right. I remember her especially because Mike Lutazzi had always pictured himself as this lover, and was working desperately to seduce her. And she seduced me.

Naw, Mike didn't believe it. He didn't wanna believe that it happened, you know, because here he had been working so hard, but it was kinda funny. And after that, then I went out with her younger sister.

We'd go to the show. And we'd go to the lake. And I'd rather go to the lake than go to the show, because we had bathing suits on and I could take her bathing suit top down and I remember how wonderful that was. I mean there was nothing like that in the world. But that's all we did. You know, I didn't have intercourse. You know thinking back, I could have. But I wasn't sophisticated enough. And my idea back then was that you didn't do that with nice girls. Or with somebody you liked or you were going out with. You just did that with the girls in the neighborhood who hada reputation for being promiscuous. And they were several, you know. I'm not going to mention their names. But man, they were promiscuous, you talk about promiscuous. There were at least two girls in the neighborhood that got laid by everybody. And I mean everyone was laying 'em. You know.

Dates? Well I always had somebody that I was doing something with. We did things. I went to the show. There were two or three different groups that of girls that I was involved with and had been dating. I'm trying to remember her name. Liz Masterson. I don't remember that group. And who was her girlfriends? Peggy, Peggy McCullough. There were six or seven of them and we hung around as a group with them and then there were the Italian group.

I was on a blanket with Joanie at Schiller Street at the lake swimming. And I was making out with her on the blanket and somebody asked her why she was fooling with that little kid, and she was only a year older than me, you know. In all my life I've been hearing that crap and I still hear it.

So there was a group of girls there that we did hang around. I said we didn't but that's not true because we did kinda hang around with them. What other group was there? There was the group that called themselves the Ramettes from Mundelein. I don't remember their names, but they were kinda the nicest bunch of kids that I can remember. But they very quickly became disillusioned because you know when they really got to know us we were pretty coarse, pretty rude. All right, pretty vulgar. You know. That didn't last very long. But at least it was, you know, something.

The drinking was a real problem. In fact I'm thinking maybe for the first time just to what extent that drinking problem was underlying some of that destructive behavior. Because we'd get drunk and that's when stuff would happen. And probably sober, you know we may not have gotten into some of the problems that we had.

Joe Olita

Here I am like a god damn idiot chasing her up the stairs with my schwanz hanging out.

I never had one girlfriend in high school. No. No. No. As a matter of fact none of us did. No, we liked to play the field. As we got older, you know, we had a term, "If you're going home with the Tribune tonight we'll meet ya at the restaurant." And there was a restaurant called Patsy's restaurant. "Going home with the Tribune" means you didn't pick a girl up.

Yeah if we didn't pick up a girl, we would go to Patsy's and we'd sit there and ah have a little dish of pasta before we went home. At any given Saturday night there were always be two or three guys there out of maybe six or seven.

But I liked clothes a lot. 'Cause I always thought that if you looked good, the women came for you. I mean that was really the motivation. How can I make myself attractive so I can have a lot of female friends, you know. And of course the object of female friends was to have a lot of sex. You know, basically that's what it was. I mean, it wasn't to fall in love or anything like that you know. And not to talk to. Who the hell wants to talk to a female? I mean, that would be ridiculous. It would be way out of context, you know. So that was really the only motivation for having female acquaintances, you know.

The place that we frequented was Paradise Ballroom, which was located on Pulaski Road. I think it was just north of Washington Boulevard. And we went there a lot. The reason we went there it was a big place in an Italian neighborhood. They'd have a big band that played. There were twenty-four numbers that they would play.

Never, never took a gal to the ballroom, never. But what I would do is I had a place where I stood all the time. That was my spot, see. And then I had numbers that I would have with certain women. Well, you know if it was dance number five, six, seven, eight. They'd come and they'd say, well our dance is number five. And another one would say ours is seven and I'd say okay, fine. They'd know where to come and get me. I never went to them. I would just stand in my spot and the girls would come and say come on this is our dance and I say okay and we'd get out there and we'd dance. Now if I had an empty slot, then I would go looking around. See. But generally I would say, half the time, more than half the time, the dance numbers would be filled up.

I was a pretty good dancer. The majority of the women that I actually had dance numbers with were women that I was not interested in sexually. I might even consider them like a sister to me. And were they involved sexually with somebody else? I don't know and I don't care. That never occurred to me, I never thought about it. But that was not my bag with them. It was just to go out and dance.

I never had a car during this time. Couldn't afford it. If one of our friends' parents had a car, he would take the car on a Saturday night and we'd all jump on to the car and go. You were always risking how you were gonna come home. Because if the fellow that had the car got lucky that night, you had to find another way to get home. And we understood that; there was never a question of, no you take us home. That's not the way it was.

I remember the oldest of my two buddies, Mario. He would tell me "Every woman will say 'no,' but every woman wants to get laid." One day I took a gal home from the dance. I had to take her home on a streetcar 'cause I didn't have any means of transportation. I had to be something like maybe nineteen years old at the most. I had to be older than that, maybe twenty. So I get her home and she lived on the third floor of this building. We were exchanging a few kisses and, pretty soon I'm trying to get a few feels on her and she's not going for this.

This friend of mine, Mario, who was a short little guy and had said, "When they refuse you," he said, "zip your pants down and pull it out." And you'll be all set. And so I said, well I'm gonna use Mario's strategy. So I zip my pants down, I pull it out and she starts running up the stairs and here I am like a goddamn idiot chasing her up there with my schwanz hanging out. And I went up two and half flights of stairs and I said, "What the hell am I doing, her father'll come out with a goddamn gun and kill me." And immediately ran down the stairs and went out. I saw Mario the next day. I said, you know Mario you're the biggest goddamn asshole I've ever known in my life. I tried that strategy; I almost got myself killed yesterday.

"Well I didn't tell you it was gonna work with everyone."

I said, "You did." But that was one of the stupid things that had occurred, yeah.

Frank DeMonte

Did I have sex? You mean did we have any trim?

There were no girls in our neighborhood. There was just boys. At least that's what I remember. I know there were girls in my grammar school, but they weren't in my neighborhood, they came from other neighborhoods. No girls involved. Not at all. Never. There was one maybe and that was Carol Guerney. Carol Guerney was in our class and there's other girls like Maryellen Feeney, Charlene Condon. But outside of class there was no association. I don't think I remember going on a date in grammar school.

I was three years at De Paul High School. No girls were ever involved. Nope. Now that doesn't mean we didn't have dates. Sure we got dates. I dated in high school but did we have girlfriends? No. Friends that were girls? Not really.

On a date was the only time we were involved with girls. Otherwise, we were mostly around the guys. Maybe they came to DePaul High School games. But there wasn't like a crowd ... no, no. I mean, all I was thinking about in grammar school and high school was sports. Sports and being around guys that I know. And having a good time.

Maybe in my senior year I had a steady girl. Yeah. I did go to the prom. In high school who did I take to the prom? Yeah, I took a girl by the name of Patty Bonine.

Did I have sex? You mean, you mean did we have any trim? Did we have any trim? Let me tell you something...tried a lot. I had some encounters, but it wasn't intercourse it was just some petting stuff. I was always afraid I was gonna get in trouble. All the people knew our family, you know. You weren't gonna fool around with somebody.

John Owens

We'd sit and drink and then I'd screw her, you know.

No, no girls hung around with the guys in grammar school. Not in grammar school. We had nothing to do with 'em. Well, yeah I did. There was one. But she lived on, I guess on Evergreen. Julie was her name. There was a little grammar school there. I started going out with her a little bit, you know. Franklin School, yeah, yeah. Probably my second year high school. I never took her out.

I used to go over to her house. When her mother and father were not home during the day. I used to go over and fuck her. And she had an aunt that lived on, you're talking about the Gold Coast. She lived in a hotel right off of Elm and State, right on the corner. A really nice place in those days. And her aunt would be out of town sometimes and I used to go by her house there, you know. We'd sit and drink and then I'd screw her, you know. But I don't remember if I ever took her out to the show or anything.

Charlie Martinez

Patti Irwin assumed the role of our group's literary leader. He read books we all longed for but that needed to be hidden from view of teachers, parents, most other adults, priests, and nuns. He was the unnamed official selector of what books to read and therefore dictated our tastes in literature. His selections did not stray from Mickey Spillane paperbacks, *I, The Jury*... and similar writing. The *Amboy Dukes* interested us because we identified with the gang lifestyle of the hero but of course our existence didn't involve that much bloodshed or sex.

How we pored over those pages sniffing out the most violent, macho passages and the most sexually explicit paragraphs. Patti gave his official explanations and deep critique to these areas. We were in awe. The plots were a tolerated part of the books as long as they moved the violence, machismo, and sex along. We spent many happy hours in his class and of course never questioned his conclusions. He gave these freely in a benign, pleasant way that left no need for questions.

Jim Sullivan

Never had a girlfriend in high school. Not really.

In grammar school I had a couple girls that I had like a crush on, you know. Girlfriends like dating? Naw, no girl friends like that but a couple girls that you know, like to play spin the bottle with, you know.

There was a number of girls like Dorothy Beck, Barbara Donavan, Audi Mauon, ah, the LaDulci girl that hung around where we hung around. We'd all hang around at Muzzie's and that's where they were. You know they were part of like the clique, you know. And later on they moved to Mason's, a candy store, which was on the corner of Wells and Goethe. And later on, Third Base opened up just south of Evergreen on Wells.

Never had a girlfriend in high school. Not really.

Bunny Byrne

She says "you guys wanna watch me take a bath." And oh, yeah, yeah. We go for that.

Yeah, well we hung out everywhere you know. The Heimsoth's drugstore was on the opposite corner. And Mary Joyce's was up on North Park. Then we had Tanke's drugstore was were Foley worked and got a lot of supplies for the club. That's where the jars of marshmallow and chocolate and everything came from.

But anyway, we had some great parties. Angela Scaletta lived just south of Evergreen. We had a big party at her house when her parents weren't home once. The mother and father came in the front door and we all went out the window. From the second floor. Dove into a grass yard next door to it. About seven of us went out that window. Yeah, we all ran, you know. That was probably just about grammar school. She went to grammar school with us. So that was grammar school.

The girls hung around our crowd. And you know believe it or not that's exactly the way it was. The girls were the followers. We never followed a girl around anywhere it seemed like. They followed us. They invited us to all their parties. And we'd go to the parties and eat the food.

We all had girlfriends. We went pretty steady. When I was in senior year, a girl just came to the school brand new. Brand new. Her and a, three of them came. Two in our class and one in the class behind us. And she just happened to be sitting in front of me. And I didn't know her from a bale of hay. Well, we started bullshitting and talking and we started going out together.

Took her to the prom. I was from the North Side, she was from the West Side. See, we did all our planning in school. I'd say, "Okay, you want to go to the movies Friday night. All right." The Marlboro Theater was out there by her house. Oh, we'll go to the movie. I'd go get her at her house. I knew her parents. I mean, that was from like from September when we went to school, I went out with her till the day we left. And then when we left, she was gone. I went out with her steady and never saw her again.

We had a club. A club over on Sedgwick and Evergreen, behind Vince's house. It was just our club. It was a, a shed, we called a club. We just played cards, hung out. In grammar school, yeah. Everybody got in. But you know, it was usually to do mischief; we washed Zummo's hair with chocolate and it was like … certain guys got in just so we could abuse 'em.

Wally's was there too. That was a hangout. Wally's right, right at the corner there.

Another time, there was a woman gonna take a bath. And ah, she invited us all up. We had the club downstairs. She was right above the club. Yeah. She was renting from Vince's uncle. She had told us this one day when she was coming home. She says, "You guys wanna watch me take a bath." And oh, yeah, yeah. We go for that, so. It didn't happen then, but when it did happen, I didn't happen to be there. But I guess three or four of the guys did go up. They told me they hadda jump out the window 'cause the Filipino husband who was a waiter came to the door and was pounding on the door. "Who's in there? Who's in there?" And they were in the bathroom watching her take a bath.

Yeah, we used to play pinochle in the club. Well it was Vince's uncle's shed. And there was a dirt floor. It was a club that's all, you know. You hadda give a word. We used to have the word in Italian and you'd go … you'd knock and, and then the guy on the inside would say "Guchi." And then you'd have to holler, "Juno." That was the password. And then you and the guy inside would both have to go (bugle sound). If that didn't happen, you didn't get in. That was the password. It was just a magic time. It really was. Like I said, it was just a absolute magic time.

Ken Martinez

Sent me a Dear John letter with the ring when I was on top of a mountain in Korea during the war.

In grammar school the only girl I remember is Kathleen Maloney. She was the prettiest girl in the room and she had long blond hair. Later on, I went out with girls but not in grammar school, no. We went and had a couple a parties. You know kids have parties and stuff, yeah.

Then there was Kathleen O'Donnell. She lived on Wieland Street. I don't know what happened to her. Never seen her anymore. But ah, I went to her house for parties and you talk, you know. You don't fool around. In those days you didn't fool around because all you had to do was look at a girl wrong and nine times out of ten, she'd get pregnant. So, you never fooled around.

I was sixteen when I met Betty. She had two years of school to go to. When I was in Korea, in the Marines, she sent me the ring. Sent me a Dear John on top of a mountain with the ring. And I came home from Korea when Ma passed away and I took her to her prom.

Yeah, after I got the letter. She was happy to see me, you know. And she didn't think I was coming back and she took back her ring. Then I was in Washington D.C. Then I was ordered to the Philippines.

And then she wrote me a letter in the Philippines that she was getting married.

Charlie Martinez

I was between eight and nine when I slid down the steel tube covering a cable to the telephone pole in the alley next to George Maltezos' apartment. I was surprised by a pleasant sensation in my groin. I tried it again. The same sensation recurred. This was my first conscious sexual pleasure.

The years ten through twelve were a time of increasing interest in those strange creatures with long hair, clean faces, nice clothes and who smiled at anything said or done by boys. I don't remember any conversations with girls. There were spin the bottle games at this time. For some reason I was associated with Mary Condon, not as a boyfriend but as I don't know what.

I remember while still in grammar school, a few of us began playing near Bobby Humberg's house on Scott Street. Again for some reason I became connected with a girl who lived nearby by the name of Eleanor. She gave me her photo and I was intrigued as how different she looked from the guys. Someone drew with chalk one of those large hearts in the street with an arrow through it. Eleanor loves Chuckie was written in the heart. This was across the street from my older brother Tommie's house. I was worried that he would see it and I erased it.

For our eighth grade graduation several of us decided to go on a date to Riverview Park, a huge amusement park at Belmont Street and Western Avenue. I went with my "cousin" Nancy Kennedy who lived next door to me. I found out later she was not a cousin at all. We kissed a few times and that was that. At this time I started to hear stories of other guys have deeper relations and even the suggestion that they had been doing heavy necking. Of course I envied them but had no idea how to ever get close to a girl for this kind of activity. I was mute around girls.

This awkwardness was compounded because I was attending Quigley Preparatory Seminary for two years. This was a high school for training future priests. Of course all dating was frowned upon and if you were found to date or have a girlfriend, you were asked to leave the school. No one told us this was the rule. No one talked against sex more than in the usual religious classes of other schools but this idea circulated among the five hundred boys anyway.

So during this time I had no contact with girls my age, no dates, no necking, no hanging around with any girls in a crowd. But my brain, with hormones swirling, was very active. When not distracted by sports, school, work, or the guys, I felt this intense pressure rising in me. I didn't know what it was but it demanded an outlet. I would confess thoughts of undressing, touching and wishing for contact with girls -- but that was all it amounted to.

So for those two years I wandered again in a fog of distraction, becoming more introverted around girls and women. I marveled at guys who could talk and joke with girls and even get a laugh for a suggestive comment.

At age fifteen I transferred to a small Catholic coed school only three blocks from Quigley. This was Mundelein High School at Chicago Avenue and State Street. Now, although I was freed from the non-dating and non-contact rules of Quigley, I was worse off than before. Many of the other guys in my class at least had some conversations and on occasion even dates with girls in their first two years of high school. Of course some had had heavy petting and necking and shared these tales at lunchtime among the guys. I had no way of knowing if the stories were true but I couldn't confront them because I had no personal knowledge of these activities. It helped that I now went to parties but still no connection to a girl occurred. I just acted silly with the guys and drank a little.

In senior year the pressure was on to find a person to take to the prom at the end of the year. I probably could have asked a dozen girls and would have been accepted. Every girl wanted to go to the senior prom whether she was a freshman or senior. But I was still mute. I did secretly want to approach two girls but did nothing to start a conversation.

Finally I somehow was fixed up with or forced on a date with a sophomore and the sister of the prettiest girl in my senior class. I can't remember how this was arranged but a well-meaning buddy and his girlfriend probably set it up out of pity. I had to go out with her on some kind of group date, perhaps a hayride in the fall. I remember sitting with her on my lap in the front seat of a car. Frank Rodgers and his future wife were in the backseat. I was again mute and Frank kicked the back of the seat to try and get me to say something. I don't recall if I responded. Funny I don't remember the prom except the girl was pretty, especially in her prom gown. I kissed her once and was amazed at her thick lipstick and that was the end of the evening.

Obviously I was still a virgin while several of the guys told me of their conquests. I did not know whether they were real or not but I envied them. But I should say that many of the guys admitted that they were still virgins. Some carried condoms in their wallets, "just in case." So I wasn't totally alone in my misery but most guys still could talk and banter with girls while I was mute.

Part Two: Gays

Charlie Martinez

"All right, who did it?" she bellowed. "What bastard punctured my tires?"

The soggy summer evening brought a crush of us to Third Base, our hamburger joint hangout, for general milling around and doing nothing. Play some ledge ball and then buy a few quarts of beer and go down to the lake? This was the kind of loose planning we kicked around. But then an entertainment of sorts happened upon us. A herald spread the news that two lezies had parked their car in front of the store and went into Tio's Mexican restaurant a few doors south on Wells Street. We didn't use the words gays, homosexuals or lesbians and did not talk about alternative lifestyles; it was just homos, queers, fruits, fags or lezies.

This set off a buzzing which became a subdued frenzy that you knew would mean something's gonna happen. Something had to happen for this trespass. These women represented everything that was repugnant, laughable, foreign, detestable and threatening in some unknown manner to our male adolescent culture. We didn't discuss it; we *sensed* it.

Jimmy Foley was in his official booth at the back of the store, sitting with his captains and surrounded by hangers-on and fellow conspirators. When the whispers reached him, he gave a sly nod and half smile to a lackey. This fawning wannabe quietly left and did his duty.

No consideration or compassion was ever openly expressed for these women. We all went along with whatever punishment our chieftain judged was appropriate for this transgression. We went along with curiosity and awe. Awe for his daring and energy to take action and curiosity for the response of these aliens. We glanced at each other with knowing smugness and enjoyed the rising tension running through us.

We were a pack of wolves waiting for the dominant male to bring in the prize. Our wait was rewarded. With the door slamming behind her, in walked a stereotypic dyke. Shiny, slicked-back, male-cut hair and wearing slacks and a man's collared shirt, she moved fearlessly into the crowd. She was stocky and short.

"All right, who did it?" she bellowed. No one answered but all smiled. Jim Foley and his fellows chuckled and snickered in unison.

"Who did what?" someone shouted from the group.

"What bastard punctured my tires?"

No answer, just suppressed sneers and giggles but we relished her display of anger. Johnny Mathis wailed "little white cloud that cri-ie-ie-d" from the jukebox.

Her face contorted with rage and frustration, she charged out the door but returned ten minutes later with a baffled looking policeman. Accusations and demands for justice were piled on top of denials and alternate explanations till the cop led her out the door so she could ruminate on her hate in private.

Our appetite for intolerance satiated, we went to the lake and drank beer.

Peter Eichel

Shoes and Krupke were supposed to come up and knock him out. Roll him, and we split the take.

Bill Shoes and Krupke used to take me to Lincoln Park to set up queers. Yeah.

Well on each side of Cafe Brauer were men's bathrooms. So you'd go in there and kinda hang around. I did this once. Jesus. We didn't do this as a matter of routine. The pitch they told me I should say was, "It's my brother's birthday and I need money to buy a birthday gift for my brother." Now I don't know whether they were supposed to give me a blowjob or I was supposed to give them a blowjob. But either way, it wasn't too cool.

I went in there and this middle-aged man starts talking to me and I tell him and he says, "Well how much do you need?" And I don't remember the details from there but then we were walking, and the idea is Shoes and Krupke were supposed to come up and knock him out. Roll him, and we split the take. Obviously I wasn't gonna get a full share. But I don't see them; I don't know where they're at. And we are walking and we are walking and finally I said, "You know, I'm tired." And I didn't want to go any further. And I sat down on the park bench, and he sits down next to me and starts making all these funny grunting noises. So finally Bill Shoes and Krupke jump out of the bushes and start punching him. But they don't knock him out. And he starts screaming, like a woman.

And you know that bridge that goes over the lagoon? The big stone one? A policeman is up there with his flashlight and starts saying, "What's going on down there?" Obviously he was afraid, I think, to come over by himself. And Charlie, I started to run and I lived on Clark Street. On that night I didn't even bother to kill the cockroaches or the bedbugs, Okay. I was never so scared in my life. I mean, you talk about cure-all; right then and there I was never again gonna roll anybody.

Pat Rogers

He said you can have your money but he would have to perform on me.

At that time, I was working construction at the end of my sophomore year in high school. One of the local yokels said hey I'll introduce you too to my friend; he'll give you a job in Lake Bluff. I was up there for a week. You know, it was the hardest work I've ever done.

We were working on forms from foundations. I was sixteen at the time. I picked one up and put it on my shoulder. And if the wind caught you right it just almost knocked you off the bluff, into the lake. I was introduced to homosexuality at that time. When I went to get my first paycheck, the guy turned out to be a little acey-deucy. He said you can have your money but he would have to perform on me. Well with that I pushed the guy down the bluff. Yeah. I pushed him down the bluff towards the lake and I got to my ride, got the hell out of there and I never went back. You know. He was a big guy. He was foreman of the job and he turned out he wanted me. You know. I said, "You can't have me." That's all. That was my first job and I didn't get paid for it. I was really pissed off.

Jim Sullivan

> *When he got out of jail he was making money by rolling queers on the lake, you know.*

John Sodos went to jail for burglary. When he got out he was making money by rolling queers on the lake, you know. Once, a couple of us guys were with him and he started to roll a couple of 'em. But they started to fight back and you know, we went from I'd say Schiller Street all the way down to Division Street under the underpass. And along like Banks Street and stuff like that. And these guys are like yelling and screaming and trying to get somebody to like call the police. In the meantime John Sodos starts hollering in pain that he is having a hernia attack!

He also used to come on to a queer, have him get on his knees for a blowjob, and then punch him to knock him out and rob him. Well one time the guy didn't go down with a punch but got up and beat the shit out of John Sodos.

Pat Rogers

> *And he threw a shot in the air and we saw a flash throughout the sky, you know.*

One time in August, I visited my friends Ronnie and Johnnie Hanna. And we were walking back along the lakefront and at the first light at Oak Street, Ronnie jumped out and grabbed a guy. There was another fellow sitting next to him, a younger fellow. And Ronnie is gonna roll 'em. You know, roll a queer. And he said, "All right hit 'em, hit 'em." Johnnie and I had no intention of hitting this guy and in the meantime the guy that was sitting next to him was a cop. And he threw a shot in the air and we saw a flash throughout the sky, you know. The sky was dark at this time. So Ronnie dropped the guy and he started to run and the cop shot him in the leg. Ronnie turned up at

Henrotin Hospital. And they picked him up there and arrested him. Whatever Ronnie said or whatever story they concocted, in one paper I was the ringleader, in the other paper Johnnie Hanna was the ringleader. Ronnie went to parole school. And Johnnie and I were let go. But the papers had carried us as ringleaders depending upon, you know, whoever gave the story. I'm sure it was the police. And from that moment on I was just kicked out of Cathedral High School. And I went to the Audie Home again.

Paul Temple

Looking back it was because we were ignorant.

Remember the fag bar on Division Street; right by the alley, west of Rush Street ... the North Star?
We went in there one night and we were in high school. One smartass guy with us had a broken leg. He's got a cast and he's got a crutch. About four or five of us walk in. And this guy makes a remark to the bartender. Well this bartender was about six-four, about two-thirty. Now whether he was a homo or not I have no idea. All of a sudden the whole place gets up. Here's five of us, there must be thirty-five, forty guys backing us out the door. I thought we were gonna get our fannies whipped so bad. We couldn't get away 'cause we couldn't leave the one guy go with the broken leg. They just wanted us to get out and you know, we exchanged a few blows and got out the door. But you know, stupid things like that we would do. And this is not something that you're proud of but looking back it was because we were ignorant.

La Brasca

That was our first introduction to the fact that all queers are not sissies.

I remember one time we were walking to Oak Street Beach, and I was with Babe Viverito and a couple of other guys. And of course we always presumed that all fags were sissies. And Whitey

Blake went over and he grabbed this guy's radio. The early portable radios. Took it off his neck. And this guy punched Whitey silly. I mean he actually battered him until he was a pulp. That was our first introduction to the fact that all queers are not sissies.

Joe Zummo

I ran up to the cab, smashed the door on the guy's head and spit on them.

You know, I was probably in high school, maybe the summer before senior year. I was walking north on the east side of State Street. I was past the Cathedral and across Chicago Avenue on the east side of the street. Two guys were walking toward me. They were maybe in their late twenties. They made a pass at me. They said something, which I can't remember exactly and they smiled. I was instantly offended and felt violated. Just then they flagged a cab and got in. I ran up to the cab, smashed the door on the guy's head and spit on them. Then I told 'em they better think twice about who they're fucking with next time.

But you know, I can hardly talk about it now because I feel so ashamed for what I did.

Charlie Martinez

Two quick, short, horrific punches to the abdomen flattened Willie to the cement.

Down a ways, south from Schiller Street where Goethe meets the lake and near the queer zone of Oak Street Beach, our group of fifteen or so was lazing away an early summer evening. This was a common, pleasant interlude as the shadows from the tall apartment buildings across Lake Shore Drive oozed toward the lake and began smothering us in twilight.

Two youths, in their late teens like us, promenaded past on the upper cement walk, bisecting our group. One was big and muscular, the other small but still muscular. Their costumes of overripe tan muscles and skimpy, tight-fitting bathing trunks showing a prominent phallic bulge immediately identified them as queers. Whistles broke out, insults were cast and laughter ushered them past us.

Joe Russo stared with animal intensity and hollered, "Hey baby, want some action?" We all laughed. Once I was in Papa Milano's Italian Restaurant at Division Street and Rush Street when Joe made eye contact with two men at another table. He claimed he could tell by their non-verbal response that they were queer. He played a mind game with them and tapped his plate with his fork. They did the same. Joe had a way of making everyone uncomfortable with his seeming innate knowledge of the seamy side of a situation.

Willie Sheridan made the most fuss at the lake scene, following the fags for a short distance, making ape-like gestures, mocking their built-up muscles. He then turned to us and was rewarded with laughs, hoots and a warm welcome back into the pack. Those two guys made no comments and hardly glanced at any of us. When they were finally a long distance away, we all chuckled and congratulated each other for our display.

About fifteen minutes later, the two returned with two companions and were upon us almost unnoticed. The two new queers were larger and even more musclebound. They used the method of divide and conquer which froze us and made cowards of us all. One, with a new perfect haircut and shaved chest, confronted Willie Sheridan. There were a few words spoken as Willie was slowly backing away, watching the aggressor and hoping someone would come to his aid.

"No man, I didn't mean nothin'."

Two quick, short, horrific punches to the abdomen flattened Willie to the cement. Then this lead male looked around challenging anyone to discuss the matter further. No one responded. The four strutted away calmly, never looking back.

We buried our fears in remarks like "that fruity bastard, he's marked," "didn't think he'd do anything or I'da jumped in," "the queer bastard moved so fast." We even bickered among ourselves as to who should have led a response. I asked Patti Irwin why he didn't lead a counterattack. He said, "I wasn't sure who I could depend on except you and a few others."

So it goes when fear and shame take over.

CHAPTER EIGHT: BEHIND OUR WORLD

Part One: Crime and Police

Charlie Martinez

Quick, young hands grabbed the fruit like pigeons pecking at birdseed.

Sweat soaked, hungry and thirsty after a day of playing ball, the three of us, Joe Zummo, Jimmy Foley, and myself plodded past the Chicago Historical Society building and stumbled out of Lincoln Park onto North Avenue. Rays of heat immediately sought us out as the cement sidewalk gave up the sun it had absorbed all day.

How to get food and drink? No one had a cent. We dare not look in the direction of Hasty Tasty on the corner or the ice cream parlor next to the Gold Coast Theater. A man dying of thirst would not want to watch others drink cool water. Foley's brain was broiling for an answer. Then as we listened in awe, he outlined a plan so direct, so simple, and so doable that our spirits soared and we could feel the cool breeze coming off the oasis ahead. He noted that our route home would take us past the fruit stand next to the alley, east of Wells Street. A fruit stand in front of a store with the owner busy inside with customers. A free chicken to be plucked!

He gathered us in.

"When nobody's at the stand, we make a run by it, grab the fruit and cut down the alley. And Zummo, don't fuck up."

His confidence inspired and calmed us. We had no fear. We didn't hesitate to accept his plan. Here was the potential future Marine Corps captain leading his men in a major battle and possible head of General Motors after he left the service. Who were we to question?

This twelve-year-old had the brains, managerial savvy, and leadership instinct that were twice as good as a twenty-year-old.

Naw, no twenty-year-old could stand up to him at all. And he was our leader.

Foley acted when he judged we were at an appropriate distance and the fruit stand was empty of customers. He flew towards the store with Zummo and me following. Quick, young hands grabbed the fruit like pigeons pecking at birdseed. Then we raced down the alley laughing. We were comfortable and safe in the alley among the familiar turned-over garbage cans, scurrying rats, dog crap, weeds, abandoned cars, refrigerators, gas stoves, and occasional bums. What was really fascinating about alleys to a young boy was the delicious sense of wonder and mystery that the back entrances to restaurants, factories and funeral parlors promised us. All alleys were our secret byways. We knew adults disliked alleys but we preferred them to the streets. No one followed us. Likely no one saw us. At Burton Place we slid into a hallway and followed Foley's order to exchange shirts. Thus anyone pursuing us would be confused. We made it easily to the front of Mary Joyce's store and enjoyed our stolen fruit. No guilt, no regrets, just fun.

Peter Eichel

I'd climb in the window and open the windows and open the doors and they'd come in and they'd loot the house.

I don't remember the police being a factor. The only time we were involved with them was like this kind of kid stuff where there'd be twenty or thirty of us and there'd be a couple quarts of beer and somebody'd have an eight pager and they'd come in like they're raiding Mafia headquarters. Beat us up with nightsticks and take us to jail.

The other thing I did at nine, eight or nine years old was with this brother-sister team and they used to burglarize all the homes in the neighborhood. So I went with them one time with my older sister and they would lift me up and I'd climb in the window and open the windows and open the doors and they'd come in and they'd loot the house. I did that, you know and I cannot imagine that I was so lucky to have survived all that.

Jay Pistone

And then he would shoot the gun in the air make ya shit in your pants, you know.

We used to shoot dice underneath the streetlight, ya know I mean? Well, when the police used to come over to raid, they chased away the black kids. Ya know I mean? We all be running down an alley, or you know a gangway, and there was a policeman by the name a Walker. He always chased his own.

He was black. And then he would shoot the gun in the air make ya shit in your pants, you know. You know, boom. You know, he didn't fire at cha, but in the air.

Well of course you're gonna stop, you know. You know he slapped us kids a little bit and try teaching us not to gamble. He didn't shake us down. He didn't, you know, he just say listen you got better things to do than gamble. You know.

As I got older then they were doing shakedowns. As when I was in my twenties. But these were white police. They were not black police. They were doing shakedowns. They see you walk out a poolroom on Clark Street. They figure well maybe he's doing something illegal and then they would follow ya and ah grab ya and shake ya down. And want your money you had on ya.

Joe Zummo

Looking back our involvement with the police or crime was minor but at the time it was serious. The cops used to pick up the guys in a paddy wagon if they thought we were malingering on the streets. When I was a sophomore and it was a Saturday morning and I came home from football practice. I fell asleep on the sidewalk next to a dice game. The next I knew someone was kicking my feet and it was one of Chicago's finest waking me up and hauling us all into jail. They finally let us go but they reported us to school—De Paul Academy. They couldn't remember my name all they remembered was that I had big feet. Father Ryan the principal was wondering who the guy was with the big feet but nobody disclosed who it was. So I was able to escape being tossed out of school for that because they wouldn't have tolerated that,

I saw the police as intruders. I didn't see them to protect you---as people who were misusing their authority and pushing people around.

Jack LaBrasca

They were burning a guy at the stake like Joan of Arc!

We were playing dice in the alley on Hill Street. Right behind Dr. Zummo's house between Orleans and Sedgwick on Hill Street. And there was a kid who came over from Sicily after the war. His name was Chece, which means Frank in Sicilian. He was a nice kid. He had one eye gone and one hand gone. He had picked up a grenade from World War II and it blew his hand off. Everybody kinda liked Chece but he was a pain in the ass. I mean he was always bugging the older guys. Somebody got really ticked off at him and grabbed him and tied him to the utility post, which was wood.

We were probably about fourteen and he was probably about ten. So this guy had found some rope and tied him. Then he started throwing garbage at him. Then he lit a match and threw it and the guy was going up like Joan of Arc. The 163 squad car was just coming by. Yeah, we knew all the squad car numbers and who was in them because my uncle was in that car with his partner for years. And before him it was Foley, Jimmy's father in the 163.

The police grabbed all of us and took us to East Chicago Avenue station in front of a sergeant named Colacki. And he said in an Irish brogue, he says, "I understand what these Dago sonofabitches were just doing. They were burning a guy at the stake like Joan of Arc!" He says, get out of here all of ya. He threw us all out.

Charlie Martinez

Well, the gun did fire the bullet, barely missing several of us.

Joe Russo took his high school classes seriously, especially wood shop. He figured a way to cut and carve a piece of wood into the shape of a pistol. There was a slot on the top of the "barrel." A bullet was placed there and a powerful rubber band was made from a piece of old car tire inner tube. This was connected to a "trigger" and when released it made a nail point on the "hammer" strike the bullet, setting off the charge. This was called a zip gun. Why it was called that I do not know.

Joe announced one day on the street that he was going to test his in the Franklin School yard. 'Course we all went along not wanting to miss this experiment. Well, the gun did fire the bullet, barely missing several of us. It ricocheted off the cement and hit the wall of the school. Abba Kennedy claimed it nicked him in the shoulder. We all looked at each other and silently decided that zip guns were not a reliable or safe thing to fool with, especially with Joe being the triggerman.

Pat Rogers

I don't know where Ronnie got a hold of this acetylene torch.

There was this one friend of mine, Ronnie. He and I got in more trouble. At age ten Ronnie stole a car and we took a joy ride up and down Clark Street, from Grand Avenue to Chicago Avenue and then we deserted the car. He had jumped it. Ronnie was a very bright kid, at ten. And we never got caught for that. My brother Frankie caught me and he gave me a couple of whacks. And he said, "Stop hanging around with that kid, he's gonna get you in trouble."

We became petty burglars. Whatever wasn't locked up, we visited and took. Like Moeller's Barber Shop was a perfect example where they used to charge thirty-five cents for a haircut. We went in there and took some of their equipment and sold it. I mean there was a lot of petty stuff.

We hit offices directly across from the 18th District, the police station. We went in and took their pencils and they always had some change in their drawers and stuff like that. This was at night. It was burglary. Sometimes we'd walk up and down Clark Street and one of us would create a commotion. The other one would go into the cash register and take a couple bucks.

And then Ronnie made his big mistake. There was a currency exchange on Grand and Clark. I don't know where Ronnie got a hold of this acetylene torch. But we were under the sidewalk. We were twelve years old. We tried to burn down an iron door. Well we never got anything. We never even got even close. We did trigger an alarm. There was about seven of us down there with an acetylene torch. Fortunately, nobody got hurt and nobody got arrested. But Ronnie did get into a cleaners and he dropped his identification card. They gave him the once-over at the 18th District, and he included me as his accomplice. And like I said we did a lot of penny ante stuff and the cops had us legitimately for like four or five things but they said they solved forty crimes by blaming us. We didn't do it, you know, but they said they solved forty crimes by blaming us.

That gave us a little trip to the Audie Home for a couple of days, both of us. Ronnie later on was at school in seventh grade or sixth grade, and he broke into the Cathedra High School office and took some of the presents from the Christmas parties. Well when the nuns found out about that they dismissed Ronnie permanently from Cathedral. And he ended up over at Ogden School with Bobbie Hannon and Obie Barnes Those were guys from the neighborhood at the time who were hanger-ons over at Chicago and State. So that was our experience at age twelve when Ronnie was there to lead me on. Ronnie was a bright guy. But he turned out very well. You know. So, it was interesting.

There was so much we did though. We also at twelve invaded people's estates, just for pure mischief. Like the McCormicks' estate. The McCormicks were up across from the lake on Oak and Lake Shore Boulevard. They were gone. So all the kids would break in their homes and go around their homes. Yeah.

The McCormicks had two of them then. One was across from the Drake and the other one was down on Wabash along Rush right in there, so we did get into those homes from time to time. We just looked around. That's all. We didn't do anything. There wasn't any vandalism or any mischief or anything it was just something exciting to do. Maybe on Halloween we did it, who knows. Seemed like the place to go. Ah, but there was a lot of that, a lot of mischief I guess as young kids.

Frank DeMonte

So me and Paul Temple are running down the alley and this copper shoots.

We went to a St. Paddy's Day dance when we were in high school. We were all together, all the guys from high school. We all would dance a little bit and hang around. And somebody brought booze. One guy in our group, who will remain anonymous 'cause I saw him throw it, just heaves a beer bottle in the air. It comes down on a girl and I mean breaks apart and scars this girl. I mean she's bleeding all over the place. Of course all the other people look around and a big fight breaks out. Someone calls the police. Everybody scatters 'cause they don't want to be no part of the police, right. So me and Paul Temple are running down the alley and this copper shoots. Now whether he shot at us I don't know. But we heard, bang, bang. You know, we're like in high school. Right? What do we know about what's going on. But I wanted to relate that 'cause it was a very traumatic experience that we went through.

Charlie Martinez

But Joe had a serious character defect. He had a conscience.

"Jim, empty the waste containers into the garbage cans in the alley."
"Okay, Mr. Fry."
Not only was Mr. Fry frameless in his eyeglass wear, he was clueless in his knowledge of the boys he hired for odd jobs after school. He was a quiet, never demanding, never scolding boss. He

was a very proper pharmacist at the Tanke Drug Store at the northwest corner of Schiller and Clark Streets. The store was at the halfway point between the neighborhood and the lake and was on the direct route down Schiller Street we all took. Jimmy Foley at fourteen was as far advanced in the ways of the world as if he was Mr. Fry's father. Of course, Mr. Fry could not appreciate this and thought if he was nice and treated everyone the way he wanted others to treat him…blah, blah, blah.

And what did Jimmy empty the waste containers into before going into the alley? Why into a tall cardboard box, maybe four or five feet tall. So far so good. He looks efficient. But the lower one-third of the box did not contain garbage. It contained a mix of woman's compacts, new electric shavers, cigarette lighters, and perfume bottles. The trash was piled on top the about-to-be stolen goods. Once in the alley, Jimmy put the tall box next to the garbage can and after the store was closed, retrieved the stolen goods.

Jimmy would test us all. He would not ask if we would feel uncomfortable helping him steal from Tanke's. No, he just ordered us to help and if we backed down, well that was okay but he would get his revenge later.

"Joe, put some electric razors in the box."

Joe hesitated and said "No."

Jimmy asked again.

"No", said Joe.

Jimmy then mentally excluded Joe from the perks to come— like steak dinners at local restaurants, cuts of stolen cash and future presents for his relatives. Joe had taken some of these in previous days and passed them out all cheerfully wrapped at Christmas and Valentine's Day. No relative asked Joe where an eleven-year-old got the money to buy these presents. But Joe had a serious character defect. He had a conscience. He could not shake this burden. He confessed his thievery to the priest and received the most horrible penance. He must do retribution. Impossible! Return the gifts or their cash equivalent! The horror of it!

So Joe was marginalized to running errands and receiving the crumbs from our dinners.

I didn't have the problem Joe had. It didn't bother me to steal from Tanke Drug store. Of course, I was afraid to get caught, but I didn't think of sin or shame and did not confess it to the priests. I just blocked out the event. It wasn't that I thought I had some right to the money or materiel. I just didn't think it through that hard.

Tanke Drugs was located at a point where our areas to the west abutted the Gold Coast. This produced a collision of these two cultures at the fountain area of the drug store. There was a group of older guys and girls, maybe eighteen to twenty years old that met and socialized in the store. They were from the Gold Coast. I noted that they used better English, dressed preppy and seemed intelligent. Some were in college.

I instantly was attracted to this group. They were patient with me and one time I asked Jim Dane if he would explain to me how a car engine worked.

"Do you really want to know?"

"Yes."

I knew he was annoyed.

We were sitting in adjacent stools at the soda fountain. He patiently explained the theory of the internal combustion engine and I was fascinated.

The fountain was a pre-World War II style fountain with eight stools with chrome-plated decoration. The fountain counter was black marble. Everywhere was stainless steel and chrome. Two faucets dispensed plain water and carbonated water. This second was for making phosphates.

The cheap favorite dish was a chocolate sundae. Two scoops of vanilla ice cream with a generous amount of chocolate syrup ladled out from a chrome container. No one knew that Jimmy and I had to mix that chocolate in the back room and to add that certain touch, we spit into it as we stirred it.

I don't know what all the chemicals were, but walking into Tanke's you noticed the odors of camphor, alcohol, and liniment all mingled with soda fountain lemon, chocolate, cherry and the dank smell from the basement. But it was a clean store.

Foley did all the managing of the thievery and continually probed for additional weak spots in the drug store's antitheft system.

He discovered one of Mr. Fry's methods that only protected the store from an outside thief. To keep some money safe and out of the cash register, he put fives and tens in a cigar box hidden on a shelf beneath the cash register. This was a total windfall. That's how several twelve- and thirteen-year-olds dined on steak, chops and fish. But always Jimmy got the largest share of anything because he decided what the shares were.

I was the darling of my family, giving my sisters compacts and perfume and my brothers electric razors as presents. We also stole cases of toilet paper because at that time there was a shortage of soft paper. The Delsey brand was in demand and we generously supplied our households.

No one questioned me. I figured they thought I bought all this with money I earned from my paper route.

John Owens

The cop pulled the fucking handle off the door!

We were by Franklin School. This was in high school and this kid Dom Domonica had this Ford, a '49 Ford or something like that. This is the kid I was telling you about that could buy the beer. So we were sitting right across from Franklin School. Arnold School was on the other side. We were parked there and we had four or five quarts of beer and probably smoking pot too. All of a sudden, this cop pulls up on the side of us. He gets out and he wants to open the door but the door was locked. He pulled the fucking handle off the door! So he finally convinces us to open the door. So we open the door and get out. There were three or four of us in there. He took us to Hudson Avenue Police station. He booked us for drinking beer in the car. They locked us up. My mother had to come down with my father and I don't know if they had put up a bail or something. But we never had to go to court or anything. But they locked us up and then they wouldn't let us out until our parents came.

But the police, they were terrible. Terrible. I mean they used to roust us all the time, you know.

Michael Lutazzi

Let that motherfucker kill himself.

We were on Rush Street. We were like nineteen, starting to feel like men. We decided to get all dressed up, go to Rush Street, sit down in a restaurant like adults. Joe Russo, myself, Ditty and I don't remember the other two or three guys. Might have been George. We ate and they served us drinks and then we left. We got back in Joe's car and that's when we got pulled over. Detectives stood us outside the car. Joe hollered at the policemen for leaving the car lights on with the motor off. "You're gonna run my battery down." Real nasty. The cop says to Joe, "You're lucky you got friends with you or else somebody would find you in the alley."

They took us down to Eleventh and State, made us sit in a cell. Ditty was sitting in the cell. Ditty was trying to talk Joe into hanging himself with his shoelaces because Joe got us in this mess and Ditty was thinking, let that motherfucker kill himself. He got us in trouble and we didn't talk to him for a while. And you know he done that before with others.

Bunny Byrne

We'd open the sewer lids and put the cases of beer down there.

Foley was a winner. It's so unfortunate with Jimmy. Jimmy had a brilliant mind. He stole so much liquor out of Solomon's Drug and Liquor store that he use to do weddings. He did Louise Maltezos' wedding. He supplied every bit of liquor for that wedding. At bargain prices, that's right. You know we used to stick it down in the sewers around the neighborhood. We'd open the sewer lids and put the cases of beer down there.

He was such a genius. He used to make up an order in the store and, and I don't know exactly how he did it 'cause I never worked there. But he would send it out as the last order of the night. And the trucks were rented from Hertz. See Solomon rented all his trucks. So when the guys would make their last order, they'd return the truck to Hertz. So he would load his order up on the last order of the night. And then, whoever was driving the truck would take it where he wanted it.

The guy who delivered it'd get a little cut. He had some of the black guys working there, you know, in on the deal. These guys were grown men. Aw, Jesus, I don't think he was fifteen.

Solomon made a big mistake. He had Northwestern college students doing his inventories 'cause he was getting it free. Well, these college students 'id go down to do the inventory and they'd see a mistake. They would just make a correction on the paper. They didn't want to send this thing back to school out of kilter! Well the guy'd say, "Hey, Jesus, there's four hundred dollars difference here" … and the guy'd say, "Well switch it around, my god, you don't wanna take us back with a four hundred dollar mistake on it."

So they would switch it around to make sure they got a good mark at school! See. It was part of their schoolwork. And so, Jimmy doped out that there not gonna turn him in. They wanna just do their paper and get on with their life. God knows what he stole outta that place.

Our group really never got in any trouble of any kind. We potentially coulda got in trouble but always, you know, ducked the bullet. Like one time Vince took a fur stole off a woman over by the Astor Hotel. Pulled it right off her neck. We ran down to Lincoln Park and I says "Jesus, Vince," I said, "this is a mink stole, there's gonna be problems." So we gave it to one of the younger kids to bring back. Under threat, naturally. We told him to just say some guy gave me this over by the park. I don't even know who it was now but we always sent a little guy, a younger guy that wouldn't harass us. He went back with it and found somebody and said, "Here's your stole." Nothing happened. But I mean, those are stupid things you do. Ya get out of it, but it coulda caused problems.

Ken Martinez

Mary Joyce was the lady that owned the store at Schiller Street and North Park Avenue. She had a bad hand and she walked funny. I stole some money from her. I stole some money off the cash register.

Gus and I went to Milwaukee. We were in grammar school. We just got on the L and went to Milwaukee. I did that all the time. Just walked around. The cops sent us back.

Gus and I stole a hunk of ice off of Healey's truck. And you know how they found us? He called the cops. The cops followed the water mark as we were pushing the huge piece of ice down the street. It was so damn cold. Our hands were numb. And the two big cops are standing behind us. "Okay, now you guys can push it back."

Oh, yeah. We used to climb up on the L and then when the train was coming stuck our heads up between the ties and then pull our heads down. The motorman would be looking at us and he went crazy. They used to call the railroad dicks and chase us.

Charlie Martinez

Joe Russo calmly spits in the cop's face!

"Gimme dat quarter!"
"Fuck you and your quarter."
At the end of the counter at the Yankee Burger Hamburger Joint on Chicago Avenue just east of State Street, Joe Russo was having a discussion with the grill man. This grill man was archetypical of grill men in the 1940s and 1950s. He was of average height and about forty years old. Above all else, he was a hillbilly. At least that's what we labeled anyone with even the slightest Southern accent. His thinness made you think he was a patient in a TB sanitarium instead of a grill man in a hamburger joint. Didn't he get free food at this place? He wore a square paper cap, soiled white tee shirt and a dirty half apron that covered his lower abdomen and legs. He constantly had a spatula for flipping the burgers in his right hand, and a half-smoked, spit-soaked cigarette hung from his mouth. We were always glad to note that he had more spaces between his teeth than there were empty parking spaces on State Street.

But what of the conversation between Joe and this guy? A stare down occurred. The grill man accused Joe of stealing a tip left by a previous patron.

"Dat quarter you took off the counter is mine." As he said this, he kept glancing at two middle-aged patrons at the far end of the counter.

"You fucking hillbilly. Prove it."

More discussion and stare down between Joe and the grill man to which we really were paying no attention because this was Joe's modus operandi anyplace we went. We figured Joe did take the quarter just to get in this guy's face even though Joe was always loaded with dough.

There were six of us in the Yankee Burger, Joe Russo, George Maltezos, Nick Gallo, Jim Patac, Abba Kennedy and myself. Ignored by us were the two older guys in suits sitting at the far end of the counter drinking coffee. We had ended up at the Yankee Burger after a wedding reception had closed for the night. At the reception, to which we were not invited but attended anyway, we filled up on beer and Italian beef sandwiches. With nowhere else to go and still underage for taverns, we headed for a local late night place to have coffee and pie. This night we chose the Yankee Burger, across from Mundelein Cathedral High School. It was about midnight.

We suddenly realized that the scene at the end of the counter had been rearranged. Now Joe was standing away from the counter and the two guys in hats and topcoats were facing him and were very close. Words were being passed back and forth between them and suddenly one of the guys in the topcoats pulls out a gun and announces he is a cop. George Maltezos, by this time, has moved over to the action. He ends up holding the cop's arm with the gun in the air. We stared at Joe for his response, cause we knew a response there would be. After maybe a ten to fifteen second stare down, Joe calmly spits in the guy's face! The other guy pins Joe while the cop with the gun calls on his radio for a wagon.

Reflecting Nick Gallo's deep respect for the law, he pushes me forward hollering that they have no right to arrest Joe and that Charlie here is a senior law student at Loyola University and he knows the law. Well I go along with the con, thinking maybe I can talk them out of arresting Joe. As I blabbed some nonsense of not identifying themselves as cops before showing a weapon which violated statute blah, blah, blah ... the paddy wagon pulls up and all of us are pushed into the vehicle for a trip to jail.

We take our places on parallel benches on each side of the wagon and the doors are locked shut. Joe seems annoyed at the rough ride and proceeds to kick out the little glass window separating us from the cab. This does not sit well with the cops. They stop at the Chicago Avenue Police station about three blocks west. When we get out of the wagon, the cop handcuffs Joe and me together, figuring I might calm him down.

We are put in a holding cell at the station and told we can each make one phone call to home or whatever. All of us make our calls with no difficulty but Joe is the last one. As he goes down the corridor, we hear swearing and pounding on walls and then a loud noise. Joe is dragged back and thrown head first into our cell. He had kicked in a door in the station on his way to the phone.

Back into the paddy wagon we go for a trip to the Sheffield Avenue station where they have night court for the drunks. Now it is getting creepy with vomit, passed-out drunks and strong smell of urine. We huddle together but get to send out for coffee and doughnuts, which we share with some of the grateful alkys. We are marched upstairs to the judge at about three in the morning. He immediately berates the police that we should be at the criminal court at 11th and State.

Back into the wagon we go to 11th and State, that dreaded place of hardened criminals. We are again placed in a cell together but are worried that real crooks are all around us. Finally at seven in the morning we are brought into court. To my surprise, a group of our relatives is present. There are my brothers Bernie and Jerry, Joe's mother and father, Nick Gallo's mother, Abba's brother John, George's sister Louise, and Jim Patac's father. We were all smiling and waving like we just got first place in some softball tournament.

We are told to come forward to the bench. The judge asks one of those cops who was at the Yankee Burger to give a report. His report is all about Joe and how he damaged city property, resisted arrest and swore at the officers. What was strange, the cop read Joe's swear words out loud as if he was reading some technical paper.

The judge asked for our response. With nothing to lose and feeling like I now had some personal experience with the justice system, I gave my response arguing the unfairness of the cops, the fact that we smelled liquor on their breath and that we should be set free at once. The judge actually listened attentively. When I finished, he hesitated, lifted his gavel and said "Guilty!" They fined Joe thirty-five dollars. When we left the building, I happened to glance north on State Street. Standing half-hidden in a hallway was the other cop who had pulled the gun. So ended our encounter with the criminal justice system.

Part Two: Mafia

Charlie Martinez

> *"Johnny, I don't see you much anymore. We got to get together some time for lunch, all right?"*

"Oh Christ, Charlie, don't turn around," said Johnny.

Soft, indirect lighting; gorgeous bouquets with plaintive streamers of "Loving Mother" and "Dearest Grandmother;" appropriate mourners mumbling among themselves—the parlor scene was set at the Montclair Funeral Home out west on Belmont Avenue. Joe Zummo, George Maltezos and I stood in the entrance to the parlor with Johnny Giovenco, paying our respects for the loss of his mother. I didn't turn around just then, but was curious as hell of what was coming up behind me.

"Here comes Frank Capizzi, a cousin. He's an outfit guy. One of the toughest enforcers. He's coming over to talk to me. Don't leave. I don't want him by me too long."

Then I turned around. Walking quickly through the crowd as if late for an appointment was a large man, larger than any of the Sicilians present. He was not obese, but his body was that of an older, retired boxer. His shoulders were square and he was trim. He leaned forward as he walked as if ready for a quick response to any physical threat. He had a full head of graying hair and his face was on the mature handsome side. But could I have written a better script for this meeting? Read on.

"Johnny, Johnny, Johnny." Pathos dripped from his tongue modified by a strong Italian accent as he embraced Johnny forcibly. Johnny smiled and returned the embrace.

"I'm sorry for your mother. She was a wonderful person. Are you still in Las Vegas?"

"Thank you, Sal. Yeah, I'm still in Las Vegas."

"Johnny, I don't see you much anymore. We got to get together some time for lunch, all right?"

"Sure."

"Okay, take care of yourself. I'm gonna say a prayer."

As he walked toward the casket a path cleared in front of him, then closed as he passed. There were many nods by him and to him as he moved through the throng.

A specter was present on the Near North Side. Not among the blacks; they were real, seen almost daily. Not among the hillbillies; we knew where they were and avoided them not out of fear but out of loathing. Certainly not among the hodgepodge rest of us.

The specter was a vampire living in the Italian ghetto. After ensnaring the young men, it came out at twilight to terrorize the adjacent areas, suck their economic blood, corrupt their police and courts, and live the high life compared to hardworking Italians.

Few of us ever knew a Mafioso. Most of the Italians had no personal contact with them. We whispered about them, feared them, and detested them. They were not the benign heroes as portrayed in the movies. Some of our friends took pride in knowing or being related to them; others shunned them and were ashamed of their connection.

I was fascinated with stories about the Mafia.

"Yeah, right in Mary Joyce's store, before she owned it, the LoVecchios' grandfather was gunned down."

Of course my father never gave any more details than that and I never knew if it was true. But I did search the outside of the store for bullet holes. I found none.

We sensed they were involved in police, court and political corruption. We were not sophisticated enough to think of business corruption. They did not touch our lives directly. Several of my pals detested the smear of ethnic association.

Jay Pistone

You hadda buy off these guys or you wouldn't have no wedding cake.

And there's another thing, if you had a wedding, the bakers were little tough guys. They would go to Father Louis at St. Phillips and ask who's getting married.

"Okay Father who's getting married this week or next week or the following month?"

Now you had to buy your wedding cake off those guys. Cause they were Mafias, and they were in the baking business. They'd come over yer house. There was no telephone in those days. And they'd say, Mr. Pistone I heard your son Tom is getting married. The wedding cake was the big thing. You know, everybody bought a canola cake. Ya know I mean? The Italians. You hadda buy off these guys or you wouldn't have no cake. That was it. So most a the guys knew no use buying a cake from a friend, you know, cause you're gonna have a problem.

In the early days, they were called the Black Hands. And they caused a lot of trouble for the little people. When the Italians first came to this country, they still understood the Black Hand from the old Sicily. You know. A guy could know you, be your best friend and write a letter and put a Black Hand on it and he wasn't even a Black Hand man, you know what I mean. But because of the fear of the Black Hand organization, you would go over there, leave the money where he told ya to leave it. And then he would go pick it up. But he knew you had money and he knew you were scared of the Black Hand. You know. He'd write a letter in Italian, you know, and say listen this is what ya gotta give up or else I'll take care of your son or your daughter. If I don't get the money. See. But they weren't even involved; it could be a friend. Ah. Lot a times, you know.

Mr. Manascalco and some guys, they were very intelligent. And they taught these people not to give. Ya know I mean? They formed an organization where if anybody took advantage of older Italians or something, you go to them. And you tell them that somebody was bugging you and they would take care of that party. Well these were not the Mafia. These were the good guys. They would take care of you.

My aunt, my dad's sister, her husband had passed away and she moved in with my dad's brother. Well my dad told her, "Listen, he's gonna take advantage of you. And then put cha in a home." (old people's home)

She had a building and she had money in the bank, you know. So that's why he moved in with her. Then all of a sudden she transferred the money to his account. She had two buildings on North Park avenue. A three-flat and a two-flat. He sold the buildings and then he put her in a home. In those days they were not like today. They were, you know, they weren't as bad as today's homes. So, then she came crying to my dad. You know. My dad says, "Well I told ya what he was gonna do to ya."

So my dad took her to see these guys, you know. They're like the godfathers. You know. They were all businessmen. But their job was to take care of people that were being taken advantage of. So they went to visit my dad's brother. He gave her back all the money for the buildings. You know what I mean? All the money he had in the bank. He had to give her all back. You know, or else. Ya know I mean? So she went to live with us.

These guys, they didn't wanna see anybody be takin' advantage of. Well, they, they just enforced by word. Most times people didn't want any problems and they knew they did the wrong thing.
She knew my dad knew, you know. But she hadda explain what her brother did to her. He can't explain what his brother did to her. It hadda come outa her mouth. You know I mean? They didn't want no, you know, second opinion, you know I mean?

At longs as it came out of her mouth, they said, "Okay, don't worry; we'll give your brother a visit." There'll be two or three guys, you know. And they would tell him, "You did this to your sister? You took your sister's money? And sold her house and did all that? Well you know it's time for you to do the right thing by it." Now, you know, most of the times they didn't have a problem. Because they know the guy knew that they would take care of him, you know.

Michael Lutazzi

I would think about what would have happened if he woulda went that way.

My mother told me that back in the 30's my father had a chance to get with some of the local guys. You know, the local wise guys (Mafia, outfit). They offered him some money to do certain things. He turned 'em down. My mother was very proud of that.

And she passed that along to me. He didn't want nottin to do with them. So he was a ditch-digger and in my youth, I would think about what would have happened if he woulda went that way. I don't know. I coulda had a different life.

Paul Temple

He says to him one more time, real nicely, so he says, give 'em their money.

The old feast used to be down at St. Dominic's. The Italian feast? Do you remember it? Then they used to have the parade on Cleveland Avenue where we lived. I mean they had it every year. And a fellow that we grew up with, his father worked the carnival. He was not in the outfit but he had a relative who was. Now this is for the church. You'd play games down there. They had one; it was very similar to Chinese checkers, which I always remember. And I want to say like you had to get six and half or seven and half points. And at this time we were all in high school. There was about eight of us that went down. We had to go from our neighborhood ... it was south of us. You're talking about around Chicago Avenue. Around Montgomery Ward. Not too far from Montgomery Ward.

I was working in the Daily News then in high school. We all had part time jobs in high school. Or whatever we were doing. Frank DeMonte says to us, he says, "Don't play the game." 'Cause his dad knew that they were all fixed. They were syndicate there. That's who supplied the games ... the Outfit ... for the Catholic Church. Which I always found incongruous but I always enjoyed that side of it. So we're playing the game and this one guy we grew up with really liked to gamble. So we're down there, we're playing and this is not an exaggeration cause I remember you know, what eventually happened. We had paychecks. We had just gotten paid. It was like on a Friday night. We went through everything we had. Paychecks, everything. Tying to get this half a point. We never got it.

So we go back up to where we grew up around Sedgwick and Evergreen and there was a guy's father who used to stand on the corner with another guy. Do you remember Larry the Bum? I don't want to get too personal, you know. But they're standing on the corner and this guy says to Frankie's dad, he says, you know what these guys did? We were down at the feast and they played this you know, blah, blah, whatever the game was. And he says they lost everything. Frankie's dad says, "What did they do?" You know, he says, "Are you crazy?" He says, "Get in the car, God damn it, get in this car and we're going back down there." Two cars 'cause we had so many of us. We go back down there and again I don't want to use a name but a relative was really big in the outfit. This friend's uncle that we knew.

So he goes back down there and he says to the guy running the game, he says, "Give 'em their money." And the guy says, "I'm not gonna give 'em their money; this is for the church. If they're that stupid ..."

He says to him one more time, real nicely, so he says, "Give 'em their money." That's all he said. The guy goes in his pocket, takes out the check, all this stuff and we get all our money back. We get back up to the neighborhood, get out of the car. Frankie's father starts slapping us around the back of the head. You guys are so God damn stupid. I told you never to do that, you know.

Jack LaBrasca

My dad always said to me "You see those guys? You respect them but that's not what you want to be."

My dad and guys in the barbershop would talk in hushed tones about the Three Bells. There were three guys from the neighborhood that were in charge of the vice in our area. Guy from our neighborhood was a guy by the name of ah, was it Little Caesar? It'll come to me in minute. But these guys were mostly hanging out on Clark Street or on Rush Street. The Three Bells they were called. The Three Bells.

Then there were minor guys in the neighborhood who were like hangeroners. They were always hanging out in front of the Mark Twain Hotel. Small time, you know, wannabe hoodlums. But we knew that they were there. And they were referred to occasionally.

But they were not an integral part of our life. They were almost like, that you knew Clark Gable was in the movies, but he was not part of your life.

My dad would take me to the fights at the Stadium sometimes on Friday nights 'cause we had a neighborhood welterweight by the name of Nick Castigleone, "Blacky." He once fought for the welterweight championship. He always stopped at my dad's shop so we went to the fights when he fought. Once in awhile I would be sitting with my dad and some of these torpedoes would stop by and say hi to my dad. My dad always said to me, "You see those guys? You respect them but that's not what you want to be." See, he would explain to me that they're in their world, respect them, but that's not the kind of lifestyle you want to be involved in. So we knew who they were. But it was never, never a big thing.

We never interacted with them. Theirs was purely a commercial base. They were into, you know, gambling, prostitution. Whatever illegal activities, but they had no need to be around us. There was no, there was no relevance to neighborhood life.

Joe Olita

What the women were doing was going out and throwing bread out there so the dogs would not attack the body but they would eat the bread.

You know they talk about influences in this world today, okay? But we had influences too Charlie. Some of the influences we had were criminals.

This is grammar school. Oh, yeah, this is grammar school. They set the tone for us. We used to have a neighbor of ours whose son was connected. Okay. Now you got to realize, that we're just barely making it in the community. And he was the son of one of the people there who owned a two-flat building. He would drive up in his rumble seat car, this guy; we called him the "Sheik." He could have been a movie star. Extremely handsome. And dressed of the times with a fedora, and a beautiful suit and the tie with the high neck collar and the real pointed shoes. He was meticulous. Every time he came to see his mother he came with a different woman. Beautiful woman who would be sitting in the seat next to him. She was not allowed to enter his mother's house because she was a "butona." And a "butona" is known as a whore. When the Sheik would pull up, it was like wildfire through the neighborhood. They'd say, "The Sheik is here."

I was probably about eight or nine. He would allow us to sit in the car, get in the rumble seat, anything we wanted to do. We'd say, "Hey Sheik," and he'd say, "Enjoy yourselves." He would go, "I'm going to see mom." He would go up and see mom and maybe spend a half an hour with her or something like that. Then when he came down, he would say, "All right guys, I'm ready to go." We'd say, "Okay Sheik, we'll see ya again." He says, "Fine." And off he went.

My mother never talked about the mafia but everyone in the neighborhood was well aware of it. A kind of a ridiculous thing happened one time because there was somebody who was killed in an alley. Everybody knew in the neighborhood that a killing had taken place in the alley. What the women were doing was going out and throwing bread out there so the dogs would not attack the body but they would eat the bread. Now it would appear to me that if I were a dog and I'm carnivorous … I would go for the body rather than the bread. See it was an old tale … "Well if we threw this food out, they're not gonna touch the body."

No one called the police. We didn't have any telephones! When my sister got older, she was the only one in the neighborhood who had a telephone. That was the one you put a nickel in. Right in their house. Yeah, you put the nickel right in the box. And they would come up and collect the money, sure. And her brother-in-law would take bets. He would take horse race bets on the phone.

Let me also say this, there was a code of ethics in the community. Any young girl would have no fear walking through pitch-black alleys. They never had a fear of being molested, or being confronted. Because if it happened, it would be the first and last time. The people in the community would take care of that person.

And it happened twice. You never saw him again. That was it. Never saw him again. The river was close. Well you didn't ask. You knew that he was no longer around, and you didn't ask. You know.

There are certain things you talk about and certain things you don't talk about. Or you didn't talk about, put it that way. And you didn't ask.

Most of the stores around there did sell cheese. Okay? But we always related to the fact that any of the Italian stores you have, they'd sell provolone, they sell Romano cheese, they'd sell the parmossona cheese and stuff like that see so. They used to have all these balls hanging up in there. You know the mozzarella and stuff like that so.

We had a guy in our neighborhood whose name was "The Cheese King," and he was the guy that would operate his end of the syndicate. He used to collect protection from all the store owners. You know it was an insurance policy to make sure they didn't get their windows broken and that their business wasn't disrupted.

The thing that used to bother me about this was his son, who was a fat little shit that had a goddamn bike with damn portable radio on it. And we had nothing. Every time we saw this guy and he saw us, the fear of God got into his eyes. He immediately became extremely afraid because we'd chase him down pull him off the bike and beat the hell out of him. He never bothered us. It was just that we objected to what the situation was.

We just knew that certain people were involved. And we didn't ask. A very good friend of mine was involved. Just about a year before I moved down here to Asheville, North Carolina I met him and we had lunch together. We were sitting and having our lunch and we're talking about the old days and stuff like that. He told me he was involved and the stuff that he did. To me he was still my friend. You know, I never really looked at him as being a criminal. One of the compliments that he paid to me was, "You know what? I'm gonna tell you something, you did it the right way." And I said, "Well thank you very much." He said, "I really mean that." He said, "You can walk around and you can keep your head up high." He says, "Yeah some of us can't do that."

Joe Zummo

The mafia to me was almost nonexisting except maybe in the movies or idle conversation. Nobody in my family or anyone I knew had anything to do with them. I never heard any of the Italians I knew talk about the mafia. I think my family was so low on the totem pole that they wouldn't have any connection.

None of my family had any decent jobs. No city jobs, clout. We were totally on our own.

Pat DeVito

Remember Talk of the Town, it was a strip joint? He owned part of that.

Man, to tell the truth, I just stayed away from that Mafia stuff like the plague. See, one of the things that a lot of people don't know my uncle Tony was in the outfit. He had nothing to do with that stuff, the drugs. He was more gangland and other things. You know he owned part of the Talk of the Town. Remember Talk of the Town, it was a strip joint? He owned part of that. It was right off of Division and I believe Dearborn. Talk of the Town.

I had very little to do with my uncle Tony. We used to see him at you know, parties, and birthday parties and stuff. He was my father's brother. I found out later on, after high school, that he was involved. He lived in a nice place. In those row houses on Webster. He was in a brownstone. And you go in his house, it's very nice.

He would sit down and talk and he knew everybody in the city of Chicago. He got us jobs. He knew so many people in the Chicago Park District and in the city. I was making money in the summertime that paid my tuition in high school and college.

There never was any discussion about the Mafia or Outfit in our house, never. My father was a hard working stiff. No, we never talked about the Mafia. We all knew what it was but we didn't call it the Outfit, they called it something else, I don't know what they called it. Those were names we gave it.

They used to have something called "going to the mattresses." When they did that they had to get rid of all the weapons when it was over cause they killed people, and they didn't want anyone to know this gun shot that guy. So my uncle gave my father all the guns. He put 'em in the attic. Before my father died he showed me. He says, "Somebody's gonna come over and ask for the guns. And you have to give them to him." I thought, my God, they actually killed people.

John Owens

> *A machine gun sticks out ... bam-bam-bam ... they shot him, they wasted him.*

Yeah. We were coming out of St Phillip's Church on Oak Street. That's where my sister went to school. St. Phillip's is on Oak and just east of Larrabee. Yeah. We were coming out of church.

I gotta say I was ten, twelve years old, and my sister was little then. I would walk her to church ... 'cause my mother didn't go to church with us. My mother would tell me, "Take your sister, you go to church." So I'd take her, go to church. So we're coming out and this guy's walking down the street on this side of the street. All of a sudden this car stops and they had the doors that opened in the back. A machine gun sticks out ... bam-bam-bam ... they shot him, they wasted him. Took off and that was the end of it ... I mean, you know. We ran like hell. Yeah, I mean it was about 1945. I never forget that.

We heard people talk about the Mafia but you know they would call it "Outfit." "Outfit." Yeah. I did remember something of it. This Sam Garfola had a house on Vine Street. Dominic and myself and another kid, he would pay us to come over. They used to steal the cigarettes and they would put stamps on 'em. In his basement. Yeah.

I was probably just outa grammar school. He would pay us to do that. I mean, I don't know, I guess they stole the cigs. I don't know where he got the stamps. But there were no stamps on them when he got 'em. But then we put a stamp on it, a federal stamp. Then just open up the carton, stamp 'em and put 'em back in the carton.

Across the street from me there was one guy who was a union leader. A union organizer, Sally Grudadaro. Later somebody set a fire in his house and he died in his house.

Yeah, he was in the Outfit. Everybody knew him as the name of Sally. Salvatore Grudadaro was his name. He lived across the street from me and my little sister used to babysit for his daughter. He had a daughter that was retarded. He was very protective of her, you know, so when him and his wife wanted to go out to the movies or something, my sister would babysit for 'em, you know. For his daughter Sally. Sally Girl he called her. Yeah he died accidentally. They made sure neither the wife nor the daughter was home. This happened maybe, I want to say fifteen years ago. They finally got him.

But he used to come home the Fourth of July and we'd be playing out in the street, or standing around or hanging around. One day he came and we were throwing firecrackers. And he says, "That's not a firecracker. I'll show you a firecracker." He opens up his trunk and he's got big sticks of dynamite in his trunk. He says, "Watch this." So he takes a little one, puts it underneath the goddamn street, there was a crack in the sidewalk. He lit it and blew the fucking sidewalk up. He says, "That's how I organize people if they don't join me."

Jim Sullivan

Yeah, he died of lead poisoning.

In high school we didn't know anybody in the Mafia. No, just an awareness of you know, the Black Hand and some family members that were involved.

There were some individuals that were like tough. You know, beat up people and had guns and robberies and stuff like that.

It was like all secondhand. Secondhand information that would like be passed around the neighborhood a lot. Babe Mancini was like a goof ball. I know for a fact one day on Orleans Street he drove down the sidewalk sixty, seventy miles an hour. If anybody would have came off a curb or a stoop or out of a gangway or something like that, they'd been killed. But that's the kind of guy he was.

He was just a tough guy in the neighborhood. And he was mad about somebody or something. And that's the way he acted. But he was like a loose cannon. Everybody's afraid of him, you know.

Yeah, he died of lead poisoning. He threatened somebody and somebody took him literally, and defended himself and they killed him. So there was a couple guys like that. I forget who the other guy was that was you know, just a type of personality that would go after everybody. And they usually end up the same way. They frighten somebody enough that they'll take action against them.

Ken Martinez

They were always dressed to kill.

I had no idea about the Mafia in grammar or high school. We wouldn't know what the hell it was. We didn't pay any attention to that stuff. But there was one thing. There was a family that lived next to us before Red, who was our Boy Scout leader. There was a family that lived there when the Poges moved. They moved in under Philly LoVecchio, in his building. These people never seemed to go work. They were always home. But at night, they'd go out. It was the strangest people. They were always dressed to kill. Shirt and ties, suit. And they'd go out at night. Whatever they did I have no idea. But it was strange.

Charlie Martinez

There was a small piece of information I withheld from the restaurant manager. I couldn't drive.

"He will come up to you after ya worked a couple of hours. Give him the first twelve dollars you make."

What a strange combination banality and arrogance make. The arrogance of this nobody, whose name I can't remember, whose connection with me is lost. But arrogant he was. For me to take and keep this job I had to give up my first twelve dollars in tips to some unknown guy who would walk up to me without a word, accept the twelve and keep walking south on Dearborn Street. I agreed.

The job seemed choice. I was to be in charge of a small parking lot just south of the Embers Restaurant on Elm and Dearborn. I was in premed and any part-time job was welcome. There was no salary, therefore no records of any kind but the tips were said to be good. This was the summer of 1956 and the Democratic National Convention was in town. The drunken senators and representatives and other politicians tipped well. There was a small piece of information I withheld from the restaurant manager. I couldn't drive. I had a driver's license but I never drove a car on the street. But I figured I could maneuver a car in a parking lot.

How did I get a driver's license when I couldn't drive? Well, when I was about sixteen, I was coming out of Third Base, our hamburger joint hangout on Wells Street between Goethe and Evergreen. Walking into the place was the local precinct captain. I says, "Hey Mike, can you get me a driver's license?" He says, "You ain't got one? Okay come over to the ward office." The next day I went over and got my license. I took no test and paid no bribe.

I started my parking lot job at four in the afternoon. At six, banality arrived. He was as short as me, about forty, dressed in a quality pair of pressed gabardine pants and an expensive shirt. He was clean-shaven. He walked up to me and I looked at him. I handed over the twelve dollars and he walked south on Dearborn without a word. That was my only encounter with the Outfit. By the way, I parked the cars so tight, I couldn't get them out and the manager had to retrieve them.

CHAPTER NINE: THE PLAGUE

> Come away, O human child!
> To the waters and the wild
> With a faery, hand in hand,
> For the world's more full of weeping than you can understand.
>
> "The Stolen Child" - William Butler Yeats

Charlie Martinez

"Charlie?" The voice on the phone was hoarse and hesitant. It was 6 a.m. on a Sunday morning.

"Yeah?"

"Pete. Ah, can you come to the county morgue with me? They called and said Billy is there. I gotta identify him."

"Sure."

"I'll pick you up in twenty minutes."

Billy, Pete Eichel's younger brother, had been rolled out of a car unconscious by his buddies and dumped in a hospital parking lot after a heroin fix.

The morgue was totally nondescript on the inside. What I mean is, you couldn't tell that you were in a morgue. Everything was ceramic tile. Ceramic walls, floors and countertops. The sweet-pungent scent of formaldehyde permeated the air. The only noise was the slapping of our shoes on the ceramic floor as we met the attendant at the main counter.

"Ya got ID?"

"Yeah, sure." Pete hands over his driver's license.

It's 7:10 a.m. Sunday. I figure the attendant has been on duty ten minutes. He already looks and acts bored. His lab coat is soiled. He probably got the job when he auditioned as an official and disinterested ward heeler.

"Fill out this form."

Is it too much to expect a little sympathy? All right, you handled this a hundred times, but a little empathy or warmth? These thoughts go through my head. The attendant never even looks at me.

"Come over into the viewing room, okay? Now stand here and I will pull the drapes."

He leaves. Drab drapes separate in several jerks.

"Aw, shit."

Pete wobbles a little as I watch his reflection in the glass separating us from Billy. The glass has finger and palm prints spread out over it. There is a lip print seen in the lower half. He examines Billy for a full minute.

"Jeez, Charlie, he looks asleep."

There is our childhood, frozen in time on a county morgue gurney. The body is rigid as if at attention. Hands at side, palms flat, head positioned straight towards the ceiling. A sheet, wrinkled, gray with blotchy red and yellow discolorations, covers him from mid-chest to upper thighs. His feet are turned outward with an identification tag tied to his right big toe.

Billy is about thirty. No gray hair; no wrinkles. He has a four-inch scar in his right cheek from childhood. I notice fading purple mottling in the forearms up to the elbows. He looks pale. His lips are purplish/blue; his eyes closed.

At age twelve, those eyes were bright, the lips smiling. He had the usual non-ambition of the neighborhood guys, but no worse. School was uninteresting. No definite plans. Just wanted to live and have fun. First a little alcohol, then some marijuana. At this point, a separation from the main group occurred with him joining a fringe band of hip people. Jive was their talk; smooth was their walk. Jazz was their life; cool was their style. Disdain for the lame was their attitude.

Popping pills was the next chapter. And then. Always finger pointing in retrospect. Was it Marty who got him started on heroin? Joey? Jimmy? Who knows? Who cares? The hook was into his soul up to the shank. Pulling it out was more painful than leaving it in to fester.

He graduated to ecstatic highs. Of course the highs got shallower and then there were only the lows that made him desperate for a fix. He was fourteen.

Now came the drop out of school, odd jobs, loss of jobs, petty thievery, turning others on to drugs, stealing from family, begging. And always fooling himself.

Then there was severe illness.

I visited him at the Illinois Education and Research hospital when he was in his early twenties. He had been near death from a severe infection due to his habit. He was very pleasant and you would have thought he was recuperating from a broken ankle. On IV's and potent medicines for weeks, he pulled out of it.

I met him on a bus one day. The trees were radiant in greens, reds, oranges and yellows. It was a fall we had shared dozens of times before. I had transferred from the Damen Avenue bus to the Ogden Avenue bus. He was sitting alone in the middle barely filling half a seat with his thin frame. I smiled hello. He smiled back as if this was the most special day of his life. We talked and then rose together to leave to exit at California Avenue.

"Got a half dollar?" Billy asked me as we stepped to the curb.

"No," I said. Why did I lie and not give it to him? Would it really have mattered if he were going to parley that fifty cents into another fix? He smiled that pleasant smile. I said goodbye and went into Mt. Sinai Hospital where I was in a rotation for my medical residency. He caught the California bus south to the courthouse at 26th and California. He had a scheduled court hearing on a drug charge.

"What the fuck," says Pete.

I sense the wrenching guilt Pete must be enduring, thinking of the times he beat Billy up and threw him down the stairs when he caught Billy stealing from the apartment where the family lived.

After a few moments we go back to the morgue counter. Pete signs more forms and we leave.

Pete Eichel

You know, he spent the rest of his life working as hard as he could to stay high on heroin.

But those were not good years, my middle teens. Those were the years we had kids that were dying of overdoses. And if I remember back then the drug problem was confined to the inner city, the lower socioeconomic groups. That was before it spread out and affected everybody.

I can name the kids that were dead before they were twenty-one. Louis Nevasco and Pete Vadlecia died from an overdose of drugs. Frank Pistacho died. But eventually, almost all of those people who were doing drugs were gone. In fact it was kind of spread out and they were gone in their twenties, thirties, forties. But I don't think any of them made it to sixty. Foley's still alive. He made it through. But he would, wouldn't he? Yeah, he would. But Frank and Bucky didn't.

My brother was dead when he was thirty. Thirty-two. Something like that. But he was gone when he was fourteen. By the time he was fourteen or fifteen years old he didn't have a life. It was all over for him. You know, he spent the rest of his life working as hard as he could to stay high on heroin. Some of those people were able to get in a methadone program. And it's interesting that I hear people tell, and I don't wanna mention their names, how they kicked the habit and they're doing okay. And they've been on methadone for thirty years. You know, it's hilarious. But that's I guess better than being out stealing to stay high. Right?

Well I smoked some marijuana, but I had to be eighteen years old, at the oldest nineteen. In fact I remember I had to make a decision, between the two groups that split off of the neighborhood. I mean the people that were cool that were doing drugs, and then everybody else that was going to school and to college and were, you know, were doing some things that were a little different. I had some pot in a bag. And I made a decision as I was walking from Third Base north on Wells Street and there was an empty lot there by Scholl's shoe factory. I decided that's it. Okay. I took the bag of pot and I threw it in the lot. That's when I quit smoking pot. I told somebody that that's it, and I said in fact I threw it in an empty lot. About six guys, you know, were all coming to that area. It was like some miracle of God that I had experienced, that was enough to make me really think very poorly of these people. And it was just so stupid. They were trying to find all these little grains of pot in the field, you know. Stupid shit.

Michael Lutazzi

The cigarette burned right through his finger.

You know, dope was never a big thing for me. I smoked pot but other guys smoked it every day, you know. I just couldn't see that.

I got my pot from Sal but everybody had it. Sal, John Duncan. I used to work for Illinois Condenser on North Avenue and Throop, which is near Elston. That's another job I had as a kid before typesetting. They made condensers. There was a black guy there, got friendly with him. I was fifteen, sixteen. Yeah. It was a part-time job after school. Get on a bus. Get home at eight o'clock.

Bought a whole pound of marijuana off this black guy one time and shared it with a bunch of the guys in the neighborhood. And I said after that, I said I'm never gonna do that again. Because I put this whole thing in my pant leg and get on the bus with it. You know, it was a package about as big as a half a loaf of bread. And I never did that again. I was afraid to get arrested and go to jail. That was a lot of pot. We never carried but maybe one or two joints on us. You can get rid of it real quick.

Who did we get it from? Christ. There was a Japanese guy in that neighborhood, around Wells Street there. The Japanese guy come around quite a bit. He was a junkie. He had real good pot. Marty McDonough had pot. I wanna say Foley, but I can't say that for sure. A few other guys, I can't remember.

Sal was my best man at my wedding. I seen him at Magrini's tavern one time and sat down and he was stoned out of his mind. Smoking a cigarette, drinking a beer. All of a sudden, he's got a cigarette between his fingers, and he closes his eyes and fell asleep. The cigarette burned right through his finger. I wanted to see how far it went. So then I knocked it out of his fingers. He was burning and he was sleeping.

He came in one time and he asked me for fifty cents. One of my best friends. I told him, "No." I was so insulted. And I felt so bad for him that he had stooped so low that he was, how old were we, nineteen, twenty one? Magrini's! And he asked me for half a buck. I don't remember if I gave it to him. I thought I said "No." He was all fucked up. But he was my best man at my wedding. Yeah, he was on heroin and I knew that. But I still asked him because we were tight. We grew up together. I knew him before he was a junkie, you know. So he and I were close. Ah, Sal, fuck. Fucking Sal, he was so talented. He could draw. He was a cartoonist. Sal was a smart kid too. Sal was smart in his own ways, ah. But you tell 'em, you know … when you're young you don't know nothing but you try…you can't do that shit. "Ah, yeah you're right …" they say. But he lived another ten years.

Charlie Martinez

The problem was that although I did roll a joint, it was the size of a cigar.

The cool people would use the lames at times.
"Charlie!"
"Yeah?" Again it was milling around time at Third Base and the cool people picked me out of the crowd for a confidential conversation.
"Come here."
A handsome face topped with blond hair was calling me from inside a car parked at the curb. He kept his face in the shadows of the inside of the car because only the uncool would stick his head out of a car window. This was Jimmy Foley. Not the coolest of the cool but the natural born leader of all lames till drugs came along and now the chieftain of the cool. He had been my grammar school buddy.
"Get in."

"Sure." I had no misgivings about getting into the car. I knew that they were so far gone along a different road in life, that in my mind's eye I was totally superior to them.

The car was parked in front of the store. The car was old then, maybe a late thirties Ford. This was 1952. I was seventeen. When I got in, even as lame as I was, I could smell the sweet scent of marijuana. Joey Labello, a little over five feet tall and perhaps a hundred pounds, was next to Jimmy looking cool, staring straight ahead, totally uninterested in me. They had on new, draped gabardine pants, boxed-end shoes and short sleeve shirts with open collars. No jewelry. The hair was combed back into a duck's ass at the neck. They probably had plans for a great night of smoking pot, listening to jazz on the radio, going to a jazz joint, popping pills, smoking more pot and spending a few more hours listening to live jazz. Us lames were going to play touch football and treat ourselves to some Pepsi and later split a quart of beer between six guys.

"Can you do me a favor, man?"

"Sure."

He reached up to the overhead light fixture and took it apart. He pulled out a paper bag secured with a rubber band and handed it to me. As I fingered it, I sensed the feel of dried grass.

"Will you roll us a few joints in Third Base, man?" He gave no explanation why he picked out, a lame for this important job when several other cool people were also milling around in front of Third Base. No honor among thieves, I guess. But he had no qualms about possibly getting me into trouble with the law. He used people well.

"Yeah, sure."

Now I had never smoked a joint; had never rolled a joint; had never seen anyone else roll a joint. But I figured it was just like rolling an ordinary cigarette, right? Ken, Joe Zummo and I had rolled regular cigarettes on a little manual machine we found in the alley next to the Plaza Theater when we were ten years old. So it couldn't be that different. They must really be afraid of getting busted to trust me, I thought as I walked into Third Base and then locked myself in the bathroom. What a mistake they made!

In the john, I went about my business. Since my great grandfather was a cigar maker in New Orleans, why not me? I succeeded in spilling about a third of their goods down the toilet. Another third I laid out on the cigarette papers from the bag. When I rolled it up and licked the edges, it actually stayed together. The problem was that although I did roll a joint, it was the size of a White Owl cigar. I came out of the bathroom laughing to myself totally unafraid of how Foley and his buddies would react.

They were disgusted and did not lower themselves to berate me. The look on their faces told me everything they were thinking. "All lames were losers."

Frank DeMonte

What they were doing was they were going and having a joint. And then I had to go with different friends that you know, didn't smoke.

In grammar school, that's where I learned there was drugs in the area. I had a group of friends and we were always, always together. All of sudden, we weren't together any more. I never smoked. But we ah, we were just talking and playing all of a sudden they just left.

If I was gonna guess a year, I would say sixth, seventh grade? They stopped talking. They just got up. Didn't say nothing. They just left. What they were doing was they were going and having a joint. And since I didn't smoke, I was called ... what's the word? Lame. And they were cool and I was lame. That's what they would do. They would take off. And then you could smell that stuff from a mile away, really. They weren't fooling anybody. I only discussed drugs once with any of them. That was with Louis Navasco. He was a Filipino kid from Wells Street. He went to De Paul Academy with me and Paul. He was a year behind us. At that time heroin was the big deal. He winds up killing himself. Him and two other guys break in to a drug store. And they thought they were taking some drug for a high. He injects himself and dies. Doesn't know what it is. He was in his mid twenties.

And then I had to go with different friends that you know, didn't smoke. Guys like Paul Temple, Joe Lendino, Paul Davies. All these guys that I knew but they weren't part of my group. Now they had to be part of my group.

John Owens

Red devils they called 'em. Yeah. We used to just pop those.

I smoked pot. I never shot any smack, but I smoked pot and about once in awhile we took some pills and drop them in a quart of beer or something. Red devils they called 'em. It's like benzedrine. Yeah. We used to just pop those. But my only problem was alcohol and still is.

My stepbrother, he was a dope fiend. He ended up dying from an overdose. He ended up dying in one of those fucking rattraps, in one of those fleabag hotels on Madison Street. It was probably '58. I was older. I had to go down there at the Cook County morgue with my mother to identify the body, yeah. It was terrible.

Charlie Martinez

One of them must become the sacrificial lamb to the police.

Sal gave the outward appearance of a religious bent. He went to church regularly, but never visited the nave. Services were held on the steps of the Episcopal Church at La Salle and Maple Streets. These steps were on the side of the building, which was more discreet and hid the services from the less religious passersby. "Going to the church steps" was a pilgrimage set out on for drug exchange and drug use. But to avoid any lame from knowing any details of this enterprise, the potheads called it the "scene" when we were around.

Sal, like so many of the potheads, was a natural leader as opposed to the stumblebum juiceheads they named the rest of us. His reddish blonde hair always had a perfect brush cut. He was pleasant, polite, articulate and neatly dressed. This was the picture the potheads presented to the world. Adults thought of them as more mature than the juiceheads who frequently had no cool clothes, were silly and lacking in social graces. But the potheads were so cool!

Never in a hurry. Their church music was jazz about which they talked in hushed reverent tones. Serious discussion also occurred about pot, pills and heroin. They frequently mumbled, and chuckled as they talked and with the jive dialect it was sometimes difficult to understand them. This was their intention.

Sal and his congregation, Jimmy Foley, Chow, Joey Labella, Marty McDonough, and several other cool people, were sitting on the church steps one pleasant summer evening. Smoking joints, doing smack and jiving. During this service a black Ford pulled up. Four husky men got out and came towards the group. No chance to run or ditch any pot or pills. A paddy wagon then appeared. Oh what a desecration this was from these unbelievers! The congregation was lined up against the church wall, searched and marched into the wagon.

They were placed in a holding cell at 11th and State Streets, released and given a date for a bench trial. Of course, the police really wanted a high priest (drug dealer), not these ordinary members of the congregation.

A lawyer was hired for the trial. Discussions were held and during one huddle a plan was hatched. A plan so simple, yet direct and clear that it was sure to get them off. But to attain a good result, a price must be paid. Sacrifice must occur. One of them must become the sacrificial lamb to the police.

But which of the seven would be given over?

The lawyer had decided. Sal was called to the bench. He stood with his lawyer who whispered the concise strategy that would free all but one.

"Finger the chink."

Charlie Martinez

They called him Mike. No one later remembered a clear story of where or how he came to be in the neighborhood. He was short, looked about seventeen and had crew cut blonde hair. He knew the jive talk. He attached himself to the potheads and ignored the juiceheads. To the potheads, he was a teenager from a nearby neighborhood. He got their confidence, bought their shit and shared his shit with them. They were proud of him and pointed him out as a cool guy to us lames. I never heard him talk. Their group kept a safe distance from the juiceheads when important subjects like drugs, jazz, or clothes were discussed.

Ah, but one day Mike brought his friends to make a buy. It turned out Mike wasn't a pothead; he was a federal agent. How could this be? But it could be and the guys were busted for selling marijuana. Some had mailed it from a vacation trip in Mississippi. But the idea was to go easy on the teens and in this way enlist the parents to help stop the scourge. The teens and their parents were invited to the IC lot field house. The parents could not, would not believe their kids were involved in drugs. So the dance of death went on.

Pete Eichel

They were almost like the Moody Bible guys trying to convert everybody.

There were three or four people that first start using drugs. And then they started dealing to support their habit. Most drug addicts do eventually deal. And they skim, you know, so they can maintain their own drugs. I think the people were Joey Labella, Marty McDonough, Andy Gumps, and Jimmy Foley. Those were probably the four key people who brought the drugs into the neighborhood.

Let's see maybe I'm fifteen, Marty McDonough is nineteen. He had a job for a typewriter repair company. He'd pick up typewriters to be repaired and then deliver repaired typewriters. And I remember he had something like twelve thousand dollars in the bank. Now how much money would that be today? Lot a money.

And he used to buy a pound of what we call "dyno." It was marijuana that was really potent and it was chartreuse in color. I mean it looked so good compared to the garbage, which was brown and shitty looking. You could buy some real cheap pot for like thirty-five bucks a pound. And the "dyno" was something like two hundred dollars a pound. I'm not too sure of the prices, but he'd buy all of this huge big supply of garbage, and then he'd buy a pound of this "dyno" and mix it all in. Okay? I smoked marijuana, but I never did any of the other. I couldn't, thank God.

But Marty was doing heroin at that time. I'd be in the back of his truck and I'd be sorting all the stuff out and measuring it in Prince Albert pipe tobacco cans. A can was a Prince Albert can. A quarter can was a shot glass. He'd be delivering his typewriters and picking up and while he was doing that, he'd be stopping at all these hangouts, like Third Base where we hung out for example, like candy stores and little restaurants where the teenagers hung out. And he'd be the man. They'd all be copping their pot from him.

And here I am with no idea, no clue of what level of risk that was for me. Just never, never occurred to me that I, if I got caught that I probably would have went to jail. He certainly would've. You know, that was a serious offense back then. So, you know, something watched over me all those years. But those people were able to maintain their habits by dealing. And in order to deal they needed to turn people on. They were almost like the Moody Bible guys trying to convert everybody. You know. It was a way of life for them.

Charlie Martinez

Father Morrison gazed at Sal through the oxygen-enriched mist.

"Sal." A voice pleaded for recognition.

Sal's world had shrunk to the oxygen tent enveloping his hospital bed. IV fluids replaced the beer and pizza at Papa Milano's. IV antibiotics instead of heroin.

"Sal." A gray, featureless head, with body clad in black stared down at Sal.

"Sal." A distant, dull sound came from the specter.

"Who the fuck was this?" thought Sal. "Some brother wanting a fix?"

"Sal."

"Man can't you see I'm having a tough time? Get lost."

"Sal."

Father Morrison gazed at Sal through the oxygen-enriched mist. He saw a shrunken body, pale face and mouth gasping for air.

"Did you want to talk about anything and did you want the last rites of the Church?"

"Get the fuck otta here!"

Father Morrison left. His kindly attempt at salvation for Sal's soul turned aside.

But the effort was energizing for Sal. He rose from the bed, disconnected himself from his medical care, got dressed and made it home from Grant Hospital in time to die. He was thirty years old.

Third Base

The old sign hung over the doorway,
Still attached by rusty anchor bolts
Drilled into common brick
And bleeding lime had taken its toll
On the foundation of that sign.

One thing I recall was
"You have to stop at Third Base before going home"
The sign read.

I, being young, and all my friends
Would stop and hang out at Third Base
Which was located between Goethe St. and Schiller St.
On Wells St.
Which is a proud Old Town today.

Third Base began to be my second home,
Or, even my first home at times.

The smell of reefers was on my clothes and breath,
When taking a walk wasn't for exercise.
Shades covered the part of my eyes that weren't half shut
To hide maps of red on white eyeballs
At eight o'clock at night.

My ears would bounce
And my feet kept the beat to sounds of
Illinois Jackquet, Flip Phills, Earl Bostic,
Stan Getz, Joe Williams
And Ella belting a song of Be-bop-buta-scrook-scrook..

Satin all the way
Stan Kenton's Big Band

With Clark Terry and Maynard Ferguson
Just learning from the pros.

I think you could get six plays for a quarter
On that Jukebox at Third Base.

Then there was Josephine,
The owner of Third Base
With her long dyed black hair
With long gray hair peeking through
All the black.

Her short skirt passed above the knees
So you could see the varicose veins
Drawing maps of long years
Of toil and child-bearing
Looking to burst at any moment.

We exercised our lungs
On product of Columbia
(not coffee)
Purchased from Juan Felher

Which he sold for the reasonable price
Of a nickel a bag
For stuff that looked like twigs
That said 'snap, krackle, and pop'.

We made a killing when we mixed oregano
We got from John, George's brother,
With the Columbian stuff.

I drank beer in the Franklin School playground
On Evergreen Street west of Wells Street.

Used peanuts for a chaser
When I had to eat a false ID
In the back of a paddy wagon
So that "the Man" wouldn't bust me.

I have many memories of those past days,
Many more stories of growing up
In today's old town.

So, you see David Hernandez,
I grew up in a hood with winos, dope heads,
And beer lushes like myself.
But today, we can both write
With minds that have been clean and sober
For many years.

No matter how many townhouses
They build in Old Town today,
My heart will always remember
The 1300 block of Wells Street
And stopping at Third Base before going home.

-Nick Gallo

CHAPTER TEN: WELL MEANING

Part One: Religion

Charlie Martinez

Confession

Immaculate Conception Church was a moderate-sized brick building with a steeple top clad in copper and a statue of the Virgin surveying our chunk of the Near North Side. On a cloudy day, the only added illumination in the dimly lit church was from the vigil light candles being tended to by the old ladies in babushkas. Hanging in an elaborate metal container high up in the center of the altar area, a candle was a red focus through the Sacred Heart colored glass. This lamp alerted the faithful that the body of Christ in the form of the Eucharist was present in the tabernacle. On all sides, plaster eyes followed you as you moved in a gloomy, ill-defined monotone. A mild odor of incense mixed with the smoke of burning candles gave a soft background perfume to the air. The pews were dark brown and in the corners at the back of the church, almost invisible in the muted light, were the confessionals.

These were roughly seven feet high by two feet deep and ten feet wide wooden boxes divided in three sections. The priest sat in the middle with a penitent entering for confession on each end. The priest slid a thick wooden panel closed as he blessed a departing penitent and at the same time slid open a panel for the person next up. That person faced a thick cloth panel. We formed lines flowing away from each door but no closer than five feet so that there was a decent distance to prevent eavesdropping.

Pick the confessional by the priest. Got to get the easiest, the guy who didn't ask questions or give a sermon and also gave the least penance. You hated lines. It meant that the guy in back of you recognized you and what if he could hear you while waiting outside the door? Same way if the person in the line on the opposite side saw you and then listened hard when you were both in your boxes.

Tension. Sweat. Remember to half whisper, so the priest couldn't identify you.

To me, this identification thing was big. Once when we were about seventeen, John Giovenco and I were walking past the church on a Saturday afternoon. He said, "Let's hit confession." I said, "Okay." But as we entered the back of the church, Giovenco saw Father Morrison leaving to go into the sacristy.

He shouted, "Father, can you hear our confessions?"

"Sure," was the reply.

I said, "John are you crazy? Morrison will know who we are!"

"So," was his reply.

And thus I endured one of my greatest mortifications.

Waiting in line was the time to rehearse what you were gonna confess. Did I have the nerve to say I abused myself? All the other stuff, like disobeying your mother or missing Mass were bullshit in comparison. Dirty thoughts were the second-line crimes. You could hear the panel slide shut on the guy ahead of you in the box. He came out with his head bowed. You went in and waited, trying to decipher the mumbling you heard coming from the other side.

The mumbling ended and there was a soft swooshing sound, a second of silence, and then the noise of the panel sliding away gently on your side. Your eyes strained to see through the thick cloth facing you but you saw only the results of your imagination in the darkness.

"Bless me father for I have sinned. It has been one month since my last confession.(mumbling) I had dirty thoughts six times ... (speak up son, I can't hear you) ... and wouldn't take out the garbage once."

"May the Almighty and merciful Lord grant thee pardon, absolution and forgiveness of thy sins. Amen."

"Drink much water to cleanse your body. And for your penance say three Our Fathers, three Hail Marys and three Glory Be To God. Go in Peace."

"Thank you, Father."

Guilt gone. New slate to work with. No question I felt that something had actually taken place and I was now clean, back in the good graces, forgiven, a burden lifted.

I envied those who had interactions with priests, nuns and those in authority or were just simply older. My only interactions, it seemed, were for infractions of rules. I never was called by a nun or priest or teacher or older person to discuss my feelings, aspirations, problems or triumphs. It seemed to me that these people were as weak as I was and tended to relate to their "favorites" instead of helping the emotionally needy. I longed for this contact but at the same time avoided it.

"Want to talk to me about where you went when you ran away?" said Father Sullivan. I remained mute. He wanted to find out about the time I ran away for a week in seventh grade. Perhaps my parents put him up to it because I had shared nothing about the incident with them. But I said nothing. He did not persevere. I thought later that he was very involved with the popular, the extroverts and the athletes of the school. Why did he ask me those questions? I did not get the impression that he wanted to help me but just wanted information. He was a good example of what I mean that the priests or nuns or those in charge were just as weak as I was.

Holy Week

If Easter Sunday was the capstone of Holy Week, then Good Friday was the foundation for the Resurrection. But Good Friday always felt depressing as it was intended to be and we kids waited for the thunderstorms to occur in the afternoon as the adults said *always* happened. We listened for the sounds of "the veil of the Temple being rent in twain from the top even to the bottom and the earth quaked and the rocks were rent. And the monuments were opened, and many bodies of the saints, who had slept, arose." This was scary stuff and was supposed to happen at exactly 3 p.m. when Jesus died. But we were disappointed.

There was a shocking difference in the appearance of the altar on Good Friday. Gloom prevailed. The doors of the tabernacle of the main altar were wide open and the consecrated hosts were absent.

The altar was draped in purple. Sometimes the front of the church was also draped in purple linens.

This is when my sister and I came to kiss the body of Christ on a large cross that was lying in front of the Communion rail. Hand in hand we walked as cautious children do. The pace was fast, jerky, like puppets, eyes focused ahead on the goal, ending with an awkward plop to our knees before the crucifix. But as we were about to perform the ritual, I noticed a large woven basket with a felt bottom next to the crucifix. It was full of change and there was an occasional piece of paper money. What was this! You had to pay before you could kiss the cross! I had no money. I grabbed Lee's hand and turned her around. We repeated our walk but at a faster pace, my face burning with shame. What further possible humiliation we had avoided! At home, my mother explained that we really didn't need to give money but I refused to return till she gave us a few pennies to donate. We went back and did our duty.

I recall that Holy Saturday had a more upbeat tone. The highlight of the two- or three-hour set of devotions that we served as altar boys was the Litany of the Saints. Each saint's name was pronounced in Latin and then the priest would sing, "Flectamus genua" (bend your knees). We would kneel for a moment and say "Ora pro nobis" (Pray for us). Then the priest would command in song "Levatae" (rise). There was a rhythm to this that I enjoyed. The entire happening was like a chorus line on a hit show. After *Sanctus Jacobe*, (Saint James) I expected James Cagney to come on the altar and go into one of his tap dance numbers.

Easter Sunday, which was the pivotal day in the Christian religion because Christ had conquered death, was treated as a holiday, fit for celebrations. This day was for new clothes and a big meal. The clothes were perhaps a shirt and pair of pants as well as new shoes and socks. There was a glorious shock when we entered the church that day. All the purple of Good Friday had been removed. Everywhere was flowers. Gladiolas, lilies, carnations and roses. Hundreds of flowers had been placed in the main altar and the side altars of Mary and St. Joseph by ladies of the Altar and Rosary Society. The mild background incense odor was replaced by a wild jumble of flower perfume similar to a wake at Sullivan's Funeral Home.

The best altar cloths were laid out and the priests wore beautiful gold and white vestments. If we were serving Mass, we had on a black cassock, white surplice and a large gold or red bow at our neck.

Forty Hours Devotion

> *"This devotion, known in Italy as the Quarant ore, continues for Forty Hours, in memory of the forty hours during which the Body of our Lord remained in the Sepulchre."*

That description evokes a scene of devout Catholics kneeling in front of the Blessed Sacrament for forty hours and praying constantly. Well, you know, some people did just that in church during this devotion but to the altar boys it was a much different experience. You see the problem was how to keep twelve-, thirteen- or fourteen-year-old boys calm, attentive and pious during their two-hour stints for which they signed up. No one instructed, so we improvised.

There were two of us on the altar at one time with no priest in attendance. Each had his own kneeler on the main altar with his back to the congregation. In order to pass the time in a meaningful way we brought in candy bars and comic books hidden in our clothes. We alternated sitting and kneeling. During the sitting periods, we secretly slipped the candy into our mouths and read the comic books as they were held close to our chest. Even this food and entertainment was often not enough to keep us from fidgeting. Eventually, one or the other would snicker, or stick his tongue out or cross his eyes. To the congregation we appeared as pious boys looking at the altar for inspiration in our lives. Well, once the silliness began, paroxysms of suppressed laughter were hardly controlled. Large globs of snot came out our noses as we tried desperately to conceal these convulsions. We didn't carry handkerchiefs, so the only available material to wipe our noses was the sleeves of our cassocks.

Eventually our time was up and we walked off, relieved by a new team. Parents, nuns, priests, and parishioners were proud of our devout and generous gift of those two hours. Of course it wasn't all fun. Sometimes we didn't get to finish the Superman comic.

Serving Mass and the Altar Boy Room

"Chuckie, get up."

It was 6:30 a.m. and my mother was prodding me awake. I was scheduled for serving the 7 a.m. Mass. My mother had been up for probably an hour already. She was dressed in her cotton housedress. That's all she wore in the house and also to daily Mass. Her rosary was being fingered in the left hand. As I passed by the kitchen table on the way to the bathroom I noticed several glossy booklets half the size of book pages. These were devotional tracts she read every day. I also smelled the alcohol-iodine odor of the Sloan's liniment that she constantly used for joint pains.

A quick face wash and sometimes teeth brushing was the extent of my cleaning up. I dressed and was out of the house quickly. No breakfast was offered because I had to go to Communion every time I served Mass and we were not allowed to eat from the night before.

Johnny Nicolini and I were scheduled to serve the 7 a.m. Mass. We lived across from each other and next to the church so that we met in front of the church about 6:45.

At times we had to prompt each other to ring the bell, get the cruets, pick up the Missal, or give a Latin response. When we didn't respond on cue, there would be a silence as the priest waited or sometimes the priest would pronounce our responses himself. None of this bothered us. We didn't look upon it as a failure since we didn't want to be there anyway. The low Mass lasted about half an hour. After leading the priest into the sacristy, we went out and retrieved the Missal and cruets as well as put out the candles. The sudden quiet of the church at this time amazed me. There was perhaps one old lady left praying in a back pew. Others had left for work or to cook breakfast for the family and get the kids to school. The lights were turned out and the church reverted to its tomblike, shadowy stillness with the saints keeping their plaster vigil.

Jay Pistone

This minister then would go to Rush Street. He had a ball.

The biggest thing that we used to have fun with is they used to have tents. They had these ministers, black ministers, and they put up a tent. They're preachers, and we used to help 'em put up the tents. And fold the chairs, you know. These ministers, you know, they could get these black people to give up anything. They would have music, and then they'd get 'em going, you know. Hallalujah! Hallalujah! And then they'd pass the hat around and these people are giving money like crazy. This minister then would go to Rush Street. You know. With their money. He had a ball.

Oh, yeah, he paid us to pick up the chairs and the tent. The tents were put up on the corner of Sedgwick Street and Elm. It was an empty lot. Yeah. It was every summer they'd go out. They were con men.

You know what I mean. They were con men. They sold religion. You know I mean? These people were moved by the singing and all that and they would give their fifty cents, their quarters, and, you know, he knew just when to pass the basket around. You know. And these people would give. We used to have a ball 'cause then we know this guy's going on Rush Street.

Joe Zummo

I don't know if you could call this religion but I owe everything to the Catholic Church. When I transferred over to the Immaculate Conception I was much closer to my friends and thought they were good examples. Even parts of Jimmie Foley. It was a whole tremendous culture we had at the church—friends, altar boys. I didn't mind going to Church. We went to confession all the time. It was a little spooky, intimidating, scary. You know, letting this guy in this box know about your sins.

My parents never went to church—except my mother went to a protestant church on La Salle street. She would go there for the socialization and whatever freebies she could get. My father never went to church, however he used to make the sign of the cross before each meal and before he went to bed.

Paul Temple

They said a lot of the older nuns from the order of Sinsinawa Dominicans taught at Immaculate Conception. But you're talking about Sister Mildred. God, she was a character. That was the one that had the ruler. Put your hands on the desk and if you misbehaved, she'd crack ya. You know, I don't remember getting hit by her, but I can remember that very vividly. The other thing I know we did do to her. Remember the clocks on the wall? The big old clocks she'd set 'em and wind 'em every day? Once in awhile we'd move it ahead five minutes to get out of class. And that's true. I mean, I can remember doing that. I have no bad memories of the nuns.

I was an altar boy, yeah. Fifth or sixth grade? I can't remember. But to me it seems about four or five years that we served. We had another nun that I can't remember her name. We had her in sixth grade and had her in seventh grade again. She was a wonderful woman. She ran the altar boys at that time and the choir. There was another little nun, a little bit smaller who came and ran the choir. Little tiny nun. I wanna say Sister Maryellen. She got ticked off at the guys in eighth grade, the altar boys.

Now the big thing about being an altar boy was either the weddings or the funerals. The weddings you got money. The funerals you got out of school. So we always get out for an hour and a half or two hours. Then you'd run down to the corner to Condon's and get a cupcake or a Hostess Twinkie or something, go back to school. So it was great being an altar boy. I mean, those were the perks. So when she got ticked off at the guys in eighth grade, she demoted 'em and for two years, seventh and eighth grade, we had the weddings and funerals. It was phenomenal. It was the greatest thing that ever happened to us.

Jack La Brasca

Yeah, we did confirmation and, and you know, we did the

Baltimore Catechism. And I was an altar boy for about five years at St. Phillips so I knew the prayers at the foot of the altar.

My dad never went to church. My mother went to church but my dad never did. My mom went on Sundays. My mother didn't go during the week. It was not a thing. My grandmother, my Dad's mother, was a daily communicant, seven days a week. They had a 5:30 in the morning Italian Mass at St. Phillips. All in Italian. There'd be about twenty-five of 'em all in black and they went to Mass 5:30 every morning.

My dad was not religious. What I remember very strongly about my dad was that he was one of the guys in the neighborhood who had strong respect for his wife. He would never talk in vulgar terms about women. He would never participate when guys would talk about their gumatis, their girlfriends or things like that. And he always shied away from that sort of thing. He had a very, very, strong sense of respect for his wife. My mom.

No, the nuns in grammar school never talked to me about future plans or what high school to go to. No, in fact what I remember is that it was always a "they were there and we were here." You got there and you started at 9 and at 3:15 you split. And you had nothing to do with them. Except those people that lived right around the school. Some of the mothers would invite the nuns over for dinner or for pastry and coffee occasionally. But we were on the far northeast end of St.Phillip's. We were on Sedgwick Street. Which was really almost out of parish. And on a street that had a lot of Irish and old Germans. We were almost not a part of the Sicilian neighborhood.

There was a Sister in fifth grade name Dolorata. I was impressed with her effervescence, her upbeat attitude. Always gentle and never angry. She always talked about Brenda Starr, her favorite comic strip. For Lent,she gave up reading Brenda Starr then we'd all give her the back copies after Lent was over. But none of the nuns promoted any kind of scholarship. None of those native priests impressed me either.

Michael Lutazzi

Yeah, I went to church in grammar school. Had to. My parents went twice a year to church. Christmas and Easter. I went to church, I want to say everyday, but it can't be, you know. But I went every Good Friday and every Sunday. Good Friday was a day of fast, we had Communion and then we went to the cafeteria and had coffee and doughnuts. That was in grammar school. Didn't go to church in high school.

I can name you the nuns in grammar school. Can you believe that? Sister Leopold, third grade. Very nice woman. Sister Mathias, fourth grade. Very mean, short fat woman. Fifth grade, Sister ah, can't remember her. Sixth grade was Sister Valencia, mean woman. Seventh grade Sister Genorose, mean.

Eight grade, Sister Mary Walbirch. She was very very serious. Today I think about her and I wish I could know her today and buy her a beer. And sit and talk with her, you know. Sister Mary Walbirch. She seemed sad, sincere, smart, knew what she was doing and she paid attention to you. But when I think of her today, I want to talk to her. I want to know about her. And she was my last nun.

Yeah. I didn't get along with 'em. Fight. Sister Genorose grabbed me by the ear one time and dragged me down the aisle. That hurt, you know. She was pulling my whole body by my ear. That was in seventh grade. I was acting out a lot, you know. But, if I knew I couldn't get away with it, I wouldn't do it. And most of them teachers you couldn't get away with it. Leopold was so nice, you know. And I was only a third grader. I probably wasn't getting in much trouble then.

Joe Olita

Commandments that were not convenient were not kept.

There was a Protestant church which I believe was evangelical or something. We used to call them holy rollers. The church was located on Erie Street and I'm gonna say in around the 1400 block west. It was called Erie Chapel. Every year they had a Christmas party and they invited all the children in the neighborhood to participate in the Christmas celebration. I was probably six or seven years old.

There was a little bit of favoritism that was shown. I'm not objecting to that, but there was favoritism shown. Those children who actually were members of the church were the ones who were able to pick out their gifts first.

We used to sing a song, "The first the worst, the second the same, the third the best of all the gang." When we were going for the gifts, we would sing this song which would then give us this uplifting attitude. If you were last, it was probably the best thing that could happen to you even though we never realized that what we were getting were the gifts that were really picked over by someone else. I was probably six or seven years old.

Well I never went to Catholic school, but we went to Catechism. We went to Santa Maria Delorata, in the church itself where they used to conduct Catechism classes. Sometime during the week but it would be after school. I think it was two days a week or something like that and we would get our instruction and that. I had to go. Yeah, I had to go.

Well no, I wasn't religious. I believed in God, you know. There were certain Commandments that I kept because they were convenient. See. Those that were not convenient were not kept.

Frank Demonte

A little baby got born and he was a good dude.

Father Fleming, the pastor at Immaculate Conception Church, I thought he was 140 years old when I was young. And he may have been. Father Bracken became the assistant to the Cardinal for the longest time. Couldn't sing a note, but IC was his home parish and he taught at Quigley. Bracken was very smart. I liked Father Morrison, Father Mlnarik, Father Bracken. And a course the pastor, Father Fleming. But Fleming not as much as the other ones cause he was a older guy and the younger priests would always be very friendly and nice. Of course when we served Mass, they would tell us where to go and what to do.

The one that I like the most was Father Morrison. I guess, the word is, he didn't look down upon us. He was always trying to be like our friend. And he was the nicest guy … in fact I think he just died.

In grammar school the nuns taught us to be altar boys and the priest would come in and give classes on certain things. But we also served Mass. We had to say the Mass in Latin. We had to learn Latin. And of course that's when the repetition came in. Over and over again. Bracken and Mlnarik were kind of aloof. There were stories about Father Mlnarik, you know, that he went out on Rush Street and had a good time and stuff like that. I had no knowledge of that. You know, people say things that you can't prove.

I did religious things 'cause I had to. I did have a conscience. I got moved a little but not teary eyed. I liked Christmas. A little baby got born and he was a good dude.

John Owens

She was a very superstitious woman.

My mother never went to church but she liked to listen to these gospel programs on the radio or on television. She used to get on the streetcar and she used to go to St. Jude on the south side. Yeah. Yeah. She used to go and make candles and you know.

She favored all religions. Yeah. She'd get on streetcar and go to St. Jude's. I don't know if it was on 35th Street or something like that, on Halsted. She'd watch the programs on television with the gospel singers. She had pictures of saints and she always had candles. You know, like holy candles in the house. She was a very superstitious woman, I mean, *very* superstitious. I mean she believed that somebody could put a hex on ya so to speak, you know. She believed in that kind of stuff.

My sister and I got involved with the Catholic Church. When we were say maybe ten, twelve years old we used to go to St. Marchelo's church. That was on Evergreen; it's still there by the way.

It's all boarded up. Eventually the gangbangers took it over as their headquarters. And finally the cops got 'em outta there, now it's boarded up.

Yeah, my mother was southern and Baptist but you know what happened I think that ah, the nuns came over to the school. The grammar school. I think that's how it happened. I'm not sure how it happened, I'm not sure. But I started going to Catechism you know once a week, twice a week. I went through all that Catechism thing. And then I finally made my first Communion and Confirmation.

Yeah. My mother went to those ceremonies. A neighbor of ours who my father worked with, was an Italian guy, he was my godfather for my confirmation. He gave me a nice watch. I'll never forget that. You know. So I made my first Communion, Confirmation. My sister went to St. Phillip's grammar school on Oak Street. She went and made her Confirmation and everything and her first Communion and everything there. So she went to Catholic school. I don't know how all that came about.

I stopped going to church after I would say about that time that I got into high school. I stopped going to church.

Bunny Byrne

I was an altar boy. Everybody was. Free wine. Yeah. Two years. I really didn't take it seriously, but most of 'em did.

Yep. Both parents were religious. Both never missed church. Never.

Yeah, I went to church pretty steady up through high school. And after I got back from the service, I'd go. Yeah, I'd go, I never fell away. If I had something to do … like if I was going a football game, I wouldn't go to church. I'm getting ready to go to a Bears game or something, I'm not going to church, you know. I'm getting ready to do something else, you know. And the same way if I was out real late. If we're out to five, six in the morning, I'd get home and I wouldn't get up and go to church. You know. But if I was home, and Sunday came, I'd get up and go to church.

Ken Martinez

I was an altar boy for a very short period of time. Because Sister Seraphia, she was head of the altar boys and she caught me drinking wine and mimicking the priest. Well, see, we was on the altar. I was on the one side. This guy over on the opposite side did all the stuff and I just stood there. The only time I did anything is when we poured a little wine. And that's it and I'd go over on the other side. And then he left and I had to fold the stuff and put it in the drawers. I saw the hosts and I saw this thing of wine and I put the vestments on and I was going … Nomine Patris et Filias Sanctus … Deo Gracias … Deo Gracias … Mea Culpa … Mea Culpa … Mea Culpa … and I drank the wine. As I was eating the broken hosts that were in the container, Sister Seraphia hit me with the yardstick. She caught me. She says, "I want to talk to your mother. No, I want to talk to your father!" And I said, "I'd rather have you talk to my mother." And she was mean. She looked like a German Gestapo. Seventh grade.

Part Two: Mentors

Charlie Martinez

A personal human trusted advisor or counselor, I did not have. But somehow, in my detached, secret way, I sucked in ideas and concepts from those around me without acknowledging their contribution.

The gang taught me the satisfaction and the dangers of blind loyalty. Gratification came with a group of buddies always available to talk sex and sports and to play games and challenge the world. Our go it alone type of sports forced independence, creativity and initiative. But the heedless adherence to the group and its precepts made me act out of character. I was more antagonistic, willing to lower my personal standards and have confrontations with other teenagers and adults. Jimmy Foley helped me become a thief at Tanke's drug store. Joe Russo was the cause of our arrest at the Yankee Burger restaurant. I willingly was involved in a serious fight on North Avenue and North Park that could have gotten one of the crowd killed.

The street made me cautious, skeptical and aware of danger but unafraid. Adults had to prove themselves to me. I didn't demand this out loud but if I was offered a job, I listened intently and formed an opinion of the work, boss and pay and factored in my buddies' experiences if they had worked there. Then I decided on the job and did not hesitate to quit if it was not what I expected. The danger in the streets came from other gangs, blacks and dishonest police. My play in unregulated football, baseball, street hockey and swimming were all more dangerous than I gave any thought to. The streets held other dangers that I gave little attention but alertness for queers or shady men just not "smelling" right was always in the back of my mind.

The elders showed me the detachment power brings and the wondrous response of others to it. Father Fleming, the pastor, treated me as a nuisance problem and novelty. His only interest in me was to get the story of my running away. And yet others respected him and deferred to him.

The family gave me a sense of compassion as well as demonstrating the strength of frugality. Uncle Paul was a daily example to me of a man dedicated to duty; the duty of caring for an invalid, demanding wife. He worked sewing heavy canvas ship sails by hand. His hands were twisted with gnarled knuckles and scars and healing cuts and stab wounds. Yet he made toy parachutes for us and repaired our shoes when the soles ripped loose in play. The atmosphere of the house was frugality. No waste. No buying what you couldn't afford. Nothing extra at meals. No fruit, nuts or treats. The few Christmas presents, I now realize, were bought with sacrifice and were treasured. Anything new was a joy but new clothes, bed linens, towels and shoes were bought before toys.

I noted a greater tolerance and less of a smothering effect on a child than in other families. Johnny Nicolini was my best friend in grammar school. He was sheltered, protected, fed and watched over by his mother and father as if he were a baby eagle in their third-floor nest. He could not leave the house in the summer till he slept ten or twelve hours. He obeyed and loved his parents but you could feel the pressure on him. My parents never got involved in small stuff. Never told me how to live, what to do or when to come home by the time I was nine or ten. They had no involvement with school or work. No argument ever occurred between my parents and neighbors over me. It just wasn't done.

The nuns and priests presented discipline as the way to reach goals. Sister Seraphia, my seventh-grade teacher, demanded excellence. She confronted us daily. I always knew the answers to her questions but never studied and never took a book home, but I knew that she was giving an intense effort in educating us. Sister Eustella, my third-year high school teacher, praised my story writing, demanded nothing less than a strong effort in class work. Sister Monica, in her own way, was a drill sergeant and taskmaster in the typing classes. This skill supported my brother Jerry in his artwork and paid my high school, college and part of my medical school tuition.

The music, art, rituals, church buildings and rich religious celebrations were unknown to those in the neighborhood who were not Catholic and raised me somewhat above my social economic status.

Mr. Kiley, my English teacher in my freshman year at St. Joseph's College in Indiana, was impressed with an essay I wrote as a class assignment. It was on the Resurrection. He asked me to write a historical novel along the same lines. I did nothing. We had no more contact.

But a personal mentor I did not have.

Pete Eichel

Course the downside was, she was an alcoholic. All right?

And I'm thirteen years old. Twelve, thirteen. Bridget Malone and her husband Frank. He was a commercial artist. And he lived across from Ted Spiegal's building on Willow Street there. These were kind of arty people that had rehabilitated all those apartment buildings. Very nicely done and she kind of took me in. I kind've lived with her for like three or four years.

I have no idea why she took me in. You know I think I was this poor kid down the street and she didn't have any children. Well it was before I graduated from grammar school, so I was ten, eleven, twelve, thirteen. Right in there. My mother knew these people but there was no social relationship there, that's for sure. But she knew who they were because you know Bridget would come over sometimes and pick me up.

And I spent a lot a time there. Overnight, too. During the summers. I mean she was this lovely loving wonderful person that was like a second mother or surrogate mother to me. What she saw was this poor kid from down the street that had next to nothing. But you could imagine the impression it made on me. Maybe cause here I had these experiences with all these educated people and it never occurred to me at the time, you know, that it would make any difference but surely it did, you know. I mean I don't know who most of these people were but they obviously were well-educated and if they were middle class for us that would have been big stuff. Ok? But they were professional people and I remember they used to go mushroom hunting and they'd take me with em. And so that's an education. Course the down side was she was an alcoholic, all right? She had a real drinking problem, so did he.

Jay Pistone

> *I didn't have a mother so she took the place of my mother, you know, and watched me so I didn't get in trouble cause I was a little on the wild side.*

I had the same nun from fourth grade, for five years. Sister Mary Stanislaus. As I got promoted. Third, fourth, fifth, sixth, seventh and eighth. You know. There wasn't more than fourteen kids in a class. We had seven boys and seven girls in my class.

My mother died, so the nun sort of adopted me. Because she was worried about me getting in trouble. So she was actually my teacher and my guardian, you know.

Yeah, I was very close. When I went to the service, I wrote her. I used to always write to Sister and when I got married one time I had her over and invited a few a the fellas that went to school with me. She finally retired and went back to Canada.

I didn't have a mother so she took the place of my mother, you know, and watched me so I didn't get in trouble cause I was a little on the wild side. Matter of fact she passed away a year and a half ago. And me and Jack Flaherty went to her memorial. Yeah. And we met her family.

She was very young when she was teaching, so she wasn't more than maybe ten years older than we were, you know, when she was teaching. I was about eleven; she could be twenty-one, twenty-two. You know. She taught at a lot of schools but at St. Joseph, she was there about the longest. For about fifteen years till they knocked down the old one. They built a new one, then she went to another school. But I always kept in touch with her. In the service, I wrote her, you know. She wrote me. She used to write Jack Wallace. He's an actor from the neighborhood. He made a few pictures. When he was growing up he got on dope in those days and he got arrested.

And she wrote him even in prison. But afterwards he cleaned his act, became a movie star.

She kept in touch. She came here one time for Christmas. Yeah. I think it was about, I think my daughter was three or four years old. So that hadda be ah, about 1972. You know, we had her over for Christmas. But when we grew up, nuns were forbidden to associate with anybody outside the, you know, the convent. And the convent was right behind my house. And sometimes if I was a bad actor, after school I would go to the convent. You know what I mean? They had me kneeling there and then dinnertime would come, you know when they were all done cooking, ready to eat. They'd say, "Okay go home now." And I'd say, "Sister, well, can't I stay for dinner?" She used to say … "I never know what's gonna come out of you!" We had a good relationship. But I was sort of wild.

Jack La Brasca

And like an electricity went through me. Everything that I was seeing, I just felt like I was always a part of it. Like I was born to be here.

I was a clerk on the order desk for Westinghouse. And I realized at that particular point in time in my life that my diction was Chicagoese, dese, dems, and dose. They had a Toastmasters Club for the sales engineers. To help these young engineers to be able to speak more clearly and with a little bit more confidence. So they incorporated into the Westinghouse Electric sales staff a Toastmasters. These guys were coming out double EEs and they were pretty introverted and they had to be salesmen. So they decided that they were gonna bring in Toastmasters for these salesmen. Well, turns out that they could never get enough guys to constitute a quorum so they started inviting the clerks.

None of the clerks were interested. I was. I was about twenty. So I joined Toastmasters and they still didn't have enough guys so they invited a bunch of guys from the third floor, Quaker Oats. And the guys from Quaker Oats invited a bunch of guys from the Board of Trade where they bought oats from or corn in the futures. And they came over.

That's how I met Dave Mann of Cereal Byproducts, the company I later became president of. He sat next to me at Toastmasters and he liked me. And he said, "What do you do for Westinghouse?" And I told him. He says, "How would you like to be a grain trader?" I said "Ah, I don't know." I says, "You know, I never been exposed to that world." So he says, "Why don't come down and talk to us?" So I went to the Chicago Board of Trade. They took me down to the exchange floor and they took me to the cash market.

And like an electricity went through me. Everything that I was seeing, I just felt like I was always a part of it. Like I was born to be here. I swear to God, I mean I really felt like I had arrived at somewhere I was familiar with. I had never seen it but I'd been in it and it was like déjà vu. I says, "Yes I'd like this job." He says, "Don't you want to know what you're gonna make?" I says, "I don't care, I just want the job." So they interviewed me in June. And I didn't hear from them. And then in August they called me to come to work there. And I took the job. They sent me to Buffalo, New York for awhile and then they sent me to Omaha for awhile.

I wanted to get back to Chicago Board of Trade. I did. And of course, you know, I was just very lucky, just so very lucky that, you know, someone in this world finds something that fits their life as what happened for you and we're very lucky. It just happened that way for me. I was just absolutely thrilled with what I was doing. And because I liked it so much, it was easy for me. And it worked out okay. I was able to make a good living with it. And that was just fine. I found out though in all those years in the 60s and 70s that I was moving into this other world and I was losing contact with everything that I was attached to and there was nobody left that could understand, you know, where I was coming from nor did they care. They were in their own lives. So I really became a separate entity from everything that you and I knew as growing up. I just got lost in another vacuum. But it was okay. That was good for me.

Joe Zummo

There was one guy—Father Regan at the cathedral. Somehow

we hooked up even though we were totally opposite. He was Irish, I was Italian. He was educated, I was not. I was rough around the edges. I loved him very much and I even went to confession to him. And he said I got to get away from myself—go out and do something for somebody. I stayed close to him and he married me and baptized my kids. But my mentoring came from my teachers and some of my friends and my best mentor was Chuckie Martinez.

Michael Lutazzi

So he was like a god in the linotype business. And I was learning under him.

They saw something that I was good about. I had an understanding and a love for type. They said, "You wanna be a linotype operator?" I said, "Yeah." I didn't know what was going on. They steered me. An Irishman, Joe McGinty, he was one of the best. To appreciate linotype you need to understand it. It's like appreciating anything, you know, that's worthwhile. And it was quite a thing, this linotype. McGinty, was a master. He could not only set type beautifully and masterfully but he was a great mechanic of the machine. Which is a very complicated machine. The man who invented it went nuts after he invented it. And then they stole his idea. This was at the turn of the century.

And McGinty was just great, you know. He was consulting with the Tribune 'cause they would have like a hundred of these things. He wrote a book about how to maintain these things. So he was like a god in the linotype business. And I was learning under him. I began to understand that this guy was pretty good. I was having a really good teacher here. I got serious about myself. When I was sixteen and I started to learn something about printing, I got a part-time job in a print shop.

At the Paragon Press was a guy who was a captain in World War II. His name was Bob and his last name may come to me. Somebody told me I needed a hero. I didn't decide that by myself. Somebody said, you need somebody to look up to, like a hero. He was a captain and he saw combat and he was kinda my hero. He had this background, military background and he was a real nice man and he was a salesman in the company. He eventually bought part of the company and yeah, he was one of my heroes. I respected him. I liked him. When he talked with you, he listened to you, you know. You could sense it was a one-on one. He was sincere and either he was sincere or he was very good at being sincere. But I liked him a lot.

Pat Rogers

> *Frank McGrath asked me to go to De Paul Academy. It really saved me.*

Everybody thought me to be a gangster and I wasn't. I left this guy, Lefty Rosanthal because I had gotten myself into a few problems up there. I handled myself so concisely and violently and viciously in a number of incidents up there involving physical confrontation. At that time I started drinking heavily too. I was going downhill fast and the only one who kept me relatively sane was my new girlfriend. For her I tried to control myself as well as I could. But for that year I got into a number of scrapes. Cathedral wouldn't accept me back and I wasn't going to school. Ed Kelly, park district director, knew I was a good athlete. I was going no place fast so when Ed Kelly introduced me to Frank McGrath and Frank McGrath asked me to go to De Paul Academy, I went to De Paul and it really saved me. Really did. Turned me around.

John Giovenco

> *She said, "You know you got a pretty good head on your shoulders you oughta go to college."*

One day Sister Sharon walked up to me. I'll always remember this. She said, "You know you got a pretty good head on your shoulders." Now that's the first time anybody had ever told me anything like that. She said, "You oughta go to college." I said, "I don't know anything about college." I never met anybody that had ever gone to college. No one in my family had gone to college.

People at the advertising agency, you know, some of those had gone to college. I said, "No I got to go and get a job. My mother and father want me to go to work." She said, "Well you oughta go to college, think about it."

There was *The New World*, which was a Catholic newspaper, which everybody in the school had to go out and get subscriptions for. To bring them in for revenue. They had a contest in the city of Chicago and who sold the most subscriptions won a scholarship to college. And what Sister Sharon did was take all of the newspaper subscriptions for the entire school, sent them in under my name, and I won a scholarship to college. To the last scholarship given. Christian Brothers College, Memphis Tennessee.

John Owens

She said, "You should probably go into something like mechanics." I guess she had a lot of faith in me.

Mrs. Savage's husband worked for Boeing Aircraft. She used to bring me these nice photographs of these airplanes. Boeing aircraft, you know. She said, "You should probably go into something like either mechanical repair or something like that or aircraft." I guess she had a lot of faith in me. She wanted me to get involved with the aircraft industry, and I was only a kid. I would say fourth or fifth grade. Every day she'd bring me different pictures. You know her husband would bring 'em home for her and she'd give 'em to me, you know. Later on I started to build aircraft, miniature, from kits. So I did quite a bit of that. I always liked planes. I don't know why I got interested in planes. I think maybe because of her. You know.

Paul Temple

No, I never had anybody mentor me, no. You know when you look back and you think of all the things you didn't do that you should've done, you know, *who ever had anybody?*

CHAPTER ELEVEN: THE GROUP

Part One: Going to the Lake

An' I was thinking about all the times I used to walk up Schiller Street to the Lake. And I would think of a thousand things that, you know, the way buildings look at ya. Like the way they were painting a building; it would look like a face or something, you know. And your imagination could just go. I mean ... I enjoyed my childhood.

Ken Martinez

Charlie Martinez

Always the air was still and warm in the summer morning with a sweetness we tasted. All was quiet. Car horns blaring, streetcars clanging, elevated trains screeching on the turn at North Avenue -- these anxious city noises that so distracted the adults were merely background murmurs to us. A gathering on a midsummer's morning was about to begin for our journey to Lake Michigan. There at the corner of Schiller Street and North Park Avenue was the beacon that drew us -- the red fireplug in front of Mary Joyce's store.

Patti Irwin was one of the first to arrive, all neat, handsome and our revered time-waster. We were in awe at his perfect brush haircut. His Luckies pack was secure in the rolled-up right sleeve of his white tee shirt. His khakis had a modest crease and the penny loafers were buffed but not too brightly. He carried his towel and trunks folded and tucked under his left arm, which we, of course, immediately copied. His talent for seeming to do something while doing nothing was much admired and impossible to duplicate. And going to the Lake best showcased this art.

Boys walked from all directions to the red fireplug. Some were washed, with hair combed, and wore neat tee shirts and wash pants. Others wore dirt, gravel, and broken-glass-damaged clothes and appeared little different from the evening before when we had finished playing softball in the alley under the L. A few reluctantly went to rouse Johnny Nicolini, knowing it was futile. His mother demanded that Johnny get at least twelve hours sleep a night. Johnny was the respected nerd in the neighborhood. He was mediocre in all outdoor activity but he didn't "drag the street" with us and therefore avoided crime, drugs, alcohol, and danger. But we welcomed his calm, cheerful personality. Along with Johnny, Jimmy Foley, Patty Irwin and myself comprised the "Big Four." We set the intellectual and social tone in the eighth grade.

"Nicolini with the pimple on his weenie," we shouted at his third-floor window. But there was no response, and in fact, none of us had ever seen that pimple on his weenie.

Several more showed up in that slow but deliberate, "I have all day to waste" stroll. In case of want, there were two or three swimming suits drying out on the stack of Pepsi cases just inside Mary Joyce's front door. They were yours for the using. An important discussion ensued on how much each had to chip in to create a Dago sandwich. For the right amount, Mary Joyce would slice open a large loaf of Italian bread and stuff it with salami, boloney, and American cheese. Then she'd wrap it in a bag and we'd go down to the lake. We'd stay there the whole day. And then whenever you got hungry you'd go take a bite out of the sandwich. And finally the sandwich would be gone, sometime around noon or earlier. Then scrounging and conning would begin for more food or money from the girls or peripheral adults present.

Mary Joyce served the odor of oil with her Dago sandwiches. An Irish immigrant and middle-aged spinster, she ran the cramped general store at the corner of North Park and Schiller streets. She walked with a marked limp and had a shriveled left arm that she used as stick when wrapping, weighing and slicing meat. Her left leg she dragged along. She sold heating oil from a tank in the back end of her dollhouse-sized apartment, which was an extension of her store. She filled the five-gallon can you would bring and then she bounced and dragged the can to the front. Her hands were stained with and smelled of oil. I never saw those hands without their oil stains.

Whenever we really got her angry, she knew how to get back at us. She would grab the small hairs on the back of our necks and twist them. We would scream and holler as she twisted. She would ask with a thick Irish brogue, "Are ye gonna stop now? Are ye?" We would say "Yes" and when she let go we would laugh and run out. Now came Joe Russo. A short, muscular boy-man with a swagger and a chip on his shoulder as big as an L track tie, walked importantly into the group. He had handsome angular Italian features. He actually shaved and seemed several years older than us.

"Joe, you wanna get in on the Dago loaf?"

"Naw, I don't want that Mary Joyce shit. I'll get me a bizza or Italian Beef sangwich somewhere at the Lake."

Of course we agreed. No one wanted to risk being at the receiving end of one of Joe's unpredictable outbursts. He could be sweet, kind, gentle one moment and in a second he was at the throat of a stranger walking by who didn't break off a stare quickly enough.

But there were other ways to get food. A grocery store on North Avenue near LaSalle Street was right by an alley. The owner had some of his goods in stands on the sidewalk. Ken (my slightly older brother) and his buddy Gus used to steal carrots and potatoes from the stands and roast them at the lake. Or they'd go over by Gus's house and if his grandmother would be cooking spinach pies, they'd steal one. 'Course Gus would later get the hell beat out of him.

When we reached an undefined critical mass, the group began to overflow toward the lake, moving east on Schiller Street. We started in the shadow of a bleak four-story apartment building directly across from Mary Joyce's store. We called it Uncle Gocki's building for Patti Irwin's uncle. He was Maryellen Feeley's father. Scholl's Shoe Factory and B & B Shoe Factory formed a canyon that led us to the empty lot at Weiland Street and Schiller Street.

From this spot you could look into Patti Irwin's back porch. There was a long, steep stairway going up to Patti's rear apartment, the back third of the second floor. Inside, the apartment appeared as one large room divided into a bedroom, bathroom, kitchen and living room. It was crowded with doilied furniture. Framed saints peered down on us as we read through Patti's treasure of comic books. Patti, Ooner, and their widowed mother stuffed themselves into this limited space.

Below his apartment was the roof of a ten-foot-high utility building. We jumped from that roof many times into the mud of the yard, a snow bank, or a pile of old Christmas trees. The empty lot next door was the back yard of a black tenement building. We knew no one in that building.

Phil "Ooner" Irwin waved to us as his mother was just finishing combing the back of his curly brown hair. He was a couple of years younger than Patti. He was soft and handsome. In a few years he would be as tall as Patti. At which point the two had a vicious, bitter fistfight and wrestling match almost daily.

"Hey, come here you, Zummo! You don't need all that food you stole from your mother. Share it with me (I will take it all) and I'll let you ride in the raft today (the raft you paid a third for and I won't let you ride in anyway, sucker)."

Here was Bunny Byrne joining the flow at Wells, just coming from his apartment. He was a likable, gentle bully, con artist and all around fun guy as long as you weren't the con-ee. Joe Zummo quickened his pace. What to do? Joe carried a bag filled with a pound of salami, loaf of bread, Hostess cupcakes, and several bottles of Pepsi. All of this he put on his mother's "bill" at Mary Joyce's store. His mother knew nothing of the purchase. Joe hurried but was now a wounded deer and Bunny eventually tracked him down and his food was forcibly "shared."

Now we are just passing Magrini's Tavern on the corner of Schiller Street and Wells Street. That's where the "older guys" drank and vomited. In a few years we would also spend our time there in a beer-brain muddle. Across the street from Magrini's was the "old peoples" tavern called the Friendly Tap. A dreary place, its décor and patrons frozen in time in the 20s or 30s. In our late teens, they weren't careful in checking our fake ID's and we would show them our Selective Service card with altered birthdate, printed on only one side. But early on we'd get one of the bums who hung around outside to go in and buy our booze. The bums got a few beers for their troubles.

Past Wells, there was a block of modest-sized, tired apartment buildings, then the path opened to the broad, sunny expanse of La

Salle Street. From here to Clark Street was a gas station and the backs of tenement-like apartment buildings.

Tanke Drugs was at the northwest corner of Clark Street and Schiller Street. Jimmy Foley introduced us to, and seduced us into, thievery and early sexual debauchery in this drugstore. Although our age, he was socially precocious. He could talk to and charm kids, girls, and adults with an ease that a seasoned politician would have given up several large, stuffed envelopes for. He was smooth as the moss on the old wooden lake piers. He did well by accepting no moral code but his own best interest. And still we were drawn to him like ants to a dropped Dreamsicle. He would show up at the lake later in the morning with his entourage of fawning fellow potheads. He was magnetic. He was danger, evil, adventure, hope, daring, even good -- all in the handsome body of a natural leader.

Kitty-corner was the Schiller Lounge, a place that eventually claimed several livers from the group. Here we come to Dearborn Street, to State, then Astor and the Inner Drive. Now we pass elegant greystones, chic apartment buildings and stately single-family residences -- all with clean, curtained windows. Some were partitioned off from the street by a brick wall. This area seemed deserted. We seldom saw passersby unless they were deliverymen. This was the Gold Coast.

Steve Russo led a subgroup as the crowd stretched out to half a block. He and his brother Joe were similar physically but opposite in temperament. Both were short but muscular beyond their years. Steve's tan, collared short-sleeve shirt with the one roll of the sleeve to expose his biceps coordinated with his brown slacks and penny loafers. The upper two buttons of his shirt were open. His black hair was perfectly sculpted back to a duck's ass at the neck. He talked little, at least to the several lames walking with him. He was into jazz, dancing, and marijuana. When he spoke in his soft voice we leaned forward to catch the words of this envied one. He stopped. "Don't do that man, it ain't cool."

He looked right at me, not menacing but with an absolute feeling that he knew what was cool and I was violating that rule by throwing pebbles onto an expensive car. I threw a few more pebbles.

He walked ahead of us and to him and me I was the lamest of the lame.

While we walked, John Owens was bringing a few of the guys to the lake in his '42 Hudson Coupe. It was a powder blue ghost of a car with blue dot brake lights. The car moved silently except for a delicious rumble of the dual exhausts. This was a reflection of John who was tall, quiet, smooth and agreeable, and generous with his car and mechanical knowledge.

"I bought that car for ninety bucks, Charlie." His own car! I listened in awe. At the lake his group immediately organized a dice game on the cement. They watched the broads go by and once in a while took a swim.

There were no front lawns in our journey, only pitiful fenced-off areas along the curb with weeds and dog crap sharing the space. The tang of an open garbage can as we passed an alley would cause us to turn our heads away. Occasionally we caught the sweet scent of a decaying rat but mostly car and truck exhaust fumes filled the air till we got close to the lake. Then a cool, clean breeze reached us and lured us on.

The end of our journey was signaled by a huge, dreary, red brick wannabe mansion on acres of land surrounded by a five-foot brick wall. Slippery topstones set at an angle thwarted our attempts to walk it. This was the Potter Palmer Castle. A mercantile baron's attempt to outdo his fellow Joneses. Nancy Constable, a girl in our class, lived above the huge garage. Her father was the chauffeur. We didn't get to see the inside of the mansion, but we did play tackle with the girls on the lawn. This game fed our imagination and led to further discussions and arguments at the lake about the softness of the girls and who had almost touched some forbidden fruit.

And there, seen across Lake Shore Drive through a chain-link fence intended to prevent us from crossing at this point, was Shangri La. Lake Michigan. We had overcome sloth, parental indifference, hunger, boring jobs, boring school, feuding, fights, leadership problems, poverty, police, drugs, religion, juvenile detention, and beer drunks, to arrive. All that was left was to terrorize motorists as we ran the gauntlet of speeding cars on Lake Shore Drive. Ken led the way but ran in front of a bus and was hit by a Cadillac coming up on the other side of the bus. The guy was going slowly, and Ken went right over the hood, got up, and ran like hell. We scaled the chain-link fence and began to gorge ourselves on wasted time.

Cement and water was all a person ever saw in that area of the lakefront. The cement was hot and clean, and there was no odor. The sun had burned off all the spit, urine and other garbage left behind from the night. A few dead fish were drying themselves out in the sun. The water was now a beautiful blue but most of the time it was a pale green, and when the wind blew southwest, a gray-black, smelly foam accumulated near shore. The guys would then cannonball open a clear area for swimming.

A few years before I had walked alone near Goethe Street at the lake. This was the beginning of the deep water. I was eleven. The ladder drew me. I climbed down, pushed off and dog-paddled out about thirty feet. After I turned around, I could not figure out what to do next. I slipped under the surface of the water and at the same time I saw a red blur coming through the air towards me. The red blur was the lifeguard that brought me to the surface and pulled me to the ladder. I got up on the cement and walked away from my first deepwater swim. My parents never knew. Others learned to swim in a similar frightening manner. Jim Sullivan simply jumped in the deep water when he was six and swam back to shore, to the shock of his companions. Ken learned to swim by being physically thrown into the deep water by the older guys. He thrashed about and dog-paddled his way to shore.

And it was not just in the summer that we went to the lake. We made trips when the Schiller Street area was our Arctic frontier. No crowds, just a frigid wind in our face and blocks of ice rising and falling gently with the swells of the slush-thickened water. The ice-covered footing was slippery and treacherous. But young boys were not at the lake in the middle of winter for the beauty. Adventure was the calling. And a dare became contagious until all undressed and jumped into the lake for one instantaneous blast of shock and pain. While dressing we began the delicious retelling, laughing, and shouting about our triumph.

Bunny Byrne, his brother John and Patty Irwin were the rock divers. The water was about eight feet deep at Schiller Street. There were big stones down at the bottom where it was murky and they found them by feel. Sometimes they spent the whole day bringing stones up. They would bring a hundred and fifty large stones up. The stones were light underwater. Then they'd have to struggle to get 'em up on the cement. But they'd have piles up there. Then before they'd go home at night, they threw them all back in.

A sand beach at North Avenue and a sand beach at Oak Street set the north-south borders for our five-block island of cement. From here at Schiller Street you could look north or south for blocks. On a clear day, you could see tall apartment buildings in the south seemingly floating in the lake as the shoreline curved eastward in the Jackson Park area miles away. At the southern end of Oak Street Beach, the cement wall starts in again. The twenty- to thirty-foot expanse of cement on the lakefront wasn't always neatly hemmed in by steel pilings. Earlier, the Schiller Street area was a dangerous jumble of slippery, moss-laden, rotting timbers scattered through blocks of cement, broken and tossed as if by a giant. None of us could swim but we jumped among the cement chunks where a slip could mean a bashed-in skull or death by drowning.

We were hunters. In the crevices of broken cement were creatures we sought. Two- or three-inch brown crabs. We threw in pieces of stale bread and grabbed the crabs when they went for the bait. I don't recall that we ever took them home, just threw them back.

And on a certain day a blue spinning light caught our eye. A police patrol wagon had pulled onto the cement past Oak Street Beach. A Fire Department ambulance could be made out. A cluster of bodies was forming near the vehicles and I imagined people were peering out their windows from the Drake Hotel. This was something to look into. A group of us began a slow trot, then a run towards the gathering. We climbed the front of the cement wall and stumbled into a scene of unexpected calm. Several of us, unencumbered by social constraints, worked our way to the front of the crowd, where firemen and policemen were talking quietly, almost reverently, among themselves.

On the cement was a man lying on his back. His arms were stiff and stuck out to the side from his shoulders. His elbows were bent with his forearms across his chest and his hands clenched. This was the pose of the little boxing men at the penny arcade next to the Windsor Theater. He was pale green and looked like a marble statue that had been placed on its back while the workmen were getting its pedestal ready. The skin was wet and the cement under him was dark where the water had run from his body. A small trickle of blood ran from his left nostril to the corner of his mouth. His towel was near him with a pair of shoes. Pants and a tee shirt were neatly laid out on top of them. Several beer cans were standing by the shoes. Wave riplets made slight splashing noises against the cement wall.

A fireman replaced the pulmotor into its case where each piece was put into a space that was shaped to receive it. He closed and locked the red box marked "Chicago Rescue Squad." The crowd diffused back into their niches on the beach but we stayed. Our fascination had not decreased. A fireman and a policeman rolled the statue up on its side as another policeman pushed a canvas stretcher, stained from previous occupants, as far in as he could and then they lowered the stiff body and settled it on the stretcher. The statue's earth-life paraphernalia, including the beer cans, was placed between his feet. A gray sheet, dappled with yellow and red blotches, was brought forth and placed over him and at the same time he was lifted and placed in the police meat wagon. We watched as the wagon moved at a solemn pace, with blue lights blinking, towards the opening in the fence at Oak Street and disappeared up Lake Shore Drive.

We walked north toward Schiller Street. Silence was our shield against awkward discussion. Dead rats, horses, ants, caterpillars, mice, dogs, and cats were a curiosity or object of fun -- but they were not of us. This wasn't the movies where John Wayne killed ten outlaws with bullets from one six-shooter. We knew that was fake. Make-believe and real were separating out in our minds. I thought of Bobby Humberg who lost his leg then his life to cancer in the seventh grade. At Schiller Street we got dressed, and climbed the chain-link fence. The wind had shifted to the southwest and behind us the water turned gray-black with a foamy scum.

We again dashed crazily across Lake Shore Drive and then began the trek back to the neighborhood. We were quieter with the group more strung out along the sidewalk. But after a few blocks the talk started on whether we would be able to con Mary Joyce or some of the little guys out of enough money for a Pepsi and Hostess CupCakes. Life was full of hope again.

Part Two: Fights

I mean, he kicks him in the face like he's kicking a football.
Frank De Monte

Charlie Martinez

Fights of different intensity, cause and duration were an everyday occurrence. To call something a fight, physical contact had to be made, not just swearing and hollering. Just nasty looks and a little shoving really didn't constitute a fight. Then there were several types of fights. Gang fights were generally a short, sometimes prearranged free for all that usually was broken up by police or dissipated because the crowd thought the police were called. Occasionally the gang fight ended because one or several guys received a serious injury.

Spontaneous fights between members within a gang could be vicious and even end up with the loser being banished or badly humiliated. Fights between people on the street who did not know each other occurred because of some imagined or real insult. Similar fights occurred in theaters. Fights at parties and wedding receptions happened often because of the presence of liquor and drugs. These fights were between guys from different neighborhoods and not always between gangs. The two groups just did not know each other or barely had contact but each thought the other was a dangerous usurping stranger. Fights over girls were rare and usually just an excuse for a gang fight.

An unusual and usually vicious type of fight was the one between brothers or close friends. These could be recurrent and seemed senseless. Neither party would back down or totally forgive the other. The fight did not settle the argument because the disagreement was a deep hatred and usually could not be stated.

As there were different types and intensity of fights, there were different types of fighters. Most people in a gang fight were not really fighters on their own. They were just taken up by the excitement and need to feel involved and not "chicken." Usually in each gang or group there were several fighters in the sense they would decide on the battle and lead it. They would pull along the rest of us. Then there were guys who weren't necessarily leaders but were known as tough guys just the same. They were in and out of a gang or group and sometimes just fought their own battles.

A special few vicious guys, who were "thugs" to us, were total loners who fought to rob people and tolerated no insult. These were dangerous people and most ended up dying of lead poisoning or going to prison.

A peculiar additional type was the instigator. Surprisingly, these were frequently the smaller or smallest person in the group. He depended totally on back-up from the stronger group members. He would start an argument and throw a punch when the guy was not looking or unaware. Then the others would finish things up for him.

Fighting was not an action that bothered most of us in a moral sense. We felt righteous and it was as much or more fun than winning a baseball game. A few people with sensitive souls shrunk from the combat, but most enjoyed it. For most the joy was a rush of fear and excitement, strong bonding with your buddies, and the glory of talking about your role and the whole affair endlessly afterwards.

Charlie Martinez

He pulled out a screwdriver and plunged it into my right eye.

Joe Zummo walked toward me and we met in front of his house at the south side of Monteleone's red brick three-flat at the corner of North Park Avenue and Schiller Street. I was with my older sister, Patsy. Imagining that he was about to be attacked, he stopped, pulled out a screwdriver and plunged it into my right eye. He was five years old and I was six. Immediately there was a large group of kids taunting him at his front fence. He cowered in the house, terrified. I don't recall any particular discomfort or pain. I was taken to the eye doctor and I remember a cool ointment being placed on my eye. I suffered no permanent damage except a scar on my iris. The instigation for the attack was unknown and the event not thought of during the thousand summer days we spent together in our childhood. We have been friends ever since.

Jay Pistone

We're running trying to ketch the streetcar. And there's parents coming out of the homes chasing us

We were in the *Herald American* softball tournament and we played at Kosciusko Park. Now that's all Polish. Now, us Italian guys we started shaving at fourteen or fifteen. This was ah seventeen or under tournament. We were playing a game and whoever wins this game plays for the championship for the *Herald American* newspaper. The Polish guys said we were all over seventeen and they start coming over, start swearing at us, pushing us around. So I got all the guys together, I says, "We better take a duck before we get hurt." Well we were lucky we got out a that neighborhood with our lives. Ya know I mean?

The game got outta hand and they're chasing us down the street with baseball bats. And we're catching it; we're running trying to ketch the streetcar. And there's parents coming out of the homes chasing us. You know, we couldn't get out of that neighborhood. Several of our guys got beat up pretty bad. You know wha' I mean?

So I sent in the score that we won the game. They sent the score that they won the game. Ya know. Actually they won the game, but we didn't finish it. So the *Herald American* calls us in and asks what happened. I said, "Well, what happened was you can ask the umpires, I mean the game got otta hand. We showed our birth certificates to *Herald American*." I says, "Look, here's every guy on my team. There's our birth certificates."

So now the game has to be played at Seward Park to decide on who plays in the championship game. I know all the black guys at Seward Park. So I told all the black guys from Seward Park that our ball players are gonna have tapes on their noses. So the black guys could recognize youus. We all had double tapes on our noses. I says you gonna have about ten carloads of Polish with their parents coming to play the game. You know wha I mean? And they were having race riots like crazy at Wells High School between the Polish and the blacks already. So the minute the ball game started, here comes about two hundred black guys, with chains, you know. And gun and knives.

See what in those days the big weapon was the switchblade. What they do is, if they didn't have the button knife, they would put toothpicks inside where the knife blades were. Ya know? So the knife would open faster. They'd practice all day long. I used to laugh. Ya mean ya waste all yer time on that, you know. But that was their thing. Knives were their thing. I tell ya they really beat the hell out of those Polish guys. They never made it to their cars. They start beating 'em with chains. They started knifing 'em. The police finally came.

Ya, we, ha, ha, ha, we won the tournament. I mean they asked for it, ya know I mean? We didn't lay a hand on 'em. We were just sitting there with our tapes on our noses and all the black kids in the neighborhood, you know, were laying on 'em boy. They were beatin 'em up.

Jack La Brasca

Yes I was part of it, but you know I don't know if I was throwing punches just to be part of it or not to be tagged as a sissy.

One night, it was late winter early spring; we were on Cambridge and Chicago. Cold night, under the lights, shooting dice on the sidewalk. And a big black guy named Joe Miller walked over by the crap game, picked up the money, put it in his pocket. Anthony Manascalco hit him from behind, Lenney Lapaglio gave him a punch and he fell in the gutter. We jumped in Anthony's 1951 Buick and they ran over him. Bump, bump, bump. I says, we just committed a murder. I says, we're all gonna go to jail for life. So we all went home. I was trembling. I was scared to death.

I was sixteen. About three weeks later, it was a warm summer day, we were playing ball. Who walks up to Seward Park? Joe Miller with his head bandaged. He's got a little Babe Ruth souvenir baseball bat and he's chasing Anthony Manascalco with it. He wanted to kill him. In fact he did catch him. He gave him a beating. He came back from the dead. I remember that like it was yesterday because I remember, thinking is this really happening, we're running over a, a human being? I mean, we ran over the guy with a Buick,

Another time there was a couple of girls in the neighborhood that said that these guys were bothering 'em. They were two Latino guys and got caught by Seward Park, these two Latino guys. They caught such a beating that you couldn't recognize them. Their faces were so battered. All I can remember is the brutality of it. I mean. It always bothered me. I mean I was in the middle of all this but it always bothered me. Yes I was part of it, but you know I don't know if I was throwing punches just to be part of it or not. I might have, out of, you know, just not to be tagged as a sissy.

There was a real famous fight between a group of hillbillies from around La Salle and Elm and the guys from the neighborhood around Schiller and Sedgwick. The leader of the hillbillies was called Nick Adeamus. Our guys were Moonus, and Domonic Ferello. Domonic Ferello was stabbed about seven times in the lungs. Well, from north of Division. It was more your neighborhood. There was about three, four guys in the hospital. Domonic Ferello, they gave him the last rites.

Later, we were hanging out in a joint called the White Castle. It was on Division and La Salle. Anthony Maniscalco who thought he was a minor torpedo, got into it with this Nick Adeamus. The next thing you know there was about fifty hillbillies out there with motorcycles and we had to get out through the back door. So Anthony Maniscalco went and told his nephew Nicky what happened. This guy Nick Adeamus lived in a wooden frame house on Elm just east of La Salle Street. And Nicky told another guy by the name of Turps. And Turps got one of those big shotguns and kept shooting at the guy's house till the boards were coming off. Nobody would believe this!

On Oak Street, near St. Phillip Benizi, there was a candy store named Jim and Els. A bunch of guys hung out in there that they referred to as the Eagan Rats. There was a sociologist major from Menominee, Wisconsin, Ray Raymond, who was working at Seward Park during a summer internship. He had no idea what kind of neighborhood he was involved in. He found out about these guys who hung out on Oak Street at Jim and Els called the Eagan Rats. He started writing a newspaper, a monthly newspaper about their exploits.

These were the roughest, toughest, dead end kids you ever saw in your life. There was Red Foley, Willie's older brother and Spike. They were almost famous -- street fighters. A guy by the name of the Beak, Carl Jondolia , Jeeps, who was gonna be a priest and came out of it. Ah, Fingers Burke. These guys were tough, tough, street fighters. I don't know where it came from, but they called them the Eagan Rats.

They cornered this guy by, ah, by Jenner school on a hot summer night. And they had one of those mops that they used for tarring roofs but the tar had turned hard. They were whacking him with this thing. And skin was flying. I mean there was chunks of flesh all over the place. And no one ever saw him again. Either he disappeared or he died. So, I mean, I saw some brutality. I saw some serious brutality.

When I was a senior at Waller 'cause I had left Holy Name after my junior year, there was a problem. Some guy from the Italian neighborhood around Ogden and Chicago was romancing one of the girls. Which is a different clique. And they had a guy by the name of Phil Polito. He was like major league in that neighborhood. Big time tough guy. People said his name and people shivered. Well, it turns out they were coming. The guys from Ogden and Chicago, they were gonna come on a Thursday night to our neighborhood. We were gonna meet on Division and Orleans to fight. It was all planned. Then we got some guys from Webster and couple black guys from the neighborhood, and another clique from around Fullerton. We had about forty guys underneath the L waiting for them. And then their cars came.

There was a kid from Webster named Timmy McDevit, and he was supposed to stand in front of the coffee shop where this was all gonna go down underneath the tracks. He was the first guy, I mean like nine guys were punching him. And all of sudden the blacks were coming from underneath the L. They were on our side and they were slamming the cars with big boards and throwing bottles at them. They all took off. I mean it was a flash, bang, and boom. One car flipped over. There were guys all over the street. I was kinda huddling in a corner. I was pretty scared. I was really scared.

Charlie Martinez

We rolled in the glass-strewn alley and our clothes got tattooed with dog shit.

There was no glory in fighting Tommy Walsh. First of all the fights were expected once a week. The audience grew bored with the fight, although they were the instigators. An older guy (e.g. thirteen or fourteen) would shove Tommy against me or say that Tommy beat me last time. If I didn't respond with a shove of my own, they'd say, "What's the matter, Charlie, ya chicken?"

Vile swear words were exchanged. Faces turned red. Sweat beads came out as we pushed against each other saying, yeah go ahead you asshole. Then after dancing around like this for a few moments, one of us would throw a punch. After about three or four wild ineffectual punches by both of us, the wrestling began. This pitted one red faced, sweat-soaked stinking body against another red faced, sweat-soaked stinking body. We rolled in the glass-strewn alley ground and our clothes got tattooed with dog shit.

This went on for a few minutes till we tied each other up so that no punches could be thrown and we tired. No signal was given but somehow we released our grips simultaneously, stood up, and walked away. The instigators would compliment me on this ridiculous exhibition, but Tommy walked away alone.

Joe Olita

It was obvious to me that he had carried this hostility in his heart from our original meeting.

When I was about nine years old my brother-in-law was driving a truck for a trucking company. And it was during the summer time and I loved to go with him because he would always buy me lunch. And this one time that I went with him we went just about a block away. My brother-in-law had a friend there that he was very friendly with who was also a truck driver that drove for another trucking company. His friend had a kid there that was about my age. And I didn't know this guy from Adam.

So through the course of the conversation my brother-in-law said to his friend "My brother-in-law will beat the hell out of your friend there, your little friend." He says like hell he would. And he said, oh yes he will. You want to bet? And he says, yeah I'll bet you. So they go ahead and they make this bet. And I don't know who this kid is! So the next thing I know here we are, we're fighting. So my brother-in-law collects the bet.

I saw the kid after that and I thought we were friends. We had a relationship for many years. We used to call him "Pigeon Tony" cause he was interested in pigeons. We went through, I would say Charlie fifteen years of what I thought was a friendship and a friendly relationship.

One day, it was on a Sunday, we were at the gas station. Pigeon Tony happened to be there. There must have been maybe seven or eight guys there. There were other people, grownups like my brother-in-law and the gas station owner and people like that. So I would say all told there might be maybe fifteen guys. I was probably about twenty-three years old. So, for some reason, Tony starts to pick on me.

I says you know. "Tony, knock the shit off, you're really getting me pissed off." He'd, you know, make remarks like "Fuck you." I said, "You know you're going a little far Tony I'm not gonna take too much of this." It was obvious to me that afterwards that he had carried this hostility in his heart that I never knew from our original meeting. I didn't want to have any problem with him. You know. And as this thing went on I tried to avoid him. He says, "You're a motherfucker." I said "You sonofabitch, you better take that back right now." And he says. "There ain't no way I'm taking that back." I said, "Well get prepared to get your ass beat."

He says, "Just a minute; I gotta go home and change my shoes. I have new shoes on." Stupid. And I says, "Okay." So now, yeah because I figure by the time he goes home, I mean this is a friend of mine, he changes his shoes and comes back, he's gonna say, "Jesus Christ, I'm sorry." But he didn't. And now you had to pick a second.

You always had a second, see. All the guys that were there actually formed a ring. Whenever there was gonna be a fight, it was Charlie, it was like somebody got on the radio and spread it with a loudspeaker. Pretty soon there had to be I'd say a hundred guys that were standing around. Okay. So then I said to one of the guys, you know, I said "We are gonna have to have somebody who's gonna set the rules on this thing to make sure that we don't break the rules here." So then we said to one guy, "You're gonna be like the ref. Now you're gonna be the ref and watch what's going on here. But we'll set the rules. So the rules were is it gonna be a clean fight or is it gonna be a dirty fight and anything goes." When in an anything goes fight, if the guy goes down you can kick him, you can stomp him, you can do anything you want. But if it's gonna be clean and you knock him down you wait for him to get up. See. So we decided on clean.

I said, "My brother's gonna be my second." And then Tony picked somebody. So we get in the ring and then we start it. I had a really great reluctance to hit him, I mean really and truly. So we were going around and he would throw a punch and he'd hit me and he'd throw another punch and I'd block it and he'd throw another punch. I never returned it. We did this for about a minute and a half.

As I was going around, I saw my brother standing there. I looked at him and he had the fear of God on his face. What that told me was, "What the hell is the matter with you, are you afraid of him?" That's all I had to have. He had thrown a punch and I blocked him and I gave him a right and I came through with a left and I knocked him down. See the fact remains that he would never say he had enough. So I let him get up and I hit him a couple of more times and I said, "You know what, I've had enough, Tony. I don't want no more of this, I've had enough." And he said, "Okay."

He never talked to me again. He would come down the street and if I were walking towards him, he would cross the street to avoid me. And that was the tragedy of the situation 'cause I liked this guy. Absolutely bizarre. The truth of the matter was that last time I ever hit anybody. Yep, the last time.

Charlie Martinez

Fists flew and the other guy crumpled to the ground.

We were young. Ken, my brother, was maybe fourteen and I was twelve. Just walking north on North Park Avenue on the IC lot side. We were heading to the Plaza Theater on a Saturday afternoon to catch the cowboy movies and get a free comic book if you left without staying for a repeat of the movies. That's how they got the kids to leave the show; otherwise everybody would have stayed seven, eight hours.

A guy we did not know, was walking toward us on Ken's side of the sidewalk. He was about Ken's size, six foot, a hundred and fifty pounds but maybe a year older. Now there was an unwritten law in the neighborhood that when two male teenage strangers are walking towards each other, one has to give way. Of course this would seem gutless if you were the one who moved out of the way. The gap was closing fast. Neither Ken nor the other guy shifted their position on the sidewalk. Fifty feet, thirty feet, ten feet then both stopped about three feet apart. No words were exchanged. Fists flew and the other guy crumpled to the ground. We went on to the Plaza, saw the cowboy movies and got our comic books.

Frank De Monte

And before George even knew it, the guy hits 'em, and flattens him

Do you remember at that time in the late fifties what was the big thing on Chicago and Division streets? The beatniks. Well they had these restaurants where you sat down and they would tell poetry and then you would drink beer and stuff. We went to one of 'em called the La Moi ... whatever that was. So there was Ezzie, Joe Lendino, Dom Faraci, me, Zummo, Mike Bonifedi, George and Paul Temple. We had a bunch of guys. And there was two girls. There was Ezzie's wife, Jackie and Dom's sister Vivian.

So we went in there just to spend some time. You know, the deal was you sat around these little pillows, and the guy would talk, and it was like a Jack Kerouac type thing, you know. All we were gonna do is sit down and have a beer. And I had a fake ID. All the other guys were twenty-one and me and Joe were like twenty. Now when you sat on these pillows they had these little tables with the candles on 'em. To make it feel like you're cozy. But at that time the candles were in the glass and they didn't have those plastic things. So if you picked up the candle, ya burned your hand.

So when George sat down, he wanted to move the candle to another a small table. He burns his hand. He goes "Ow," and throws the candle and the wax on another guy in a different group. Okay?

You can see it coming, you know what's gonna happen. Now the guy gets mad, he jumps up and George says, "Oh, oh, I'm really sorry I just burned my hand on the candle." He says, "Let me buy you a drink." He says, "My fault." The guy says, "Okay." I mean he's got the wax on him, but it was, you know, it was an accident. Now George goes up there and not only gets his drink but gets the guy's buddies a drink. There's two other buddies with him. He's got all these drinks in his hand (chuckles) and it's dark in there, so he trips over the pillow and the drinks falls on the same guy. Now he's not only is he loaded with the wax, but the drinks as well.

So then the guy says, "Outside." See, I don't think that these guys knew how many guys we had. We were eight. Eight of us and I think three or four of them. So we took it outside.

Well what happened is George was following him, right? So the guy comes out, and before George even knew it, the guy hits 'em, and flattens him. And after that we just started fighting. You see I didn't know you could really hurt somebody in a fight at that time. A fight used to last a punch or two.

Joe Zummo jumps on the guy who hits George. Then another guy tries to get Joe, but before he got to Joe, Paul gets him and he virtually picks him up and he throws him so far he lands on the hood of a car. The other guy is gonna fight all of us but before he gets to fight me and Joey and Dominic Bonafedi hits him in the jaw, knocks him down. I think he hits him about two or three times. But he says to him which I thought was very nice of Michael at the time. "Don't get up. Stay there."

The guy, he's not listening. So he starts to get up. But before he gets up, Michael kicks him right in the face. I mean, he kicks him like he's kicking a football. And I thought he killed him. He snapped his head back and he went down and hit himself on the cement. And, I mean, Mike musta hurt him.

There was another guy that was there that me, Dominic, Essie and Joe hit at the same time. It was one guy and we would like punch at the same time. But Dominic missed and he hits me. And then he's swinging like crazy and I said, "Dominic, over that way." So we got on this one guy. There was four of us on this one guy. I don't think we were really hurting him. I think I pulled his hair one time and I think Dominic wanted to punch him and missed. But the thing was over in like ... if I was gonna say it lasted more than a minute it was a lot. So it ended very quickly but then we all took off. Did I tell ya the two girls that were there? Never stopped screamin'. Jackie and Vivian. Never stopped screamin'. Ya, they're killing these guys!

Then we all jumped in a cab and we took off. But I gotta tell ya something, I look back and I gotta tell ya something, it was just like a Damon Runyon film. Dat's how funny it was. It wasn't funny for the guys who got a beating but it was funny for us when in retrospect we looked back.

John Owens

This kid, Patac's cousin, grabs a full bottle of Pepsi and he hit this guy on the side of the head and cut his whole fuckin' neck open.

There was a restaurant across from Marshall Field Apartments. Maria's, just north of Evergreen on Sedgwick Street. Right. East side of the street, yeah. And we used to hang out there quite a bit too. At lunch hour from high school we used to go over there.

Things happened in there too. I don't know if you know Jim Patac? Yeah? Do you remember Moose the big broad, from Washburn? A real tall woman.

She was a good looking woman. Real nice shape on her, you know. Big.

Once a week the apprentices would come. The union would send them to school the whole day and they would pay 'em for that day. So there was a tavern on the other side of the street and these guys had left school … I guess they were in their late twenties or something, and were in this bar drinking all morning probably. So lunch hour they come over to get something to eat in this place. Well Jim Patac's cousin was here from Detroit. So one guy is really getting hot and heavy with Toni, ah, Moose we called her.

Yeah, one of the drunks from across the street. She's telling him, leave me alone, you know. And he's starting to grab her and everything. This kid, Jim Patac's cousin, comes up and says, hey, you better leave her alone. And the guy says, fuck you, you know.

In those days they used to have the Pepsis in the wood cartons. The bottles were stacked in the cartons on the rack. This kid, Patac's cousin grabs a full bottle of Pepsi and he hit this guy on the side of the head and cut his whole fuckin' neck open. We all scattered. I mean we just ran. Fucking siren, you know. The cops were coming and we were running like crazy. I left my car there. I was scared to go get my car. And I went home. I didn't come out till maybe eight o'clock at night, you know. I went back and got my car. And the next day, we're like, what happened, you know. So, you know, I don't know. I'm sure the guy's still alive, I don't think he died. But, I mean, he was cut pretty bad, you know.

Charlie Martinez

Ken tapped Frank Corbett on the shoulder. Corbett turned and was greeted with a right fist to the face that knocked him backward over the fireplug at the corner of Orleans Street and Schiller Street. That was the only good punch Ken got in.

Earlier, Corbett, who was a few years older and about twenty pounds heavier than Ken, although they were the same height, had beat up Ken for reasons that have been blown away with a summer thunderstorm.

When Ken came home after the first fight, Bernie, our older brother, would not accept the fact the fight was over. He took us back to the crowd, instructing Ken to hit Corbett first, with no discussion. Well, Ken followed Bernie's plan but unfortunately Corbett got up and pulverized Ken. And so another legendary fight was added to the stories of the neighborhood.

Bunny Byrne

I says, you know, it'll be over my dead body you'll get this basketball.

It all started with Tommy Walsh stealing money at the bingo games. I still don't know how he did it. But he used to have a wallet full of money. He used to have thirty, forty bucks in that wallet, which was an enormous amount of money in our day. And one day we're walking home. He lived on Weiland. I lived on Wells.

We were walking home and this big fat woman was coming up the street. I knew he had this fat wallet. I figured, he might hand it too me. So, I says, Jesus Tommy here comes your mother.

"Where?"

"She's coming up the street, a big fat woman."

It wasn't her. I knew it wasn't her, but I knew he couldn't see her, see. He was cross-eyed. She was about half a block away. And he went, "Jesus, Holy Christ." He took the wallet out of his pocket. We were walking right along the back of Immaculate Conception grammar school and there's a green fence there where the nuns lived. And he pitched the wallet over the fence. And he kept going. And naturally when he got down there he says, "That wasn't my mother." And I says, "I thought it was her, you know." And he went "Okay, I'll see ya" and he went into his gangway to his house. Well I just doubled around, went back and jumped the fence and got the wallet. Now, luckily enough, there was about twenty-six bucks in the wallet. The next day we all made the trip over to Montgomery Ward's. And they just came out with an outdoor rubber basketball. They never had 'em before. You know if you played on the leather one it was gone to hell in no time. This was the rubber one. And I says, guys, we're gonna get the rubber basketball. So we went to Ward's and we got the ball.

We go over to the Olivet and we're playing basketball. Now, all of a sudden we get in the locker room and one of the guys says to me, "Bunny, where's the basketball?" There was Corbett there, my brother, Mike Cavatio, Roy Fabri, I don't know who else. Some guy says, "There's a guy outside with the ball. There's one of the guys from the Cleveland Aces got the ball out in the gym." And I says, "Well, I gotta get the ball."

The Cleveland Aces was an Italian gang that hung around the Olivet. And that's just about all they did. You know, they didn't move outa that area but you dasn't go into their area, it was like that. So what happens is, I went back out and this guy Joe Vanilla has the basketball and he's down at the other end playing. So I went down, I says, "Joe we're gonna go now, we gotta have the basketball." And he says, "Hey, you'll get the basketball when I'm done." So just about that time he threw it up, and it hit the rim and bounced over his head and I got it. So, I says, "We're going Joe, we gotta have it." So away I go back into the locker room.

Well three minutes later, there's forty guys in the locker room where we're at. I mean, it's jammed. It's like everyone of them was in there see, so. He wanted the basketball. I says, "You know, it'll be over my dead body you'll get this basketball. So you want the basketball? You're gonna have to take it." Well, boom, the shit hit the fan. So anyway, there was nobody really helping me because there was like forty of them and about five or six of us. So as it turned out after it was over, I still had the basketball and I stood up there. Course I got a cut in my eye, my nose is bleeding and someone says, "Are you gonna give up the ball?" I says, "No." I said, "No way." I says, "You're not getting this ball, guy." So then somebody said, "Aw come on, let's go and they walked out."

And that was it. See and a funny thing happened too. 'Cause I said to him, "Someday we'll meet again, Joe." And I came out of service. This is like five, six years later. There was a bar on Ogden Avenue. I was up there with my cousin Eddie Boyle. He was Billy's brother. He was huge, you know. But who walks in but this Joe Vanilla. Well, I, I mean it was like, "My god the chicken's come home to roost." Here he comes and he's about your size. And I walk up to him and I says, "Joe?" He looks at me and he says, "What?" I says, "Remember me?" And he goes "No." I says "Yes you do." "Naw, I don't."

And I says, "You don't remember the basketball, huh, Joe." And he goes, "Ah, the basketball?" And he says, "You know I don't know if you're aware of it," he says, "You know, I got a paralyzed left hand." And I says, "You had a paralyzed left hand back then." I said, "But you had forty guys with ya." I says, "I don't see anybody here with ya now." He goes, "Well, I just wanna tell I got a paralyzed hand." I says, "Alright, Joe," I said, "forget about it." I says. "Go ahead and have your drinks, enjoy yourself." You know, I was gonna give him a pass. I wasn't gonna beat him up anyway. But, I just wanted him to know, 'cause I remember saying that to him that day. I said, "We might meet again Joe."

But that's what it was in that neighborhood. See, you didn't mess around over there. They wouldn't come over to Lincoln Park where we were playing football or anything 'cause we had a lot of guys there, see. And they wouldn't come to the Plaza Theater in a big group 'cause we were usually in there with the Rams. They'd come in two's and four's. They never came in a gang. But if you went over to the Olivet where they hung out, they would like, you know, they would congregate see, where they had numbers. See.

We had some fights there in the high school cafeteria too. Yeah. The year ahead of us. You know, Vince Gullo got into it with a guy that was a year ahead of us in school. It was over seating, see. The seniors supposedly sat at the seat next to the door. Well we beat 'em there, we sat in the seat. They came in, this guy Rothamel, he comes to our table. Jim Rothamel. He says to Vince, Get up." And Vince says, well you know how Vince was he had a temper anyway. He says, "Fuck you, I ain't getting up." You know, and he says, "Hey this is where we sit." Bernie McCauley was there, Marty Barnes. They were all with him and they weren't about to mess with any of us. None of 'em. But ah, he grabbed Vince by the jacket and Vince jumped up and punched him and down they went. Vince threw the guy down the stairs and threw him out on the basketball court. Holy Christ, I mean, we really went at it. There was a, I can't think of this little guys name, he was like an Indian or something. I had aholed a him. Vince had this Jim. My brother was fighting with somebody. Dick Ryan and Tom Ryan too and you know we really got into it. And the nuns were screaming "stop it."

The only fight my brother Johnny was really in that meant anything was his fight with the Walshes. He beat Johnny Walsh up over some argument they had. And Johnny went home and the father came back with Tommy who was older. He told Tommy to beat my brother up. So, my brother beat Tommy up. While he was giving Tommy a whipping the old man stepped in to stop 'em and he punched the old man in the groin, which knocked the old man down, and then he punched him in the face when he was falling down. And so that was the story of John fighting the Walshes.

John Giovenco

He smashed a Coca-Cola up against my head.

I remember and this is later. This is Third Base. I had a fight with Jimmy Foley at Third Base. We were sitting there and having a discussion and he took a Coke and he poured it on me. So I took my Coke and I poured it on him. He stood up and took a glass, a Coca-Cola glass and smashed it up against my head. And it broke. It dazed me. I just stood there, dazed. You know, cause he hit me with the glass. And there were three or four other people in the room. The next day I came back to Third Base and brought a knife. If he touched me, I was gonna stick him with the knife.

I went to the lake about a week later ... remember Carl Madonia? Carl said, if I wanted him to, he would beat the shit out of Foley for me. He said he didn't like Foley anyway. He didn't like the idea that Foley beat me up and that he would fight him. I said "No," I really didn't want him to do that.

Ken Martinez

His father hit me 'cause I beat the hell out of Jimmy. So the next day I beat the hell out of Jimmy again.

I didn't get into too many fights in high school. Grammar school yes. Grammar school I got in a lot of fights. I used to beat the hell out of Jimmy Foley. His father was a cop and he hit me across the ass with the nightstick. I went home and told my father and my brother Clement. Clement went over and talked to him. I don't know what he said to him. It hurt. Man that hurt. He hit me 'cause I beat the hell out of Jimmy. So the next day I beat the hell out of Jimmy again. He was a pain in the ass. He always wanted to be boss of everything. And he would put his face close to you and start talking and that just used to aggravate me. And I just beat the hell out of him. I hit him three or four times.

Charlie Martinez

I told him that Jimmy was no longer the leader of the gang.

You know, I don't remember any discussion. No preliminary comparing of notes or evaluating each other's points of argument. There was Ken pounding Jimmy Foley into the ground right next to the fireplug directly in front of our house on North Park Avenue. I vaguely think Ken was protecting me from Jimmy "always wanting to be boss." At any rate, after the beating, I walked east through the alley between George Maltezos's apartment and the priest house and continued across Weiland Street into the empty lot behind the black peoples' apartment buildings facing Wells Street. I went up to the fence to the north and hollered for Patti Irwin. I told him about the fight and that Jimmy was no longer the leader of the gang. I was a little premature. The next day there was no question that Jimmy was back in his familiar role as the boss. He just resumed the position as if nothing had happened because, in retrospect, Ken had no followers or, as we would say now, no political power.

Frank DeMonte

...you got to have a badge of honor.

Just north of us at DePaul Academy, there was a hangout of hillbillies. They used to come down and pick on some of the guys at DePaul. I guess they did it one time where they picked on the wrong guys and it was our group. So we all got in two cars, went down … you know where Lincoln and Sheffield is? There was an L station. There was a restaurant that the hillbillies stayed in. We went inside, we had about fifteen guys. We went inside; beat the shit out of fifteen guys. And I mean we laid them out. It was one of these things where I was scared to death but I had to go because … it was the group. It was almost like you got to have a badge of honor.

Charlie Martinez

To show you how a "non-fight" occurs, I will relate an occurrence in the Gold Coast Theater located on the west side of Clark Street almost at North Avenue. I was in the movie theater with Joe Zummo and Joe Russo. I was sitting in the middle. We were about sixteen. Three or four guys who were perhaps a year or two older than us were in the seats directly behind us. One of them leaned forward.

"How you guys doin'?"

"Okay, okay."

We all looked at each other in a nice friendly way but we didn't recognize them and they didn't know us.

He asked about the movie and made a few more comments.

"Do you guys know Bill Fortunato?"

About here I felt uneasy because this was like an opening line for a fight.

I said, "No, I don't know him."

The guy mentioned the name a second time and again I answered in the negative. Then this guy swings, hits me in the side of the head and I fall off of the seat onto the floor. The two Joes each take off and out the show up opposite aisles. I am on the floor and these guys are climbing over the seats trying to get to me. People are screaming. Suddenly it gets quiet. I get up. Standing next to me was the most feared thug in the neighborhood. Frank Gimarici and he was on my side!

"What's goin' on here?" he said.

I blurted out, "I'm from the Rams, you know me." Which of course he didn't know me but he must have known that the Rams were a local group. The four guys trying to get to me ran up the aisle and out the front door. I had a bruise or two but nothing really hurt. Gimarici went back to his girl without a word and I began my search for my two buddies. Years later, Gimarici and his wife were shot dead over an Outfit business disagreement.

Jim Sullivan

I just always backed myself to the wall and said, you know, take it and they never did.

Yeah. I had quite a few fights in grammar school. I don't know why, but my nature was that if I knew I was gonna get into a fight I usually swung the first punch. Yeah. I didn't screw around. If I saw that it was going down to the point where it was going to be pushing or shoving or punching, I usually did the first punch. I was smaller, you know, in grammar school in the first grades and I started to get a little bigger and stronger. When I got a bigger and stronger, I didn't take any guff from anybody.

I didn't get into a lot of fights in high school. You know, most fights were like local neighborhood fights. But there used to be like high school bullies. They would try to say, let me take a dime off of you. That would be like their approach, you know. And they would intimidate people, you know, younger kids. And I would always stand up to them and tell 'em if you wanted to get a dime from me they have to take it from me. And you know, they never gave me a problem. We had couple guys like that, but whenever they tried it with me, I just always backed myself to the wall and said, you know, take it and they never did. And, you know, I'm not a fighting guy except that if I know I'm gonna get into a fight, you know, I don't back away from the fight. I don't look for the fight.

It was like a couple times I went out with you know, some of the Cleveland Aces. You know Donny Ferrela. And like Joe Labella and stuff like that. Joe was the smallest guy in the place and he'd always pick a fight with the biggest guy in the place, you know. And his favorite mode of attack was like to cold cock the guy when he wasn't looking. Just to punch him or to throw a chair at him or something like that and there was quite an uproar. And you know, I'd say I'm smart enough to say this is the wrong kind of guys to hang around with because you know you're gonna end up in jail or you're gonna end up hurt or end up whatever. I just never hung around with those guys.

Charlie Martinez

Just then Pete runs into the group as a blur and hits another big guy on the head with something.

Joe Russo was suspended in the air and was about to be dropped into a cement stairwell, down maybe ten feet.
How did Pete Eichel, Joe Russo, and me get into this mess? Well add one part Joe Russo, three parts testosterone and three or four beers each and you got yourself volatility. There is now a small step to outright craziness.

The three of us, underage for taverns at about nineteen, were doing what they call pub-crawling in England. Hitting a few places and having a beer in each. At about midnight we ended up in a tavern at North Avenue and North Park Avenue on the northwest corner. This was a low-class place, peopled by motorcycle riders, hillbillies and other drifters. We're sitting at the bar, killing time, not knowing what to do next when I hear, "Hey that's my beer you're drinking!" Joe Russo responded in the most gentlemanly way possible.

"Tough shit, man."

There was general mumbling and staring. We decided that we had enough of this place and walked out the front door. We went across North Avenue and stood on the southwest corner of the intersection, next to Benny's Toy Store. Glancing over our shoulders, we noticed three or four guys come out of the tavern and start across the street. Aw, shit. Now we can't run 'cause the stupid beer drinking made us braver than normal.

They come over and after some more staring, one guy grabs me and tries to drive his knee into my groin area several times. This has no effect. I hit this guy once and he rolls over against a parked car. I see Joe being lifted up. Now there was some kind of sidewalk construction going on in the spot. I picked up a two-by-four and broke it over the head of a guy who is getting set to drop Joe to at least a month in the intensive care unit at a local hospital. Joe is released and starts swinging at people.

Throughout this several-minute episode (and these fights always seemed to be only a few moments), I hear this screaming coming from south on North Park Avenue. It gets louder and louder and eventually I realize some woman is screaming, "Peter! Peter!" Just then Pete runs into the group as a blur and hits another big guy on the head with something. At this point, Joe, Pete, and myself take off running south under the L tracks in IC lot. As we get safely away we began laughing at our good fortune. Pete shows us what he hit the guy with. It is some type of curved knife about eighteen inches long. Pete had run to his home about half a block away, grabbed the knife and headed back. The screaming woman was his mother chasing him to try and stop him.

Well we laughed and laughed and told the story to ourselves twenty times. The next day was Sunday and the three of us decided to take in a matinee at the Windsor Theater on Clark Street near Division. We were across the street when we saw several of the guys from the fight buying tickets. One guy has his head wrapped in a turban like bandage. We instantly referred to him thereafter as the "Arab." We then discreetly walked away to find another movie house. And we never made contact with those guys again.

But, wait. A covert operation was in motion that we knew nothing about. The boys we had the fight with were out for revenge. The rumor was passed around that they had acquired guns and were trying to locate us. Fortunately, Pete's sister found out about their plans. She tipped off her boyfriend, Nino, who was "connected." Suddenly the plans to come after us were dropped. We went on our way, blissfully ignorant of a real possibility of a shortened lifespan.

Part Three: Buddies

An hour for play,
An hour for sport.
But for a friend
Is life too short.

> *Anonymous*
> *Framed poem hung above Joe Zummo's*
> *parents' bed,*
> *in their Wells Street apartment.*

The excitement for me back then was being part of the group of kids that we hung around with. Okay? Now, you know, just knowing that you could go somewhere that took ya out of that terrible home environment, and then be with people that you could talk with and laugh with and share things with and feel like, you know ...

- Pete Eichel

Charlie Martinez

Summer camp

> *"Over hill, over dale, we will hit the dusty trail*
> *As the caissons go rolling along.*
> *For it's hi, hi, hee, in the Field Artillery...*

Here comes my brother Ken, arms pumping, knees kicking, voice booming, marching alone down the middle of a creek fully clothed.

This was camping at its best. No rules, no parents, no Boy Scout leaders. Just ten preteens on their own in the Forest Preserve. 'Course the equipment such as tents, knapsacks, axes, and knives were "borrowed" from Boy Scout Troop 142. But what did that matter? The stuff would be returned in almost as good condition as when we took it. The point is, we were camping. And how did all this start? Probably word of mouth with Foley buying in and becoming the unofficial leader.

There was no discussion with parents. I don't think they knew where we were for that whole weekend and likely they thought we were going on a supervised Boy Scout outing.

Travel to the Mannheim Woods Forest Preserve was simple. We caught the L at the Schiller Street station on a Friday morning. The train took us through downtown and turned west south of the Loop. It continued to the Westchester stop. This was the end of the line. We marched off and into the Forest Preserve entrance a few blocks away.

We did not apply any complicated Boy Scout training in selecting our campsite. We just picked the first open spot we found and pitched our tents. This was a few yards from a creek. Hot dogs, buns, cans of soup and beans as well as candy and pop was all the food we carried. No need to even start a fire for cooking.

After setting up the tents, the rest of the outing consisted of just fooling around and we followed whatever our ten- and eleven-year-old minds led us to. Ken caught a snapping turtle that first afternoon. We tortured it with sticks and bait for a while and then released it back into the creek. We did some minimal hiking and of course Ken wowed us with his dramatic march down the creek. Also, since we had plenty of food, we got into our foolish heads that it would be fun to put all our hot dogs up in the trees. By the next afternoon we were hungry for those hot dogs. So Patty Irwin climbed the trees, retrieved the hot dogs and we all had them for supper.

I hiked alone once and came across some older teens at a campsite. As usual, they acted like I was invisible because of my age and went about their business. One girl was hitting a boy and saying as she laughed, "Jerry's a jagoff, Jerry's a jagoff." My imagination went crazy trying to figure out what other things went on between them if she could shout something so intimate. How lucky can you be?

Late Saturday afternoon, Foley decided to organize us into a sexual orgy. He had us lie on our sides, bellies to butts, with our pants pulled down. He instructed us to put our erections (always a thought away) between the legs of the guy in front. This lasted about a minute till everybody got secretly embarrassed and the orgy broke up. Foley was hard to resist, no matter what crazy plan he suggested.

Sunday morning came. We had not washed for two days and had the musty smell of canvas in our clothes and hair. But what a wonderful outing it had been. Before leaving, we disposed of our garbage in the trash cans. However, one last ceremony had to be performed to make it a perfect adventure. We threw our leftover full cans of soup and beans into a campfire that belonged to another group. We watched with our faces a foot away as the cans swelled and then in a glorious moment, burst, sending boiling hot soup and red ashes into our faces. We laughed and howled at the wonder of it.

We retraced our route on the L and got home late Sunday morning. Our parents said and asked nothing, but likely were pleased that we had had a chance to experience nature under the careful guidance of the Scoutmasters.

Pete Eichel

> *Geez, we had people that ranged from wasted drug addicts that were isolated, to people that went on to be very successful. Academically and professionally.*

What the hell did we do at sixteen, seventeen years old? We drank beer and sat on the school steps. We were hanging out. I mean there would be as many as forty or fifty of us sitting around that little Guerney's restaurant on Evergreen at North Park Avenue. The little hamburger joint with a jukebox. Everybody, all just sitting around, you know, like one happy big-time congregation. Remember the crabs from the fish store on Sedgwick? We'd all go over and get crabs and we'd break those things up and we'd all eat them together.

And of course Jimmy Foley would come with a case of some kind of booze. He'd be stealing all that stuff from Solomon's when he worked there delivering. And he'd bring a case of beer and a couple bottles a booze. A course they'd all be smoking pot, you know, the other side, the cool guys sitting with the juiceheads. They're all right, those juiceheads, you know but they're lame. They don't smoke pot, you know or do heroin or whatever they were doing. But yeah those were great times, you know. Just hanging together as a group and doing all that stuff. Where the hell were you? You were in college. But you were there. You weren't in college yet.

I had a lot a different people that I had a good relationship with. Because I knew Michael Lutazzi and I got to know Joe Spiza and those guys from the Wildcats and the Tigers and the Cleveland Aces. And then they had the Junior Aces. And John Catini was in my class in IC and I got to know them. Tony was with the Tiger group and so I kinda got to know them. Those groups were gangs. Italian gangs. Yeah, little Mafia gangs. It had to be before I was sixteen. So it had to be twelve, thirteen, fourteen, fifteen. Right in there, right during that period. Then later in high school we were the Rams.

You know, with people being different, they were different relationships. There were people that I grew up with who made better decisions than other people. They were little more capable of looking out and preparing for the future. Geez, we had people that ranged from wasted drug addicts that were isolated, to people that went on to be very successful. Academically and professionally. And I had friends across the whole range of those people.

Sal and I were very good friends, And of course Sal became addicted to drugs when he was maybe about my brother's age. Which woulda been a year or two before my brother was addicted. In his early teens. And I'd forgotten him. An he was one of those people that instigated and dealt, you know, influenced other kids. He was dealing drugs to maintain his habit. He died in his thirties.

Jack Flaherty

They was just group of guys with some common interest or common neighborhood that just gave themselves a name so they knew their association.

Well, back then of course there were a lot of us guys around. There were six, seven young guys that just lived on the block, so. There was always someone to play ball with or do anything with.

Here I'm talking of guys who lived on Wendell Street. Eddie Wagner, Tom Tarrant, Marty Barnes, and Joey Aguila.

Joey Aguila, his father was a doctor. He used to take care of everybody in the neighborhood. When they had a problem, you never had to wait in line like with the other patients, cause he would always bring you in the other door to his dad's place and you'd get a quick treatment and be gone again without the people in the other room, the waiting room, knowing about it. We spent a lot of time at Joey's house. He had a pretty big apartment and it was just a place to hang out. Just talk, watch TV. Maybe play a little cards.

Near school at Division and La Salle there was a hamburger place. Then near the high school there was this malt shop that we always went to usually after sporting events. Right by Loyola University. Probably Pearson and Rush. Also some football activity. We picked up with a group a guys, called ourself the Rams and we played a lot of football in Lincoln Park. We were pretty good really. I think we went two, three years undefeated.

Joe Zummo

My proving grounds in life was my friends. Guys like Chuckie Martinez, even Jimmie Foley, Johnnie Nicolini and Patti Irwin—four different personalities but involved in friendship vis-à-vis school. I learned very early in life what a friend really means. Without them I might be nothing. I still carry my childhood friendships with me internally and realize what they did for me and gave me a platform of substance on which to build. I think I got my intellectual curiosity from all these guys. They were just my heroes.

But I really enjoyed the guys. My whole life was the guys. I enjoyed them and their parents and if you were lucky enough to get in the house you might get a free meal. In high school Jimmy Fischera had parties in his basement and some of the girls had parties. The guys used to just hang out. You would just hang out in front of Mary Joyce's store after you were thrown out and tell stories or go sit on Chuckie Martinez's steps and tell stories.

Somewhere along the line, in my freshman year, there was a store that opened up called Third Base. The owner Josephine Bogan had a sign over the door saying 'You must go to Third Base before you go home.' We spent the lion's share of our free time at Third Base all through high school. I used to go there with my own tea bag, buy a cup of water for a nickel and a donut and that was my breakfast before I grabbed a streetcar or bus to go to school. I remember Chuckie Martinez and I ran up a bill of thirty or forty dollars. We had a job painting this woman, Miss Mundy's floor and then threw a party. We moved a wrought iron table and scratched the floor. We eventually paid the bill when we got the money.

Summer was filled with softball tournaments. In fact a guy named Bobby Johns organized a tournament for fifteen and under and we ended up winning the tournament. And the opposing pitcher in the championship game was Isaac Putrus who played with the Menomonie club.

Charlie Martinez

The *Sunday Sun-Times* reached the crest of its flight, hesitated, then spread its wings, exploded and morphed into two hundred black and white and colored birds. These pages of the news, comics, sports and advertisements fluttered and floated down on a summer morning breeze into the alley, back yards and tops of garages of Goethe Street houses. I knew Mr. Catalano wouldn't appreciate the beauty of the scene. He might even be angry when he realized he would have to search the alley, backyards and garage tops for those two hundred pages of his Sunday newspaper. Of course, I knew when I threw the paper it had no chance of reaching his third-floor back porch.

But adventure was calling. "Come on, come on," my brother Ken hollered from the street. I ran to the end of the alley and jumped on my bike. Ken and I raced to catch up to Joe Zummo, Abba Kennedy and Patty Irwin. Whose idea it was to make this trip I don't know. But we decided on the spot to ride our bikes to my sister's house in Lockport, Illinois. This was about a forty-mile ride. My sister knew nothing of our coming and our mothers knew nothing of our going. Ken was twelve years old; Patti and myself were eleven. Zummo and Abba were ten years old.

Our preparations were as complete as for anything. We had a total of seventy-five cents, a lunch Zummo hurriedly grabbed from home, no extra clothing, and only a vague idea of our route to my sister's. I can't remember whose bikes we used. None of us owned a bike, so they must have been borrowed without the owners knowing about the trip. They were cheap Schwinns with balloon tires, coaster brakes, and single speed.

The caravan rode southwest on Ogden Avenue for a while, then headed south to catch Archer Avenue and then southwest again towards Lockport. After a few hours, our hunger couldn't be ignored. We stopped on a grassy slope next to a cemetery. Zummo was behind us taking up the last place. We waited eagerly as he pedaled up to us.

"All right, get the food out Joe," said Ken.

"What food?" said Joe.

"The shit you packed at your house!"

"I ate that an hour ago."

Now we knew why he stayed at the end of the column. Disaster. Hours more of pedaling with no chance of food. We were able to buy pop at a picnic we passed -- but the smell of grilling hamburgers, hot dogs and Polish sausages made us feel like the prisoners on the Bataan Death March we saw in the movies at the Plaza.

At the end of the ride we had to pedal up a steep hill to my sister's house on 13th Street. She was surprised to see us but welcomed us without hesitation. She may have called my mother to let her know where we were, but that was irrelevant to us. She couldn't have contacted Joe's or Patty's mother because they had no phones. Patsy fed us well. Freddy, her husband, was a husky ex-Marine, badly wounded at Iwo Jima. He looked at us. No smile, no greeting. He walked away.

That night we slept on the living room floor with Joe crawling under the dining room table. The next morning Freddy came downstairs to eat breakfast before catching the train for work. I didn't want to meet his eyes because the odor from our dried sweat-soaked clothes and shoes and socks was awful. He passed us by without comment.

Lockport was a separate small town a few miles from Joliet. Archer Avenue bisected the "downtown." We took a bicycle tour of my sister's neighborhood and the downtown. We marveled at the absence of anything that resembled the Near North Side. No ghettos, no tall buildings, L, streetcars or buses. No crowds. No blacks. Just calmness.

Adventure turned to danger on our return trip. Darkness overtook us halfway back. The highways were all two lane and we rode with the traffic without lights or reflectors. The car and truck drivers must have been shocked when they happened on us suddenly around a curve. The rush of noise, bright lights and gusts of wind of the semi's kept us pedaling and terrified. Occasional horn blasts made us pedal faster. We had no bike breakdowns during the entire passage.

So we came home without mishap. I recall no discussion of "where were you" etc. I just went to bed, savoring another adventure with my buddies.

Jack La Brasca

We'd go buy a loaf-an.

As we got a little bit older we started having clubs in a clubroom. You know, there'd be an empty apartment. You know how that worked. Everybody went in on dirty furniture and we would roast potatoes with paper and did that sort of thing. We were probably about eight or nine.

In the summertime it seemed like the streets were empty on Sedgwick Street. I was always with Sal Randazzo. We started together in first grade. My mom and his mom were very close and we were always together. We hung out constantly and sometimes we'd go in the hallway and lock the door and fight. And punch each other silly.

In the real early days I remember there were bullies in the neighborhood. There was a family called Mole. They were all older. Sicilians. There was Frank who was about our age. He had an older brother named Sammy who was like, seven years older and then an older brother named Phil. They moved into the neighborhood from another neighborhood and they were like bullies.

Probably I was about six. And I remember they knocked my brother down. He was gonna make his Confirmation or Communion and his face was cut up from falling on his glasses. They were always mischievous. And they got away with murder. I was scared to death of that family. They were always abusing people, you know. And the neighborhood wasn't fun in those days.

Well, in fifth and sixth grade we started going downtown to the movies. We took the 163 streetcar on Sedgwick Street. It took us right to State Street. We went downtown usually on Sunday afternoon.

We were eight, nine, ten, that area. My brother and I and a couple guys from the neighborhood get on the streetcar. We'd go to the Woods, or the Oriental or the Chicago. That was a big thing. Really a big thing. Especially around the holidays.

During the summer vacation we hung out in the neighborhood. It was kind of boring. You played softball. Ah, maybe three, four games. Then you'd go buy a loaf-an. Which was, you'd get a loaf of Italian bread, slice it in half, put lunchmeat and tomatoes and cut it three ways and then get a Pepsi. And you'd do that and then start another ball game. Maybe we'd open up the water hydrant. And get underneath that for a while.

See that culture on Oak Street was dramatically different than on Sedgwick where I lived and it was dramatically different than Third Base and IC. And dramatically different from Cleveland Avenue. It was a different, as you went from block to block, it was a different scene. Different scene.

Charlie Martinez

"A terrified. crying face was plastered against the back window."

Wandering the Gold Coast was a pleasant waste of time. You might find treasure in the "rich people's" garbage. Once we did find a battered trumpet, which we used for entertainment up and down the neighborhood. This weekday afternoon we decided to taunt the "rich kids" from the Latin School. Tommy Walsh, Joe Zummo and I worked our way over to North Avenue and Clark Street. I say worked our way because we never just walked along like adults. Twelve- and thirteen-year-olds constantly inspected gangways, stairs, alleys, and front and backyards looking for any goods that we could confiscate.

We saw our prey milling around a nondescript building. Parents in cars were picking some up. New cars! How could this be? We taunted several well-dressed teenagers as they came by. We made fun of their collared shirts, khaki pants and polished shoes. They said nothing. We were proud of our actions.

We laughed and carried on but didn't notice a car pull up alongside us on Clark Street. We heard a scream and Tommy Walsh was gone. Swallowed up into the car as we ran like crazy. We ran into alleys, up side streets and worked our way back within a block or two of the school. We stood there wondering what the hell happened to Tommy. Just then the same car came rushing past us. A terrified, crying face was plastered against the back window. He pounded on the window and was screaming something we could not hear. It was Tommy! Of course we ran in the opposite direction. We never asked Tommy what happened or what they did with him. We assumed the "they" were security people from the Latin School. At least that is how we rationalized our cowardice for years.

But over sixty years later, I saw the movie *Mystic River*. A similar incident occurred where two men pretending to be policemen grabbed one of three boys playing in the street. As the car drove away, the boy looked out a car window and pleaded for help. The boy was taken and sexually abused. The incident with Tommy Walsh came back to me in the movie house. I thought, what if the guy in the car was not a security person from Latin School but just some pervert. We never knew and Tommy never said.

Michael Lutazzi

We even didn't care if he went out with a white girl.

My existence was unique because I grew up on Cleveland Avenue, had a bunch of friends there. And then I grew up on Wells Street and I had a bunch of friends there. So I had friends in two neighborhoods and I grew up knowing a lot of guys. When I was living on Wells I was still going back to the Olivet on Cleveland Avenue.

The Olivet was a boy's club. Big boy's club on Cleveland and Blackhawk. The Olivet Institute. There was social things, you know, dances. There was basketball. The Harlem Globetrotters would come there every once in awhile. We would play basketball. We had softball leagues there. They had everything. It was a big social center for kids. And, there was a lot of Irish and Italian guys. You know the Cleveland Aces. The Tigers, of which I was a member of and the little Junior Aces. They had like five clubs. Above the Cleveland Aces it was the Lashers and then you go way back, your Lucania Elks. Going back to the '30s. These are all social clubs and gangs.

I loved Wells Street. We had Beverly, and Marilyn, and Diane, and Marsha. They were girls that lived on the street. They was our friends. Then we had us guys. And we all hung around together. We did a lot of things together. Went to Lincoln Park a lot. You know, just climbed on Abraham Lincoln. Or went to the second lagoon, you know. Wintertime went ice-skating at the lagoon.

John Owens was a special buddy. I met John in high school. He was a great mechanic. And he was a car racer and he just was a nice guy. He was half black and half white and it didn't seem to matter to us. We even didn't care if he went out with a white girl. He was one of us. How did it happen?

Joe Russo and me were pretty close friends in high school. Our game was standing toe-to-toe punching each other in the arm. To see who was stronger. I always liked Joe. He was a hard worker. As a younger guy, it was easier for me to understand the violence. As you grew older, there were things that would go into your head that would say to you, do you want to be with this guy. You know, you don't want to cut the guy off completely but you don't want to hang around with him a lot either, so in your mind you say, this guy was a good guy but now he just stopped growing, you know. He's still going around fucking whacking people. He still wanted to be a tough guy. When he was young maybe that was his appeal. Not for me. Cause I used to do that to. That's why we used to punch each other; cause there was shit going on. His appeal was he was one of the guys. He wasn't special. Steve his brother and Joe used to fight a lot. Everyone fought Joe. He fought with the world. Steve was more saner. He was older about two or three years. He was older than me. He was a more sociable person. Everyone talked about how much Steve was liked and Joe was fucking trouble.

Gus Johns was called "Dirty Gus" 'cause he was dirty. I didn't think he was dirty until I heard someone call him "Dirty Gus." He was just a great softball player. I knew him and his younger brother Bobby was a good friend of mine. Gus, I didn't know him well. He was a little goofy, a little weird. But a wonderful ballplayer and that I respected. But you know he looked like an ape, you know, with them long arms. Never did anything socially with him but watched him play ball. Loved to watch him play ball. He could hit it a mile.

And the story I heard was that his father was a frustrated ball player and he made Gus play ball. He wanted Gus to be Babe Ruth. Years later, Pete and I were about thirty-five. We took a ride to the old neighborhood and went to the Earl of Old Town on Wells Street, which is where Gus worked, but we didn't know that. Lot of big name folk singers went through there and Gus was there through all that. And here's Gus behind the bar and it was a beautiful thing. So the three of us are at the bar shooting the shit. Gus gets up and sits at the piano and starts playing jazz. And I asked him how he knows that. He says he taught himself. And we were impressed.

I didn't like Jimmy Foley. He seemed to be arrogant and I didn't like the way Pete kissed up to him. People kissed up to Foley, I didn't like that. Why they did that, I don't know. He was the son of a cop. Everybody liked him so everybody wants to be around a guy everybody likes. He treated people arrogantly. Joe Filpi was a good man. Filpi got involved with Foley. Jimmy started doing drugs.

Jimmy's father blamed Joe. Joe never did drugs. He never smoked a joint. Joe says the old man was mad at me. I think that's why Filpi joined the Navy at seventeen. I smoked some pot with Foley in his apartment years later. He was fucked up. He had a wife and a kid. Pete, Sal and me went to his apartment and he was messed up.

Went to high school with Ike Putrus. He was a good car mechanic. He loved cars like we all did. We became friends in high school. He lived on the other side of North Avenue. I can't forget his drinking. Him and Ooner were big beer drinkers. He didn't smoke cigarettes or pot but him and Ooner drank beer like, you know, by the truckload. But he changed, doesn't drink now. But a great guy. Honest. Nothing wrong with Ike.

Pat Rogers

We were outside all the time. Absolutely outside all the time.

When I was at St. Joe's, in early grammar school, we had a tremendous amount of activity in that community. Anywhere from La Salle Street over to Seward Park. I don't even know what the heck the western boundary was at that time. Cleveland? I don't know, I can't remember, Chuck. But it was not uncommon to be playing all the time or going into people's homes.

Yeah, we went home for supper. You see our brothers and sisters were on the street too. I just cannot impress on you enough of the young people that I met then. Like Babe Veverito. We went to school together. Ralph Commano. I don't know if you remember Ralph Commano. Eddie Rose was a very famous catcher at Wells High School at the time, a great athlete, and his dad was the manager at a hotel on Hill and Wells. He had a sister, lovely. And even though I was only in third grade I really admired her. She looked like an angel.

For our activities we would watch teams like the Goldies, which was an all-Italian team playing over at Seward Park. Later on we'd go to Lake Shore Park and see a variety of the teams play.

We were outside all the time. Absolutely outside all the time. And like I'm saying, could have been four, five, six of us and we'd end up at somebody's house and there was always a slice of bread and butter or sugar or something. Always a treat. It was a very friendly community. Very friendly. I didn't mention this initially, but I received First Communion at Holy Name Cathedral in first grade and was confirmed at St. Joseph's in second grade. Yeah. Second grade.

My parents didn't want me to play with Ronnie. Ronnie was very confused. He was an interesting story unto himself really. His mom was separated or divorced from her husband. Had two brothers who were absolutely straight-laced guys. One became a warrant officer. Entered the service as a private and got out as a warrant officer. That was Wilbert. And Jerry came out as a, I think was he a tech or a master sergeant. Anyway he worked for the CIA. And these guys were two straight-shooters and Ronnie was a loose cannon.

Ronnie and I had engaged in a number of weird incidents. Ronnie went away to a parole school. St. Charles, I think. Yeah, I think he went to St. Charles. And I went to the Audie Home. Ronnie told me later on in life, not too long ago, that he really felt badly about it. Once he was waiting outside my door and he wasn't welcomed in. So. No. He was verboten. You know. Sammy Marchetti was part of that group. Do you remember Sammy? But he wasn't part of the organized crime cartel we had. He lived on Wells, and he was, he was a Cathedral kid. Yeah. He was in Joe Zummo's class. Incidentally he plays saxophone to this day and he's a court reporter for the state. Yeah. In fact, we had some fascinating characters.

Joe Olita

An unspoken code of ethics that we had for each other.

Actually we didn't have a name for our gang like they have today see. It was just a group of guys that we knew. I mean you talk about rat partners; well that's what we were. An unspoken code of ethics that we had for each other. Would we challenge other gangs outside the community? Yes we would. We would actually go to their territory but one thing we never did. We never had clubs and we never had guns. All of it was done with fists. That was it. No knives. No. No. No one was ever physically damaged to the point where there was some permanent damage done to the individual. Never. It was never done that way.

My mother would sometimes say to me, "You know I want you to go over to the store over there because there's something that is a couple pennies cheaper and I want you to go over and get this for me." The store was across the border. My mother didn't know about these borders. Otherwise she wouldn't send me. Then what I'd do is I go and pick up a couple of friends. I'd say I'm going over and I need a couple of guys. Okay, we'll go with you. And then we would all go there. You know the idea of, of the feeling of protection even though we might confront three times as many.

John Owens

So we just, you know, we would hang around, go over to Third Base.

I used to hang around with a kid named ah, Lane. It was like a little clique. There was a kid name Tony Patito, and Dom Domonica, and who else was there? Real quick. And Vic Rebondo. Yeah. Right. And you know, we would fool around on the corner and just hang around. A lot of times we would roast potatoes on the street. You know, build a little fire, and take the potatoes and just throw them in the fire. And till they cooked, and you know. You just eat 'em after you got 'em otta there. But that was a big thing with us, cooking potatoes in the street. Right by the curb, we'd build a little fire. You know, between the curb and a little bit away from the curb in the street. I forget what we put on there. We didn't cover them up or anything, just threw them in the fire. Then pretty soon, the fire would die down a little bit, and they kinda steamed in there, and then we'd take' em. Somebody would go and get some salt or something. We put some salt on 'em.

Yeah. There was a candy store next to our grammar school. I can't remember the name of that one. We'd go in there after school and hang around in there. Not in there all the time but out around there outside, you know.

Yeah, we gambled some in high school. We used to shoot dice on the corner all the time. Yeah. We used to shoot dice at that restaurant on Sedgwick. There was a restaurant.

We didn't have a gang in high school, just a crowd of guys. It was just a like Tony Provenzano, and Ike, who else was there? Frank Delarosa, and there was one Polish kid, Dan Pasowitz. He used to hang around a lot with us. So we just, you know, we would hang around, go over to Third Base. Then I started going to the lake at night.

Charlie Martinez

Sitting on the curb at Sedgwick and Schiller, we used up our summer nights discussing sports, politics, sports, gang problems, sports, girls, and sports. This was the glorious time after ten o'clock when only an occasional car rolled by with its tires slapping the cobblestone paving between the steel streetcar rails. Sometimes the car would catch its tires on the rails and slide, the driver swearing out the open window. The red number 163 Sedgwick streetcars came careening by regularly. We knew all was well. Our parents were tucked into bed or had their heads cocked toward the glow of the radio dial, priests and nuns asleep or praying, Mary Joyce's grocery store closed, Morrealle's fish and Italian goods store darkened, and Heimsoth's pharmacy and soda fountain now empty and lights being turned off. Blinking Blatz or Miller beer signs of the taverns let us know that there were still souls in those secret, dank, dark places smoking and sipping beers with a whiskey chaser deciding important issues and swearing that Any Pafko of the Cubs was the best fucking right fielder to ever play the game.

Patti Irwin was the moderator for this impromptu meeting. He signaled the start by walking to the curb and inspecting it for a clean spot to sit on. We all followed his lead and took our places. These meetings occurred late, after games, wanderings, eating, and fights had ended. Usually the group consisted of four to six of us. Sometimes a quart of beer was produced which was passed back and forth.

"When the fuck are we gonna start practice?" Joe Russo meant of course, football practice for our Rams team. Our interest in football was aroused in July when the *Tribune*, sponsors of the College All Star Game which pitted the National Football League champions against the College All Stars, began blasting the public with articles on every play and every conceivable aspect of the past games and possibilities for the new game. The game was usually played in the middle of August at Soldier Field.

We looked to Patti for the response to Joe's question. This was like asking Eisenhower to give an answer to the question of when D-Day would occur.

Patty took his new pack of Luckies from his left rolled-up sleeve of his tee shirt and went through the ritual of "getting a cigarette out for a perfect smoke." This was another one of his performances that awed all of us by its perfection. After hitting the pack against the side of his closed fist to bring the tobacco into a denser condition on the eventual mouth end, he pulled the red string to release the cellophane wrapper, pulled up on the folded tinfoil, ripping off about three quarters of an inch, exposing three to four cigarettes. He tapped the pack against his left hand so that one cigarette would pop up about an inch.

He removed the cigarette, tapped one end rather vigorously against the fingernail of his right thumb and placed that tightly packed portion between his lips. (How he knew how long to tap was something we could not understand but we assumed he had instinctive knowledge). Reaching into his tee shirt pocket he pulled out a Zippo lighter. The top was flipped open and the friction wheel engaged. All was done in a continuous motion. The cigarette was lit with one draw and the smoke was set free through his nose as a silky, luscious cloud.

Despite being the obvious leader, Patti allowed us to be involved in important decision-making by developing a pseudo-consensus.

"Well, Joe do you think August first is too soon? You're always in good shape, but some of us need a little more conditioning."

"Yeah, dat seems okay with me." Joe was pleased with this compliment.

We all nodded in agreement, knowing if we had a real argument against August first, Patti would ask about our problems, but he would settle the alternate date.

Ken Martinez

Roasted a lot of potatoes.

Before grammar school, I used to play with Walter Gibbons, and the other kid that lived this side of Mueller's. I can't remember his name. Mueller's Bakery was in that big building on Schiller and Sedgwick. On the north side. Then we used to go over on the other side of Schiller and climb up and look in the window of a health store. There was a lot of people with doctors in white uniforms and everything.

And then there was Gus Johns. Gus used to live over on Sedgwick Street. He used to come over and visit his Grandmother. And he would stay all day in the summertime. Then his mother left … 'cause I used to go over there. On the second floor he lived. We'd come down, and then he started living over with his grandma so I saw him all the time.

During the winter, Gus and I threw snowballs at cars and played with our sleds. We would build a hill under the L. We'd push all the snow together.

Roasted a lot of potatoes. We used to steal the potatoes. From the grocery store up on ah, North Avenue and Sedgwick Street.

They'd put the potatoes and stuff outside so we'd steal 'em. Gus would run by, I would run by. He'd grab two potatoes; I'd grab two potatoes. And then we'd run under the L, build a fire, roast potatoes. Nobody told us not to use that salt that's up on the elevator platform. So we would put that on the potatoes.

We used to play on the L all the time. Mr. Culbertson was in the elevated station. He sold newspapers. He lost his leg in World War I. Newspapers, cigarettes, chewing gum and magazines.

Charlie Martinez

Nick Gallo was a six-foot-two, curly-haired, handsome, smiling Italian. He was also gentle, friendly, good natured and adverse to almost all arguments or fights.

He did talk jive and used marijuana and a few pills but somehow he was able to be a bridge between the potheads and juiceheads. He was into jazz. He was smooth, smooth, smooth. One talent of Nick's that we all envied -- he could dance. None of us had any grace but he actually followed the beat, taught himself steps, and looked good at the wedding receptions we crashed on our Saturday night social outings.

He understood music far above our "listening" level. We followed him to the Blue Note nightclub to listen to the great jazz people of our day. Of course I didn't know what the hell I was listening to and I couldn't tell the difference between a tenor sax and an alto sax or a xylophone (vibes) and a piano. But Nick knew.

School, sports and work were just distractions to his living for jazz and popular music. He had a sharing nature. On a Sunday in 1953, we asked him to give us a gift of himself. He said okay. He would teach us to dance! The dance he decided on because of its ease and popularity at the time was the Cha Cha.

Pete's apartment was selected as the school. No parents or adults were home. Pete, Zummo, Nicolini and me spent two hours being taught by this master. He was cool and we became cool, if only for those few hours. We imitated his every move, of course never as smooth as Nick but we tried. He never gave up on us. At least now we could dance one dance with some class at the next wedding reception we crashed.

Part Four: That Summer Vacation

Charlie Martinez

THE PLAN

We *did* have a plan. Now, you might call it an idiotic teenager idea. You see, Jim Patac and his friend we can only remember as "The Mexican" were going to Patac's cousin's place in Menasha, Wisconsin. We didn't know where the hell that place was but for five guys who never got as far as the suburbs, it sounded like a great place to have a vacation. Not that we ever had vacations. None of us had ever been on one in his life and we were all seventeen or eighteen. Patac and his friend were going to hitchhike up there and then hitchhike back in a week. The three of us, Joe Zummo, Joe Russo, and myself, could only stay the weekend because of work. But, we said, why spend all that effort hitchhiking when we could con Tex into driving us there in his new car?

We didn't know his real name or where he was from. He had a Southern drawl, so naturally we called him Tex. He was taller than any of us but heavy and soft. We figured he was old, maybe thirty-five or so. But he had one thing that drew us like yellow jackets to a Forest Preserve garbage can -- he had a car! And for five conniving teenagers from the Near North Side of Chicago, that car was our passage to a grand vacation. To us, his new, 1952 Dodge Coronet with Gyromatic Drive looked like a black, thirty-foot, gangster sedan. Tex was reluctant. We told him that three of us would come back on that Sunday so he wouldn't have to stay the whole week. We felt he was probably dumb enough or naïve enough, or both, to go along with this plan. And you know what? He swallowed the whole idea like it was a dish of his mama's grits.

We met at our hamburger joint called the Third Base a half a block north of Goethe on Wells.

DEPARTURE

At six sharp, Tex arrived. He stayed in his car, windows down with the radio bellowing hillbilly music. He constantly adjusted a Western-style hat. It was about five gallons rather than a real ten-gallon hat. I got there just as Joe Russo was sitting down on the top step of Third Base.

"Charlie!"

"Joe!"

"I feel like shoving that radio up his ass." Joe got annoyed easily but this time he didn't act out his annoyance. Later in life he would have us in laughter one moment and fear and embarrassment the next.

"Dumb fucking hillbilly. Where's Zummo and Patac?"

"They both said they'd be here at six. They'll come."

"Look at this. My old lady made me take all this shit."

He opened a shopping bag from the Fair Store. He pointed out an extra pair of pants, a shirt, socks, underwear and two bananas. I had rolled up my shirt, socks, and underwear in a pair of pants.

Jim Patac and his Mexican friend turned the corner from Goethe Street onto Wells. Jim was medium brown in complexion with an Oriental shape to his eyes. I didn't know his nationality but assumed he was at least part Filipino. He had a constant half-smile and talked in short, energetic bursts. His Mexican friend only talked to Patac and we never heard a distinct sentence from him. We acknowledged each other with the usual grunts and smiles. Patac carried a brown, wicker trunk. It was about five feet by two feet by two feet deep. The Mexican had his clothes in a small, old-fashioned suitcase with a bold stripe down the middle. None of us had greeted or acknowledged Tex in any way.

"Where's Zummo?" asked Patac.

"Don't you know nothin' about Zummo yet?" said Joe Russo. "He's probably bullshiting with some guy and trying to con him outa a suit or fifty bucks. He's never on time."

And then came Zummo. The front entrance to his apartment building was only twenty steps away. You passed a used clothing store, which I never remember being open, before entering his long hallway. He bounced out, tucking in his shirt. He had come home from his construction job and of course spent about an hour taking a bath and getting dressed. He carried a shirt and pants on hangers. Extra socks and shorts were stuffed in his pockets.

"You guys ready?" said Zummo.

"What the fuck do you think?" said Joe Russo.

We all walked slowly to the car. You knew everyone was jockeying around to avoid sitting next to Tex. Tex got out of the car to open the trunk. We mumbled a greeting to him. He was about five foot eleven and two hundred fifty pounds of blubber. His Western-cut denim shirt and large belt with a bighorn steer buckle went along with his Levi's. In those days, in our neighborhood, only hillbillies, motorcycle riders, and queers wore blue jeans.

He opened the trunk. Inside were two cases of liquor. The boxes were labeled Gallo's Upstate New York Sherry. That impressed us. 'Course we thought he was an ass for carrying that much liquor. A guy like Joe Russo could make an illogical claim on the liquor and then there might be trouble.

"Got to get rid of one of these here cases of Sherry so's I can get all your shit in the trunk," Tex said.

"Why don't we put one in my house till we get back?" said Zummo. We all suppressed a smile. Joe Russo's eyes lit up.

The case was placed safe and sound on Joe Zummo's fire escape which was just outside his bedroom window. We could hear some of the yelling and swearing of his mother out the kitchen window as she argued with him about the case of liquor. "Whose is this? What are you doing you lousy sommamabitch? You want me to call the police?" But Joe came running out the hallway and jumped into the front passenger seat. Oh yeah, Joe Russo got the seat next to Tex.

"Go down Division Street to Lake Shore Drive. That's Route 41. Go north and it'll take us all the way to Menasha." Jim Patac hollered out the directions in his cheerful, confident manner as we all laughed and joked about the trip.

Jim had never been to Wisconsin before, let alone Menasha. He had only a vague idea where his cousin's house actually was. We quieted down as we turned north on Lake Shore Drive. Even though we all had driven on the Drive before, it was still the most beautiful drive any of us was ever on. There was the blue lake on the right and green Lincoln Park and high rises of the Gold Coast on the left. In those days Lake Shore Drive ended at Foster Avenue, just at the pink Edgewater Beach hotel. We jogged west to Lincoln Avenue then north to Skokie Boulevard, following the Illinois Route 41 signs.

"I worked on some of these two-flats last summer," said Joe Zummo. He pointed to a series of nondescript Fifties-style two-flats with coach lights and mismatched stonework on the front.

"Yeah, you built dem all right," said Joe Russo. "Shit, all you did was take nails out of two-by-fours and probably slept half the time, driving the boss crazy."

"Yeah, and what a boss he was," said Joe Zummo. "He was a fellow Sicilian. He picked me up at my house. We talked broken Sicilian to one another and he called me his paison. But then a black guy came along that he could cheat out of twenty-five cents an hour. He fired me."

THE PROBLEM DEVELOPS

Joe Russo made a comment when we passed Lake Bluff that changed the history of our vacation entirely.

"You thirsty, Charlie?" he said.

"Yeah."

"Well, let's see, we ain't got no pop. Then what else we got to drink Patac?"

"I didn't bring no pop either and I don't see no stores outside," says Patac, going along with the con.

"Why don't y'all buy some soda and beer if I see a store?" said Tex. That was his first full sentence since we left Third Base.

"You know Tex, why spend the money? You got a case in your trunk that I'm pretty sure didn't cost you much. Am I right?" said Patac.

Again we were amazed. Tex pulls over, goes to the trunk as we all smile and pat each other on the back. He gets out two fifths of sherry and gets back in and takes off. Now this really feels like a vacation. The bottles are passed around freely and after a while, we all start talking freely. Naturally some of the talk is likely to upset a Southerner since we made them the butt of a few jokes. Well, anyway, things started to deteriorate. Joe Russo, next to Tex, is swearing and laughing at him. Zummo falls asleep after a few drinks and Jim Patac gets oiled up and talks like crazy.

MILWAUKEE EXIT

I guess at this point, somewhere in Milwaukee, Tex decides he wants rid of us. He pulls over to the curb.

"Get out," he says.

"What are talking about, you fat asshole?" says Joe Russo.

You can see this is not going well. Tex goes around and opens the trunk. He is really going to dump us with our clothes at midnight in Milwaukee.

Then Tex does something stupid. He hollers that all of us better get out of the car and grab our stuff from the trunk or he'll toss all the shit out on the street. This did not sit well with us. Joe Zummo decides to clarify the situation to Tex. He picks up a full bottle of sherry and says, "You throw our stuff out and I'll break this bottle over your head".

A stare-down occurs between Joe and Tex. Tex backs off and we grab our stuff from the trunk. He slams the lid down, gets in the car, presses the gas and pulls away with tires squealing. The pretty 1952 black Dodge Coronet with Gyromatic drive just disappeared into the Milwaukee night.

Out on the street at midnight in a strange city. What to do? We picked up our goods and started walking. Tex had dumped us in a residential neighborhood. It was pleasant but we had no idea where we were.

"Ya think that asshole would have let us out on a main drag," said Joe Russo.

We walked for about fifteen minutes and were no closer to knowing where we were or what we were gonna do.

So I asked, "What are we gonna do?"

CHURCH DOORWAY AND A NEW PACK OF DOGS

"I know what I'm doing," said Patac. And he headed to a church entrance with his Mexican friend helping him carry his trunk. The rest of us joined them on the church steps.

We heard a distant chatter. Couldn't make out the words right away but picked up on the occasional laughter, swear words, oaths taken, and the sound of shoes hitting the cement.

Then it was quiet.

They were across the street, standing still and looking our way. We never could agree on the number but figured there were ten to twelve guys, our age, staring at us. We had a common thought but only Patac said it out loud, softly. "Aw shit." We knew they were discussing the situation, sizing us up, counting. But all we heard was the rustle of leaves in the trees and rumble of distant traffic.

They started a slow walk across the street, all of their eyes on us. They were our height and none very husky. They stopped at the curb, some on, some off in the street, about ten feet from us. We didn't worry about guns in those days. Occasionally a knife would be a problem. But this figured to be just a fist-to-face brawl.

But Patac, with his pleasant half smile and no fear in his voice said, "What's happening man?" to no one in particular.

A guy in front wearing greasy hair, a tee shirt with rolled-up sleeves, khaki pants and Frankenstein shoes asked pleasantly, "Where you guys from?"

That did it. Guys from both sides started talking all at once. Some outsider would have thought we were all part of the same gang.

"We was traveling with this asshole, Tex. He got a little nasty so we dumped him," said Joe Russo, rearranging the facts slightly. Joe explained that Tex was an older guy and kinda weird. The new group immediately developed a dislike for this "older guy."

Zummo explained our new predicament in that we didn't know where the hell we were or how to get either to Menasha or Chicago. One guy said, "No problem man." A sharp-looking 1949 Nash Ambassador appeared.

After a discussion, Patac and his Mexican friend decided they wanted directions to Route 41 so they could continue hitchhiking to

Manesha. The two Joes and me were going back to Chicago. After setting Patac in the right direction for the few blocks to Route 41, the three of us got in the Nash for a drive to the North Shore train station.

They let us out and there was a round of "tanks a lot," "look us up in Chicago," "don't mention it," and "if you see Tex, beat the shitass up for us."

DRESSING FOR THE OCCASION AND ARRIVAL AT THE STATION

Before we climbed the marble stairs of the train station, we figured out a way that made carrying our extra clothes easier. We put on the extra pants and shirts right over our clothes and stuffed the socks and shorts in our pockets. But then, halfway up the stairs, the sherry caught up with Joe Zummo. Up came the two hot dogs he had eaten at Third Base, plus potato chips. All of this glob was laced with the aroma of sherry. Joe couldn't move for a while. But then he wiped off his face with his extra shorts and continued the climb like a guy on the last few yards to the top of Mt. Everest, vomiting his way to the top.

Inside this dark, 1930's station was an oversized birdcage where the ticket seller sat. He was a gray haired guy half asleep.

"Dis ting go to Chicago?" asked Joe Russo.

"Yeah."

"Where in Chicago? Near North Side or near the Loop?"

"Chicago Avenue good enough?"

"Yeah. Gimme tree tickets. When does the next one leave?"

"Three o'clock."

"Tree o'clock? We gotta spend more den two hours sitting here looking at you?"

After another vomiting demonstration, Joe Zummo passed out on a long wooden bench.

When the train did arrive it was empty. Joe Zummo got up, went into the train and passed out on a double seat. As we got closer to Chicago, people started getting on the train. They went by us as if we were invisible.

RETURN TO JOE ZUMMO'S APARTMENT

We got off the train at Chicago Avenue and Wells sometime after six. We caught a Wells Street bus and went straight to Joe Zummo's apartment. As we walked into his musty-smelling hallway and up the unpainted stairs to his door, I realized we were now finishing our eleven-hour vacation. Joe didn't have a key. He just pounded on the door. He must've scared the hell out of his mother. (His father was not living there at the time. He had moved in with his own mother on Dickens Street near Waller High School).

"Who the hell is it?" Joe's mother shouted at the door from the other side.

"It's me, Joey, let me in."

"Joey?"

The locks were thrown and Mrs. Zummo, two hundred pounds of Italian motherhood with her hair in curlers and in a housedress, looked out in puzzlement. There was her son, Joe Russo, and me wearing all the clothes she saw us leave with the night before. "What the hell are you doing here?" she said.

Joe gave no reply and no explanation but just walked by her towards his bedroom. We meekly followed and settled down to sleep.

ENCOUNTER WITH THE WIFE OF TEX

A couple of hours later we heard a faint knock on the door.

"Who the hell is it?' bellowed Mrs. Zummo.

We couldn't hear the reply, but she opened the door. There was a low-volume exchange of words. We heard the door close. Mrs. Zummo came into the bedroom.

"Joey! That Tex guy's wife is here. He wants her to get that other case of sherry she says you got."

Joe says, "Okay" with no fuss. He opens the bedroom window, climbs out on the fire escape and retrieves the case of sherry. We follow him into the kitchen. There was Tex's wife. A sad-looking little woman with a ponytail, faded housedress and no makeup.

Joe says to her, "You want this sherry?"

She whispers, "Yes."

"Okay." He opens the kitchen window and asks again, "You want this stuff?" She nods.

"Well here it is." And in a smooth motion, like shoveling wet cement at his construction job, Joe floats the case of sherry out the second-story window to its grave on the gangway sidewalk below.

Hysteria!

"Joey, you somamabitch!" cries Mrs. Zummo. Tex's wife is frozen in her spot. We burst into shrieks of laughter. Joe calmly puts on a clean shirt and buttons it. But he realizes his mother is looking for a chair, or frying pan to throw at him. Finally she does throw a pan and then grabs a broom and starts beating him. He laughs as we all run out the front door. Mrs. Zummo screams, "I'm calling the police, you somamabitch!"

WATCHING THE PARADE

We knew Mrs. Zummo was not averse to calling the police. She had done it several times before. Being streetwise and cautious, I suggest we watch the unfolding circus from a safe vantage place. We select a house, with steep front steps, across the street from Third Base. No one from Zummo's apartment would be able to see us and we would be partially hidden from anyone searching from the front of Joe's building. We were laughing and retelling the events when a Chicago police car pulled up in front of Third Base, directly across the street from us.

Two policemen, who looked like they never ate anywhere but at Roma's Italian Beef stand, plopped out of the car. They went through their ritual of adjusting their gun, belt, billy club, radio and undershorts. They then began a search for the building's address. Just then Mrs. Zummo comes out of the hallway with her flowered housedress on and her hair in curlers. She gestures wildly as the police are obviously trying to calm her down. Tex's wife appears and they ask her a few questions. One cop is led up into the apartment by Mrs. Zummo. We can see him stick his head out of the kitchen window and look down into the gangway. This results in uncontrollable laughter for us. Eventually the police pull away, Mrs.

438

Zummo goes into her hallway and Tex's wife starts walking east on Goethe Street.

It was over.

But was it? Without saying so, we were worried about the hillbilly. What if Tex came after us? He might kill us, the crazy hick. But our archangel in the form of a five-foot-ten, 220-pound Japanese American tackle on the Navy Pier University of Illinois football team appeared. It was Harold Domoto. We hung around with Harold all that day.

We never did see Tex after that morning. He never came back to Third Base as far as we know. He just drifted out of our life and is probably making the same mistake somewhere else by cozying up to a group of streetwise teenagers who are ready to go on a vacation.

CHAPTER TWELVE: THE END OF THE LINE

Part One: Runaways

Father, father, where are you going?
  O do not walk so fast.
Speak father, speak to your little boy
  Or else I shall be lost.

The night was dark, no father was there,
  The child was wet with dew.
The mire was deep, & the child did weep,
  And away the vapour flew.
            The Little Boy Lost - William Blake

Charlie Martinez

Wanderaways and runaways. Many of the kids I grew up with engaged in one or the other or both methods of disconnecting from their family and or friends. The disconnect lasted sometimes for a few hours to days and into weeks.

There was a difference between the age, motives and goals of these acts. In general, the wanderaways were younger, usually in early to mid-grammar school. They sought adventure and were led by their natural young boy curiosity. They wanted to see what was in the river, across the lagoon, or even just to walk in a direction they hadn't gone before until they tired. They would get on the L or streetcar and go to the end of the line just to find out where that was and what was there. Parents or older siblings knew none of this. The action was spontaneous and usually it involved a buddy or two. After some anxiety for the parents but usually none for the boys, police or older siblings brought them home. Frequently physical punishment was given out but they all felt it was worth it. The delicious part was to relive that adventure for your pals the next day and to dream of the next one.

Joe Zummo was five years old, I was six and my brother Ken was seven when we hit upon the idea of an adventure. No complicated plan. Joe wanted to find an ice cream parlor on Division Street next to the 152 Theater. He had heard older boys talking about a new wonder. They whispered among themselves that this store had a machine that could dispense ice cream as a soft, cream-like material. That we must search out and find this machine quickly became our goal. We didn't have any money to buy the ice cream but Joe thought that a soulful con may deliver this treat into our hands. Three young boys. A warm summer morning. No obligations for work or school. Parents only knowing that we went "out." They wouldn't miss us for lunch because we usually were not home anyway for lunch. They might start wondering where the hell we were when seven or eight hours went by.

Joe decided we should start off walking down Wells Street and turn on Division Street. From there, he thought we should turn toward the lake. We never used north, south, east, or west in our directions. We walked to Wells Street from Mary Joyce's store and then walked past Joe's apartment building toward Division but stayed on the opposite side of the street to avoid any chance encounter with his mother. We were strung out along the sidewalk with Ken always in the lead. Unfortunately he led us across and past Division Street. As we walked, Joe looked in vain for the ice cream parlor that gave out soft ice cream from a machine.

We continued along Wells Street for about eight blocks until our path was blocked by a glorious unexpected structure. We stumbled onto the Chicago River. In those days the river was dark, with an oily irregular sheen. Pieces of lumber, beer cans, tree branches, kitchen chairs, paint buckets, occasional dead cats or rats and condoms floated by on the mild current. There was the aroma of sewer water. Sewer water did not smell the same as toilet water. No, it was a combination of the smells of mud, decaying vegetation, some excrement and dead animals.

We ran to its edge and our young minds were flooded with marvelous noises and sights. Large open sightseeing boats, beginning to fill with passengers, were tied up at the Michigan Avenue Bridge to our left. Sailboats with sails furled moved on inboard motors to and from the lake. We waved to the brave captains going out to challenge the lake. They waved back, filling us with longing to go along. Bridges were clanging, raising, lowering for the tall masts of the sailboats. Cars were beeping and the L to our right was rumbling across a double-decker bridge at Orleans Street just past the Merchandise Mart building.

And right in front of us, as if planted by the good fairy, was a tied up derelict wooden boat, maybe twenty feet long. It had a canvas tarp over half the open deck. Joe and I jumped into the boat and into a few inches of standing water. The paint was peeling but the boards were intact. Maybe our jumping and moving irritated the river gods because just then the rope holding the boat to a wooden post on shore began to loosen and unravel, threatening to send us down the river. Ken, still on shore, grabbed the rope, pulled us back and tied up the boat. This rescue by Ken was very fortunate because none of us could swim.

Deciding to look for other adventures and still not sure where the ice cream shop was, we worked our way along the river to Michigan Avenue and north toward the Water Tower. We were now hungry. In front of the Drake Hotel at Oak and Michigan Avenues was a small pagoda-like building. This was a temporary summer office of the Park District Police. A policeman, probably surmising by our dress and confusion that we weren't from the Gold Coast, steered us into the station. A friendly officer at the desk asked us a few questions, got addresses and then offered us coffee from his thermos and gave each of us a sweet roll. With a smile he said he would have to arrest us. Ken and I laughed but Joe was scared and peed in his pants. Actually it was a one-piece suit called a "tank suit" given to his mother by the welfare department.

The next thrill was when we were told to jump into the back seat of a squad car. This was big time. A murderer may have sat on this very seat! The police drove us back to the neighborhood and, seeing a large gathering in front of Mary Joyce's store at North Park Avenue and Schiller Street, he pulled to the curb.

We had left the area about eight hours previously. There, milling around, was a crowd of relatives, curious onlookers, and of course our buddies who wanted to hear about our adventure but also were eager to see what kind of beating we would surely get. My sisters Patsy and Lee, as well as my brothers Jerry, Bernie and Bobby were there. But as we got out of the squad car, a commotion was occurring in the back of the crowd. The people, in fear of being trampled, parted quickly as a large woman in a print dress and hair in curlers was running forward and screaming "you sommomabitch, you sommomabitch." Joe's mother grabbed him by the neck and her other fat hand slapped his ass all the way home. Ken and I just enjoyed the attention and received no punishment for our adventure.

Ken Martinez

The policeman told Pa, he says, "Well if he comes back again, we got a cell."

I don't know why Gus and me were always wandering away. I think it was to see, just to go. I don't know. We'd just start walking. I got in a lot of trouble. I mean, the cops brought me home a couple times ... three, four times for wandering away. I went to Milwaukee, went there, went here. I had no idea where I was going. I guess I had to see the critter.

One time Gus and I were in the Chicago River paddling this rowboat when we got lost. This big boat. It was next to the pier. Nobody was on it. So we untied it and we started to go up the river. A boat came and got us and took us home.

And then we got on the Bluebird bus somewhere, and we went and we just had enough money to come back.

We got lost once. Really lost. We didn't know where the hell we were. We got on a streetcar that kept changing ... you know how the streetcars used to transfer back and forth? We got on the wrong streetcar on Wells Street and it went west on Lake Street underneath the L. Then it swung around a different way. And then it went all the way somewhere else, and somewhere else. And we don't know where the hell we were and we didn't know what the hell to do.

Another time, I got on the North Avenue streetcar and went all the way to the end and I didn't have any money to come back. I was out at Mannheim Road and the police took me all the way back. Pa had to come over to the police station at Hudson Avenue. The policeman told Pa, he says, "Well if he comes back again, we got a cell." I had to sit there and I was watching the cop make the baloney sandwiches for the guys in the back. I says, "They got baloney sandwiches." Pa says, "That's all you learned? Come on let's go."

We did all this in grammar school.

Joe Zummo

It was pretty exciting...not coming home.

The summer between eighth grade and high school, I left home for almost the whole summer and I was working at Solomon's Liquors and I was staying at Jimmy Foley's house overnight. It was boring at home and I needed some action. I would go back during the day and wash up and put on clean clothes. My mother didn't say much at all. My Dad would come over to Jimmie's house calling for me. He said I had a home and a bed and I should be at my own place. It was pretty exciting working at Solomon's and not coming home. Foley's mother and father were in their summer home and didn't know I was staying with Jimmie. I eventually did go home part way through the summer and I had to get home and get a lot of sleep. I was fourteen at this time.

Vinnie Marino

Instead of cheering me, they were killing me.

Well, when I was about twelve years old, there was a guy in our neighborhood. His name was Kiley Davis. He moved in from the West Coast. He was an oddity in our Sicilian neighborhood but I thought he was a big deal. I was twelve and he was about fourteen. And he said to me one time, "You know it's pretty bad; it's January, why don't we get the hell out of here?" So we went down to Montgomery Wards. We took some stuff with us. We took sandwiches. Peanut butter and jelly. We had a couple bucks. We took a jacket. We jumped on a freight train and we wound up in

Oakland, California.

Took us about five days to get there. Yeah, this was a freight train. We froze our buns off going through the Rockies. The train discharged in Oakland and we walked into San Francisco.

We lived on, you know, the automats. We went in there and got stuff. Then we'd often go in restaurants and grab ketchup off the table and mix it with a little water and make soup a couple times. I finally called home about a day later. My parents were frantic there. My father answered the phone. He says, "Where are you?" And I says "California." He says, "California and what?" You know, he's thinking California Street in Chicago. "No Dad, California on the coast." He says, "What are you doing out there!" So he wired us money and I took the dog back, the Greyhound back to Chicago. I mean he busted my buns. My dad was really upset. Never hit me in his life. Yeah, he kicked me in my butt. And my mother was whacking on my head.

Kiley Davis stayed. I took the bus back. And I never saw him again. They moved. They, you know, they were like transients. Like hillbillies. Trailer park people. I came back by myself, yeah. It took about two and a half days.

Yeah, twelve years old on the bus. I was beside myself, I didn't know what the hell was gonna happen. I got off the bus downtown around ah, Clark and Lake, and they were waiting for me. My older brother, I mean he grabbed me. I mean I got off that bus and he was on me like a hawk. Yeah. My uncle was there. He was a cop. Yeah they were all waiting for me. It was like a reception committee. I was like Sergeant York coming home from World War I in reverse. Instead of cheering me, they were killing me.

Charlie Martinez

The runaway was a more serious matter. It is possible that this disconnection could be permanent. This boy was usually in his early or mid teens, but could be younger. He was typically alone but again that was not an absolute characteristic. A crisis between him and the family usually occurred and this crisis may be only in the young boy's mind. No serious preparations or planning were made and the runaway's naiveté was obvious. Since this was a serious disconnect there was no intention to return and an active search was instituted. Sometimes police were involved, but usually only the family did the searching and praying.

Pat Rogers

You were too tough to go home...

There was a time I even took off for a week when I was fourteen. It was nothing to get a rental saying you were sixteen and you could get a day-by-day rental over by Chicago Avenue and State Street. In one of those rooming houses ... you know.
Yeah, I lived there for a week and my mom and my sister finally found out where I was and they came in and brought me home. I don't know why I ran away. I think my dad was harassing me. The rooming house was facing Cathedral, actually. Just on the other side of Yankee Burgers. Yeah, there was a little rooming house there. You could get a four-by- eight room whatever it was, for a couple bucks. And you thought you were a big shot. You were too tough to go home so mom and dad had to say, "Come on we'll take you home." And of course they were real eager so I had to go home. I mean you could survive for a week. It wasn't as bad as it is today. The drugs were not paramount. Nobody was out there. You didn't have as many fruitcakes on the street as you do today that could take a young girl or young guy and turn you into prostitution. They didn't exist as far as we knew.

Charlie Martinez

I pulled back to hide myself behind the brick wall of a warehouse in the alley between Wells Street and La Salle Street. This was straight east from Joe Zummo's apartment building, about a half a block north of Division Street. I was sure that the front of a 1946 Ford Coupe I saw turning up the alley belonged to my brother-in-law, Freddy. He must be searching for me, I thought. My sister Patsy was probably in the car pushing him on.

I had just turned twelve and was running away from home. This was during the Christmas vacation in seventh grade.

I peeked out after a few moments. Nothing there. No rats, no cars, no people. Just miscellaneous junk and garbage strewn on the cobblestone pavement. I had no money, was already hungry and dressed in a thin jacket without gloves or hat. December was not a good time to pick to run away.

I had run away once before about a year previously. That was only an overnight outing. I stayed all night in a third-floor hallway five doors north of my house on North Park Avenue. This was in a hillbilly tenement. I remember urinating down the steps. I slept on and off during the night. I had no anxiety. Why I ran away is not clear, but I felt this terrible burden of having disappointed my parents. It had something to do with my newspaper delivery job and not bringing home my pay or not making enough pay. I took these burdens on myself because neither my parents nor my siblings ever asked me about my jobs or expected me to turn over the money. I left the hallway in the morning without being seen and went home. There were questions and mild threats but no punishment. I answered no questions and gave no information on where I had spent the night.

In keeping with my way of thinking and acting, I had made no plans for my new escape. I had no idea where I was going, how I was to eat, sleep or stay warm. I never thought of leaving the immediate neighborhood. I had not confided in anyone else; not my friends, siblings, parents, teachers, or priests. I just did not go home that Saturday afternoon. Although the exact timing and dates escape my memory, I stayed away about a week. Again the reason had to do with my job. I had promised my brother Ken that I would take him to the circus and pay his way. But I just couldn't come up with enough money till the circus was half over. I just walked away from the house to avoid facing him.

When I felt sure that Freddy's Ford coupe was gone, I followed my nose north through the alley to North Avenue and turned east toward Lincoln Park. In the park I worked my way over to the zoo. Inside the Lion House the air was warm but unpleasantly humid with a vague animal smell but I was comfortable. The big cats marched quickly back and forth, rubbing their fur against the bars of their cage.

They always looked into the distance, never looking me in the eye. They wanted to escape too. Eventually huge chunks of raw meat were thrown into the cage. The cats licked the meat tenderly before quietly ripping off pieces and swallowing them.

I went to the zoo daily during my absence from home. Sometimes I stayed all day in the monkey house or occasionally I spent a few hours in the reptile house. The large animals on the outside I avoided because of the cold.

It is hard even now for me to believe, but I cannot recall eating at all during that week. I had no money. I don't recall begging for any food. However a strange incident happened halfway into my odyssey. Somehow, I ended up on Evergreen Street at Muzzie's candy store. I must have stolen some comic books and tried to sell them to a kid in the store. He may have bought them and that's how I got a little food but I am not sure.

I slept at several different places but can't remember all the nights. My first night I wandered back into the neighborhood about ten o'clock. I found myself in a backyard opposite Jimmy Foley's house on Evergreen Street, just east of the L tracks. I stood behind a garage to get shelter from the wind. After a while I heard my brother Jerry hollering up to Jimmy's house.

"Is Chuckie with you?"

"No."

"Have you seen him today"?

"No, not all day," came the reply.

I heard Jerry crunch his way in the snow back to North Park Avenue and north toward home.

I went up the back steps of the house in front of the garage and snuggled into the stairs just before the top landing. A few moments later, the door to the top apartment opened and a medium-sized dog came out. He stopped at my stair and growled and barked. I did not move. I heard a woman and man arguing on what the hell was the matter with that dog. Finally the door opened and the dog was let in. I waited till all was quiet again and then went back down the steps to the first floor. A pile of garbage, cardboard and paper was on the porch and I burrowed my way into it and fell asleep. I awoke with the morning light and wandered over to the Lincoln Park Zoo.

One of the nights I walked up the back steps of Patti Irwin's house and went into their unheated back porch. It was dark and I pushed my way back into their boxes and containers till I had shut out the obvious air leaks. It is a strange sensation to burrow in the dark because you have no idea what you are pushing against or how far to go, but I was not afraid. You do stop when your feet are within the burrow. A few moments later, Patti's younger brother, Ooner, came out of his back door. His mother was telling him to be careful and not slip on the ice. I heard him chopping the ice off the long stairway down to the yard and after an hour or so his mother came out and called him in. She praised him for the job, promising hot chocolate. With the dawn, I climbed out of my hideaway and went back to the zoo.

I was in a trance, suspended in confusion all during my journey. There was no thought-out plan for shelter or food. I thought no deep thoughts and had no conscious sensation of missing my family or friends. Except for the encounter in the candy store, I saw no one I knew although I was in and out of my neighborhood daily. Of course, I avoided all places where I might be recognized. Throughout, I was not approached by any stranger and never felt in any danger. Isn't that amazing for a boy of twelve?

Late one night, possibly ten o'clock, I found myself standing in a store at Armitage Avenue and Clark Street. The zoo, a few blocks away, had closed, and I was in the store to stay warm. I talked to no one. It might have been a drug store. I'm not sure.

A man I assumed was the manager was counting up the cash and getting ready to close the store. How I must have looked! I had worn the same clothes for three or four days. I had not washed or eaten in that time. I had no hat, no gloves and this in the middle of the winter. My shoes were likely falling apart. I stood mute. The man continued to count the change that was spread out on the counter, occasionally glancing at me. When he had finished he flipped a dime along the counter towards me. I picked it up and left the store. Not a word had passed between us. I didn't use the dime to buy food. I got on the Clark Street streetcar and rode it all night back and forth from one end of the line to the other. It was warm on the basket weave seats with a good heater underneath each seat. Neither the conductor nor the motorman questioned me or disturbed me. In the morning I left the streetcar at Armitage Avenue and worked my way back to the zoo.

Another night I found myself in the Schiller Street L station. The station had a large cast iron stove that shot out a lot of heat. It was a small station and it felt cozy. The station attendant in his cage never asked what a twelve year old was doing at midnight in the L station. He may have assumed I was waiting for a sister or brother or parent to come home on the L from work. That was not unusual in those days. But I was getting anxious that he might call the police if I stayed any longer. I went out into the winter night and was suddenly chilled but after a few moments I was not uncomfortable. Now at this point I was about a hundred feet from the house I grew up in at 329 West Schiller Street. Eddie Kennedy's family had bought it and lived on the first floor. My Aunt Nini and her husband Paul lived on the second floor. I don't recall if my grandma Teen was still there or had moved around the corner to our house on North Park Avenue.

Without thinking it through, I walked toward the Schiller Street house, entered its narrow gangway and opened the gate to enter the backyard. I had slammed that gate into my brother Ken's face when he chased me a few years before and it cut his face badly.

The door to the back porch was unlocked and I made my way up to the second floor landing. I looked in the kitchen window. I could not see into any of the bedrooms and since I saw no one, I assumed all were asleep. There was a minimal light, probably a nightlight, on at the far end of the apartment, likely in my Aunt Nini's room. She was an invalid, tenderly taken care of by Uncle Paul who slept separately in a bedroom at the street side of the house.

I tried the door but it was locked. I could not raise the bottom sash of the window but with a few tugs the top sash gave way and I lowered it about twelve inches. I scrambled through it with much noise and jumped down on a chair. I stood there in near darkness listening. I heard my Aunt Nini say at first softly, then louder over and over again, "Paul, Paul, Paul."

After a few moments I heard Uncle Paul's heavy, tired footsteps coming towards the kitchen. I quickly ran to the back door, flipped the bolt and ran out and down the stairs. I ran across the backyard and into the back house. This was a one-story unoccupied, unfinished wooden house that had window holes and door openings but no windows or doors. I went deep as I could into a corner and waited. The smell of urine came up from the wood. A chill settled into me from the fright and exertion. Anticipation of my uncle calling the police about a burglar made me worried but not panicky. I was still able to look for an escape like an animal, not thinking but acting on instinct. After a time, which was hard to measure in the cold with no watch, nothing happened. I don't recall how long I stayed in the back house, but I must have left for the zoo before dawn in order to avoid being seen by relatives, friends, or neighbors.

Looking back, I had no interest in food. I didn't scrounge in the garbage cans at the zoo or pick up discarded peanuts in the monkey house. I probably got my fluids at the drinking fountains. Each night I left the zoo in the cold and dark with no idea where I was to spend the night. I walked the park path from the zoo toward a tunnel under the street. Wind, snow, and leafless trees are all I remember. I encountered no one. Through the years I have lost track of how many nights I was away, but it was at least the better part of a week. I can only recall clearly how I spent four of those nights as mentioned above.

On the last morning of my wandering, I had walked west in the alley between Weiland Street and North Park Avenue in the direction of my house. I may have slept under the loading dock of the B & B shoe company the night before. I emerged from the alley at George Maltezos' house. I turned and started to walk north in front of the rectory when someone put their arm around me and said "Chuckie?" It was my sister, Maryellen. It was probably difficult for her to recognize me in my disheveled appearance. She began to cry and gently guided me to the entrance of the Immaculate Conception Church. This was exactly across the street from my house. We went in and knelt down. She prayed for a few moments and then took me home.

I was still in a daze and don't recall all that happened. I do remember sitting on a kitchen chair with my mother asking me questions. I said nothing. I don't recall any contact with my father. I was probably given something to eat and then put to bed. Soon the family doctor, Schmehil, came and did an exam and then I heard him tell my mother that my ankles and feet were swollen likely from exposure but otherwise I was fine.

No punishments were handed out to me; no curfew or restrictions were placed on me. Matter of fact, life was unchanged. My friends or siblings did not question me and I gave out no information. I did meet the boy from Muzzie's candy store where I had the incident with the comic books and he said with a sneer, "Chuckie, got any comic books for sale?" I did not answer. I returned to school, and my schoolmates asked no questions of me. The only hateful, foolish person was the pastor, Father Fleming, but to his prying, hurtful, embarrassing questions in front of the class, I answered nothing.

Several years later, Joe Zummo tried to bribe me with a candy bar for information on my trip as we stood waiting for the bus near Newberry Library. He also told me some secrets about Jimmy Foley to try and tempt me, but I told him nothing.

In the Newberry Library, when I worked as a cloakroom attendant and later as a page, I had access to the old copies of Chicago newspapers. I looked up the dates when I had runaway in the Chicago Daily News. There was a three line item about me and it also mentioned a teenage girl. I don't believe names were mentioned. I was just identified as a young boy who was missing

> *The little boy lost in the lonely fen,*
>   *Led by the wand'ring light,*
> *Began to cry, but God ever nigh*
>   *Appeared like his father in white.*
>
> *He kissed the child and by the hand led*
>   *And to his mother brought,*
> *Who in sorrow pale, thro' the lonely dale,*
>   *Her little boy weeping sought.*
>
>   *The Little Boy Found*
>   William Blake, 1789

Part Two: You Can't Go Home Again

"To lose the earth you know, for greater knowing; to lose the life you have, for greater life; to leave the friends you loved, for greater loving; to find a land more kind than home, more large than earth."
You Can't Go Home Again
Thomas Wolfe

Charlie Martinez

   Late in life, I revisited the now-alien neighborhood of my youth. I parked on Orleans Street and looked over my shoulder as I locked the car door. I walked along the same sidewalk cement as I had over fifty years before. Schiller Street seemed no wider than an alley. The Schiller Street L station was gone, with only a cement pad in its place. My mind's eye saw the turnstiles and the attendant's cage where an always elderly blue-suited man with a white shirt and dark blue tie sat with his pile of coins in front of him, holding a paper puncher in one hand and transfers ready in the other. Against the opposite wall was Mr. Culbertson's cramped newsstand that smelled of peppermint gum, candy, and newsprint. He hobbled around on his wooden leg -- a gift from the grateful taxpayers for his service in World War I.
   The absence of the L station anchor was bothersome -- but the worst was just ahead. A one-hundred-foot wide empty field had replaced comfort, memories, childish adventures, friends' dwellings, grass and gardens.
   My early childhood space had been flattened, measured, and sold. Degnans' frame three-flat, Johns's tilted bungalow with the never-visited ghostly second floor, their cottage which the artists rented, Kennedys' well kept frame two-flat with the perfect unused back lawn, and my tired two-story frame with the unfinished "spook" house in back were all bulldozed, burned and hauled away. The north side of Mr. Bartoli's red barn was visible for the first time in a century. In the space were several stony outcroppings, giving the impression of an ancient cemetery, unattended. The vile developer,

swearing to do the community good, would soon come with his hoard and replace these gentle homes with memory-extinguishing gentrification.

I wandered over the homeless landscape. In this spot my mother's mint grew and here she coaxed four o'clocks every year to add some life and color to the backyard. The Tree of Heaven, which had survived insults from dozens of kids, was now a charred stump. No evidence of puppies or chickens. Over there, in Gus Johns' luxurious backyard, I once went with my mother at night. She carried a flashlight and we searched for Gus and Ken, both 10, who had "run away." We found them hiding in a hydrangea bush. Now not even a weed grew. The dreaded back house torn down without a trace left. Our circus area in the backyard now furrowed by bulldozer tracks.

All the happy Christmases and Easters; the sadness of my mother; the meager meals; the happy poverty of my childhood; the burning shame of poverty for my older brothers and sisters; the long suffering of Uncle Paul; the sorrowful, invalid life of Aunt Nini; the sightless and near-deaf final years of my grandmother Teen; the adolescence and young adult joys of my brothers and sisters; all these memories were searching the heavens for a resting place when they went up as smoke in the burning of the house.

The Conasentis' brick house still stood with its memory of Mrs. Conasenti who stayed too long and was murdered in a robbery as a reward for her loyalty to the neighborhood. Across the street was the neat cottage behind Mueller's bakery. Then there was a little piazza-like grouping of two houses that the Bushalacis lived in. They were volatile Italians but otherwise good neighbors. The Schlaws lived on the corner with the daughter who was to be badly injured in a factory fire. Johnny Schlaw was my older brother Tommy's best friend. These people were all gone. Sold out to eventual developers. Memories traded for real estate profits.

Around the corner and up North Park Avenue, I visited the place where I had spent my teenage years. The back house where I stayed with my Aunt Nini was torn down. Its footprint was so tiny that a stranger would have thought a child's playhouse had stood there. The front house was stripped naked of its walls. All that worry about being part of the group, relationship to girls, shyness, wasted school years, the happy times playing sports with my older brothers, unexpressed feelings about being lower class -- all this pent-up emotion was released to the air when the walls were removed. The dreaded basement was exposed and sunlight entered into all its crevices for the first time since the birth of the house a hundred years before. I noticed that rough, irregular tree trunks, rather than sawed lumber, were holding up the house. All that remained was a shell. It was on its deathbed, ready for the bulldozer. The 1428 sign was still tacked up on the left side of the doorway. I ripped this off and took it as a souvenir. Later I found out that the house was not torn down but a floor was added and it was sold as condominiums.

Bunny Byrne

Everything was over.

And it was such a short period of time. When I go back and I think of all the things we did with the cars, going up to Foley's cottage. Hitchhiking up to Wisconsin and going to the Lake Shore Club to work. Going down to Schiller Street at the lake every summer. Then we get into high school. All the basketball games, all that and then we had to grow up, yeah. I went in the service six months after I got out of high school. Well that ended it for me. See, for the rest of them in the neighborhood, it continued for a while for the simple reason: they were still there. But I was just like plucked out and I was gone for two years. Well, by the time I got back everything was over. Everything was over.

Jack LaBrasca

Yeah, it was different for us because only a short time after we moved, they tore down the houses. And that was the time when I began to find guys from north of us. Guys from your neighborhood and guys from Webster Avenue. All the guys, you know, from different neighborhoods north of Division because my neighborhood was no more. It was literally torn down. And it looked like Berlin in '46. Cabrini Green was built. Yeah we moved out in '54. And ah, by the end of '55, it was decimated.

Jim Sullivan

Yeah, it all changed.

I got out of the service, and when I came back, everybody was gone. You know, it was like a functional place to be, and when I came back there was nothing there. Third Base was closed and everybody moved away. Everything that I knew before I went in the service was gone. Yeah, it all changed. You know, there was like no place to hang out. So we moved out of the area. We moved to 2100 Cleveland Avenue. We used to go back to Magrini's Tavern every now and then. You know, like on St. Patrick's Day and everybody would be there. I started seeing Barbara at that time. Let's see that was like in '55 or even '57. So I saw her for a year or two and then got married. So that's it, Charlie.

Jay Pistone

It was just different.

When I got out of the service I was about twenty-one, twenty-two. In that neighborhood you either were a drinker or a gambler. You know, there wasn't that much to do. So all the Irish guys were big drinkers and a few Italians. And most of the Italian guys were gamblers. They either shot dice or played cards. When I was in my twenties and thirties I hung around with guys that shot dice, played cards, or went to the racetracks. See. That was our outlet.
But most of the guys had grown and then they went their own way. You know, we didn't play ball that much anymore. Some guys were married, you know. It wasn't the same group, you know. We weren't the same. It's hard to explain. It was just different.

456

Charlie Martinez

And the guys. The premature dead had thrown snake eyes. The living scattered into different lives. Not far geographically but functionally. The comradeship of the early years gave way to a loosening of relationships. Soon girlfriends, wives, kids, jobs, houses, cars, ambitions, and worries, began eating away chunks of time and energy previously reserved for the guys. The casualness and time wasting of youth were gone. We still met but only at certain times and for predefined activities -- baseball games, nights at the tavern, occasional dances on special days, wedding receptions. We still had contact—but as one guy said, "It's hard to explain, it was just different."

No more taking the aimless walks for junking, no more petty thievery, no more staring down a strange boy approaching on the sidewalk, no more stupid two-minute gang fights, no more long talks late on a summer night, no more taking advantage of any adult, no more sneaking beer to the park or lake, no more wandering slowly in a car, no more running to stand in line or to a car for crude sex, no more spontaneous ball games with little or no equipment, no more touch football or ledge ball, no more freedom to take any job or go to any school and quit either anytime. Gone was belonging to a group, the smell of grass at Lincoln Park, wandering around on Sunday afternoon downtown in our "cool" clothes, and wasting minutes as if they were countless drops of warm summer rain.

Thus the gray, two-headed monster of goals and responsibilities snuck up on us. We were unaware. It was a monster called adulthood, severing us from our childhood forever. Fellowship was gone and we were bonded only by memories.

Part Three: The Passing Bell

On Pembroke Road look out for my ghost,
Disheveled with shoes untied,
Playing through the railings with little children
Whose children have long since died.

                If You Ever Go to Dublin Town,
                Patrick Kavanagh

RECOMMENDATION OF A DEPARTING SOUL

The priest, vested in surplice and violet stole, enters the room of the dying person, saying, "Peace be unto this house."

Patrick Irwin (he who we wanted to imitate)
Phillip Irwin (late bloomer, Irish curse)
Jimmy Foley (God gifted him--the Devil destroyed him)

He then sprinkles the dying person, the chamber, and all the bystanders with Holy Water in the form of a cross.

John Maltezos (Johnny we hardly knew ya)
Jerry Martinez (never made you feel uncomfortable)
Pat Rogers (talented survivor)

He next presents a crucifix to the dying person to be kissed and exhorts him to look forward to everlasting life; leaving the crucifix before him, that beholding it, he may be encouraged to hope for eternal salvation.

Joe Filpi (the mature one with gracious smile)
Nick Gallo (happy man, the music man but hid deep sorrows)
Jay Pistone (everyone's friend)
Paul Temple (the steady one)

Then, having lighted a candle, the priest kneels, and with the bystanders devoutly recites The Litany For The Dying.

Then while the soul is in the agony of its departure, the priest recites the following prayers … Go forth, O Christian soul, from this world …

Eddy Kennedy (the pleasant, handsome buddy)
Roy Fabri (the friendly, hidden political talent man)
Jack Flaherty (humble, natural leader)
Frankie DeMonte (best joke teller in the world)

Here, if the soul still linger, may be read the Passion of Our Lord According to St. John.

Steve Russo (the coolest of the cool)
John Nicolini (the much admired nerd)
George Maltezos (found his second career late in life)

When the soul is about to depart the body, then more than ever ought they who are by to pray earnestly around the dying person's bed; and if he be unable to speak, the Holy Name of Jesus should be constantly invoked, and such words as the following again and again repeated in his ear: "Into Thy hands, O Lord, I commend my spirit … "

Ditty Bury(talent with a monkey on his back)
Bobby Johns (that short, sad life)
Ken Martinez (friendly extrovert, wounded Marine)

When the soul has departed, the following responsory may be said :
"Come to his assistance, ye Saints of God, come forth to meet him, ye Angels of the Lord."

Marty McDonough (demons devoured his future)
Jimmy Fichera (always the friendly little brother)

Tony Provnezano (the late blooming intellectual)

Meanwhile, according to the custom of the place, let the Passing Bell be rung, reminding all who hear it to pray for the Christian soul. Then let the body be decently laid out, with lighted candles near. Let a small cross be placed upon the breast, between the hands, or else let the hands themselves be folded, one upon another, in the form of a cross. The body is sprinkled with holy water, and thenceforward until the time of burial, let all who are present pray for the repose of the departed soul.

Louis Provenzano (the pleasant, successful Sicilian)
Hankie Kuhn (half American Indian, all-American boy)
John Owens (survived with a "B" around his neck)

THE MASS FOR THE DEAD AND THE BURIAL OF THE DEAD

The Priest, being vested in a surplice and black stole meets the corpse at the church door. Standing at its feet, he sprinkles it with holy water and then says the Antiphon:

"If thou, O Lord, wilt mark iniquities; Lord who shall abide it?"

Death came to old people. We looked on their faces in the coffin when our mothers dragged us to a wake. We served the priest at a funeral Mass. But we were life; they were death.

The body is then borne into the Church; meanwhile the Priest recites the following:

"The bones that were humble shall rejoice in the Lord."

"Bobby Humberg fell off his bike and smashed his knee. That's how the cancer started and it got into his whole leg. My dad says it happens all the time."

Who was to question this? I was silent. There were several among us who could imitate the authority of adults and back up their claims with an adult imprimatur.

The Bier is then set at the head of the nave of the Church, with the feet of the Corpse towards the Altar. Lighted candles are placed about the Bier, and forthwith is begun the Mass for the Dead.

Brethren: --We will not have you ignorant concerning those who sleep, that ye sorrow not, as even the others who have no hope. For if we believe that Jesus died and rose again, so also those who are asleep through Jesus, God will bring with him.

Bobby was out of school for months and returned on crutches. The lower two-thirds of his left leg was missing. Even with several surgeries, he tried to play football with us and rode his bike with weights on the left pedal.

After Mass, the Priest receives the sprinkler from the assistant, and, having made a low bow to the crucifix, goes round the Bier and sprinkles the Corpse thrice on each side; Then, returning to his place, he receives the censer from the assistant, and in like manner goes round the Bier, and incenses the Corpse in the same way as he sprinkled it; then having returned the censer to the assistant, he says …

I wondered about him at a distance and observed his movements with interest but never talked to him. He suddenly was not one of us but seemed suspended somewhere out of our time and place.

From the gate of hell deliver his soul, O Lord.

Then, after all, he died. There was an empty desk and whispers. Sister Seraphia had us pray daily for his soul and told us he surely had gone to heaven.

After this the Body is borne to the Grave, if it is to be buried then: meanwhile is said or sung:

May the Angels lead thee into Paradise; at thy coming may the Martyrs receive thee, and bring thee into the holy City, Jerusalem. May the Choir of Angels receive thee, and with Lazarus, once a beggar, mayest thou have eternal rest.

The entire seventh grade class was taken to the wake at Sullivan's funeral parlor. Sister Seraphia placed us in rows and ordered us to kneel. She began the Sorrowful Mysteries of the Rosary ...

I.   The Prayer and Bloody Sweat of our Blessed Savior in the Garden... We were to respond in kind ...
II.   The Scourging of Our Blessed Lord at the Pillar ... But then. Who is to say how it started?
III.   The Crowning of our Blessed Savior with Thorns ... Spontaneous combustion, most likely. There were little flickers, then quiet. Then more flickers from a different area.
IV.   Jesus carrying His Cross ... We couldn't stop the spread. Attempts at snuffing it out by holding our breath only resulted in explosions of tears and snot and more laughter ...
V.   The Crucifixion of Our Lord Jesus Christ.

On reaching the Grave, the Priest sprinkles with holy water, and afterwards incenses, the Body of the deceased and the Grave. The office then continues as follows:

I am the Resurrection and the Life: he that believeth in Me, although he be dead, shall live: and every one who liveth, and believeth in Me, shall never die.

The parents stared ahead, generously ignoring our irreverence. This boy, this young angel, was their only child. We felt some shame but did not understand, did not understand.

Suffer the little children to come to Me. For of such is the kingdom of heaven.

From: RECOMMENDATION OF A DEPARTING SOUL Page 511
THE BURIAL OF THE DEAD page 541

> The Manual of Prayers
> For the use of the
> Catholic Laity
>
> The Official Prayer Book
> Of the
> Catholic Church
>
> Prepared and Published
> By order of the
> Third Plenary Council
> Of Baltimore
>
> 1888 Baltimore and New York
> John Murphy Company

So ends our tale of growing up in the Near North Side in the 1930s, 40s, and 50s.

> *"So we beat on, boats against the current, born back ceaselessly into the past."*
>
> *The Great Gatsby, F. Scott Fitzgerald*

Author- Charlie - age 4.

Epilogue of how some of the guys turned out.

John Giovenco: Dropped out of high school but then returned to a different high school and did well. Walked three blocks in downtown Chicago to Loyola University. Studied accounting and became a CPA. Went to University of Chicago at night and obtained a Masters in Finance. Worked at a firm and was chosen by one of their clients, Baron Hilton, to work for him. He eventually became Executive Vice President of Hilton and President of the Gaming Division.

Joseph Zummo: Dropped out of a college prep school and transferred to the high school I went to. It was a mediocre school for lower class Catholics. (this was where Giovenco and Charlie Martinez went) He was drafted to Korea and did much charity work with the nuns there as a private. He came back and became a social worker and also went to Loyola and received his Masters in psychiatric social work. He became head of a school for emotionally disturbed kids. He went on to get PhDs in child psychology and social work.

Bunny Byrne: After high school, he and his brother worked on tugboats in Chicago. They bought several large apartment buildings together.

Pat Rogers: Had a difficult youth but woke up when he was rescued by a coach at De Paul high school. He became a history teacher in Chicago public high schools.

Ken Martinez: He had a troubled youth but self-taught himself TV repair and had a shop of his own. He eventually became a stationary engineer at several institutions.

Charlie Martinez: Majored in English and then pre-med at Loyola. Became a physician and was boarded in internal medicine, nuclear medicine, and nuclear cardiology and retired at age 72. He then founded a free clinic for the uninsured with his boyhood friend George Maltezos. The clinic is in its thirteenth year.

George Maltezos: He was a high school dropout but then returned and got his GED at the YMCA. He had a successful career in business at a large merchandise company. At age fifty, he went back to school, got a Masters in counseling and retired at age 70. He founded that free clinic for the uninsured with Charlie.

Tony Provenzano: Learned to run the linotype machine in high school. He went on to several printing firms and eventually opened his own print shop.

John Owens: Finished high school and then became an automobile mechanic. He went on to selling and servicing office machines and equipment.

Jack LaBrasca: Could not afford college. However, he began work as a grain commodity dealer at the Chicago Stock Exchange and became president of his company.

Jim Sullivan: He became a draftsman and continued in that career until retirement.

Joe Olita: Terrible poverty as a child. Went to college at night and eventually owned a company that warehoused manufacturing tools.

Frank DeMonte: Had a lifelong career as a successful insurance salesman.

Jay Pistone: Had a long career working for the Chicago Park District.

Paul Temple: Worked his entire career in the Chicago Daily News circulation department.

John Kennedy: Went to college and taught history in Chicago Public High Schools;

Jack Flaherty: He had a long career working in the office of a large corporation dealing with distribution of commercial papers.